# SOCIOLOGY TODAY

# SOCIOLOGY TODAY

Susan and Peter Calvert

HARVESTER
WHEATSHEAF

New York   London   Toronto   Sydney   Tokyo   Singapore

First published 1992 by
Harvester Wheatsheaf
Campus 400, Maylands Avenue
Hemel Hempstead
Hertfordshire, HP2 7EZ
A division of
Simon & Schuster International Group

© 1992 Harvester Wheatsheaf

Typeset in 10/12 Times
by MHL Typesetting Ltd, Coventry

Printed and bound in Great Britain at
the University Press, Cambridge

British Library Cataloguing in Publication Data

A catalogue record for this book is available from
the British Library

ISBN 0-7450-0871-2 (hbk)
ISBN 0-7450-0872-0 (pbk)

1  2  3  4  5    96  95  94  93  92

# Contents

# Preface

We would like to thank all those who have made this book possible, above all Margaret and Leslie Whitehead who looked after our two children while we were both working. Special thanks must go to Graham Allan and to John Scott, as well as to two publisher's readers whose names are not known to us, but whose full and helpful comments were much appreciated. The responsibility for what to put in and what to leave out is, of course, that of the authors alone.

Our outlines of some of the most examined and examinable themes at the beginning of each chapter may be of assistance as a guide to revision, especially for those studying sociology at A-level. They should not be taken as definitive, and certainly should not be followed so rigorously that they prevent the development of an overview of the subject. Similarly, the suggestions for further reading at the end of each chapter are only selections from a vast literature. The interest-value of sociology lies, at least in part, in two facts: that nobody can know everything there is to know and that no two sociologists will ever agree completely over what there is to be known!

Sue Calvert
Peter Calvert

# Acknowledgements

The authors would like to thank the following for permission to reproduce copyright material:

Professor A.B. Atkinson and the Syndics of the Cambridge University Press for part of Table 6.5 from A.B. Atkinson and A.J. Harrison, *The distribution of personal wealth in Britain*; Benn's Business Information Services Limited for material on newspaper ownership and circulation; Central Statistical Office for tables from *Annual Abstract of Statistics*, *Regional Trends* and *Social Trends*; Conservative Political Centre for a table from *The future of the welfare state*; Department of Employment for an extract from *The Yearbook of Labour Statistics* © Crown Copyright; The Economist for an extract from 'Stereotypes don't fit' from *The Economist*, 15 October 1983; Guardian News Service Ltd for tables from David McKie, 'Charting a dealignment decade', *The Guardian*, 3 June 1983, and 'Mortgage arrears and repossessions, 1980–1991', *The Guardian*, 17 December 1991 © *The Guardian*; The Comptroller of Her Majesty's Stationery Office for Table 11.1 from *Criminal Statistics for England and Wales*, 1989 © Crown Copyright; International Thompson Publishing Services Ltd for an extract from Michael Young and Peter Willmott, *Family and Kinship in East London*; Thomas Nelson and Sons Ltd for an extract from Jack Nobbs, *Sociology in Context*; The Observer Cover Stories for an extract from Adrian Caudrey, 'Mixed progress for girls in science', from *New Society*, 22 October 1986 © New Statesman & Society 1986; Simon & Schuster International Group for tabular material from Michael Hardey and Graham Crow (eds), *Lone Parenthood*; Times Newspapers Limited for the chart 'Swing to Labour in local by-elections and opinion polls since 1987 elections' from *The Sunday Times*, 15 September 1991 © Times Newspapers Ltd 1991.

# Chronology

## Before 1850

| | |
|---|---|
| 1753 | Lord Hardwicke's Act — established civil basis for marriage |
| 1776 | American Revolution |
| | Publication of Adam Smith's *The Wealth of Nations* |
| 1789 | French Revolution |
| 1792 | Publication of Mary Wollstonecraft, *A Vindication of the Rights of Woman* |
| 1795 | System of mass production first devised in United States |
| 1799 | Income tax introduced in Britain |
| 1801 | Union of Britain and Ireland |
| | First UK Census |
| 1818 | Karl Marx (1818–83) born |
| 1819 | 'Peterloo Massacre' and the Six Acts |
| 1820 | Frederick Engels (1820–95) born |
| 1830 | Opening of the Liverpool to Manchester Railway |
| 1834 | Poor Law Amendment Act — workhouses introduced |
| 1843 | Publication of J. S. Mill's *A System of Logic* |
| 1844 | Engels' *The Condition of the Working Class in England* |
| 1848 | *The Communist Manifesto* |

## 1850—99

| | |
|---|---|
| 1851 | The Great Exhibition |
| 1855 | Limited liability legislation introduced |
| 1857 | Matrimonial Causes Act |
| 1858 | Emile Durkheim (1858–1917) born |
| 1859 | Publication of Charles Darwin's *On the Origin of Species* |
| 1864 | Max Weber (1864–1920) born |
| 1868 | Trades Union Congress (TUC) founded |
| 1870 | W. E. Forster's Education Act |
| 1873 | Publication of Herbert Spencer's *Is There a Social Science?* |
| 1882 | Married Women's Property Act |

| | |
|---|---|
| 1888 | First major strikes by dockers and by women in match factories |
| 1889 | Publication of volume 1 of Charles Booth, *Life and Labour of the People of London* |
| 1893 | Women obtain vote in local elections |
| | London County Council (LCC) established |
| | Publication of Emile Durkheim's *The Divison of Labour in Society* |
| 1895 | Publication of Max Weber, *The Rules of Sociological Method* |
| | Foundation of London School of Economics and Political Science |
| 1896 | Motor car freed from legal restrictions |
| 1897 | Publication of Emile Durkheim, *Suicide: A Study in Sociology* |

## 1900−9

| | |
|---|---|
| 1902 | Balfour Education Act |
| | Talcott Parsons (1902−79) born |
| 1904 | Report on poor health of army recruits to the Boer War |
| 1904−5 | Publication of Max Weber, *The Protestant Ethic and the Spirit of Capitalism* |
| 1905 | Liberals return to power |
| 1908 | Old age pensions introduced |
| | The Children's Act |
| 1909 | Royal Commission on Divorce |
| | The Labour Exchange Act |
| | Bleriot flies the Channel |

## 1910−19

| | |
|---|---|
| 1911 | National Health Insurance Act provided for insurance against unemployment |
| 1913 | First Ford plant with assembly-line production of Model 'T' |
| | The Osborne judgment — trade unions finally legalised |
| 1915 | Publication of Robert E. Park's *The City* |
| 1917 | Russian Revolution |
| 1918 | Representation of the People Act — votes for women aged 25 and over |
| | Fisher's Education Act |
| 1919 | Housing and Planning Act |
| | Alcock and Brown fly the Atlantic |

# 1920—9

| | |
|---|---|
| 1920 | First regular radio broadcasts |
| 1922 | The Treaty — Irish Free State established |
| 1923 | Matrimonial Causes Act — women same grounds for divorce as men |
| 1924 | Wheatley's Housing Act made local authorities responsible for housing people in their areas |
| 1926 | The General Strike |
| 1927 | First traffic roundabout built |
| 1928 | Representation of the People Act — women vote on same terms as men |
| 1929 | Local Government Act |
| | The Great Depression begins |

# 1930—9

| | |
|---|---|
| 1931 | National Government — Gold Standard abandoned |
| 1932 | Unemployment at 22 per cent in England, 36 per cent in Wales |
| 1934 | (Posthumous) publication of G. H. Mead, *Mind, Self and Society* |
| 1937 | Matrimonial Causes Act |
| 1939 | Outbreak of Second World War |
| | First regular heavier-than-air service across Atlantic |

# 1940—9

| | |
|---|---|
| 1942 | Beveridge Report |
| 1944 | R. A. Butler's Education Act |
| 1945 | Labour government elected |
| 1946 | National Health Service introduced |
| | National Insurance Act |
| 1947 | Town and Country Planning Act |
| 1948 | British Nationality Act — right of all citizens of Commonwealth countries to enter Britain to work or settle |
| | National Assistance Act |
| | Representation of the People Act |
| 1949 | Legal Aid and Advice Act |
| | Publication of Edwin Sutherland, *Principles of Criminology* |

## 1950–9

| 1950 | Matrimonial Causes Act |
|------|------------------------|
| 1951 | Festival of Britain |
|      | Conservatives return to power |
| 1956 | Publication of Antony Crosland's *The Future of Socialism* |
| 1957 | Publication of Robert K. Merton, *Social Theory and Social Structure* |
| 1959 | M1 opened |

## 1960–9

| 1961 | First space flight by USSR |
|------|---------------------------|
| 1962 | Commonwealth Immigration Act restricted immigration from the new Commonwealth |
| 1963 | Local Government Reform Act — new counties created, GLC replaces LCC |
| 1966 | Race Relations Act |
| 1967 | Abortion Act — legalised abortion for medical or social reasons |
|      | Troops withdraw from Aden |
| 1968 | Commonwealth Immigration Act — excluded East African Asians |
|      | Enoch Powell's 'rivers of blood' speech |
|      | Civil rights movement in Northern Ireland |
| 1969 | Divorce Law Reform Act — sole cause 'irretrievable breakdown' |
|      | Outbreak of fighting in Northern Ireland |
|      | First moon landing |

## 1970–9

| 1970 | Equal Pay Act |
|------|---------------|
|      | Matrimonial Proceedings and Property Act |
| 1971 | British Immigration Act |
| 1973 | Oil crisis |
| 1973–74 | The miners' strike |
|      | Finer Committee on One-Parent Families |
| 1975 | Sex Discrimination Act |
|      | Publication of Edward Wilson, *Sociobiology; the new synthesis* |
| 1977 | Foundation of the Anti-Nazi League |
| 1979 | Conservatives return to power |

# 1980−9

| 1980 | Employment Act |
| | The Black Report on inequalities in health |
| 1981 | First media report of AIDS |
| | Race riots in London and Bristol |
| | British Nationality Act |
| 1982 | Falklands War |
| 1983 | Privatisation becomes general government policy |
| | Mental Health Act |
| 1984 | Matrimonial and Family Proceedings Act |
| | Trade Union Act |
| | The miners' strike |
| 1985 | Broadwater Farm |
| | Death of Rock Hudson |
| | Swann Report on the education of minority children |
| 1986 | Greater London Council abolished |
| 1988 | Education Reform Act |

# 1990−

| 1990 | Independent taxation for married women |
| 1991 | Gulf War |

# 1 Theories and Approaches

## Theories and Approaches

Discussion of these topics tends to cluster round a few central themes:

- The differences between positivist and phenomenological sociology — sometimes the expressions 'social structure' and 'social action' are preferred.
- The possibility of a science of human behaviour (sometimes the adequacy of comparing society to a living organism). The problems of uncertainty of results and the difficulties of measuring 'meaning'.
- The contributions of the Founding Fathers; sometimes a critical examination of one major work, e.g. Durkheim's *Suicide*, sometimes an examination of a concept or theme in one writer's work. Occasionally, candidates may be asked to set their work in its historical context, e.g. to consider whether sociological theory is really the history of a debate with Marx.
- The relationship between perspectives, areas selected for study and methods used.

## Why Theory?

People who know little or nothing about sociology are often heard to say that it is 'too theoretical'. However in sociology, as in science or engineering, it is true to say, as Maurice Broady says, that 'there is nothing so practical as a good theory'. Theory is what gives *meaning* to what would otherwise be a mere jumble of unrelated facts. It is not social theory that is confusing, but society itself, which is so large and complex that simple explanations, though popular with both the press and politicians, are often incorrect. As a result, the strategies or *policies* for dealing with social problems sometimes produce results very different from those originally intended (Chapter 12; see also Halsey 1989). Properly understanding society requires us to be, in the broadest sense of the word, *scientific*.

# Is Sociology a Science?

Is sociology a science? This is not a new question. It was John Stuart Mill who outlined the sort of methods that would be appropriate for social scientists in his *System of Logic* as early as 1843. Herbert Spencer wrote *Is There a Social Science?* in 1873.

'Science' simply means a specified body of knowledge, which can be applied to the real world. Science can be either *deductive*, when one fact may be deduced from another, or *inductive*, when general statements are inferred (or assumed) from specific instances. All science contains both forms, but natural sciences, like physics, chemistry or mathematics, use mainly deductive methods, while the social sciences involve much greater use of interpretative methods.

Sociology's claim to scientific status rests primarily on its use of the *hypothetico-deductive principle*, although the actual way this process is used varies from the natural to the social sciences. Investigation begins with the establishment of a proposition concerning what is to be tested. This is then refined into a tighter statement, or *hypothesis*. Frequently, this is in the form of a question rather than a statement: Is A associated with B? Does C affect D? Thus far, much sociology does not differ a great deal from the natural sciences. It is during the next stage, the testing of the hypothesis, that the subject-matter of the social sciences, that is, society, decrees a different methodology. The social scientist clearly cannot for the most part conduct inquiries in the controlled environment of the laboratory or use society itself as a subject for experiment. To do so would not only be unethical, it would also distort, perhaps beyond recognition, what is to be studied. Thus sociologists must use methods appropriate to their subject-matter: social surveys, questionnaires, interviews, observation, and so on. These will be discussed further in Chapter 2.

The specific methods used are generally suited to the hypothesis being tested, though inevitably they will also to some extent reflect the theoretical perspective of the investigator. (This latter point is perhaps the major weakness in the sociologist's claim to scientific status and reflects the division between *positivism*, the view that the social sciences must be scientific in the predictive sense, and *phenomenology*, which will be discussed later.) If the inquiry does *not* confirm the hypothesis, then the social sciences follow the same course as the natural sciences: the hypothesis is reformulated and tested again. If the initial hypothesis is confirmed, then, while natural scientists may be able to express their findings in the form of *laws*, the social scientist can only report *probabilities* or, more usually, tendencies. Human beings are unpredictable creatures and even the most hard-nosed positivists would not deny them some element of freedom of action.

However, it is the degree to which the individual is free to act that lies at the heart of the division between positivist and phenomenological sociology. It is positivist sociology which claims scientific status, the term 'positivism' deriving from Auguste Comte's claim to be establishing a 'positive science of society'. This style of sociology is large scale, viewing society as having an existence of its own, which can be subjected to scientific study. When such sociology is *empirical* (factual) it tends to examine big issues and large numbers of people. When *theoretical* it constructs broad theories, which attempt to explain the development of society and important elements within it. Phenomenology is a reaction against positivism. It takes the view that individuals create the social world around them. It is how people interpret social facts that is important; in other words, how they see the world. In order to study society, therefore, phenomenologists study individual perceptions. Hence they tend to study smaller groups of people and to use methods designed to achieve a deeper (rather than broader) understanding of society.

It should be noted that it is not only phenomenologists who reject the notion of a scientific study of society. Some philosophers also do so because they reject the notion of objectivity and with it even the possibility of impartial natural sciences. Sir Karl Popper holds the concept of universal laws to be illogical and suggests that we cannot rely on assumptions about things that have not yet happened. Thomas S. Kuhn, in *The Structure of Scientific Revolutions* (1970), went further. He argues that all scientists seek the data that will confirm their theories rather than seeking information that will test and possibly disprove them. They cling in this way to major organising theories (which he calls *paradigms*) long after they have proved quite incompatible with observation.

## The Relationship of Biology to Sociology

It is indisputable that human beings are individual biological entities who have certain basic needs that must be satisfied to ensure the survival of the individual and of the species. What is much more controversial is the precise extent to which human behaviour is determined (or controlled) by biology. Desmond Morris, in *The Naked Ape* (1967), writes that *homo sapiens* is just one of ninety-three different species of ape and that human behaviour can be explained in terms of the same biological impulses that drive other species. Lionel Tiger (1969), in *Men in Groups*, similarly suggests that much of human behaviour is controlled by our ape ancestry; that males dominate females in human society because such an arrangement was biologically advantageous to the early apes, and a message of dominance and aggression is attached to the short Y-chromosome, which determines maleness in humans. But biological explanations of human behaviour go much further back in human history than the work of these and other twentieth-century *ethologists* (those who study the behaviour of animals).

Obviously, cultural and social activities will tend to encourage rather than discourage the fulfilment of our basic needs. If they do not, the society concerned will either die out, or such activities will give way to other more appropriate modes of behaviour. However, many philosophers and early sociologists were more dogmatic than this, seeing human society as an organism with an existence of its own. Such an idea is found in the work of both Plato and Hegel, but it is particularly well developed in the thought of Herbert Spencer (1820–1903), and some aspects of it would be taken up and extended by later writers, such as the American sociologist Talcott Parsons (1902–89) (Haines 1987).

# The Organic and Mechanical Analogies

As Kuhn reminds us, thought develops by the use of *analogies*, or parallel cases. But analogies carry with them, as well as the specific meanings intended, other meanings which may well be misleading.

Society is *not* a living organism. So those who have found it useful to study it as though it were one, have constructed an analogy which points up the similarities between society and biological organisms. These similarities are then used to explain how society survives by fulfilling certain *functions* (performing tasks required to ensure the satisfaction of its members' basic needs and hence the survival of both the individuals and society).

The first of these similarities is *growth*. The history of a society is seen as being like the life-cycle of a plant or animal. It starts small, gets larger and more complicated, then decays, withers and dies. As with a living thing, parts of society get more specialised as it grows. Some individual parts die, as do cells in an organism, but the whole outlasts any one of them. In other words, it has a *structure* which remains constant over time. In terms of structure a society is like a living thing, because the way that its parts relate to one another is important. Individual members, like individual cells, are not isolated units behaving in a random way. They are contributing to the maintenance of the whole. Society, like any living thing, therefore, also has regulatory mechanisms through which normal functioning, or *equilibrium*, is restored after a crisis of some kind, in the same way as antibodies counter disease.

The notions of structure and equilibrium used in the organic analogy of society form the basis of a competing interpretation, in which society is likened to some kind of *mechanical* device, most often a watch or a self-regulating part of an engine, such as a thermostat. The watch is a useful illustration of the importance of structure, since anyone who has taken one apart and has not been able to put it together again will be aware that the parts on their own are useless. It is only in the relationship of the parts of a watch to one another that the watch is able to function. The watch is more than the simple sum of the parts, it is the sum of the parts plus their interrelationships. The thermostat illustrates the principle of equilibrium. As used by some modern sociologists it forms an analogy of the way in which society responds to a threat to social stability by the operation of self-regulating mechanisms which restore a steady state.

# The Influence of the Theory of Evolution

When the founders of sociology were establishing the ground-rules for the study of society in the latter half of the nineteenth century, they were not only influenced by long-standing biological concepts but by the new and exciting theory of evolution propounded by Charles Darwin. The importance of this theory was not that it showed that one species had evolved from another — that had already been suggested — but that it gave a reason why the process took place: 'the survival of the fittest'. Soon the evolutionary perspective was applied not just to human beings as a species of animal but, as an analogy, to human social structure. The origins of modern society were debated as travellers reported from all over the world on the strange customs of the 'primitive' peoples they had 'discovered'. Intellectuals in Western Europe and the United States saw themselves as having achieved the pinnacle of social development. An interest in *anthropology* (the study of the human species) was therefore engendered by the belief that studying tribal peoples could help explain the evolution of modern industrial society. But the conclusion reached was that modern society had appeared because it was better fitted to survive, and from that it was a short step to assuming that it was the duty of advanced societies to displace primitive ones.

## Criticisms of Rigid Biological Assumptions

Modern sociologists would argue that a human being is not just a biological animal but also a social one. Hence human society is markedly different from that of our ape relatives and our behaviour must be explained in different terms. Some aspects of human behaviour, such as religious customs and ceremonies, are simply not explicable in narrowly biological terms and can only be understood by reference to our social world. People can reason and some of our actions have complex meanings. For human beings, blinking is a biological reaction, but winking has a social meaning. Unlike the majority of animals, we are 'instinctively underdetermined'; that is, we have few *instincts* so much of our lives are not affected by them, and we choose an action much more often than we react to external stimuli.

The view that society can be likened to a living organism also rests on assumptions that later sociologists would generally find unacceptable. Organisms have a predetermined genetic blueprint (a small cabbage cannot choose to grow up to be a horse) and they grow according to an inevitable and irresistible pattern. The same cannot be said of human society. Even the most closely ordered human society comes nowhere near the completeness of integration that is an organism. Societies can undergo very far-reaching changes in a very short time. These changes can also take most people completely by surprise — witness the events of 1989 in Eastern Europe. Of course, living things suffer injuries and illnesses, but for the most part the constituent cells function automatically for the good of the whole. It is as well they do, for they cannot survive separately. Each cell has a specialised purpose from which it cannot depart, but if a cell becomes cancerous and therefore dysfunctional (works against the survival of the organism) it cannot by will be restored to its proper function. On the other hand, in society people, and the institutions they form, may and probably will vary in the nature of their contribution according to impulse and circumstances.

The evolutionary aspect of the biological approach also presents some serious moral dilemmas. The idea of a steady pattern of development towards a predetermined model, if taken literally, would imply that human efforts to improve society are pointless and that the present situation must simply be accepted as it is. Similarly, the assumed unilinear (one inevitable line) nature of development from primitive to modern society is an assumption which clearly claims the superiority of more developed and more complex societies over less developed and simpler ones, and one which rules out the possibility that different societies could evolve in different ways. It has also led to unpleasant assumptions about the genetic superiority of certain 'races', since, it was argued, they predominated in the 'better' societies of the developed world.

# Functionalism

The importance of the contribution of biology to early sociological theory is seen in the main ideas associated with one of the most important schools of sociological thought: functionalism. Although some of the problems other sociologists find with functionalist explanations may be said to mar functionalism, it is less crudely deterministic than simple biological explanations of human behaviour. Like most intellectual disciplines, functionalist sociology has become more subtle and sophisticated with time.

Functionalism sees society as a whole, a 'seamless web'. Society is viewed as a functioning entity, with phenomena (things happening) being explicable in terms of their contribution to the survival of the social system. Expressed simply, a social institution, such as the family, exists for functionalists because it performs functions, such as controlling adult sexual behaviour and socialising children, which contribute to the well-being of society as a whole. All institutions have functions to fulfil and these mesh together with those of other institutions.

Functionalism dominated American sociology between the 1930s and the 1960s, but it has origins further back in European thought. It derives in part from the ideas expressed in the work of early sociologists such as Comte, Spencer and Durkheim. The first of these three writers, Auguste Comte (1798−1857) (sometimes known as 'the Father of Sociology' because it was he who invented the term itself) insisted that society was a self-contained reality, which functioned as an integrated whole. Herbert Spencer (1820−1903) argued that sociology should study how each particular part of society contributed to the well-being of the social system. He saw the evolution of human society as essentially a struggle for existence, changing in much the same way as a species adapts in order to survive. 'Survival of the fittest' (from Darwin) was, for Spencer, the key to both 'organic' (biological) and 'superorganic' (social) phenomena. The superorganic aspect of human existence was a realm beyond the control, or even comprehension, of the individual, and it acted as a constraint on all human activity. From this debate emerged the towering intellectual contribution of Emile Durkheim.

Emile
Durkheim

Emile Durkheim (1858–1917) dominated French sociological thought for the first half of the twentieth century. But, more important still, the professional methodology he devised for his work established patterns for modern research work in the field. From Durkheim's approach comes much of sociology's claim to scientific status.

Durkheim developed further the theme of society as a reality in its own right, more than the sum of the parts which comprise it, constraining the individual within it. However, Durkheim is more critical of biological concepts than most previous writers. His work is more sophisticated. For Durkheim, although individual life derives from collective life, the individual is both creator and product of society. Society depends for its continued existence on shared *values* (understandings of what is usual, right, proper) and *norms* (certain organising principles of behaviour by which values are to be realised). The absorption of these values and norms he termed 'socialisation'. Shared values and norms give rise to social structure, which in the form of laws and rules forms an *external* constraint on the individual. They also collectively constitute 'culture', which is an *internal* control operating on the individual. In the work of Durkheim, *consensus*, or agreement on what is to be done, is essential to the operation of the social system.

Durkheim was critical of Spencer's rather simplistic explanation of a phenomenon in terms of the functions that it performs. He pointed out that the cause of something is not the same as its effect. Social institutions could not be seen as arising solely to perform certain functions since they had other effects as well. He drew attention to the *unintended* consequences of a phenomenon. These, he argued, could not be held to be its cause. In his best-known example, he argued that the function of the division of labour in society was not to produce civilisation, yet this was what has resulted. Durkheim was still a functionalist, and tended, in spite of these reservations, to account for a phenomenon in terms of its desirable and intended consequences. This tendency is clear in most of his major works: *The Division of Labor in Society* (Durkheim 1964, first published 1893), *Suicide* (1966, first published 1897), *The Elementary Forms of Religious Life* and *The Rules of Sociological Method* (1938).

# The Division of Labour in Society

In *The Division of Labor in Society*, Durkheim argues that industrialisation results in a greater division of labour and a new pattern of social integration. Specialised and clearly differentiated tasks integrate individuals into *organic* society in contrast to traditional or *mechanical* society, where it is what people have in common that creates social solidarity. Durkheim recognises four types of society, but mechanistic and organic are the two kinds that work best and therefore tend to dominate. Of the other two kinds, *forced* integration has individuals pushed into social roles for which they are unsuited. (In this Durkheim is recognising the importance of coercion, which is the basis of Marx's analysis of society.) *Anomic* integration is something of a contradiction in terms, since in it a very complex division of society lacks any guiding norms and people cannot relate to what they are doing or to one another. All four kinds are *ideal-types*, that is, theoretical constructs which cannot exist in a pure form, and therefore every society has elements of each form, although one kind will dominate. (Here Durkheim is using, albeit in a very limited way, a tool of analysis, the ideal-type, which is primarily associated with the work of Max Weber and which will be discussed later.)

For Durkheim, the interaction of individual consciousnesses produces a synthesis or mixture termed *collective consciousness* (or collective *conscience* — the French term means both), which has an existence of its own and is a binding force on society. This Durkheim describes as 'the totality of beliefs and sentiments common to average citizens of the same society' (1964: 79). Religious beliefs form part of this collective consciousness; they are the social expression of social needs. Like other social institutions, religion is functional for the maintenance of social order, though the form it takes varies with the complexity of societies. In advanced societies, the spiritual declines in influence and secular forces such as nationalism become more important in promoting social solidarity.

## Durkheim and Empirical Social Research

Durkheim is perhaps most famous for *Suicide* (1966), because it is in this work that he is at his most empirical. *Suicide* was a pioneering work in scientific sociology, which challenged the notion that the explanation of suicide was to be found in the disturbed psychology of the individual. By the use of statistics, Durkheim showed that there are patterns in suicide rates which suggest that it is a social act. Although he found that rates varied from community to community, rates in each were fairly constant over time. He concluded: 'Each society has a predisposition in its own right to contribute a definite quota of voluntary deaths' (1966: 51). The different rates for different religious or geographical communities were explained in terms of varying social characteristics. In particular the degree of social integration of a community is the main factor for the quantity and type of suicide.

For Durkheim the dominant mode of social integration (mechanical, anomic, organic or forced) gives rise to different kinds of suicide (altruistic, anomic, egoistic or fatalistic). *Altruistic* suicide occurs when social relationships are intense, when the individual devalues him/herself relative to the social groups to which s/he belongs. Such suicide could be an act of moral courage or self-sacrifice when the individual feels s/he has disgraced his or her institution. Durkheim found that altruistic suicide was high among military officers. *Anomic* suicide characterises an unstable social structure where traditional norms are breaking down and expectations exceed the means available for their satisfaction. Such suicide would be more likely during economic crises, although it would also increase in economic booms. It is the product of disorder and uncertainty. *Egoistic* suicide is the virtual opposite of the altruistic form. Instead of reflecting the over-integration of the individual in his social group, it indicates lack of integration and is more common where group cohesion is low or declining. Groups which offer less security and support to their members are likely to exhibit higher rates of egoistic suicide. Durkheim suggested that such groups included Protestants, town-dwellers, industrial workers and the more educated.

Durkheim's *Suicide* has been the subject of a colossal amount of criticism for two main reasons. First, it was an early study breaking new ground and, as such, has the weaknesses of a prototype. It has received much criticism on method-ological grounds. Durkheim had a theory and set out to prove it, rather than seeking diligently to disprove it, as the application of scientific method decrees. He used second-hand official statistics from France and Germany. These were not collected for serious sociological study. Indeed, many recorded suicides were officially known as such only through declarations made by the family of the deceased. Some families may very well have had more reason than others to conceal a suicide. Status and/or religious belief influence the amount of family shame associated with death by one's own hand. Likewise, in using official figures, Durkheim could only consider 'successful' suicides. Of course, it is possible to argue — and many now accept — that unsuccessful suicides are cries for help rather than serious attempts to die. But some no doubt are genuine cases only prevented by third-party intervention. Similarly, some of the suicides may not have intended to succeed. In addition, Durkheim assumed a direct relationship between suicide rate and social integration without exploring the possibility of third factors which could influence both suicide and level of integration: for example, economic recession.

The second reason that Durkheim's study has been so controversial is that it provides an obvious battleground for the competing interpretations of the relationship between the individual and society. In other words, Durkheim's categorical assertion that society determines individual behaviour has been challenged by those who stress the importance of the individual's interpretation of his world. Phenomenologists would wish to ask how an individual comes to *perceive* the social world in such a way that s/he wishes to leave it. They would also want to know how doctors and coroners come to *define* one death as suicide and another as an accident.

## Modern functionalism

Building on the work of early anthropologists, in particular Bronislaw Malinowski (1884–1942) and A. R. Radcliffe-Brown (1881–1955), during the 1940s and 1950s American sociologists became the most important source of functionalist thought. In particular the works of Talcott Parsons and Robert K. Merton have contributed a good deal to the development of functionalist sociology. Parsons was much influenced, not only by Durkheim, but also by the emphasis on *social needs* found in the work of Malinowski. Parsons (1964) established a general theory of social systems in which he identified four *functional prerequisites*, or fundamental social needs, which must be met for a society to continue to operate. Each corresponds to a system within that of society as a whole.

- *Adaptation* is the process by which a society caters for its members' physical needs, such as food and shelter. The economic system supplies this prerequisite.
- *Goal attainment* is the establishment of agreed social priorities, and includes the political system.
- *Integration* reduces conflict by setting up norms and rules which may in some cases be enforced by the legal system.
- *Pattern maintenance* is, however, more often achieved because the process of socialisation within the family and through the education system ensures that members understand and generally wish to conform to the norms of their society. It is through the process of socialisation that culture is passed on to each new generation and this process is of key importance to all Parsonian social science.

Like Parsons, Merton also recognised that certain needs always have to be satisfied for society to continue to exist, and that institutions which meet these needs are generally compatible with each other. But Merton picked up Durkheim's idea that not all effects of social phenomena are intended, and developed it into the concept of *dysfunction*. In doing so, Merton shows himself to be much more flexible than traditional functionalist thinkers. He states that the consequences of any action can vary and that some consequences will be dysfunctional or detrimental for society in its present form. He distinguishes between obvious and intended functions of social institutions on one hand, which he termed *manifest*, and *latent*, or hidden functions on the other. He suggested that other, more appropriate institutions could sometimes be possible. These ideas make up Merton's theory of *functional alternatives*.

Merton's revision of functionalist theory was an attempt to overcome some of the problems associated with the perspective. But, despite his work, the heyday of functionalism was over by the 1960s and increasingly the perspective — which Alvin Gouldner disparagingly called 'academic sociology' — came under attack. Criticisms came both from phenomenologists arguing that functionalism devalues individuals in their relationships with society and from conflict theorists who argued that it ignores problems in society and in particular the inherent conflict between the more powerful and wealthy groups and those who are weaker and poorer. In largely ignoring conflicting and competing interests in society and emphasising shared values, earlier functionalists failed adequately to explain social change and encouraged the preservation of an existing situation.

# Marxist Theory

Conflict theorists have tended to see 'positivism' as a dirty word because they have equated the term with functionalism. Nevertheless, both functionalism and conflict theory are macro-theories which offer a general explanation of society, which is seen as a system. They see an individual's behaviour as largely socially controlled. Both claim to be 'scientific' in their approach and may therefore be seen as separate and opposed tendencies in positivist sociology.

There, however, the similarities end, and on almost every point functionalism and conflict theory are diametrically opposed. While functionalism is about consensus, integration and stability, conflict theory stresses conflict, coercion and change. The most important and best known of conflict theories is *Marxism*.

Karl Marx

> Marxism pre-dates functionalism, since it derives specifically from the work of Karl Marx (1818–83), although it has been subject to different interpretations subsequently. Its importance to sociology has grown as the dominance of functionalism has waned.
>
> Whereas social norms and values control individual behaviour for the functionalist, it is economic arrangements which fulfil this role in the Marxist model of society. The means by which we satisfy our basic needs for food and other material objects, the productive process, is the most important characteristic of society. Production rests on the interaction of land, labour, capital, raw materials and technology, which Marx terms 'the forces of production'. The way that these forces interact produces particular kinds of social relations, which in turn divide society into *classes*. The productive process and the class structure resulting from it make up the *infrastructure* or economic base of society. Other aspects of society, values and norms, culture, politics, education, and so on, are determined by the economic base. They make up the *superstructure* of society. When the economic base of society changes, the superstructure will adapt.
>
> The theme of Marx's work is instability and change. History has shown that social structures do not survive forever. Marx holds that the reason for this is that all historical societies contain within themselves contradictions, which will eventually destroy them. These contradictions are exhibited in the social relations arising out of the productive process. As society develops beyond a very primitive level in which production is at subsistence level and all goods are commonly owned, one social group comes to exploit and coerce another in order to further its own economic interests. Under slavery, slave-owner exploited slave; in feudal society, landowner exploited peasant. In capitalist societies, the *bourgeoisie* (capitalists) exploits the *proletariat* (workers), which owns nothing but its labour-power, which it is forced by economic necessity to sell for wages.
>
> The capitalist is a victim of the system too, since he must maximise his profits in competition with other capitalists or else be broken by the system and sink into the proletariat. His profits are

based on *surplus value*, which is the amount for which he can sell his products less the costs of production. Marx saw surplus value as declining over time as competition for a diminishing market already saturated with material goods became more and more cut-throat. Dwindling profits produce economic crises and depressions, periods of high worker unemployment and poverty. At first capitalism has some capacity to adapt. Technology enables larger-scale production, and cartels are created which protect the remaining capitalists from the pressures of competition. But work, which Marx sees as essential to human dignity, 'Man's prime want', is more and more alien to the worker. The capitalist decides what is profitable and therefore what is produced. To maximise surplus value he must keep costs down, and this determines what productive method is used. This in turn controls what work actually consists of for the workers and the speed at which they are obliged to labour. They suffer *alienation*. The whole process, including the product itself, is separate from them. Work has no intrinsic value for them. They labour only for the wages which enable them to meet their basic material needs. In these circumstances the main contradiction of capitalism, the existence of an increasingly impoverished mass exploited by a minority, becomes more glaringly obvious to the exploited class. This class becomes aware of its common situation and its grievances against the system that exploits it. It has been living in a state of 'false consciousness', persuaded by ruling-class ideology disseminated through education and socialisation that its exploitation is for the common good. It sheds these notions and becomes 'a class for itself'. Because the economic base determines the values and institutions of society, it is no easy matter for the proletariat to resist cultural indoctrination and to seek to overthrow the capitalist system. It eventually develops a revolutionary consciousness, however, and the overthrow of capitalism results in the Marxist end-state: communism.

The main features of the communist society, as envisaged by Marx, result from the ending of conflict. International competition and conflict cease as communism is universal. The worst effects of the division of labour disappear as technological advances make human beings supervisors of machines. Thus they continue to do socially necessary labour, but enjoy much more free time in which to develop all aspects of human capabilities. The economy flourishes as technology creates new options; the old cycle of boom and slump disappears. In its place a continued growth in productive forces eventually ends the scarcity of material things, making it possible to move from rewarding workers according to their abilities to a situation in which all can receive what they need. When everyone has what they require, money ceases to have any meaning and is abolished. Democratic planning replaces the coercive government of the people. The state ceases to exist in its repressive form, although a central organising body survives to administer production. There is no class other than the proletariat to exploit or be exploited and a classless society is established.

# Application of Marxist Theory

The general inadequacy of Marx's explanation of the development of capitalism that Max Weber identified will be discussed later. However, by the early years of the twentieth century Weber had already begun to point to specific developments that contradicted Marx's predicted course of capitalism. He suggested that the relative position of the working class was in fact improving and that the polarisation — or moving apart — of the two main classes as described by Marx was simply not happening. Weber pointed out that a much more complex class structure already existed and indeed would continue to develop as bureaucratic organisation became more important. Classes may act together but it is not inevitable: there is no certainty a class will develop the collective mentality Marx had envisaged. Weber also does not see class as the only basis for political action and the organisation of power: *status* (social honour or esteem) and *party* (groups working together to further common interests through political action), for him, are also relevant (see Chapter 3).

Further developments in capitalist society have also contributed to the critique of Marx. In particular, some modern economists, sociologists and political scientists have countered Marxist ideas with 'supersession theory'. The basic argument is that the early industrial capitalism on which Marx based his analysis has been superseded by a new form. Some even suggest that we have entered a post-capitalist phase. The separation of ownership and control of capitalist enterprises and the growth of share-holding are taken as evidence of this change. The spread of ownership has been seen as indicative of a 'decomposition of capital' contrary to the development of an increasingly small and homogeneous bourgeoisie which was envisaged by Marx. Technology, rather than pauperising and homogenising the proletariat, has led to a more diverse and more fragmented working class, some of whom have acquired increasingly complex and well-paid jobs. The middle class of non-manual workers has increased in size, contrary to Marx's prediction that it would decline and sink into the proletariat.

No advanced capitalist society has had a proletarian revolution. Revolutions of the Bolshevik type, claiming Marxist inspiration, have been successful only in less developed peasant states with autocratic governments. In those countries which have experienced such revolutions there was little evidence of movement towards the characteristics of communist societies Marx described. Cuba remains dependent on sugar and cigars and remains dominated by the charismatic figure of Fidel Castro. Castroism has not created a harmonious society. The political prisoners remain. The Soviet Union, until the advent of General Secretary Gorbachev, was dominated by a repressive state, which imposed its model of society on its Eastern European neighbours by force of arms. From the outset the history of the Soviet bloc was characterised by regional and nationalistic disputes which provoked the coercive powers of the Soviet Union. Despite Stalinist modernisation in the USSR itself economic problems continued and scarcity of material goods persisted to such an extent that shops were empty and queues endemic. After 1984 the government began to stress the need for economic incentives especially in agriculture and to seek economic aid from the West, and in 1991 following the abortive coup of the hard-liners, communism itself has been blamed and the USSR has since disintegrated.

Other Eastern European societies, such as Hungary and Yugoslavia, had gone much further in decentralising control of the economy even before the general collapse of the Soviet system in Eastern Europe in 1989. In China privatisation of aspects of the productive process was well under way, but when, led by students, millions began to protest about the lack of democracy, brutal repression was used against them and the future of China remains uncertain in 1992. Of course, it would be possible to argue that until all capitalist nations have experienced revolutions, movement towards communism is impossible, but the antagonism even between nations professing adherence to Marxist ideology (e.g. the Soviet Union and China at least until very recently, China and Vietnam, Ethiopia and Somalia) has been strong, in places strong enough to lead to armed conflict.

Viewing Marx as the final authority on society, explaining everything that happened, was to do him a disservice. This is what C. Wright Mills termed 'Dead Marxism'. Despite what may or may not have happened since his death, Marx was a great thinker who sought to explain the development of society as it existed in his day, the mid-nineteenth century. He could not know the future and should not be ignored because he did not predict it precisely. Much of what he wrote can help us in our understanding of modern society, and his theory offers an intellectual challenge which must be faced whether we agree or disagree with his conclusions.

## The Alternatives to Positivism

While positivist sociology, including functionalism and Marxism, does not deny that people have choice in how they act, it does see this choice as quite constrained. Although for Marx people 'make their own history', how they do so is in his view largely controlled by the economic infrastructure. The options available are so limited that the direction of history is determined, regardless of the actions of individuals. Generally, much early positivism accepted the view that social evolution occurred according to certain patterns. The behaviour of people might be objectively measured in the same way as the behaviour of matter. That which is observable and measurable in human behaviour is what is important.

Other sociologists have rejected some or all of these positivist assumptions. They argue that people are fundamentally different from matter as we have consciousness and do not simply react to external stimuli in the way that matter does. Our actions carry intentions, we attach meanings to our actions and to those of other people. For some modern sociologists of the various phenomenological schools this difference between people and matter makes natural science principles and procedures totally unsuitable for the study of society. For others, it implies the need for extensive modification of natural science methodology to allow a deeper understanding of human behaviour. At the forefront of this latter group stands the great German liberal, Max Weber.

**Max Weber**

> Weber (1864–1920) accepted many of the insights of Marx and Durkheim, but he emphasised the importance of seeing individuals as reasoning and motivated actors. Weber believed that social science could benefit from the objectivity brought to it by natural science methodology *combined with* the depth of understanding achieved through the sympathetic, subjective interpretation of social action. For Weber, the individual's role in creating social and historical situations is central. The meaning an individual attaches to his actions is the foundation of any sociological explanation of those actions.
>
> As Weber explained in *Economy and Society* (*Wirtschaft und Gesellschaft*) (Talcott Parsons, intro. to Weber 1965, p. 79), he was not seeking to disprove Marx's idea that economic structure was the main determinant of any social or historical situation. He did not disagree that economic structure was important, but he did reject the idea that it was the *only* important factor. He disliked the one-sided explanation offered by Marx, but stressed that he had no wish to establish an equally one-sided opposing interpretation. For Weber, the infinite complexity of society and history make simple, one-sided explanations inadequate. He believed, moreover, in *causal pluralism* (many different reasons for the same phenomenon).
>
> Weber saw the understanding of action as being dependent on the understanding of the actor's intentions which he termed *Verstehen* (understanding). Social action occurs within a social context. The social scientist too has a social context and that affords an inherent understanding of the actor's intentions. Although the investigator may not have shared precisely the same experiences as the subject of study, the social scientist's own experiences will enable him or her to imagine the actor's situation and to develop an understanding of the actor's intentions. The actor's beliefs, then, are part of any analysis of society. They are not independent of social or economic pressures, but to discount intentions is to offer an incomplete explanation of any social or historical phenomenon.
>
> Of course, reasons for actions will vary. Weber produces a TYPOLOGY, or classification, of social action:
>
> - *Zweckrational* ('goal-rational'): action is rational in relation to a goal (*der Zweck*). The individual selects the best means available to him to achieve his intended goal.
> - *Wertrational* ('value-rational'): action is rational in relation to a specific value (*der Wert*). The individual acts according to what he perceives as right; to do otherwise would be shameful.
> - *Affective*: action is emotional behaviour.
> - *Traditional*: action is dictated by custom.
>
> These kinds of action are IDEAL-TYPES, theoretical constructs which do not exist in their pure form in the real world. They do, however, help us to analyse an actor's reasons for his or her actions.

# Weber and the 'Ideal-Type'

It was Durkheim who suggested that it would be impractical to study all social phenomena and that therefore a statistical average of the characteristics of such phenomena should be constructed. This method is evident in Durkheim's typology of suicide. Weber refined this method of study. For him, an average of the kind proposed by Durkheim did not necessarily embody the essence of the phenomenon he sought to study. Weber proposed that the social scientist should construct pure types of intentions or action by isolating and listing their characteristic traits. An ideal-type, for Weber and his successors, is an extreme form of one or more particular aspects of a phenomenon. It is supposed to provide a measuring-rod for reality, not a picture of reality. The ideal-type makes the extraction and comparison of various facts possible; it is not itself fact. The object is not to compare an empirical situation with the ideal-type, but to compare several empirical situations with one another through the medium of the ideal-type. If realities are compared in this way, Weber suggested, then one or more factors should emerge as not being common and therefore possibly as being causal. Weber's most notable work involving the use of ideal-types was his study of organisation which led to his emphasis on the concept of *bureaucracy* and to his great works on the relationship between religious ideas and the development of capitalism.

For Weber the maintenance of authority in any society depends on the constant legitimisation of that authority. This means that those who occupy positions of authority must be seen to have a right to do so. In *The Theory of Social and Economic Organization* (1965 — only part of the much larger work, *Economy and Society*, left incomplete at his death), Weber describes legitimacy or right to rule as being of three kinds:

1. *Traditional* authority is stable because of society's emphasis on preservation of traditional culture and values. Long-standing customs determine how members of society relate to one another and important decisions are taken according to historical precedent.
2. *Legal-rational* (or rational-legal) authority is, as its name suggests, the most rational mode of domination. Authority is vested in offices not the persons who occupy them. Those who hold office should be selected for their capacity to fulfil the functions of the office. Rules and regulations govern relations between members of society and rationality is the basis of decisions.
3. *Charismatic* authority (from the Greek word *charisma*, meaning spirit) is revolutionary and unstable. The leader's 'right' to lead stems from personality and outstanding personal qualities. Relations between members of society are volatile and irrational. Decision-making is arbitrary, resting as it does on the whim of the leader. Charismatic authority depends on the person of the leader. If the leader dies or loses popularity this form of authority will give way to one of the other two forms.

It was, however, from the notion of legal-rational authority that Weber derived his concept of *bureaucracy*. For him, legal-rational bureaucratic organisations are the characteristic institutional form in modern industrial society. No matter what the political and economic structure, bureaucracy will come to dominate modern society. Even in communist societies, modernisation will mean bureau-cratisation. Bureaucracy is the institutional embodiment of legal-rational authority and of rational action. It displays a number of characteristic features which together make up the Weberian ideal-type.

Bureaucracy consists of a hierarchy of officials, each official having his or her own area of decision-making within a system of labour division. The rules governing decision-making leave little room for discretion. Both they, and the decisions they give rise to, are recorded in writing. Officials low on the organisa-tional hierarchy are supervised by higher officials, but each official has the right of appeal to someone above the original decision-maker. Officials are selected on merit and paid according to a predetermined scale and keeping one's office and gaining promotion depends on sticking closely to the rules that govern official conduct. The individual's organisational role is separate from all other roles. In particular the official must not use his or her position for his or her own advantage.

For Weber the 'technical superiority' (Gerth and Mills 1957: 215) of bureaucratic organisation was the factor which would cause its spread in modern mass society, but he was no simplistic functionalist limiting himself to the desirable consequences of the social phenomena he studied. Weber recognised the disadvantages of bureaucracy. He saw it as destroying traditional values and culture. It reduced the professional bureaucrat to 'a single cog in an ever-moving mechanism which prescribes to him an essentially fixed route of march' (*ibid*.: 228). It sapped initiative and creativity and tended to promote 'good company men' without these qualities. As a result, if things go wrong, the successful bureaucrat, who is used to dealing with routine matters according to clear rules and regulations, is unlikely to be an effective trouble-shooter. Bureaucrats must themselves be supervised especially in state bureaucracies. Weber was concerned that civil servants might obstruct the will of their political masters because they placed institutional convenience above their obligation to serve. Weber would undoubtedly recognise the character of Sir Humphrey Appleby, from the television programme *Yes, Minister*, attempting to manipulate politicians in the interests of the British civil service.

Social change for Weber is generally in the direction of greater rationalisation of social life. Traditional, sentimental, customary ways of doing things tend to give way in modern societies to specific but abstract rules. Such changes are epitomised in the growth of bureaucracy and in the development of capitalism itself. Marx's explanation of the development of capitalist society stressed that economic factors were the main source of social change and of the ideological features of capitalist society, such as culture, religious beliefs, politics. Weber suggested in his most famous work, *The Protestant Ethic and the Spirit of Capitalism* (1974), that the causal chain could work the other way round. He actually believed that both explanations could only be partial and should really complement each other. Thus Weber never claimed that Protestantism *caused* capitalism, only that there were affinities (similarities) between the ideal-types he constructed for the two variables.

What Weber actually wrote was that the existence of technical possibilities such as raw materials, labour, etc., made the development of industrial society possible, but that their existence did not necessarily lead to such a development. In other words, industrial capitalism could not occur without certain physical resources, but even if those resources were present it did not follow that industrialisation would always occur. Weber cited India as an example of a situation in which such technical possibilities existed but were not used until British rule changed cultural assumptions. He points out that legal-rational administrative structures are also necessary for capitalist development. Certain belief systems may constitute obstacles to rational economic conduct and therefore to capitalist development. Although Weber is aware that capitalist development may influence religious beliefs rather than the other way round, he does point out the various features of Protestantism which make it more sympathetic to capitalist development than more traditional Catholicism. Weber accepted that capitalism became the dominant form over time and then itself became a socialising force on new members of society. But he pointed out that such developments must begin somewhere and they do so among groups of people. In particular, he believed that Calvinist Protestantism provided an ideology particularly conducive to the initial development of capitalism. The Calvinist belief that worldly success was evidence that one had been chosen by God provided an impetus to sustained commercial effort. The short span of years available in which to prove one's 'election' led to a resentment of time-wasting activities. Calvinism was a self-denying or ascetic doctrine. The combination of the needs to acquire success to show one is chosen and to avoid 'sins of the flesh' led to the accumulation of capital. The idea of some being chosen and some not itself provided religious justification for unequal material rewards, which characterise capitalism.

# Phenomenology

Weber's methodology in *The Protestant Ethic and the Spirit of Capitalism* was at least partially subjective, in that he tried to see the world from the point of view of the Calvinist/capitalist. He explained his theory in terms of the ideas actors hold of their actions. He combined in his work large-scale comparative historical studies with *social action theory*, the examination of intentions behind actions. Weber did not deny that choices of action arise from historical circumstances, but he stressed that actors choose between alternative actions. Individuals may not write their own parts, to extend the theatrical analogy, but they extemporise a good deal. Thus Weber provides a bridge between positivist and phenomenological methods in sociology. Apart from social action theory, there are two other main schools of thought which emphasise the phenomenological perspective. They are *symbolic interactionism* and *ethnomethodology*.

What social action theory has in common with these two later developments is its stress on action rather than reaction. Understanding behaviour requires an understanding of the meanings or intentions of social actions. These meanings are not fixed for all examples of the same action. In different circumstances the same action may be performed for different reasons. For example, a punch delivered by a heavyweight boxer in the ring is clearly a different action from a punch delivered by a drunk in a pub on a Saturday night. The context of the action is the key to understanding it. Likewise, actors may change their understanding of their social surroundings, and their actions may vary as a consequence. The bright but hostile lower-school pupil growing into the conscientious and co-operative sixth former is not an unknown occurrence. School has not necessarily changed that much, but the student's perceptions of it clearly have. Perceptions change during the course of interaction with other people. These changing perceptions include the actor's self-image. This self-image is a crucial element in the meanings an actor gives to his actions.

# Symbolic Interactionism

This school of thought derives primarily from the work of the philosopher and psychologist George Herbert Mead (1863–1931) at the University of Chicago, though the term was coined much later. Mead stressed the process of *socialisation*, during which the child comes to acquire awareness of the behaviour expected by other people. The spontaneous, reacting self, which Mead calls 'I', acquires a distinct, parallel aspect, or 'Me', which includes knowledge of behaviour expected. In early contact with 'significant others', such as its mother, the child absorbs or internalises meanings through symbols, the range of which includes language, facial expressions, gestures, physical contact, etc. Its understanding of other people is extended through play, especially through adopting adult roles and exploring them in play. Organised games and sports promote development of the concept of order and rules. Through this growing awareness of his social context, the child develops its self-image, the 'Me' part of its personality which moderates and adapts the actions of 'I'. The 'Me' component was a theme taken up by another social psychologist of the Chicago School, Charles Horton Cooley. Cooley emphasised that in interaction with other people, the individual was constantly imagining how he or she would appear to those others. Cooley called this 'the looking-glass self'.

It was a student of Mead's, Herbert Blumer, who took symbolic interactionism a stage further. Working from Mead's assumptions, Blumer distilled the three main propositions which characterise the symbolic interactionist approach:

1. Actions rest on meanings held by the actors.

2. Meanings develop out of social interaction with other people.
3. Group action is the sum of individual actions; the collective level exists, not in its own right as something separate from individuals but as a product of the shared symbols and meanings held by individuals which influence their behaviour.

In constructing these characteristics, especially the last, Blumer was presenting the symbolic interactionist perspective as a direct challenge to the view that society determined behaviour. He was confronting mainstream sociology and offering a critique of functionalism.

Erving Goffmann was also a student at the University of Chicago in the 1940s, much influenced by the legacy of Mead. In *The Presentation of Self in Everyday Life* (Goffman 1969) he examined how the individual's *social identity* was self-defined and maintained through the adoption of *roles*

In the late 1950s, Goffman spent a year observing interaction in a US mental hospital and went on to study behaviour in other *total institutions*, where inmates were effectively 'cut off from the wider society for a period of time' (Goffman 1961) and had to learn to make sense of a strange world and deal with staff they saw as hostile. The total institution removes many of the roles which an inmate has played outside it, he ceases to participate in family life, for example. This changes his or her identity or self-image. Even those aspects of his or her identity which remain to him, such as physical appearance or name, may be adjusted, through uniforms, haircuts, the use of numbers, etc., to reduce individuality and make the inmate more easily controlled by the institution. Goffmann also wrote about how people labelled by others as abnormal or deviant, whether because of a physical disability or some other breach of social norms, are affected. Their abnormality comes to be the main feature of their identity. In this latter aspect of his work, Goffmann is providing a bridge between symbolic interactionism and the third main strand of phenomenology, ethnomethodology. (More recent symbolic interactionist work is primarily concerned with *deviance* and will be discussed in Chapter 7.)

# Ethnomethodology

Ethnomethodology is sometimes seen as the 'sociology of everyday life'. Of course, all sociology concerns itself with everyday life, but what distinguishes this particular school of thought is the shared understandings which are essential to the most mundane of social circumstances. Without these shared meanings, everyday life is disrupted, it is not susceptible to common sense. Sociology should study what we take for granted in our everyday life. What this involves is perhaps best illustrated by the experiments the American sociologist Harold Garfinkel, who coined the term 'ethnomethodology', encouraged his students to carry out. They were asked to play different roles within their usual social settings, to behave as lodgers would in the family home, to act as strangers in their friendship groups. The unsettling effects of behaving out of context, the surprise and irritation expressed by the students' families and friends showed the extent to which the individual's behaviour is taken for granted.

As in Goffmann's work on stigma (Goffman 1986), how labels come to be attached to some people and not to others is an important aspect of ethnomethodological study. Aaron Cicourel (1968) concerned himself with how US police departments apply to juveniles their 'common-sense' definitions of what constitutes delinquency. Some juveniles caught in deviant activity fitted the police image of delinquents and they were subsequently arrested and charged, thus becoming official statistics (see also Chapter 2). Others were seen as youngsters from good home backgrounds who could be handed over to responsible parents without the need to take action against them.

## Criticisms of the Phenomenological Methodology

Just as phenomenology is itself a critique of positivist methodology concerning itself with social structure, so the opposite is also true. While *positivism* underestimates the importance of the individual, so phenomenology undervalues the impact of social forces. In its emphasis on small-scale interaction and indeed on social trivia in the case of ethnomethodology, it is devaluing the discipline of sociology by reducing its explanatory powers and failing to confront major issues. Like functionalism, phenomenology, if it were interested in doing so, would have difficulty in accounting for systemic change. Ideological opposition to interactionism stresses that not all people have the same life-chances/options. Individuality is more constrained for some than for others. Thus for conflict theorists, the main weakness of interactionism is its failure to confront the question of social class/power. Those who label others and those deviants who manage to avoid labelling tend to have more influence than those on whom deviant labels are effectively hung. Labelling is by no means a random activity.

## Social Theory Today

It would be a mistake if at this point we turned to the discussion of individual themes leaving the impression that the development of social theory ended in 1960. One purpose of all social investigation is to contribute to our better understanding of society. It would, however, be invidious to single out only some specific writers of the more recent past and present. It would also require us to repeat much that will be discussed in greater detail in the chapters that follow, where the different theoretical perspectives will reappear in the context of actual social problems, and it will be possible to re-evaluate their respective contributions.

# Suggestions for Further Reading

A lively and interesting collection of essays on key figures in sociological thought is Timothy Raison (ed.) (revised edn 1979), *The Founding Fathers of Social Science*, and extracts from their writings can be found in many convenient collections, such as J. H. Abraham (1973), *Origins and Growth of Sociology*. Weber wrote extensively, but much of his work has remained untranslated until recently. Many of the key ideas will be found in Max Weber (1965), *The Theory of Social and Economic Organization*, ed. and intro. Talcott Parsons. Marx's writings, on the other hand, have been made available in many cheap editions. On the foundations of interactionism, see Erving Goffman, *The Presentation of Self in Everyday Life* (1969). E. Livingstone (1987) explains the basic ideas involved in *Making Sense of Ethnomethodology*.

# 2 Research Methods

## Research Methods

**Discussion of this topic tends to cluster around two central themes:**

- **Critiques of various research methods or comparisons between two different methods, sometimes within one area of study.**
- **The relationship between perspectives, areas selected for study and methods used.**

## Perspective and Method

Sociologists normally work within a defined *perspective*. In turn this perspective will influence their choice of *subject*, and both the perspective and the choice of subject will to a considerable extent determine the *method* or methods by which they will study it (Allan and Skinner 1991).

All research begins from the choice of some area to be investigated. With this choice comes some tentative idea or ideas about why that area is either important or interesting. The aim of research is to build up a body of information that not only makes sense in itself but can be communicated to other people. Not all research, by any means, can be expected to produce new or surprising conclusions. But nothing new can be discovered unless people systematically examine every aspect of their knowledge, however ordinary it may appear to be. 'Common-sense' notions about society are quite often correct, as far as they go. But 'common sense' can be very unreliable — people believed for thousands of years that the sun went round the earth. Our own views on society are formed by a real knowledge of only a very small part of it. Hence our views on why it operates the way it does are to a very large extent merely personal conjectures.

Research begins with these conjectures. These conjectures may in turn be based on the generally accepted views of the world which we have learnt ourselves. If these views are reasonably systematic, and have stood up to some degree of testing in real life, then, whether or not we know it, they are in fact theories. However most, if not all, of people's views about the way society works are in fact unproven, even though they are widely believed. And not everybody thinks in a systematic way about society — people can hold quite contradictory views at one and the same time. However, all this shows is the need to test all theories, however widely accepted. A theory can only continue to be legitimately accepted and defended if it repeatedly survives testing — if it is tested, and the tests show it is defective in any way, it must either be amended or rejected in favour of a new theory.

## Theory and Hypothesis

In practice this means that research begins by *defining a problem*. The researcher then reviews the available literature and makes a survey of the evidence already available which leads to a general idea about why things are as they are. The researcher has then to formulate a question or questions to be answered. Ideally, each question should be couched in a rigorous form, as a *hypothesis* which can be tested.

A hypothesis is an untested explanation, either modifying an existing theory or seeking to extend it in some way; it has to be tested before it can be accepted, and this means that it has to be formulated in such a way that it can be tested. Sociological research will normally test quite a number of hypotheses, not all of which will necessarily have been spelt out in advance. Society is so complex that new hypotheses often emerge in the course of research and demand their own answers. The *hypothetico-deductive* method does not in any way require that we should have a positivistic world view; it is simply the necessary path to building up a connected systematic view of the world, and it cannot be avoided.

| | |
|---|---|
| The hypothetico-deductive method | 1. Forming hypotheses.<br>2. Operationalising hypotheses.<br>3. Gathering data.<br>4. Analysing results. |

The method begins with the *formulation* of hypotheses to be tested. The nature of the hypothesis to be tested dictates what sort of data has to be collected, and various methods will be considered in a moment. Hypotheses should be as clear as possible. They need not, however, involve direct statements of the 'If you do not drink water, you will die' type, and society being as complex as it is, it is in fact very unlikely that they will do so. They can be (and often are) put in the form of probability statements: 'If children come from poor homes, they are less likely to achieve educational success.' In practice, much British sociological research is concerned with seeking fairly general answers to a series of open-ended questions. From these, in turn, however, hypotheses can be derived.

Once formulated, hypotheses have to be *operationalised*. Operationalisation is the process of making explicit what a hypothesis is and finding suitable methods to test it. Ideally, the hypothesis will be expressed in terms of one or more *independent variables* (things that change in the social environment) and a *dependent variable* (a pattern of behaviour of groups or individuals that these changes are believed to affect). The *direction* of the influence will also be stated: whether the pattern of behaviour increases or decreases. The next step is to decide the *research design*, how the *data* necessary to test the hypothesis can be found. Some may be already available in the form of official statistics. The problem will be to find a way to measure the others. If, for example, it is decided to conduct a *survey* specially designed for the purpose, thought must be given to the practical problems. The respondents may be too old, too ill or too frightened to answer, or the cost of the exercise may be prohibitive. Only once the terms of the research are established clearly and unequivocally, in a way that everyone taking part in the project can understand, can the sociologist begin *gathering data*.

Many writers distinguish between data that are *qualitative* (views, notes, recorded speech, individual observations) or *quantitative* (statistics, figures, repeated observations), but this is in many ways a misleading distinction. Qualitative data cover a wider range of human experience, but deal with relatively few examples. The value of the quantitative data obtained from a large number of observations is that it is possible to apply to them *tests of statistical significance* which indicate how far their information is applicable to society as a whole. However, quality and quantity are interrelated — to take a simple example, the quality of a linen cloth is determined largely by the number of threads per inch. Worse still, many apparently qualitative statements turn out on closer examination to be simply inexact. Key words to look out for in so-called qualitative statements are: a few, much, more, many, most, everybody knows, all reasonable people agree, the bourgeoisie, the ruling class, educated people, the whole of society — and indeed any word which implies an indefinite or unconfirmed proportion.

Carrying out the *research design* depends on the methods chosen.

1. *Surveys* involving administering a questionnaire to a sample of people, the choice of the sample like the choice of questions being determined by the topic. The size of the sample should be large enough to carry statistical conviction. There is a direct trade-off, however, between the size of the sample and the number of the questions that can be asked. Given the personal nature of some sociological research, other methods may be more appropriate.
2. *Interviews* give more opportunity to probe into people's motivation. They may be *structured* or *unstructured*. A *structured* interview can be delegated to a number of different interviewers with less risk of bias, but can miss important information. On the other hand, *unstructured* interviews need great experience to keep the respondents to the point, and there is a greater risk that answers will be biased by the circumstances of the interview.
3. *Observation* raises ethical questions, since once those who are under observation are aware of the process, their behaviour is likely to be affected. Again, it is important that observers (if there are more than one) are properly briefed and that conditions of observation are as far as possible constant. Full records have to be kept as the research proceeds.

Analysis of the *results* follows. Sociological research often involves interviews with rather small numbers of people, often well below the threshold for reliable statistical analysis. Hence both the analysis and the presentation of results must be done in such a way as to avoid making too much of the evidence.

**What sort of data?**

Indirect observation:

1. Primary and secondary sources — documents.
2. Oral history.

Direct observation:

1. Field study or ethnography.
2. Participant observation
   entry, gatekeepers, key informants, problem of reliability.

Quantitative research:

1. Official statistics.
2. Surveys
   random, stratified, cluster, quota questionnaire, coding and analysis, validity and reliability.
3. Unobtrusive measures.

## What Sort of Data?

The first general rule is to look for the sort of data that are most likely to be of use in answering the questions. Such information, however, is not always directly available. The researcher may instead have to find out just what information is available and then see if it can be adapted without distortion to the purposes of the investigation. Crucial to this exercise is the concept of an *indicator*. Many sociological variables, e.g. social class, cannot be directly measured in the way that we use a thermometer to measure how hot a body is. Instead, we have to choose one or more indicators, such as occupation.

A second general rule is to try to get information where possible from more than one source. Thus official figures can be supplemented by direct observation, or survey information checked against the results of previous surveys, if available. The more sources from which the same information comes, the higher the degree of confidence that the deductions drawn from it are likely to be valid.

The third general rule is that future researchers must as far as possible be able to follow the same trail and if necessary to replicate the research. Given the intense and often acrimonious debates that have raged within sociology about the validity of certain approaches, other workers in the field expect to be able to 'decipher' the research, to uncover the assumptions on which it was based, to see how the data were obtained and analysed, and to determine how far the results presented are based on the research and how far on other sources.

The main options between which the researcher has to choose are between direct and indirect observation. Establishing a sound basis for quantitative research involves additional problems, which can be treated separately.

# Indirect Observation

Indirect observation is often the basis of a new research project and in the form of historical sources is the only way in which we can now establish what the pattern of life was before sociology came into existence.

For the sociologist it is essential to understand at least something of the strengths and weaknesses of *historical sources* (Scott 1990). The historian distinguishes between primary and secondary sources. Primary sources are documents, etc., which were produced by the people being studied during the time when the historical action was in progress. All other books, papers and documents technically are secondary sources — they represent only indirect evidence about the events of the time. The published or unpublished memoirs of participants come in a special category of their own. They are not primary sources, but they are evidence of a very special kind about how the individuals concerned wanted their actions to be seen by others. Generally speaking, the historian will hold that the evidence of primary sources should be preferred to that of memoirs, and that of memoirs to that provided by secondary sources.

Yet the author of a secondary source is likely to have had access to information that was not available at the time to the participants. This in turn will have come from other primary sources. Hence if a secondary source is to be preferred to a primary source, it must be because it provides evidence from some other primary source that the researcher has not been able to use personally. For this reason, generally the *later* the secondary source is, the more likely value it has to the researcher.

**Types of sources**

| *Primary* | *Memoirs* | *Secondary* |
|---|---|---|
| Letters | Autobiography | Academic studies |
| Recorded speech | (Oral history) | Talks |
| Debates | | Commentaries |
| Raw statistics | | Official statistics |
| | | Statistical analyses |

However, few sociologists are likely to need to make use of the primary source materials which are the stuff of historical research, and the main purpose of these points is simply to alert students to the need to approach *all* documentary material critically. Every document read should be assessed with six questions in mind:

1. Is the document what it purports to be?
2. What is the relation of the author to the event?
3. What is the document trying to show?
4. How representative is the document of the written record?

5. What does the document mean?

6. What is the researcher's relation to the subject?

Traditional, document-based history has often been criticised, sometimes unfairly, for dealing with kings and queens, and battles and other public events to the exclusion of the lives of ordinary people. Oral history is therefore of particular interest to the sociologist who needs information on 'the past behind the present'. In the technique usually used, the subject is interviewed and the entire interview recorded; a skilled interviewer, directing questions towards specific areas, can elicit information that the subject might not consider important or simply have forgotten in the course of time. However, there is a strong tendency for respondents to put the best possible light on their previous actions, as in the case of the writers of memoirs.

# Direct Observation

For many if not most sociologists, the prime concern is with the present, and historical material of this kind is likely to be seen as mainly preliminary to the serious work of direct observation. However, it is important to remember, even when engaged in field study, that what happened last week is already history.

## Field study

Field study or, as it is sometimes called, *ethnography*, that is to say, study of sociological phenomena by direct observation, is a loose term covering what originally was one of the main techniques used in British sociology, now largely superseded. Early sociologists took up the task of studying the poor of Limehouse in the same tradition as anthropologists setting off to observe the Nuer of the Sudan or the Ashanti of the Gold Coast (Ghana). They learnt the language, set up camp in the area, made friends with the local inhabitants, and while seeking to retain at all times the position of a detached and impersonal observer, asked them (if all went well) a series of increasingly intimate questions about their work, upbringing, childhood, family and mating habits.

Apart from the risk of contracting malaria or typhoid when travelling or living abroad, the main problem for the anthropologist is to know whether or not answers obtained in this way are true. The work of the American anthropologist Margaret Mead has recently had to be fundamentally reappraised when it was realised that her account of female adolescence in Samoa just did not tally with other evidence, including the accounts of women who had grown up in Samoa while her research was in progress. Mead might not have accepted their claim that they were encouraged to engage in vigorous sexual experimentation had that view of Samoan life not fitted her own preconceptions. Possibly she had been the victim of systematic practical joking by the young Samoan girls she interviewed (Freeman 1984; see also Freeman quoted in *The Guardian*, 29 November 1989).

## Participant observation

Participant observation involves the researcher actually becoming a member of a community in order to study it 'from within'. This method also has anthropological precedents in the form of the intrepid nineteenth-century explorer H. A. R. Philby who disguised himself as an Arab and penetrated the Holy City of Mecca. The penalty for disclosure as an infidel being immediate death, he first prudently had himself circumcised to ensure that his disguise was complete. Participant observation gained its present standing in sociological research from work such as William F. Whyte's *Street Corner Society* (1956), a classic study of a mainly Italian immigrant male youth group ('gang') in the slum districts of an industrial city in the United States in the years before the Second World War, which well illustrates the main problems of participant observation and the ways in which researchers try to overcome them.

*Entry*

The major problem for the would-be participant observer is to gain admission to the group or organisation s/he wishes to study. Entry has to be unobtrusive, or the results may be prejudiced, so the researcher has to adopt an acceptable role and maintain it throughout. In many cases the researcher can simply be a researcher and pursue inquires *overtly*; in others, where a researcher might not be welcome and research has to be *covert*, a satisfactory 'cover' has to be evolved and maintained throughout. In Whyte's case his 'cover' was that he was writing a book about 'Cornerville'. However, there are obvious advantages where settings can be explored and questions put quite openly.

Observers must not only maintain their roles throughout their research, they also have to ensure that as far as possible their presence is unobtrusive, i.e. does not disturb the normal functioning of the group. In social research it is not necessary to be a clumsy participant to affect research findings, the mere fact that members of the group are aware that they are being studied may be enough to distort the results. Exit is nearly as important as entry — the disappearance of the observer must also be satisfactorily accounted for if it is not to create 'waves'.

*Gatekeepers*

Whyte's success in getting accepted by the group depended crucially on his acceptance by 'Doc', the leader of the 'Norton Street' gang, who ensured he was accepted by the others and subsequently acted as a key informant. Gatekeepers are those people whose co-operation is essential for the researcher to be accepted as a member of the group. In the case of a formal organisation, permission will in any case be required from the senior authorities — the head teacher, in the case of a school, or the governor, in the case of a prison.

### Key informants

As in the case of Doc, gatekeepers may also be key informants — those whose information is of particular importance in making sense of the whole. Over reliance on one source of information, it goes without saying, presents its own risks.

### Interviewing

If the participant observer needs to maintain cover, formal interviewing will have to be confined to gatekeepers and the ability to make satisfactory use of opportunities for unstructured interviewing (persuading people to talk freely) or semi-structured interviewing (asking people questions based on a brief prepared list) is essential to further success. However, Whyte saw this not as a problem but as a strength of the technique, arguing that the unstructured situation provided him with answers to questions he never would have thought of asking.

### Field diary

It should go without saying that the participant observer must maintain a field diary of events and responses as they are still in progress, in as much detail as possible. This record forms the essential starting point for all further analysis. In addition, the field diary acts as the central evidence for other scholars of the reliability of the field work. Even where the researcher's role is overt, it may not either be appropriate or convenient to take notes, or to be seen doing so. In covert research, as Whyte makes clear, notes may need to be taken surreptitiously in order to maintain the researcher's 'cover'.

Participant observation is well established as a technique for research in sociology, but it has three main drawbacks:

1. It is only applicable to small groups.
2. It is impossible to repeat.
3. There is a considerable risk that the participation, rather than the observation, will become central.

# Quantitative Research

## Official statistics

Official statistics have long been an important source of information for sociologists — Emile Durkheim, for example, used police records as the basis for his work on *Suicide*. The annual census that has been carried out every ten years since

1801 (except, for obvious reasons, 1941) forms an essential reference point for much research conducted in the United Kingdom. In fact, statistics and sociology in Britain grew up at the same time and for similar reasons, concern at what was then known as 'the Condition of England Question'. Mayhew's *London Labour and the London Poor* (1851), which despite its largely impressionistic nature is regarded by some as the first British social survey, and the work on London's poor of Charles Booth, between 1886 and 1903, was paralleled by the work of Edwin Chadwick, Sir John Simon and Beatrice and Sidney Webb, as well as a long series of reports by government agencies, the findings of commissions of inquiry and statistical papers. Collectively, such data helped form the basis for new legislative initiatives in the later nineteenth century. Today, official figures are available from all government ministries and departments, and *Social Trends*, an annual survey first published by the Government Social Survey in 1970, is for the student sociologist a particularly useful reference source.

However, official statistics are subject to various kinds of error. Some, like the census itself, are gathered by asking people questions. Until 1991, the census did not have the problem of widespread non-response as reply was a legal obligation and a large number of census enumerators were employed to organise distribution and collection and to offer help. Otherwise, however clearly questions are worded, possibilities of misunderstanding are always present. In addition, the questions posed are asked not for the benefit of the sociologist but of the administrator, and the sociologist therefore has to accept both the assumptions on which the questions are based and the nature of the questions themselves. Official statistics can be used, therefore, only after it has been ascertained how far they are *reliable* and *valid*.

For statistics to be *reliable* there needs to be an assurance that all incidents as defined have actually been recorded. For example, official statistics for strikes are based on reports from employers, and hence they may vary a great deal in accuracy from one industry to another. Much of the media attention given to strikes in nationalised industries, for example, results from the fact that they are so public. Further problems arise where, as in the case of unemployment statistics, the basis for counting has been altered (see also Chapter 11). Until 1982, unemployment figures recorded the number of people known to be out of work whether or not they were claiming unemployment benefit. Since that time only those in receipt of unemployment benefit have been recorded. As many people, especially married or cohabiting women, are not eligible for unemployment benefit as the law now stands, this meant that, at a stroke, there seemed to be very many fewer people out of work, and the government's refusal to continue the old series as a basis for comparison made it very difficult to estimate just what the difference was. British government statistics for unemployment in the 1980s therefore are not reliable as they stand.

For statistics to be *valid* they have to measure what they actually purport to measure. Crime statistics, for example, measure crimes reported to the police. So the figures for crime go up not only when the actual number of crimes goes up, but when more are reported. Theft and burglary top the list of reported crimes, but this may well be because insurance companies will not meet a claim for theft unless a report has been made to the police. Crimes of violence, which attract a great deal of attention from the media and are believed to be very common, are in fact relatively rare. The fact that in the 1980s their number appeared to be rising may reflect a growing incidence of violence. But it may also mean that the police themselves, who were better paid and better resourced than before, were discovering crimes that previously were overlooked. Critics have drawn attention to the fact that so-called 'white-collar' crimes such as fraud and tax evasion attract little attention from the police while attacks on 'social security scroungers' were an unattractive feature of the press of the early 1980s. Yet at that time social security fraud was estimated to cost the country only £50 million a year compared with the £7,000 million lost each year to the Inland Revenue by tax evasion. The ethnomethodological approach explains this discrepancy — the middle-class white-collar worker does not fit the police 'image' of a 'criminal'.

## Surveys

The researcher who requires data which are not available from official sources has to be prepared to find it out. It is not practicable to study the whole of the population of the United Kingdom or even the population of a large industrial town such as Southampton, and fortunately it is not necessary to do so in order to be able to draw valid conclusions. Even the government finds sampling a useful way to gain vital information. Many lay people find it hard to believe that a sample of 1,200−1,500 people drawn from the entire population of the United Kingdom can give an accurate representation of, for example, people's voting intentions. The bigger the sample, they think, the more accurate the results must be, and many would give greater credence to (for example) the 'Newsnight Poll-of-polls' than to any of the individual surveys of which it is made up. But they would be wrong on both counts. A bigger sample is not necessarily more accurate and neither is an average of polls, the individual basis of which is very different. In fact, averaging polls over a period of days or weeks will tend to eliminate the trends as people change their minds up to polling day, to the disadvantage of any party which is tending to gain support at the last minute.

Sampling deals with probabilities, not certainties. The *standard error* indicates how far the sample is likely to differ from the population from which it is taken. It does not guarantee that the sample is correct; and, indeed, in the nature of sampling, there is always some chance, which can often be precisely calculated, that the sample may be very atypical indeed. We can reduce the standard error by increasing the size of the sample, though it will be necessary to quadruple the size of the sample to halve the standard error. But beyond a certain point there is little point in doing so, since we can never be sure that any given sample is typical, and the safest course is to make sure the sample itself is as accurate as we can manage and state the degree of confidence that can be placed in the results.

The advantage of conducting one's own survey, of course, is twofold. The assumptions behind it can be clearly established and every care taken to ensure that data gathered are both reliable and valid measures of the aspect to be studied. Hence a researcher's social survey can be used not only to amass a series of figures but to explore the relationships between the things measured in a way that will help show what the causes of a social phenomenon actually are.

The first step in any survey is to identify the 'population' to be surveyed, which can, of course, be the whole population of a country or region, but is more often a sub-set such as 'married women' or 'people over 60'. Life for the sociologist would be much simpler if the list of the people to be studied, termed the 'sampling frame', could be guaranteed to be accurate. However, finding out whether women are married or men over 60 is not necessarily as easy as it looks. From the sampling frame there then has to be drawn a sample such that what is true of it is likely to be true of the population as a whole. There are five ways in which this can be done:

*Random sampling*

This may be done using the electoral register as a sampling frame and a table of random numbers to determine which individuals are to be interviewed. (At one time every xth name was selected from the list, but this process, known as 'systematic random sampling', is not sufficiently random.) The main problem is that the individuals concerned may not be available for questioning, and that this may affect different strata differently, in which case the value of random sampling is impaired. In addition, the numbers are so large that this method is not available to the social researcher at reasonable cost.

*Stratified random sampling*

A stratified sample, therefore, is one in which the target population is divided into strata or groups, and individuals selected at random from each stratum. This method ensures that all groups that may have clearly distinct views on an issue are sampled and their views ascertained. Again, the main problem is to get hold of the individuals concerned.

*Cluster sampling*

Cluster sampling means interviewing in certain areas because they are typical of a category in general. It is not representative of the population as a whole, but provides a more detailed view of a particular segment of the population. The advantages of the method are the detailed picture that can be built up; the disadvantage is that it is not clear from the survey material alone how far the findings can be generalised or applied to other parts of the country. Cluster sampling is not in any case to be confused with:

*Quota sampling*

Quota sampling is the method used by most commercial surveys. Surveys of this kind, intended to establish the size and type of market for a product, likes and dislikes for given products, what people own, buy or read, or the impact of advertising, are usually carried out under contract by large commercial undertakings. These organisations interview on a regular basis and contract surveys are usually 'piggybacked' on these routine surveys. To make maximum use of the limited time and resources the interviewers employed then select the respondents to be interviewed according to pre-determined instructions as to sex, age, income, etc. This in turn means that the sample is liable to bias from the tendency of interviewers to select interviewees who are congenial or merely available, and if interviews are carried out in a public place, such as a railway station or a shopping precinct, not only do other biases creep in but interviewees are often in a hurry and give hurried answers. Fortunately, given the dire state of educational finances, sociologists can seldom afford to employ commercial firms to do their interviewing for them, even if they should wish to do so.

*Panel studies*

In panel studies the same carefully selected sample of the population is surveyed repeatedly over a period of time to determine changes in their views. This technique, first used in the United States in a pioneering study, *The People's Choice?* of the voting behaviour of residents of Erie County, Ohio, during the 1940 Presidential election (Lazarsfeld, Berelson and Gaudet 1948), is the obvious way to try to keep track of alternations in voter preferences as an election approaches. It is now the basis of the ongoing British Election Survey begun at Nuffield College, Oxford, and continuing at the University of Essex.

The next step is to draw up the *questionnaire*. A questionnaire is simply the list of questions to be asked, taking account of all the possible responses to each question. The length and detail of the questionnaire will depend not only on the amount of information needed but also on the way in which responses are to be obtained. Where a questionnaire is to be administered by interviewers, the interviewers have to be particularly careful not to introduce *their* own views — if a question is not understood and they repeat it in a different form they can easily distort the sense of the original. And a big survey brings substantial problems of handling, coding and analysing the data generated, so that it becomes particularly important that all the interviewers involved should work to the same pattern and record their data in the same way.

A short simple questionnaire can be administered to a large number of people by post: 'Questionnaires can be sent through the mail; interviewers cannot' (Jahoda *et al.* 1951). But there are problems also. Response rates are often low — unless the people concerned feel they have something to gain from answering they can drop a questionnaire in the waste-paper basket. Indeed, this is the reason that commercial mail questionnaires frequently elicit responses with offers of 'money off' coupons or 'free gifts'. If response rates are low the sample may be seriously biased, and there is a general tendency towards bias in favour of the educated and upper income groups. And if a question is ambiguous or misunderstood for any other reason there is nothing the researcher can do about it. However, with these limitations, good response rates have been attained and formed a satisfactory basis for many early studies, such as Political and Economic Planning's survey of graduate employment (PEP 1956).

Problems with the wording of questionnaires are one of the best reasons for prefacing any serious study with a so-called 'pilot survey' which should show up any difficulties, not only with the questions but also with their coding for numerical analysis. If processing is to be handled quickly and accurately coding too must be quick and accurate, and the most reliable way to do this is to incorporate the coding on the questionnaire form itself and get the interviewer simply to mark the relevant boxes. However this restricts the nature of the questions that can be asked to closed or multiple-choice questions.

Closed questions must:

1. be short;
2. make it clear exactly what they are about;
3. weigh alternative possibilities equally;
4. provide for 'don't know' and 'no opinion' (not everybody is a sociologist or wants to be one!);
5. exclude ambiguity — if something other than a 'yes' or 'no' is possible then someone will want to use it.

Multiple-choice answers are best listed on a card and presented to the respondent for comment. The order of choices should be rotated on different cards since experience shows people have a tendency to pick the one at the top or the bottom. If more than one answer is possible the form of the question should make it clear that it is possible to give more than one.

A properly drawn questionnaire achieves its accuracy at a cost, and what it loses is the chance for individuals to state their own point of view in their own words. Hence fieldwork, where open-ended or semi-structured interviews can be conducted, forms a valuable addition and corrective to the numerical data generated by a survey.

*Interviewing*

*Interviews* have many advantages for the sociologist over the rigid questionnaire, and interviewer-based surveys are therefore the norm in British sociological research. The mere presence of an interviewer can ensure questions are understood and increase likelihood of a return. With a co-operative respondent much longer and more detailed surveys can be undertaken. However, interviewing is an art and interviewers have to be well trained in order to conduct long and complex interviews successfully.

The main requirement is to have a sympathetic personality and to be a 'good listener'. The two main possibilities are *open-ended* and *semi-structured* interviews. In the former, the respondent is encouraged to talk as freely as possible, though the interviewer will seek to guide the discussion through a set number of key points as unobtrusively as possible. In the latter, a list of questions is employed openly, but of a more general nature than the questionnaire format would allow, and the answers recorded in as much detail as possible. Obviously, the more freely the respondent is encouraged to talk, the more productive is the interview likely to be, but it is also likely to be a more accurate reflection of their own views and this may be a problem if they have very obsessive personalities or wander endlessly around the subject. Another problem of interviews is the tendency for interviewees to try to 'please' the interviewer by supplying the sort of answers they think the sociologist will want to hear.

There is much controversy about whether or not to record the interview. This can, of course, ethically only be done with the knowledge and co-operation of the interviewee, and the sad fact is that even today many people who are good conversationalists 'clam up' in the presence of a microphone. The sociologist should therefore cultivate the ability to remember the key points of interviews and to record them *immediately after* the conclusion of the interview while they are still fresh in the mind.

## Unobtrusive measures

The popularity of surveys as a method of social research has often tended to obscure the fact that there may be other methods of obtaining the same information. In any case, use of other measures forms a useful cross-check on the data obtained from survey material; the process known among sociologists as *triangulation*. Asking people is one way of finding out what products people buy in different neighbourhoods; another method, pioneered by sociologists in the United States in conjunction with civic cleansing departments, is to empty out the contents of their trashcans (dustbins) and see what is actually in them. Not only is this information likely to be more accurate, but it is *unobtrusive*. By unobtrusive measures we mean those which do not alert the people being studied to the fact that they are under observation (Webb *et al.*, 1966).

Though rooting through dustbins is not to everyone's taste, there are many other unobtrusive measures of social behaviour and a sociologist should always give consideration to those available. Wear and tear on library books has been used to determine not only which books have been consulted but how well they have been read. The influx of Cubans into Miami after 1959 was reflected in terms of the amount of Spanish used in street signs and other public notices; similar methods can be used to determine the proportions of language use in other ethnically mixed areas. A Chinese researcher was made welcome in many restaurants that on the telephone had previously indicated that Chinese visitors were unwelcome; these and similar findings confirmed a marked discrepancy between verbal and actual discriminatory behaviour. (Unfortunately, this problem can also happen the other way round.)

## Suggestions for Further Reading

A comprehensive but accessible guide to research methods is Graham Allan and Chris Skinner (1991), *Handbook for Research Students in the Social Sciences*. Another good introduction is Martin Bulmer (ed.) (1984), *Sociological Research Methods*, 2nd edn. The annual publication *Social Trends* is a mine of information for the sociologist, and Myra Chapman (1986), *Plain Figures* an excellent guide to statistics and their presentation. C. Hakim (1987), *Research Design: strategies and choices in the design of social research* deals with the planning and organisation of surveys in the British context, while R. G. Burgess (ed.) (1984), *In the Field: an introduction to field research* discusses the problems of interviewing and assessing qualitative data. The classic of participant observation, William F. Whyte (1956), *Street Corner Society*, illustrates both its problems and its value.

# 3 Social Stratification I: Class, wealth and poverty

## Stratification

Most questions on this area of the syllabus centre on changes in the class structure. There are some variations on this basic theme and the most usual of these are as follows:

- The extent to which Britain remains a class society or the more theoretical examination of whether inequality is inevitable (and/or functional).
- The class position of particular groups — the favourite such group remains the routine white-collar worker.
- The changing class structure obviously involves consideration of studies of social mobility, but these may be more specifically examined by questioning how open British society is. (If a very general question on 'openness' is asked, the very clever candidate may score highly by making some comment on the other senses of the term: the absence of secrecy and international interdependence, for example.)

## Wealth and Poverty

This topic is generally examined by questions which counterpose change and the lack of it:

- Changes in the distribution of wealth in the twentieth century (or, possibly, since the Second World War).
- The persistence of poverty and the related questions of whether it is inherited or constitutes a culture trapping future generations.
- The changing relative importance of the various factors for poverty.

# What is Stratification?

Inequality has been a feature of human societies since the earliest times. For the sociologist, it is not just the fact that inequalities exist in advanced industrial societies that is interesting, but the fact that these inequalities form regular patterns, and that within each society these patterns are associated with almost everything that an individual does.

*Stratification* is not just differentiation. We use the term to refer to different levels which can be ranked in order from top to bottom; the inequalities are *structured*. The word comes from the geological term *stratum* (plural = *strata*), meaning a layer of rock. However, as with most analogies in the social sciences, this one creates problems, for as Worsley (1971: 283) points out, social strata are quite different from geological ones. Though age and type may in some cases differ, what makes social strata different is the fact of superiority or inferiority between them. They are not wholly separate from one another but connected. They are not permanent. Human beings can perceive their own inequalities, and this in turn gives rise to the emergence of new groups and brings about change over time.

# Types of Stratification

The question of whether or not early societies were stratified is still debated but we can never know the answer. Some modern pre-industrial societies appear to have no *stratification*, even though there may be differentiation of other kinds. Examples are the Andaman Islanders and the Bushmen of the Kalahari. However, otherwise all modern societies, and certainly all complex societies, are stratified, though they can and do vary in how *open* they are. By 'open' we mean the possibility of mobility between groups, which varies according to the type of stratification that exists.

Types of
stratification

- Age sets.
- Gender (see Chapter 4).
- Kinship (Caste, for Race, see Chapter 4).
- Estates.
- Social class.
- Party.

## Age sets

Just as schools are divided into classes according to age, so some pre-industrial societies are stratified by *age sets*. The Australian aborigines and the Nandi of Kenya are stratified by both age and sex. Young men move from one age set to the next as they grow up, the move being marked by 'rites of passage' for a whole group in which signs of their new standing are often marked physically on their bodies. Different age sets are responsible for different tasks, though there is little difference between them either in terms of production or of consumption. This type of stratification has rigid divisions but very high mobility — every man, if he lives long enough, occupies each male stratum in turn and can expect in time to receive the respect due to age, though not always — the Eskimos, like some other nomadic peoples, ceased to support old people when they became unproductive.

## Gender and kinship

Gender and kinship also differentiate other pre-industrial and many more advanced industrial societies (see Chapter 4). The most rigid form of stratification by kinship is *caste*, familiar to us from India, where it rests on religious sanctions and hence has been modified but not destroyed by action of government. The word 'caste' is a European word, from Portuguese 'casta' meaning 'pure stock'. Hindu caste society is stratified in five closed groups: the Brahmin, the priests, the Kshatriya, the warriors, the Vaishya, the merchants, and the Shudra, all others; historically, there were also 'outcastes' who performed the most menial duties and were shunned by all castes. Discrimination of this kind has been formally banned by the Indian government but it survives, as does discrimination against the so-called 'scheduled castes'. A recent attempt to give more jobs to members of the scheduled castes ran into furious resistance and resulted in the fall of the government. Each individual is born into a fixed position within the caste system. The hierarchy of castes itself is fixed and defined at any point in time but though neither movement nor intermarriage between one caste and another is possible, changes in the relative standing of groups (jatis) within each caste are possible, and seem, indeed, to be a major aim of some groups.

This system is not unique. Among the Ankole of Uganda the main division was between the tall, fair-skinned, cattle-rearing Bahima and the darker-skinned, agriculturalist people they conquered, the Bairu. The Bairu, effectively a subject people in that they could not hold political office, bear arms or own fertile cattle, were forbidden to intermarry with the Bahima, whom they served. Conquest also explains those characteristics which the system of *apartheid* (separateness) of present-day South Africa shares with caste society. The law has established rigid distinctions by birth between 'Whites', 'Blacks' and 'Coloured' citizens, who were formerly forbidden to intermarry and to live in the same areas. These distinctions are now breaking down under pressure from the international community. The issue of race in British society will also be dealt with in detail in the next chapter.

## Estates

Estates, which were formerly the basis of social order in most of Europe including Scotland, are legally defined groups with different obligations and rights. The three main groups were the nobility, the clergy and the commons, and for each group there was not only a specified set of tasks in the division of labour (Bottomore 1965), but specified rights and duties towards the other estates. The individual, whether noble or commoner, was born into a fixed position. Though the Church preached the duty of accepting one's place in society, kings took care to keep the legal sanctions against the breaches of the system under their own control.

The whole structure was maintained by the work of *serfs* or (in England) *villeins*. However, even villeins had rights as well as duties — they were not slaves. Mobility was very limited, but from generation to generation movement did take place, more rapidly after the growth of towns. Also a commoner could be moved to a higher estate by legal act of a superior (an example of this being the tinker's elevation in the 'induction' of Shakespeare's *Taming of the Shrew*). With the rise of towns and the emergence in the High Middle Ages of a merchant class, merchants could buy titles for themselves and some intermarriage took place between them and the nobility. In addition, the Church (whose priests were forbidden to marry) recruited from both nobility and commons — Cardinal Wolsey, for example, was a butcher's boy from Ipswich. In the end the system broke down because it could no longer accommodate the emergence of new social groups.

From the age of estates we derive the notion of *status* — visible signs of one's position in society which confers consequent rights and obligations (see Turner, B. S. 1988: 6). Status remains an important basis of stratification in modern Britain, where titles are still given as rewards to those who have served the state in various capacities, e.g. Viscount Tonypandy, Viscount Whitelaw, Sir David Steel. Though titles are still used in some republics (e.g. Ireland) they are no longer conferred, and in the United States the giving or accepting of titles was prohibited by the Constitution of 1787. However, status remains very important in helping to stratify American society, even if it has been largely detached from older connotations of kinship.

## Social class

Social class is the main type of stratification in modern industrial societies, e.g. United Kingdom, France, Germany. The term 'class' came into use to denote social strata in the mid-eighteenth century (Calvert 1982) and was never clearly defined. However, classes are best regarded as 'spontaneous configurations' (MacIver and Page 1931) arising from economic inequalities, whether of wealth or income. Though terms differ from one country to another, most recognise the existence of an upper class, a middle class and a lower or working class. Some distinguish rural workers or peasants from urban workers, as in France.

Classes, at least in Western societies, have no legal standing and in theory all are equal before the law. Hence mobility between classes is possible both up and down, but the chances of upward mobility are in each case greater for those who are better off. Similarly, while intermarriage between classes is possible, it may result in social disapproval. The sanctions that maintain a class system are neither religious nor legal, but social.

### Party

The most recent basis of stratification has been that of *party*. Political parties first emerged in their modern form in Britain and Sweden in the eighteenth century, but it was the German economist Max Weber who first noted their role as stratifying society by regulating access to political power. As such party membership became important in Eastern Europe after 1945 (Djilas 1957). When class distinctions in communist states had been formally abolished or were regarded as having been eradicated, membership of the single ruling party carried with it special privileges and duties. At the same time a distinction was maintained in the USSR between two classes of urban and rural workers, and a separate stratum of the *intelligentsia* was identified, consisting of those educated people from which the Communist Party (CPSU) members were largely recruited. It seems very likely that with the break-up of the Soviet bloc, party will again give way to class as the dominant form of stratification in the countries of Eastern Europe, though ethnic divisions may for the time being prove more important. In Lithuania, for example, ethnic discrimination has already been introduced to protect the position of the majority.

# Why Stratification Survives

Given the formal equality of citizens in most modern states, the fact that stratification survives in all advanced industrial societies needs explanation. Approaches to the study of stratification are in fact defined by the way in which they seek to explain its origins: according to whether the authors concerned are *consensus* theorists or *conflict* theorists, in the terms discussed in Chapter 1.

# Consensus Theories

The first writers to use the term 'class' in the mid-eighteenth century tended to see stratification of society as natural and even desirable, and today functionalist writers — those who hold that a social phenomenon exists because in some way it helps the society to survive and maintain itself — see stratification as a key reason why advanced industrial societies have survived and prospered. Thus, Davis and Moore (1945) argue that stratification exists in every human society because it is a 'device by which societies ensure that the most important positions are conscientiously filled by the most qualified persons'. Special rewards must be offered to individuals who take on positions of responsibility, or have the most advanced education/training, to place and motivate individuals. Differential rewards are therefore functional for society since they contribute to its maintenance and well-being. Inequality is seen as fulfilling a positive role in all human societies: it is *integrative* (helps hold society together) and *adaptive* (helps societies to adjust to new needs and new challenges).

Among sociologists the leading exponent of the functionalist view was the American Talcott Parsons. He argues (Parsons 1964) that order, stability and co-operation in society are all based on 'value consensus'. *Consensus* is the extent to which all the members of the society share a common set of ideas about the purposes and goals of society. Parsons believes that stratification systems derive from these common values and are 'the ranking of units in a social system in accordance with the common value system'. US society, for example, 'puts primary emphasis on productive activity within the economy', and believes those who perform best should be rewarded accordingly. The division of labour means that some must direct and others follow. This leads to inequality in terms of power and prestige. Those with the power to organise and co-ordinate the activities of others will have a higher social status than those they direct. Without social inequality members of society could not co-operate effectively or work together. Hence inequalities benefit all as they further the shared goals of society as a whole.

Of course, Parsons, like other consensus theorists, recognises that not everyone will see it this way and so there will still be some conflict in society. However, he fails to examine just how significant this apparently minor detail may be. As Tumin (1967) points out, who is important in society is not a constant; it depends what service is required at any given time, and in any case 'some labour force of unskilled workmen is as important and as indispensable to the factory as some labour force of engineers'. Nor is it clear that any special skill is required for those positions of power which Davis and Moore consider important. Educational inequality and lack of opportunity suggest that there is a much larger pool of talent available than is ever actually used; hence 'stratification systems are apparently inherently antagonistic to the development of full equality of opportunity'. It is not those with talent who are elevated to positions of authority, but rather the children of those who already hold such positions. Hence as Michael Young earlier argued, in his influential *The Rise of the Meritocracy* (1961), even stratification by merit may be 'dysfunctional', as it can lead to conflict rather than co-operation. In Young's vision of a Britain of the future, in which the most able use their talents to perform the most important social roles, ambition is frequently frustrated amd those who fail to achieve the top posts are demoralised.

The argument that divisions in society are apparently accepted by the majority of all classes is equally easily refuted. As Frank Parkin (1972) points out, the fact that people are fairly consistent in the relative value they attach to different occupations merely reflects effects of their individual socialisation. Berger and Luckmann (1967) put it bluntly: 'he who has the bigger stick has the better chance of imposing his definitions of reality'.

Research does suggest, however, that the main contention of the functionalist writers does have some validity: that stratification will emerge in complex societies, whether people want it to or not. An example is Eva Rosenfeld's (1974) study of kibbutzim in Israel, which showed that, despite the care that had been taken to establish them on a fully egalitarian basis, two strata had emerged. However, she rightly points out that this does not of itself mean stratification is inevitable.

# Conflict Theories

As Hindess (1987) indicates, class structures are very resistant to change and those who benefit from superior positions within them will not favour change. Conflict is necessary to social change.

## Marx

Karl Marx is the best known, if neither the first not the last, of a number of writers who can be grouped as 'conflict theorists'. Interpreting what Marx himself wrote is complicated by two things: (1) he lived for a long time and changed his mind at different stages; and (2) some of the key evidence is fragmentary. Though he stated that 'classes' were central to the organisation of society, Marx did not define what he meant by class. We can, however, infer that he saw class position as an objective economic relationship defined by an individual's relationship to the *means of production*; which is to say, whether or not the individual owned tools, machinery, land, etc., or worked for someone else who did.

Marx was primarily concerned with what he termed 'capitalist' society, which was the developing industrial society of Western Europe in the mid-nineteenth century. He saw the past as an historical sequence of economic development, from a prehistoric stage of 'primitive accumulation', through ancient societies based on slave production and feudal societies built on the work of serfs, to capitalist societies, in which most individuals sold their labour power in return for money. Consequently, he saw capitalist society as being increasingly divided into only two main classes, the bourgeoisie (owners) and the proletariat (workers), whose interests would inevitably conflict.

A society in which the bourgeoisie would have all power, and the proletariat none, implied that the proletariat would slowly lose mobility, while intermediate classes would sink into the proletariat and ultimately be reduced to destitution. At this point, he believed, when the proletariat had developed *class consciousness* and become aware of their own deprivation, they would overthrow the bourgeoisie and take their destinies into their own hands, establishing a classless society. Classes do not promote social change until they become subjective groups as well as objective ones. Only through class-consciousness will they begin to organise themselves and act effectively in political affairs. By bringing the proletariat together in factories the bourgeoisie are fostering this sense of class-consciousness and hastening their own downfall. This political view was originally one of a number of versions of *socialism*, though since the Russian Revolution of 1917 it has more commonly been known as *communism* to distinguish it from other, usually non-revolutionary socialist ideas.

For the sociologist it is in the many and complex implications of Marx's theories for the development of industrial societies that his main interest lies. For example, despite his belief in the ultimate survival of only two classes, in a number of studies of societies of his own time Marx clearly also saw:

1. Divisions within classes, e.g. that the bourgeoisie was not homogeneous, being divided between industrial interests and finance capital.
2. Transitional classes surviving from feudalism, e.g peasants, or early stages of industrial capitalism, e.g. the so-called 'petty (petit) bourgeoisie'.

It was Marx who established definitively the meaning of the word 'class' as a primarily economic term, giving us the notion of stratification by position in relation to the forces of production and the important concept of class consciousness. He is important because he shows how economic position affects everyone's life chances. Though he is the best-known conflict theorist, not all conflict theorists are Marxists. Moreover, the refutation of aspects of Marx's theories does not necessarily imply that conflict theorists are wrong. This is particularly important since it is generally accepted that universal education and progressive taxes have led in the twentieth century to the decline of material inequalities between classes. Yet major differences in life-chances remain between classes, e.g. in infant mortality rate (the number per 1,000 who die before the age of one year) and health generally. Although the pauperisation predicted by Marx himself has not occurred, poverty and inequality are still with us and have important social consequences.

## Weber

Max Weber was only one of a number of writers who showed that Marx did not adequately explain the complexity of late nineteenth-century society. However, his views are of particular importance to sociologists as he offers an effective alternative way of looking at the problem of stratification. First of all, Weber accepts the concept of class which he defines as a group of individuals who share a similar position in a market economy, and by virtue of that fact receive similar economic rewards. He accepts that the basic division in society is between those who own the means of production and those who do not, but argues that all the various skills and services offered by different occupations have different economic values. Skills and qualifications, therefore, operate to distinguish the classes in the same way as ownership or control of the means of production.

Weber sees no evidence to support the idea of the polarisation of classes. As capitalism develops, the white-collar middle class expands rather than contracts, so there is no proletarianisation. Nor does he accept that class is the only basis for political action and the organisation of power. It is possible that classes can act together but it is not inevitable. There are other bases for action. In 'Class, Status and Party', a chapter from Weber's book *Economy and Society* (Gerth and Mills 1957), he identifies two.

1. *Status*, which he equates with social honour, the common view of a person's position in society, which includes their style of life and their pattern of consumption, and so tends to go with class but not necessarily so. Unlike classes, members of status groups are almost always aware of their common status situation. They share a similar life-style, identify with their status group and feel that they belong to it. They often place restrictions on the ways in which outsiders may interact with them. Status may be *ascribed* (given as a consequence of who a person is) or *achieved* (earned). For Weber, more 'modern' and more 'rational' societies tend to stress achieved rather than ascribed status, but this judgement is controversial.

2. *Party*, which for Weber means groups working together to further common interests through political action, and he uses it in a very loose sense to cover both what we would now call parties and what are now more correctly termed 'pressure groups' or 'interest groups'. Parties often represent the interests of classes or status groups, but not always. Like status, party is class influenced but not rigidly determined as in Marx. The bases of party may in fact cut across class alignments, e.g. religious, nationalist affiliations. Some modern US writers have modified Weber's original typology to replace 'party' with the more general term 'power', but for Weber class, status and party were three dimensions of the organisation of power, and power was therefore common to all of them.

Weber's analysis of class, status groups and parties suggests that no single theory can adequately explain stratification in complex societies. The interaction of social groupings is both involved and variable, and must be examined in particular societies during particular historical periods. In fact, Weber's three bases of stratification are to some extent separate and in other respects go together so that there is some trade-off possible between them. Weber was the first writer since Boethius, at the time of the fall of the Roman Empire, to recognise that status varies according to society and time period.

Weber's position as one of the founders of sociology should not and does not exempt his theories from criticism and testing by later researchers. Class and status are so closely interlinked, that, as Parkin says, 'there is a marked congruence in the two dimensions of inequality based on the division of labour' (Parkin 1972). Ethnic and religious groups however yield differences between the status and class hierarchies. So too does the fact of whether you are a man or a woman. In fact, stratification of modern societies by *gender* and *race* is so important and raises so many interesting issues that they have been dealt with separately in Chapter 4.

# The British Class Structure

Class, then, is about the totality of an individual's economic position. However, all empirical studies of class as an economic concept are plagued by three problems.

1. There is no firm definition of classes on which all agree. Hence in analysing the British class system researchers resort to *indicators* of social class, such as income and occupation, and what they describe, whatever their own views on the matter, is really a class/status system (Calvert 1982).
2. Mobility between classes is a constant fact of social life. Hence at any given moment quite a large number of people are in a state of transition and there are many households in which (to take the most obvious example) husband and wife come from different backgrounds. Stewart *et al.* (1980) emphasise the importance of career patterns — a person's perception of class depends on where they started from.
3. Given the interrelationship between class and status, it may not be one's *actual* class position that matters so much as other people's perception of it. All observers agree that one of the most marked distinguishing features of British society is its class structure. The modern British class system is generally held to be less open, having a lower rate of social mobility than that of the United States with which it is often compared. Partly this is because of the survival of privilege based on birth and wealth. The monarchy and the House of Lords are vestiges of the division into estates, based on birth, and the class system itself is the continuation of that formed by nineteenth-century trade and industry, based on wealth but protected by heredity. Individual advancement on merit has increased in the twentieth century, and through education there is more equality of opportunity, though this is severely limited by differential access.

The old upper class survives to some extent in Britain, but in all respects except status it is hard to distinguish as a separate entity. There is in fact a very marked tendency to see British society as divided into two main classes: the middle class and the working (never the 'lower') class. This would give a class structure shaped like a blunted pyramid resting on a broad base. But the differences between the middle and working classes are certainly not based on one simple factor.

Empirical research on British society has resulted in many attempts to group individuals according to where they fit on various axes of classification. This should in turn give rise to an *aggregative model* of class positions determined by how many individuals turn out to occupy a common position. However, in practice the picture of class affiliations that this gives is a confused one. There are two problems: even in the short term the boundaries are not clear, and in the long term classes outlast the individuals who are in them, and the aggregative model cannot explain why this should be so without some overall theory about what is going on. At least seven criteria for distinguishing class membership are used by different writers.

The Registrar General's Classification (RGC), the method of determining social class used by the Office of Population, Censuses and Surveys, is the basic starting point for all modern empirical studies of social class.

**Criteria for distinguishing class membership**

1. Income and wealth.
2. Occupation.
3. Education.
4. Family background.
5. Pattern of expenditure.
6. Lifestyle.
7. Self-identification.

The basis of the RGC is the job held by the 'head of household', usually the senior male member. All jobs recognised as such are ranked in six categories termed 'social classes'. There are two criteria used for ranking. The first is broadly by income, though there are certain anomalies owing to long-term historical movements. The crucial division, however, comes in the middle, between *manual* and *non-manual* occupations. Occupational rewards on both sides of this line are, in fact, very similar. Worse still, it is precisely at this point that the debate over the present and future evolution of the social class structure is centred. And the classification presents serious problems in assigning class positions to women.

**The Registrar General's Classification**

Social class

| | |
|---|---|
| I | Professional |
| II | Intermediate occupations |
| IIIn | Routine non-manual |
| IIIm | Skilled manual |
| IV | Partly skilled manual |
| V | Unskilled manual |

Why, then, is the RGC still so widely used? There are three main reasons, apart from familiarity:

1. It identifies the *images* of society held by its members (Goldthorpe *et al.* 1969).
2. Many other social attributes relate to it to a quite striking degree, e.g. education, fertility, health, housing and voting behaviour. Hence it is an effective predictor of social behaviour. It is also of practical value in determining what people will use and consume (e.g. manual workers will spend proportionately more of their income on food than members of the middle class, and this information keyed to census data is of direct value to planners of a new supermarket). Its six categories are used essentially unchanged by the advertising industry to 'target' their campaigns.
3. It has been able to accommodate to new occupations, though as with others before (e.g. chauffeur, garage hand, aircraft engineer) these new occupations offer the most open opportunities for upward mobility, e.g. computer programmer, advertising executive, research chemist.

What it does NOT take into account is:

1. *Gender* — it assumes that an unmarried woman is of the same class as her father and a married woman of the same class as her husband (see Chapter 4).
2. *Race* — census data on racial origin have not been collected in the past in Britain and it is very hard to draw reliable deductions from other material (see also Chapter 4).
3. *Status* — there is no place for the 'upper class' or for that matter, for the 'poor'.
4. *Change* — the RGC by its nature can only describe, not analyse. It cannot tell us why the social structure is like this and why it continues to reproduce itself. As Giddens (1982) points out, social structuration can only be explained by the way people see classes, that is, with *class consciousness*. Understanding why people see classes in the way that they do is one of the main unsolved problems facing the sociologist.

Dissatisfaction with the limitations of the RGC has led to various attempts to develop other models of the British class structure. One of these, the Hall—Jones scale, devised in 1950 by John Hall and D. Caradog-Jones, was widely used by British sociologists for many years. It was also based on occupation, but has been criticised for an alleged bias towards white-collar workers and hence towards the middle class. A new scale was therefore devised from scratch for the Nuffield Mobility Survey (1972—80), the results of which were reported by Goldthorpe in *Social Mobility and Class Structure in Modern Britain* (1980) and by A. H. Halsey, A. F. Heath and J. H. Ridge in *Origins and Destinations* (1980). It is now generally known as the *Hope—Goldthorpe classification*.

The Hope—Goldthorpe classification, which follows the same principle as the RGC in being based on occupation, by incorporating also the market situation arrives at a different categorisation of seven occupational groups grouped in three larger classes. An important feature is the explicit recognition of an intermediate class between the middle and working classes.

Goldthorpe (1983) himself has taken a 'traditional' view that class is determined by the occupation of the 'head of the family', but other writers have been readier to accept that even within the same family there may be different and contradictory class positions. Similar contradictions feature in the lives of those who occupy the intermediate class, who are subject to 'social closure' (exclusion) from both the other two classes.

# Class Structure

Class position is not in fact something on which subjective and objective assessments always coincide. Hence people's own perception as to whether they (or others) are in the middle class or the working class do not always agree with each other, or with the view of the sociologist. The Young and Willmott (1956) and Ralph H. Turner (1958) studies found that:

The Hope–
Goldthorpe
Classification

---

**The Service Class**

I   Professional
    Higher grade professionals, administrators and officials;
    managers in large establishments; large proprietors
II  Administrative and managerial
    Lower-grade professionals, administrators and officials;
    higher grade technicians; managers in small business and
    industrial establishments; supervisors of non-manual
    employees

**The Intermediate Class**

III Routine non-manual
    (a) Routine non-manual employees in administration and
        commerce
    (b) Personal service workers
IV  Self-employed
    (a) Small proprietors, artisans, etc., with employees
    (b) Small proprietors, artisans, etc., without employees
    (c) Farmers and smallholders; self-employed fishermen
V   Non-professional lower technical and supervisory
    Lower-grade technicians; supervisors of manual workers

**The Working Class**

VI  Skilled manual workers
VII Semi-skilled and unskilled workers
    (a) Semi-skilled and unskilled manual workers (not in
        agriculture)
    (b) Agricultural workers

---

1. There are significant differences in the way that people in different social
   classes tend to rate occupations in terms of prestige. Hence the middle class
   view themselves differently from the way in which they are seen by members
   of the working class.
2. Businessmen and professionals tended to think differently from one another
   as well as each from labourers.

## The Middle Class

The decline in manufacturing and the expansion of the tertiary sector has led to
a massive expansion of the middle class and in the process the term has become
almost meaningless. The middle class has so far fragmented that it is now necessary
to identify professional and administrative elements as distinct groups. It is hard
to see how the class-consciousness of a company director can be likened to that
of the humble filing clerk. Their market situations are entirely different. The

middle class contains both people in authority over others and those whom they direct. The filing clerk in this sense has more in common with the production operative on the factory floor.

The key question concerning the middle class is the relationship of ownership and control. Marx believed that it was the fact that the bourgeoisie owned the means of production that gave them control, not just of industry, but of the state and society. It was ownership that made them, for Marx, the *ruling class*. However, as early as 1945, in his seminal *The Managerial Revolution*, James Burnham was arguing, still from a Marxist standpoint, that in developed industrial societies control of production was already passing out of the hands of the owners of capital into a new group of managers. This, he predicted, would result in the need for a radical reappraisal of the class position of both.

Today in Britain the ownership of industry is extremely diffuse and much of it is in the hands, not of individuals, but of large corporations, which in turn are owned by other corporations. But John Scott, who emphasises the way in which stratification is grouped around families rather than individuals, rejects the argument that the managerial revolution has reduced the power of what he terms the *business class*. For him the business class remains the key to the control of economic processes, but it is not itself a single unified group, comprising as it does the three groups of finance capitalists, entrepreneurial capitalists and managers, or what he terms 'internal' capitalists — those who manage companies in which they have relatively little personal stake (Scott 1977).

Apart from the 'managerial revolution', the most striking feature of industrial organisation in the twentieth century has been the expansion of clerical work, many of the new posts created being filled by women. David Lockwood, in *The Blackcoated Worker* (1958), noted how this had been accompanied by the growth of differences between conditions in small offices and in big ones. As the latter come to dominate the working conditions of clerical workers, they have been subject to studies questioning the extent to which they are becoming proletarianised (see Braverman's 1975 discussion of it in Chapter 4).

There has been some doubt as to whether clerical workers can really be seen as a homogeneous group with common characteristics (Stewart *et al.* 1980). This view is reinforced by the very marked gender differences in career patterns. Crompton and Jones (1984) have shown that while there are relatively high rates of male promotion out of clerical status, women, constituting 70 per cent of all clerical workers, do not find it easy to gain promotion and relatively few do.

Roberts *et al.*, in *The Fragmentary Class Structure* (1977), examined 243 male white-collar workers, and from their findings argued that the middle class could be divided into a number of different strata, according to the various images of their class position that they held. The found four main images of class:

1. Fifteen per cent felt no sense of class loyalty; they were professionals who saw society simply as a ladder of opportunity.
2. Twenty-seven per cent had a traditional 'middle-class' image of themselves;

they saw themselves as part of a massive group between a small, powerful upper class and a small, poverty-stricken lower class.

3. Nineteen per cent sensed themselves as 'compressed' — they were small businessmen who felt their position in the middle class threatened by working-class aspirations.

4. Fourteen per cent saw themselves as working class. They felt that they were at the bottom of the class ladder.

However, more modern studies need to take account of the differential class position of women, and among others Ian Bradley (1982) asserted that the obituaries of the middle class were premature. He expected that in the year 2000 the middle class would be 'bigger and probably better-off' than when he was writing. Events since have suggested that he was right.

Cotgrove (1975) and Klein (1965) have identified distinct 'class subcultures' within the overall culture of society, and in Britain the differences in view between middle and working class take a variety of forms. Most obviously, working-class respondents differ significantly from middle-class respondents in the way they rate different occupations. On the Hall—Jones scale, F. M. Martin (1954) found that:

1. Women members of the working class were more likely than men to grade themselves as middle class.

2. Those who were regarded by others and regarded themselves as working class tended to extend the term 'working class' to everyone who worked for a living (a view, interestingly enough, shared by Mrs Thatcher, who on being questioned about the effects of her policies on 'the working class' replied: 'I'm working class — I work!').

3. Those members of the working class who saw themselves as middle class tended to rate those whom they regarded as working class as lazy and irresponsible.

4. Both middle and working class tended to estimate their numbers as larger than they actually are.

## The Working Class

Perceptions of the working class tend to be dominated by the Marxist view of it as the embodiment of the proletariat. However, Marx was not necessarily a Marxist, and so recent writers tend to reserve the term 'Marxian' to refer to Marx's own ideas, 'Marxist' to writers who have followed him.

Modern Marxists, before the collapse of Marxism-Leninism in Eastern Europe, had already moved a long way from traditional Marxist positions and in some cases had abandoned them altogether. Many were heavily influenced by Continental Marxist thought and structuralism. Structuralists argue that the structure of society constrains individuals to act in predetermined ways, and that 'key social, economic and political forces' in society create a series of class positions which differ from one another as do railway carriages. The Greek writer Nicos Poulantzas (1974) was influential in the decision to abandon Marx's own distinction between the ownership/non-ownership of capital, and to seek to understand the position of 'intermediate strata' in terms of a distinction between productive/non-productive work. This division, he argued, had created a new 'petit bourgeoisie'. This, as the US socialist writer, Erik Olin Wright (1978, 1979, 1985) pointed out, resulted in some absurdities. It would mean that we would have to distinguish between a cleaner in a bank (non-productive) and a cleaner in a factory (productive). Obviously, this does not accord with common sense.

Wright concerns himself with changes in the occupational/business structure in the twentieth century, in particular the deskilling of workers, the growth of bureaucracy and the increasing dispersal of share ownership. He concludes that, despite such changes, the US working class makes up about 50 per cent of the population, while on Poulantzas' assumptions it would only be about 20 per cent (see also Carchedi 1983).

Wright has been criticised in turn by Abercrombie and Urry (1983) and by Weberians such as Parkin (1979), who say that a structural framework does not fit how people see their own place in society.

The mainstream Weberian view of British sociology is represented by the work of Ralf Dahrendorf (1959), a German Free Democrat (Liberal) who studied in England and became Director of the London School of Economics and Political Science. For him both Marxian classes have become 'decomposed'; the working class has been divided into three main parts, and trade unions have helped to institutionalise a form of class conflict. These views seem to have been confirmed by the empirical studies carried out by British Weberians, such as Goldthorpe and Lockwood.

The two key questions concerning the role of the working class in the 1990s are those posed by Abercrombie *et al.* (1988): has the position of the working class changed relative to other classes, and has the structure of the working class become more internally divided?

## The Changing Position of the Working Class?

The belief that working-class lifestyles were changing so much that workers were effectively becoming middle class — often referred to as the 'embourgeoisement thesis' — originated in the United States with Kerr *et al.*, in *Industrialism and Industrial Man* (1962). Kerr and his colleagues had noted that as a result of the prosperity of the 1950s working-class Americans were enjoying rising living standards and mass consumption, the phenomenon named 'affluence' by the economist John Kenneth Galbraith, in *The Affluent Society* (1958). Kerr argued from this that class conflict would be reduced and traditional working-class politics decline. The same theme was taken up in the United Kingdom by Ferdynand Zweig

(1961), who in his *The Worker in an Affluent Society* argued that workers were adopting middle-class lifestyles and identifying with the middle class, because income and wealth had been redistributed sufficiently to reduce inequalities between the social classes. Thus life-chances, or the opportunities open to members of different social classes, were becoming more and more alike.

The thesis gained widespread support during the 1950s and 1960s and was even used to 'explain' the electoral defeat of the Labour Party in 1959 (see Abrams *et al.* 1963). But meanwhile it was tested in a major research project by Goldthorpe *et al.* (1958a, b; 1959), taking the relatively wealthy car manufacturing town of Luton as their area for study. They found no evidence that embourgeoisement was actually taking place. On the contrary, affluent workers were not so affluent compared with members of the traditional middle class, nor had they adopted the social patterns of the middle class. In fact, they preserved many traditional patterns of working-class life, continued to identify with the working class and did not tend to vote Conservative. Looking at the problem from the other end, Young and Willmott found that, in Woodford, Essex, whatever their affluence, the working class were not accepted as middle class. They too concluded that, contrary to expectations, affluence had not brought about fundamental change, and the degree of social mobility had been overestimated.

Some developments leading to higher living standards among the working class were not in dispute, however, and were to continue into the 1970s. They included the continued growth of tertiary industry (the services sector) at the expense of primary extractive and manufacturing industry, technological developments in automation, and the continuance of more egalitarian welfare and taxation policies producing more middle incomes and better working conditions for more people. In some respects the middle and working classes were seen as coming gradually to accept common assumptions. Thus workers were accepting the primary importance of the conjugal family and seeking recreation within it in a pattern known as the 'privatisation of leisure'. On the other hand, non-manual workers were accepting unionisation as a vehicle for voicing their demands for better pay and working conditions.

Critics say that once more the data are lacking or have been misinterpreted. On the basic point, as we shall see, there is strong evidence that no significant redistribution of wealth has taken place. Otherwise there are equally plausible alternative explanations of the observed facts. Manual work is definitely in decline, but Westergaard (1984) argues that as automation increases, certain skills will become obsolete, and the need for unskilled labourers will again increase. Similarly, some manual work is better paid than some white-collar work, but the reason why so much clerical work is badly paid may well be because the workers are female, while the high manual wages of the 1970s, as events have since proved, owed more to overtime and productivity deals than a permanent improvement in basic pay, and have fallen back sharply in the 1980s.

There has certainly been some move towards homogeneity in terms of material possessions of the middle and working classes and this may indicate a change in social relationships. But it may simply reflect the relative decline in the cost of consumer durables and the increasing value put on women's time.

Even if the view that inequalities are diminishing were not wholly supported by the evidence, the view that classes are becoming more fragmentary does have more merit. Competition of this kind, long observed in the middle class, is likely to lead to a decline in class-consciousness in the working class also.

There is another sense in which the class structure has become increasingly fragmentary and this has been especially important in the analysis of voting behaviour (see Chapter 5). There are fewer and fewer people in Britain who fit neatly into the traditional views of working- and middle-class lifestyles (Reid 1977). The expansion of home ownership has been the most marked development, which has undermined the traditional simplistic view of the two classes. Now some 70 per cent of people own or are buying their own homes, home ownership is no longer a clear, middle-class attribute. This and other factors have led some commentators to pare down their estimates of the size of the working class to some 35 per cent in Goldthorpe. It is perhaps more realistic to think in terms of a working class of something just over 50 per cent but which must be far less rigidly defined than in the past. Hence the middle-class school-teacher in south London may be a Labour voter living in a council flat while the working-class lorry-driver in Barnsley is a home-owner and has started to vote Conservative.

Class awareness, despite predictions, has not much changed; 90 per cent of British people will still place themselves in a class/status position. However, in the 1980s, there have been further pronounced changes in the market, work and status situations of the traditional working class. Most striking has been the disappearance of the old primary extractive industries such as steel (between 1979 and 1982) and coal (between 1984 and the present). The traditional working-class communities, such as the mining villages of South Wales and Durham, which depended on them and on which they depended have long gone. As the traditional working class has decreased, there has been a fall in political participation among its members.

## Divisions in the Working Class?

As the foregoing suggests, it appears that the structure of the working class has indeed become more internally divided. Divisions within the working class have been examined both from the point of view of their own perceptions of themselves and the way in which they are seen by others. In interviews in Banbury in the 1950s, Margaret Stacey (1960) identified three distinct groups into which the working class divided themselves, which, using their terms, she called the 'respectable', the 'ordinary' and the 'rough' working class. These it seems are not far removed from the three categories named by Lockwood (1966): 'prolet-arians', 'privatised workers' and 'deferential workers'. The last, being nearest in working conditions to the middle class, are most likely to share their assumptions, but the concept of 'deference' requires more explanation. It means that many members of the working class accept the class structure as it is and assume that those who rule have a right to do so. We shall return to this question in Chapter 5.

Differences in occupational skill levels have increased and industrial disputes frequently involve 'differentials'. The major cleavages now include gender and ethnic divisions. Research consistently shows that racist and sexist attitudes are particularly strong among male members of the working class, and discrimination against women, both because it is more widespread and because it fits in with the working-class male pride in hard manual work, has proved difficult to overcome. The proportion of unskilled workers is declining but new work opportunities for the unskilled exist and are being disproportionately filled on a part-time basis by women. Not only do these women tend not to join unions, which they associate with the defence of male interests, but there is a general decline in union membership as new industries, e.g. computers, emerge on a non-union basis. This process has been aided by the retention of the traditional demarcation of work patterns between many trade unions, and in the most celebrated case of the 1980s, the movement of News International (including Times Newspapers) to Wapping, the management was able to defeat resistance from traditional print unions by the support they received from the Electrical Trades Union (ETU). It has been further accelerated by government policy directed at weakening the power of trade unions to put pressure on employers as well as reducing the privileges of special interests in the middle class, including lawyers, doctors, nurses and teachers. At the same time the perceived interests of the employed working class have moved away from those of the unemployed and many believe that an *underclass* has re-emerged (see below).

## Social Inequality

Though, as we shall find in Chapter 12, there is no doubt that social inequality has increased in the 1980s, there remains considerable debate about how far the reduction that occurred between 1945 and 1979 was the result of government policy and how far it was effective. Since Victorian times it has been a conscious aim of social policy first to ameliorate and then to reduce the gap between rich and poor, and both wartime and postwar governments sought to use the tax system to reduce inequality, so that R. H. Tawney, writing in 1952, could say that he already saw 'distinct advances towards the conversion of a class-ridden society into a community in fact as well as in name' (Giddens, *New Society*, 4 October 1979). It was certainly possible to find an economic basis for this belief, Crosland (1956) claiming that postwar legislation had transferred '10% of disposable income from property-owners to the working class'. But Titmuss (1962) showed that such reliance on official statistics produced misleading results as they took no account of changes in the relative size of the groups concerned. As Abel-Smith and

Townsend (1965) were later to show, it was the middle class, and not the working class, that benefited most from postwar legislation. Consequently, such changes in income as occurred were not being translated into changes in wealth.

Westergaard and Resler (1975) agreed with earlier writers, and with Lockwood, that affluence had become more widespread in postwar society, but they challenged the statistical base for the assumption that the overall shape of the class structure had really changed. They pointed out that the Registrar General's statistics were based on gross income and made no allowance for the effects of the tax structure. When tax was taken into account, they argued, wages had not in fact doubled since the 1920s, and the cost of the welfare state had been largely borne by its recipients. Nor had the gap between rich and poor narrowed as much as was often thought. The richest 1 per cent of the population still had as much income as the poorest third, the richest 10 per cent getting five times the national average income, and the poorest only one-third. The tax system, it appeared, was not functioning to reduce inequalities of income.

Even less was it effective in reducing the inequalities of wealth on which inequalities of income so largely rest. In 1960 the top 20 per cent of the population had 89.8 per cent of the wealth; the bottom 80 per cent shared a mere 10.2 per cent between them. In 1976 the figures were 83.9 per cent and 16.1 per cent respectively. But these changes were less due to any important effect that the tax system had had in reducing the concentration of wealth than to the general improvement in prosperity resulting from technological change. The wealthiest families of Britain as measured by the number of members of family that have left over £500,000 — the Rothschilds (banking), Wills (tobacco), Coats (thread), Colmans (mustard), Palmers (biscuits) — have retained the positions of wealth and influence established by the trading strength of their Victorian ancestors.

The Labour government of 1974−79 established a Royal Commission on the Distribution of Income and Wealth (the Diamond Commission). In its Report published in 1979, the Commission confirmed that there had been an apparent increase in the equality of distribution of *pre-tax personal income*. However, though the share taken by top 1 per cent had been halved since the 1920s, and there had been some reduction in the share going to the top 10 per cent, the share going to the bottom 50 per cent was largely unaffected. Similarly, Atkinson and Harrison (1980) showed that the share of national wealth held by the top 1 per cent fell from 61 per cent in 1923 to 32 per cent in 1972; that held by the top 20 per cent only declined about 10 per cent in same period, so that what had happened was not a redistribution of wealth from the rich to the poor, but from the rich to the merely well-to-do! (See also Scott 1982.)

At the other end of the scale, in their study of poverty Mack and Lansley (1985) estimated that between 1960 and 1977 the number living below the level at which they became eligible for supplementary benefit had remained more or less constant at 2 million; however, between 1979 and 1983 the number at or below the supplementary benefit level rose by 43 per cent to 8.6 million. They found also that:

1. There was surprisingly general agreement among all social classes as to what constituted a decent minimum standard of living.
2. There was also widespread acceptance that individuals would be happy to see their taxes raised to pay for necessities for the poor.

When Mack and Lansley excluded from consideration those people who did not have things because did not want them, e.g. dieters and vegetarians who did

Table 3.1   *Inequalities of wealth*

| England and Wales | | | | |
|---|---|---|---|---|
| | Top 1% | Top 5% | Top 10% | Top 20% |
| 1923 | 60.9 | 82.0 | 89.1 | 94.2 |
| 1924 | 59.9 | 81.5 | 88.1 | 93.8 |
| 1925 | 61.0 | 82.1 | 88.4 | 93.8 |
| 1926 | 57.3 | 79.9 | 87.4 | 93.2 |
| 1927 | 59.8 | 81.3 | 88.3 | 93.8 |
| 1928 | 57.0 | 79.6 | 87.2 | 93.1 |
| 1929 | 55.5 | 78.9 | 86.3 | 92.6 |
| 1930 | 57.9 | 79.2 | 86.6 | 92.6 |
| 1936 | 54.2 | 77.4 | 85.7 | 92.0 |
| 1938 | 55.0 | 76.9 | 85.0 | 91.2 |
| 1950 | 47.2 | 74.3 | — | — |
| 1951 | 45.8 | 73.6 | — | — |
| 1952 | 43.0 | 70.2 | — | — |
| 1953 | 43.6 | 71.1 | — | — |
| 1954 | 45.3 | 71.8 | — | — |
| 1955 | 44.5 | 71.1 | — | — |
| 1956 | 44.5 | 71.3 | — | — |
| 1957 | 43.4 | 68.7 | — | — |
| 1958 | 41.4 | 67.8 | — | — |
| 1959 | 41.4 | 67.6 | — | — |
| 1960 | 33.9 | 59.4 | 71.5 | 83.1 |
| 1961 | 36.5 | 60.6 | 71.1 | 83.3 |
| 1962 | 31.4 | 54.8 | 67.3 | 80.2 |
| 1963 | not available* | | | |
| 1964 | 34.5 | 58.6 | 71.4 | 84.3 |
| 1965 | 33.0 | 58.1 | 71.7 | 85.5 |
| 1966 | 30.6 | 55.5 | 69.2 | 83.8 |
| 1967 | 31.4 | 56.0 | 70.0 | 84.5 |
| 1968 | 33.6 | 58.3 | 71.6 | 85.1 |
| 1969 | 31.1 | 56.1 | 67.7 | 83.3 |
| 1970 | 29.7 | 53.6 | 68.7 | 84.5 |
| 1971 | 28.4 | 52.3 | 67.6 | 84.2 |
| 1972 | 31.7 | 56.0 | 70.4 | 84.9 |

*Notes:* — denotes outside the range of estate duty statistics.

\*   The estate data were not available by country for 1963; this means that we could not calculate a figure for Great Britain comparable with those for other years.

*Source:* A. B. Atkinson and A. J. Harrison, *The Distribution of Personal Wealth in Britain* (Cambridge, Cambridge University Press, 1978), Table 6.5, p. 159.

not eat meat and fish at least every other day, they still estimated that between 6 and 12 million people were significantly deprived (unable to buy some of the basic necessities of life), and that about 1 in 20 (including children) were seriously deprived. Finally, they found that a significantly smaller proportion of the deprived were now pensioners. This, however, did not reflect any improvement in their conditions or numbers (which are increasing as the population lives longer), but only the fact that the number of unemployed had risen so much between 1979 and 1983.

These facts should have tended to strengthen the traditional Marxist position. However, at that time the Marxist view was already under attack, not just from the traditional Right but also by continental New Left writers such as Habermas (1976), Touraine (1981), Gorz (1982) and Offe (1984). These writers concurred that the traditional Marxist 'trench warfare' between proletariat and bourgeoisie was not taking the course predicted by Marx. They differed in their reasons. However, led by Habermas, all agreed that the state was becoming more, not less, important. Most too agreed with Gorz that technological change meant that mass unemployment was set to increase, and with Offe that the ruling class would be more effective because of the importance of new axes of stratification.

In Britain Bauman, in *Memories of Class* (1982), emphasised the significance of increased state regulation of the economy and the fact that in the new stage of economic development, monopoly capitalism, 'the growth of competition ends competition'. He noted that significant numbers of the working class shared the Thatcherite enthusiasm to cut taxes and hence services in 1979, as they were to do again in 1983. The losers, he argues, have been 'new pauperized groups' like the old, the unemployed and the inhabitants of the inner cities, for which Mrs Thatcher was to promise to do something in 1987. Some Marxists, however, have considered it somewhat premature to accept 'the end of class', as, for example, Westergaard (1984), who reminds us that it is easy given the many changes around us to lose sight of the continuity of wealth and power among a few in British society. In considering the development of wealth and poverty in the 1980s and 1990s we have to look at what has happened in Britain to both wealth and income.

The 1980s saw deliberate and repeated alterations in the tax structure to foster the accumulation of wealth. As Mrs Thatcher said in 1979, the philosophy of her government was that 'Opportunity means nothing unless it includes the right to be unequal.'

## Why Poverty?

As noted above, the definition of poverty is not fixed, but changes in relation to the general expectations of society. As David Piachaud (1982) puts it, the poor have a lack of command of resources relative to their needs. Needs change as society becomes more affluent, an obvious example being that in the United States ownership of a car is effectively a necessity. However, the statistical evidence

**Gainers and losers in the 1980s**

Three groups benefited:

1. *'Yuppies'*. Yuppies — the Young Upwardly-Mobile — who worked in the City and were paid in a year what it took a manual worker a lifetime to earn, became a role-model both admired and disliked. After 1983, the government's programme of privatisation was proudly proclaimed as a vehicle to wider share-ownership. More obviously, it was a means by which the leaders of the former nationalised industries enormously increased their own salaries, and huge profits went to merchant banks and finance houses, while the government forwent the possibility of earning a return on capital for the future. As MORI found, the yuppies represent only a small fraction of the 29 per cent of the population whom they found regarded themselves as upwardly mobile, and nearly half of them said that their parents had been upwardly mobile also. Similarly, of the 7 per cent who were prepared to admit they were downwardly mobile, the majority ascribed the same condition to their parents (Jacobs and Worcester, 1990: 143–4).

2. *Former council tenants*. The sale of council houses gave many families an opportunity to own their own homes, if they could afford to pay for them. Like the sale of council land to private developers, it has had the effect of enabling white- and blue-collar workers to live together in the same neighbourhoods in a way that was already common in the United States.

3. *Criminals*. At the same time, there was a dramatic increase in crime. Ministers expressed dismay and repeated calls were made for a tougher law and order policy at Conservative Party conferences. But as Terence Morris points out in *The Crooked Way to the Top* (citing Titmuss), crime is a method to accelerated social mobility (see also Morris 1976). A society which lays special emphasis on material success must expect many people to take what they see as the fastest route to it. The effects were seen in both middle- and working-class attitudes. Conspicuously, some of the most spectacular crimes of the decade involved very large-scale fraud, even though white-collar crime is notoriously hard to detect and seldom as severely punished as working-class crime. At the same time there was also a considerable increase in crimes against property, a typically working-class crime.

Two groups lost out:

1. *Workers in the public sector*. The postwar years had seen the emergence of the *salariat*, those who had no capital but whose skills ensured them a good income. In the snakes and ladders of the 1980s those who were fortunate enough to be in the private sector could do very well and were encouraged by a variety of means to accumulate wealth. But while incomes in the private sector were not controlled and were encouraged to rise, those in the public sector were held below the rate of inflation. Government cutbacks in public services meant a sustained attack on living standards for those who worked in hitherto secure middle-class bases in the health service, the social

services, teaching and municipal service. Defensive organisations such as trade unions were restrained by law from operating according to free-market principles and found the going tough, but so too did many members of the middle classes. Job security was attacked, for example, by the introduction of fixed-term contracts for headteachers, and professional status generally was eroded by an increasing range of rules and regulations, for example, among teachers and general practitioners. There was also a consistent refusal of professional status to intermediate groups, for example, paramedics.

2. *The poor.* The government's anti-inflation policy also forced a steep rise in unemployment, which was only partially concealed by repeated changes in the basis of calculation. At the same time, repeated attempts were made to reduce state expenditure by cutting welfare benefits, most commonly by simply failing to raise them in line with inflation. For those out of work the cutbacks meant poverty, and by the mid-1980s London gained an unenviable distinction among European capitals for the number of beggars and homeless in its streets.

presented by Peter Townsend, in his *Poverty in the United Kingdom* (1979), showed that even in the 1970s absolute poverty still existed on a scale that previously would have been thought inconceivable. There were two basic reasons why the situation of the poor worsened in the 1980s: the 'poverty trap' and the erosion of welfare benefits.

Despite the 'enterprise culture', government action failed to eliminate the 'poverty trap'. A combination of tax and national insurance obligations had long created a point at which any increase in wages resulted in a net loss of income. However, with a high rate of unemployment (three times that prevailing in the 1970s) there was an even greater disincentive to take up the increasing number of poorly paid, often part-time jobs.

Yet in Britain there emerged in the 1970s a growing belief among some politicians that the state should provide only a minimum safety net for those in dire need. The resulting changes in social security provision in the 1980s have consistently tended to:

- Reduce the total amount of money available to applicants by allowing increases in benefits to fall behind the rate of inflation. Pensions have largely kept up with the rate of inflation, but before 1979 were pegged also to the rate of increase in average earnings, which has been much greater.
- Replace standard benefits open to all and consequently easy to administer with means-tested benefits. The 'means test' had previously been associated with the slump of the 1930s and was strongly opposed by Labour.
- Replace one-off grants by one-off loans to buy essential items.

In summary, therefore, the 1980s saw a reversal of the postwar consensus on creating a more equal society in which the differences between rich and poor will be reduced if not eliminated. In fact, the gap between rich and poor has again been growing, and this trend seems to be continuing into the 1990s. The most interesting thing is that the public have consistently been shown not to share the politicians' enthusiasm for this state of affairs. The survey organisation MORI found in 1990 that 71 per cent were willing to accept rises in their own taxes to pay for more generous support to the poor, against only 15 per cent who favoured less taxes and minimal support. In fact, their respondents consistently supported 'socialistic' rather than 'Thatcherite' values, and there was evidence that, despite the verdict of three successive General Elections, public support for egalitarianism had actually strengthened during the 1980s (Jacobs and Worcester 1990: 23–34). Similar conclusions emerged fron the 1991 British Social Attitudes Survey (*The Guardian*, 20 November 1991).

## Social Mobility

A necessary corollary of the assumption that inequality is functionally desirable is that social mobility will occur freely. Social mobility is movement either up or down the class hierarchy to a different class. A society in which any member can aspire to climb to the highest positions on merit alone has been termed a *meritocracy* (rule by the most meritorious). Meritocracy is also supported by critics of the class structure on the grounds that it is more efficient and adaptable; putting a person in the 'right' niche makes the fullest use of that person's capabilities, while the belief (some call it a 'myth') of a society open to opportunity promotes social harmony. There are, however, problems also, some of which were noted by the inventor of the term, Michael Young (1961), such as the disillusionment that comes with the acceptance of failure, and the fact that high mobility (as in the United States) distorts kinship associations.

The basic problem is how to study social mobility. Somehow the researcher has to relate data on income, occupation and wealth to changes (if any) in behaviour, which are much harder to identify. Sociologists distinguish, first, between *intra-generational mobility* — how far an individual class position changes in their own lifetime — and *inter-generational mobility* — whether a given individual's class position differs from that of their parents. The latter, for practical reasons, is the usual measure. Mobility can of course be either *vertical* or *horizontal* — people can and do change their occupation without necessarily changing their class position.

Lipset and Zetterberg (1956) suggested that the *frequency* of intergenerational social mobility (i.e. the number of people who occupied a different class position from that of their parents) was very similar in the different Western industrial societies they studied. But their study referred to 'mass' mobility across the manual/non-manual barrier, and this was the result of, and hence dependent on, the speed of industrialisation itself. 'Elite' mobility, the extent to which individuals move without the assistance of such major social changes, was much lower and showed important national variations. In addition, S. M. Miller (1960) showed that when *range* as well as frequency was considered, industrial societies did show differences also in their mass mobility patterns. Long-range mobility (movement across more than one class division) was generally low, which indicates that Western industrial societies were not as open and meritocratic as often claimed. The Soviet Union and the United States both had fairly high rates of 'elite' mobility. For Britain, which had low long-range mobility but high short-range mobility, comparisons with the more highly mobile societies of the United States, Canada, Australia, etc. were and are of special importance. Nations at broadly similar levels of economic development have different patterns of mobility which seem to vary with a number of factors: the occupational structure, the type of social stratification, the educational system and cultural values.

## Social Mobility and the RGC

Whether or not we accept the assumption of the RGC that a married woman's class position is determined by that of her husband, marriage does in fact form a significant vehicle for intragenerational social mobility. As might be expected, there is a significant tendency for people to marry within their own class. However,

**Britain's first national social mobility survey**

In Britain the first national mobility survey was conducted only forty years ago by David Glass (1954), interviewing a two-stage stratified random sample of 10,000 persons over 18 chosen from the National Register. It has been noted that there were significant differences in this sample from the Registrar General's estimates of age and marital composition. Glass did not use the RGC but the concept of socioeconomic status devised by Moser and Hall, and the differences in part reflect the problems of reclassifying occupations and in particular of distinguishing higher and lower supervisory grades. In this, as in most other matters related to social class, there is a built-in discrepancy between subjective and objective class positions.

Glass showed that:

1. Britain had a high rate of intergenerational mobility and that nearly two-thirds of his respondents were in a different occupational category from that of their fathers, though roughly one-third had moved up and one-third down.
2. Mobility rates were fairly constant over time, with those upwardly mobile just exceeding those downwardly mobile, indicating a structure that was stable but not closed.
3. Most mobility was short-range and occurred in the middle of the class hierarchy, across the IIIn/IIIm divide. Long-range mobility was very rare and it was almost unheard of for someone to move all the way from Social Class V to Social Class I. There was a very high level of self-recruitment both at the top and at the bottom of the social scale.

the tendency to do so has declined very significantly in the fifty years since 1915 (when the correlation between class positions of marriage partners was 0.50). The educational status of marriage partners is also closely related. Differences are a tendency for men to marry wives less well educated than themselves, and a slight tendency for men to marry women from a class lower than their own. The degree of association between the class origins of marriage partners was greatest at both the top and the bottom of the social scale.

From the Registrar General's own figures we can see that:

1. The pattern of class has altered slowly over a long period with the slow disappearance of the former very large class V the most noticeable feature.
2. As classes I, II and IIIn have expanded, they have needed to recruit from those below them on the scale. The middle classes have tended in the last fifty years to have fewer children (differential fertility), so in the postwar period there was a demand for people to fill middle-class jobs. However, upward mobility into the highest professional classes has been low due to self-recruitment.
3. Most mobility has occurred because of changes in the occupational structure. As manual jobs have disappeared, the non-manual sector has grown markedly. In 1881 only 21 per cent of male jobs were non-manual. By 1951 the figure was still only 27 per cent, but in ten years, by 1961, it had risen by 7 per cent to 34 per cent, more than it had done in the previous 100 years.

The Nuffield Mobility Study (Goldthorpe 1980) confirmed much that Glass had said, but there were some key differences. It found more long-range mobility than Glass and more upward than downward mobility. Goldthorpe observes that the outstanding feature of the rate of social mobility in Britain today is the achievement of high social class positions by large numbers of sons of 'intermediate' and working-class fathers. Otherwise the relative chances of long-range upward mobility have remained fairly stable for different social classes over the 60 years studied. This upward mobility has resulted from changes in the occupational structure leading to the creation of a new 'service class' (the *salariat*) of professional, administrative and managerial workers. But there is little sense of class solidarity in the expanding middle class, while the working class is getting smaller and more — some claim — homogeneous, as fewer members of the middle class are downwardly mobile into the working class while the working class has lost many of its most energetic and articulate members.

Goldthorpe points out that the relative chances of upward mobility for men of different social classes reaching the top of the class hierarchy remains unchanged (only 10–15 per cent of men from working-class backgrounds rise to Nuffield social classes I and II). He believes that the class structure and the rates of social mobility have now stabilised. The reason is that if a candidate from the working class is to make it into the middle class, the most promising route is up the ladder of educational opportunity. Hence recruitment must begin early and there is less chance in later life if a person lacks the necessary qualifications. Class inequalities are persistent; there is little evidence of any significant reductions in social inequality. The differences from Glass can be explained by the dates of both surveys: the affluence of the 1950s and 1960s was accompanied by an expansion of highly skilled and well-paid jobs, particularly in the service industries and in the public sector. Later writers in turn have criticised some methodological weaknesses of Goldthorpe (see Goldthorpe 1983; Stanworth 1984).

# International Comparisons

It is a very widely held belief in Britain that its society is uniquely class-conscious. Anthony Sampson (1982) summarised the almost universally held view that the British educational system 'reinforces and perpetuates a class system whose divisions run through all British institutions, separating language, attitude and motivation'. Not only is the British class system often blamed for Britain's poor economic performance, but comparison is most often made with the allegedly more fluid and less class-conscious society of the United States. Hence it may come as something of a surprise to find that international comparisons do not support this belief. In fact, Britain is neither a particularly class-bound or class-conscious society; nor is it very different from the United States. While in Britain only 36 per cent agreed or strongly agreed that people like them had a good chance of improving their standard of living, as against 58 per cent in Australia or 71 per cent in the United States, 47 per cent reported that the level of their own job was much higher than their father's, the same as the United States and comparable with Australia (46 per cent). The difference seems to be that the British are inclined to rate themselves lower on the social scale than do the Americans, and are more inclined to place themselves near the bottom than Italians or Germans (Jowell, Witherspoon and Brook, 1989: 67, 66).

We have seen how, in mid-century Britain, upward mobility into social classes I/II was mostly structural mobility. Changes in organisation and techniques of work had created more managerial jobs, and upward mobility was a necessity if they were to be filled. At the international level the Lipset/Zetterberg thesis that overall patterns of social mobility were much the same in all advanced industrial societies has also been challenged by Heath (1981) and Erikson *et al.* (1979, 1982, 1983). By reworking data provided by nineteen of the most recent national studies, Heath found that:

1. According to the measure used different societies emerge as most open. If the focus is on the move from manual to non-manual occupations, Canada, Sweden, the United States and Norway rank at the top; if on the move from both manual and farm occupations to non-manual, first place would go to Hungary, followed by Bulgaria, Poland and Yugoslavia. This is because in Eastern Europe late industrialisation has coincided with both a sharp contraction in the number employed in modern mechanised agriculture and the growth of massive bureaucracies needed to steer unwieldy 'command' economies.

2. Correcting for changing occupational structures shows Sweden and Australia rank higher than expected; Spain, Italy and the former German Federal Republic lower than expected. Mobility in Canada, Denmark, England [*sic*], Norway, the United States and the Eastern bloc is approximately what would be expected given the advanced levels of industrialisation there.

Erikson *et al.* use the Hope−Goldthorpe seven-tier class model to conduct a comparative survey of Britain, France and Sweden. Though this has to be done with caution, given the very different perception of social class in France, for example, they find that there is a high level of self-recruitment to service class I and petit bourgeois class IV in France. In Britain the self-recruitment of working class VI is particularly marked, as is that of class VII. But in both France and Britain historic rates of mobility are constant, while Sweden has become more open to mobility with time.

Questions on people's belief about opportunity and mobility show a high range of agreement between Western European countries on what factors are most important for 'getting ahead in life'. In a comparison of seven industrial nations, Jowell, Witherspoon and Brook (1989: 68) found a high level of agreement that personal characteristics such as hard work, ambition and a good education were most important. In West Germany, Italy and the Netherlands, more emphasis was placed on education, which was ranked first, ahead of personal characteristics. Only in Italy, however, was 'knowing the right people' ranked second and 'political connections' fifth!

## Suggestions for Further Reading

On *stratification* a good place to start is with Frank Parkin (1972), *Class Inequality and Political Order* or Tom Bottomore (1991), *Classes in Modern Society*, 2nd edn. Peter Calvert (1982), *The Concept of Class*, discusses the way in which modern ideas of class have evolved and the confusion between class and status that has resulted. The arguments for the Hope−Goldthorpe classification are put in John H. Goldthorpe (1980), *Social Mobility and Class Structure in Modern Britain*. A further useful overview is Anthony Heath (1981), *Social Mobility*. The Marxist arguments are put by Erik Wright (1978), *Class, Crisis and the State*. Michael Young (1961), *The Rise of the Meritocracy* is a classic which is doubly interesting in the light of recent developments, such as the development of the 'business class' discussed by John Scott (1977), *Corporations, Classes and Capitalism*.

*Wealth and poverty* are very much live issues in the 1990s. However figures change only slowly and much background information is available. John Westergaard and Henrietta Resler (1975), *Class in a Capitalist Society*, showed how the main cost of the welfare state had been borne by its recipients, while John Scott (1982), *The Upper Classes*, confirmed that the rich were still alive and (very) well, and Ian Bradley (1982), *The English Middle Classes are Alive and Kicking* turned out to be prophetic. At the same time, Peter Townsend (1979), *Poverty in the United Kingdom: a survey of household resources and standards of living*, showed that deprivation was still widespread, a conclusion reinforced by J. Mack and S. Lansley (1985), *Poor Britain*.

# 4 Social Stratification II: Gender, race and ethnicity

## Gender

The most usual areas for examination are:

- The problems of allocating women to class positions.
- Why females are generally less successful than males — this sort of question often stresses the importance of expectations.
- The effects of employment legislation and its limited success in countering inequalities.
- The effects of increased female employment on family life.
- The male-orientated nature of Sociology itself.

## Race and Ethnicity

Changing patterns of integration and inequalities of opportunity are the most examined race and ethnicity issues, though there is a considerable variation in how such questions are asked:

- Is Britain a multicultural society?
- Why are ethnic minorities generally less successful? Such questions are frequently expressed as a comparison of the experiences and achievements of any two ethnic groups in certain specified areas; usually work, education and housing.
- The reasons for immigrant concentration in cities and the potential problems to which this may give rise.
- The increasing political activity of ethnic minorities.
- Sociological explanations of racial conflict.

One of the most contentious issues in sociology today concerns the relative importance of different modes of stratification. In Chapter 3 we looked at social class and saw how the relationships between class, status and party continue to structure British society. We now have to consider the role of *gender*, which has always been a factor in determining a person's individual social position, and *race and ethnicity*, which has assumed a new importance in recent years as a result of the wave of New Commonwealth immigration that began in the 1950s.

# Gender and Sex

By *sex* we refer to biological or anatomical differences between men and women. By *gender* we refer to psychological, cultural or social differences which vary with the nature of society itself. Though sex differences exist in all societies, the values attached to them do differ considerably, and with them the status of women as compared with men. For example, aggression is linked with maleness in most societies, but it does not follow that the link is biological rather than social; in primate species females can be very aggressive when their young are threatened (see e.g. Morris 1967).

Gender is the product of socialisation. It is true that *sociobiologists* argue that sex (rather than gender) leads to social structure, as do some *radical feminists*, e.g. Shulamith Firestone (1972), who believes that the reproductive process itself will have to be modified for women to become liberated. However, Will, Self and Datan (1976) showed that women treated the same child differently according to whether they thought it was a boy or a girl. The child learns about gender differences from adults' cues supplied either consciously or unconsciously, and this begins within the *family* (see also Chapter 8). Toys and books all emphasise gender differences; moreover, there are more male characters than female in children's books, television, etc., and they have more active roles.

Gender roles are reinforced by the socialisation effects of school and single-sex peer groups. By this stage, however, children have already absorbed the idea of *patriarchy* — the fact that men have more power and influence than women and that the key factor in establishing and maintaining this state of affairs is the *sexual contract* (Pateman 1988) — and this notion is inbuilt in later class and work roles. Hence gender relations, it is now generally accepted, have to be taken into account in all aspects of sociology (and even in the sociology of sociology itself! Maynard 1990). Hence in this chapter only an outline of the major problems appears: other aspects will be dealt with in later chapters.

# Gender and Stratification

However, the main area of debate ranges over the nature of stratification by gender and whether or not — as Firestone (1972) and other radical feminists argue — it is a more important dimension of stratification than class.

Gender stratification is historically more deeply rooted than that of class, though like status and class its form has varied over the ages. Before the Protestant Reformation in England, for example, women could own land and property, abbesses and prioresses sat in Parliament in the House of Lords, and women could succeed to the throne, though women's holding of secular titles in their own right was severely restricted in England (as opposed to Scotland). After the Reformation the inequality of women in Britain increased.

In the wake of the French Revolution Mary Wollstonecraft (1792) called for equality for women. The call was taken up in the United States by Margaret Fuller (1971) and embodied in the Declaration of the Rights of Woman of the Women's Rights Convention held at Seneca Falls in 1848 (Fuller 1971). In Britain the accession of Queen Victoria revived the issue, and Harriet Taylor published an essay on 'The Enfranchisement of Women' in the *Westminster Review*. The argument for women's equality was taken up after her death by her husband, the influential political philosopher John Stuart Mill, in *The Subjection of Women* (Rossi 1970). From then onwards it led to a series of political campaigns, the object of which was to obtain for women the same civic rights as men.

There is no doubt, however, that in key ways women are disadvantaged even today as compared with men. The question is, how far can we talk of a system of stratification based on gender. Do women *as a group* have less power or status in society than men?

## Gender as a Determinant of Status

Women are still seen as being largely confined to the 'private' domestic world as opposed to the 'public' domain which men occupy. Goldthorpe (1983) defended this 'conventional position' by saying that women's paid work was insignificant as a contribution to the household income compared with men's, so that women could properly be seen as belonging to the same class as their husbands. And,

**Rights for women**

1. *The right to vote and to participate in democratic government.* Women first obtained the right to vote and representation in county councils in 1893, but women were not able to vote in Parliamentary elections until the Representation of the People Act 1918 and then only if they were over 25 (21 for men). The following year the Qualification of Women Act 1919 allowed women to become MPs, and Lady Astor became the first woman to take her seat as an MP. The first woman to serve as a cabinet minister was Margaret Bondfield in the 1923 Labour Government, even though women were not given an equal right to vote until 1928. Though in 1979 Margaret Thatcher became the first woman to serve as prime minister, there continue to be proportionately very few women in Parliament. In fact, there were fewer women MPs in 1990 than at any time since 1929!
2. *The right to own property.* Until the Married Women's Property

Act 1882, women's property and income ceased to be their own on marriage and became effectively their husband's. In 1935 the Law Reform (Married Women) Act allowed them to bequeath their property as they chose. However, until 1990 a married woman's income continued to be treated for tax purposes as her husband's unless both were earning enough to make it worthwhile to ask for separate taxation. Even correspondence dealing with a wife's earnings was addressed to her husband, and any rebate due to her was paid to him.

3. *The right to control their own bodies.* Given the preponderance of men in Parliament, laws on matters relating to women are still effectively made by men, to the point that an overwhelmingly male Parliament legislates to control women's fertility. Until the Abortion Law Reform Act 1967, abortion was illegal though 'back-street' abortions could be purchased at a price, which could include the death of the woman from insanitary conditions and crude medical practice. Since 1967, abortions are legal provided that certain conditions are fulfilled, though there have been repeated attempts by male MPs such as the Catholic Liberal Democrat David Alton to impose more stringent conditions in the hope of ending legal abortion altogether. Restraints on the right to abortion mean that women are still effectively denied the right to control their own bodies.

4. *The right of equal access to jobs.* Women were given the right in law to entry to the professions by the Sex Disqualification (Removal) Act 1919. Formal discrimination against entry to all other occupations except coal mining has since been prohibited by the Sex Discrimination Act of 1975, which also made discriminatory retirement ages illegal. Earlier, in 1975, the Social Security Pensions Act guaranteed women equal access to company pension schemes. So great is the presumption that women's primary role is to bear children, however, that women are still asked at interviews if they have families or family obligations, a question rarely asked of men. Women are legally seen as primarily responsible for parenting and despite equal rights legislation they still sometimes lose their jobs when they have children and if they are re-employed it is on much less favourable terms.

5. *The right to equal pay for equal work.* After many years of pressure, a Royal Commission in 1946 recommended equal pay for men and women in teaching, local government and the civil service. The Equal Pay Act 1970 (which did not come into effect for five years) and the Sex Discrimination Act 1975 tried to establish the principle of 'equal pay for equal work'. Many jobs were reclassified to retain differentials, and women workers still earn less than male colleagues. For example, female clerical workers earn 60 per cent of their male colleagues' pay and sales employees a mere 56 per cent. Women, especially single women with children, are disproportionately represented among the poor, and throughout the 1980s a male-dominated Parliament has progressively cut benefits and failed to tackle the problem of the 'poverty-trap'.

as noted above, the Registrar General's Classification still allocates class position to women on the basis of the occupation of their husbands. Only unmarried women have a position in their own right. Yet 'It is far from clear why patterns of family ties and shared culture should be expected to correlate with the occupational experiences of men' (Hindess 1987: 82).

Women may be and are paid less than men, but that does not make their contribution 'insignificant'. Very few middle-class households today could maintain their distinctive standard of living without the contribution made by the wife's income; in short, their class position is the product of their *shared* income and their combined gender positions. On the other hand, as Parkin (1972) points out, it is also true that wives and daughters of unskilled labourers have very little in common with wives and daughters of wealthy landowners. In the case of the latter, their gender disadvantages are clearly overridden by their class advantages. Even those who argue the centrality of gender relations have to take account of the fact that the life-chances of Lady Diana Spencer (even without her marriage to the Prince of Wales) were certainly more like those of her brother, Viscount Althorp, than the life-chances of the daughter of a hospital porter in Hackney.

Feminists who argue for the centrality of gender relations claim that such differences are not simply reducible to class. Class culture is passed on by families. But even if the family (rather than the individual) is taken as the main unit of analysis, the identification of the family with the head of the family is certainly problematic.

## Stratification based on the family

Conventional class analysis could be modified to take account of gender differences. Such modification will need to take account of these questions:

1. Many heads of families are women, and the proportion of families where women are the sole breadwinners is increasing. In fact the 'cereal packet' household of housewife and breadwinner husband is now in a minority in Britain. Why then should it be maintained as the basis of class allocation?
2. If allocation is based on the occupation of the 'head of the family', the wife's occupation might be the lead factor in determining the husband's class position, rather than the other way round. Is this so, and if so, under what circumstances does it occur?
3. Even where the role of the husband as the head of the family is not disputed, many families *need* the wife's earnings to maintain their economic position. How far is this relevant in determining their class position?
4. Some argue that a significant number of families have different class locations for the man and the woman (Britten and Heath 1983) and so occupy a cross-class position. Others deny that this is possible. Who is right?

There are a number of objections, however, to simply modifying traditional views of class. The obvious one is that they were based on a male-dominated view of things and that this makes them fundamentally flawed. Some radical feminists argue that class hides inequalities *within* the family, and leads to a new form of stratification. This is quite compatible with the view that a modified form of class stratification also exists.

## Stratification within the family

Those who argue that gender forms a distinct system of stratification within the family argue that within the family the man exploits the woman and does not pay for the domestic and sexual [*sic*] services he actually receives. So whatever her class position, the woman is always inferior to the man.

The principal objections to this view are:

1. Given the relative absence of legal constraints, there is no evident reason why this state of affairs should continue to exist in the last decade of the twentieth century.
2. It is not clear why sexuality should be regarded as a service rather than a mutual benefit.
3. The precise nature of domestic services varies with class position and in the case of the well-to-do may be effectively non-existent. The well-to-do — men or women — seldom *have* to do their own washing, cleaning or cooking.

# Expectations and Employment

There is no doubt that women are at a serious disadvantage relative to men in most occupations, and that this affects their status in society. The reasons why females are generally less successful than males are complex. Starting with their expectations, marriage is seen as the central choice a woman has to make; a career choice as secondary. The pattern of occupation is broken to look after children. While 'working' (i.e. working outside the home for pay), women are also expected to be responsible for the housework, which is in some strange way still generally seen as not being 'real' work, even though it is often more onerous than many paid jobs. But despite this extra burden:

1. Women's paid work is less remunerative.
2. Many women work part-time.
3. Discrimination against women in pay and promotion prospects is normal and has not been effectively countered by legislation (Martin and Roberts 1984; Yeandle 1984; Dex 1985).

The question of why this should be so is more difficult. Expectations are the product of the process of socialisation, and it has been argued that it is men's control of resources that determines women's expectations. The problem is how. In the United States, for example, women own more than half the wealth of the country, yet their expectations seem to have changed much less than this would imply.

# Women's Work Outside the Home

Female employment outside the home before 1914 was largely limited to working-class single women, one-third of whom were in domestic service (Fuller 1971). After the First World War when many working-class women had been recruited for munitions production and other war work, most of them found themselves out of a job and returned to family life, so that, with changes in marriage patterns, the number of full-time housewives peaked between the wars. After the Second World War, however, the pattern was quite different. Domestic service had virtually ceased to exist as an option. Many women either stayed with or entered other work outside the home, and so contributed to the rising expectations of the 1950s and 1960s. One of them was Margaret Thatcher, who wrote in 1954:

> Every girl now has to earn her own living between leaving school and getting married. Some of them take a long training and become so absorbed in the subject that they want to continue with it after marriage. For many of these girls the kind of work involved in running a house is not sufficient to use all their abilities and they feel they are not working to full capacity. (Interview in *Onward*, April 1954, reproduced in *The Guardian*, 21 March 1990)

Today, women are disproportionately concentrated in the services sector of the economy — in 1989, 82 per cent of all female employees. There is also a strong tendency for them to be employed in what is termed the 'secondary labour market', doing temporary or part-time work (waitressing, cleaning, sales). In the Soviet Union, which lost twenty million people in the Second World War, owing to the severe shortage of male employees women drive trains, work in heavy industry and make up 75 per cent of the doctors and dentists (compared with 7 per cent in the United Kingdom). However, they are still paid less than their male counterparts and are expected to do housework as well (including the many hours of queuing which were necessary to buy scarce foodstuffs in all East European countries before 1989 and continue to be so in the territories formerly part of the Soviet Union).

# Part-time Work

Part-time working would seem an obvious way to combine housework with work outside the home. In fact, 90 per cent of all UK part-timers are women, and 40 per cent of all women are in part-time paid employment. However, this is by no means always from choice. Having broken their career pattern to have children and to bring them up, they find that their job opportunities have been sharply reduced and they have to take what work they can. Women suffered disproportionately

Table 4.1 *Women in employment*

| Year | Total employed | Men | Women | % Women |
|------|----------------|--------|--------|---------|
| 1971 | 24,031 | 15,249 | 8,782 | 36.5 |
| 1976 | 24,429 | 14,906 | 9,524 | 39.0 |
| 1981 | 24,345 | 14,573 | 9,773 | 40.1 |
| 1986 | 24,568 | 14,169 | 10,399 | 42.3 |
| 1990 | 26,881 | 15,107 | 11,773 | 43.8 |

*Source: Yearbook of Labour Statistics*, 1981, Table 3A, p. 191; 1991, Table 3A, p. 381.

in the recession of 1979–81. Much of the expansion of jobs since that time has taken the form of part-time work. The number of women with a second job doubled between 1983 and 1988, reflecting the large number of women forced by economic circumstances to take whatever work they could. In June 1989 female part-time employees in Great Britain made up 20 per cent of all employees compared with only 13 per cent in June 1971 (*Social Trends, 1990*: 72, 71).

Part-time work has other problems, too. Part-timers are much less likely to get sickness benefit, paid holidays or occupational pensions. Hence the expanded use of part-time jobs has been an effective way for employers to get round legislation intended to guarantee such provision. Part-timers are useful to management precisely because they lack job security and so can be used as a pool of temporary labour (Gershuny and Miles 1983).

International comparisons are instructive. In 1988, 44.6 per cent of the British female labour force were in part-time work. In West Germany only 29.5 per cent of the female labour force worked part-time, in France 23 per cent, in Ireland 15.7 per cent and in Italy 10.4 per cent. But then there are many more part-timers in Britain anyway — twice as many as in Italy and four times as many as in Germany (Eurostat, in *The Guardian*, 14 September 1990).

# Employment Legislation

The effects of employment legislation in countering inequalities of this kind have been very limited. As noted above, women workers continue to earn less than male colleagues, and ironically one of the problems of challenging this under the law has been the difficulty of finding men and women doing comparable jobs. The 1988 Labour Force Survey (LFS) showed that 30 per cent of employed women were in clerical and related occupations compared to 6 per cent of men; 25 per cent of men worked in craft and similar occupations compared with 4 per cent of women. This position was virtually unchanged since 1981 (*Social Trends, 1990*: 71–2).

Women find it very much more difficult than men to earn promotion. For example, in 1990 the discriminatory term 'woman police constable — wpc' was dropped, but Britain's most senior policewoman, an assistant chief constable, was arguing before an industrial tribunal that she had been denied promotion on account of her sex (BBC Radio 4, 4 September 1990). Few women are to be found in managerial or professional grades even in those occupations in which they are most commonly employed. In 1984 women made up 46 per cent of the paid labour force of the United Kingdom, but only 17 per cent of higher managerial positions. A major factor limiting the promotion of married women appears to be the continuing assumption that it is their husband's job that really matters, and it is still comparatively rare for a man to move to enable his wife to obtain promotion in her job (Dex 1987).

Women in the United States and Britain are less likely to be unemployed than men (Jowell, Witherspoon and Brook 1989: 20), though without the convention that married women looking after children are not counted as unemployed the figures would look very different (and see Coyle 1984; Westwood 1984). The effects of increased female employment on family life will be considered further in Chapter 7.

## Self-employment

The increase in the number of self-employed has been hailed as one of the success-stories of the 1980s. In 1965 only 6 per cent of the population were self-employed. By 1975 the proportion had risen to 7.2 per cent and, ten years later, in 1985, it had risen even more markedly, to 9.3 per cent, some 2.5 million people. Between September 1979 and September 1984 some 596,000 people (2 per cent of the working population) had decided to become self-employed. A Gallup survey showed that 37 per cent were seeking independence, only 16 per cent because they were already unemployed (*New Society*, 26 March 1986).

Self-employment would seem a particularly attractive career option for women, both because it reduces (if not eliminates) status problems and because it can in theory be more easily combined with parenting than employment. However, the reverse appears to be the case. Of the 2,433,000 self-employed recorded in 1984, the largest share, 794,000, were in distribution, catering, hotel and repair trades. Women formed only 25 per cent of the self-employed, and though there were signs that they were tending to gravitate more into managerial positions, especially as shopkeepers, they remained at a disadvantage. The second largest number of self-employed, 462,000, worked in the construction industry, a traditional male preserve. A survey commissioned by Barclays Bank found that in 1991 women started one-third of new small firms. Those interviewed believed they faced more problems than men in setting up their own businesses. Generally, the self-employed worked longer hours (a 60-hour week) for a below-average wage, and contacts with family and friends suffered in consequence. But, in addition, women complained that they were often not taken seriously (*Southern Evening Echo*, 14 January 1992).

## Homeworking

In 1985, 1.7 million people, 7 per cent of the workforce, worked at home. In the United States the figure is more than 10 per cent. 'Homeworking', or 'outworking' as it was then known, was a feature of the textile industry before the Industrial Revolution and remained a feature of it even after the economies of scale had concentrated the bulk of the workforce into the new factories.

However, things have not improved as much as they might since then and as things stand at present the disadvantages for the homeworker are so significant that in the 1970s the issue attracted the attention of a government body specifically set up to investigate such complaints, the Low Pay Unit. For the worker, much of the homework available tends to be onerous, boring, repetitive and extremely badly paid.

For the employer, the only practicable basis for homeworking is a contract, and such contracts, which impose only limited requirements on the employee, tend to give only limited job security in return. Like part-timers, homeworkers are on the 'periphery'; their work is essentially casual and much of it is simply an extension of their family activities. Hence women have yet to benefit much from this development, despite the sometimes extravagant claims that have been made in its favour, particularly in the United States. In some respects they are in greater need of job security and allied protection against sickness, etc., than their male counterparts, but they lack the bargaining power which would enable them to secure it (Allen and Wolkowitz 1987). Worst of all, if they have small children, women are liable to become 'trapped homeworkers' — women who are forced to accept less well paid homework because of the absence of adequate crèche facilities in British factories and offices.

Britain has the worst workplace childcare provision in Europe. In 1990 there were only 3000 places all told in workplace nurseries, and only 2 per cent of under two-year-olds received publicly funded day care, against 4 per cent in Portugal, 25 per cent in France and Belgium, and 44 per cent in Denmark (*The Guardian*, 21 March 1990). The most extensive survey yet conducted into provision for 4 million children of primary-school age showed that in the whole country there were only 300 schemes to look after pupils before and after lessons and during holidays, with only 1 child in 500 in an out-of-school club, compared with 1 in 33 in Portugal and 1 in 5 in Denmark (*The Sunday Times*, 11 March 1990).

For professionals such as doctors, veterinary surgeons, lawyers and architects, homeworking has always been possible. But today the growth of information technology is returning people to their homes; work-stations can be far away from their parent offices, and can indeed be portable. The increase in homeworking is an obvious remedy for the social problems caused by the twice-daily tidal wave of commuter traffic. In *The Third Wave* (1980), Alvin Toffler forecast that in the world of the future people would increasingly stay at home and be reluctant to venture into the violent and frightening world — a theme already explored by E. M. Forster in his sinister short story, 'The Machine Stops'. Many social scientists agree that the nature of work is changing to some degree (Gershuny 1978; Gershuny and Pahl 1979−80). However, it is not yet at all clear that this will benefit either the social or the economic position of women.

## Housework

Housework is responsible for the largest share of the 'grey economy', which Richard Rose estimates may account for 51 per cent of all labour hours worked. Other areas are 'do-it-yourself' and voluntary work for churches, hospitals, charities, etc. Though accurate figures are not available, it is generally assumed that most, if not all, housework is done by women. More significantly, for women (unpaid) housework constitutes a *career option* in a sense that it does not for men.

Oakley (1974, 1976, 1982) notes that some married and virtually all unmarried *working-class* women have had to undertake paid work since the beginning of industrialisation. But as late as the inter-war period, 90 per cent of all married women were housewives. It is the distinctive feature of the twentieth century that from the 1930s onwards there has been a steep decline almost to vanishing point of domestic servants in the home. Working-class women continue to do the family housework as they always have done, though with rising expectations there is increasing pressure for them to go out to work as well. The effects for the middle-class family are even more complex.

Erik Arnold and Wendy Faulkner (Faulkner and Arnold 1985) of the Science Policy Research Unit at Sussex University find that the amount of time spent on housework has not declined in the last fifty years despite the availability of labour-saving gadgets. The fact is that, as Gershuny (1978) has shown, capital goods in the home, i.e. washing machines, microwave ovens, videos and mowers, simply substitute for buying services outside the home in laundries, cafés and cinemas, or from inside the home, from cooks, cleaners and gardeners. And the gadgets do not use themselves; they require human operators. Married women therefore, in a very large number of cases, underpin and make possible their husbands' full-time paid labour by undertaking the work that previously for the middle classes others would have shared or even taken over entirely. In economic terms 'the servant-wife is available, domestically, to almost the entire present male population' (Galbraith 1974: 33).

A consistent criticism of housework is its boring, repetitive and unending quality. A positive feature is the freedom to choose how or when things are done, and the absence of interference from outside the home. However, despite the move of women into jobs outside the home, there has not been a similar move of men into the home to take a full-time role in housework and in parenting, which suggests that their attractions are not as highly regarded as they might be. In fact, little progress has even been made towards the sharing of domestic tasks by both partners. Most of the men who share domestic duties in this way see themselves as 'helping' their wives rather than undertaking a fair share of the overall burden. Reports in the early 1980s of the 'new man' who shared such duties on a genuinely equal basis seem to have been somewhat exaggerated (see Pahl 1984).

## Conclusion

Gender undoubtedly has very significant effects on the way an individual perceives society and the sort of lifechances they expect to receive. These differences are difficult to measure because many of them are mediated through the institution of the family, which is itself a complex term covering a wide range of situations and experiences.

The son of a doctor has a 1 in 2 chance of getting to university; the daughter of an unskilled manual worker 1 in 500. However, the daughter of a doctor is very much more likely to get to university than the son of an unskilled manual worker. So the case for gender stratification being more significant than class across British society has not been proved. However, there remains a persuasive case that gender stratification is *independently* important, and even that assumptions of inequality within the family, which continue to be largely unquestioned, continue to be reproduced throughout society in a way that *reinforces* the effects of inequalities based on class position.

Sociologists should also be wary of the residual effects of the male-orientated nature of sociology itself. In recent years, many of the assumptions of the pioneers of sociology, who assumed the masculine gender to be the norm, have been rethought, and great care is (or should be) taken to avoid gender-specific language except where it is actually needed. But as in other areas of higher education, there continues to be a disproportionate representation of men in student enrolment, and an even more marked bias in the recruitment of teachers and lecturers and in their promotion to positions of responsibility. These issues will be discussed further in Chapter 8.

## Race and Ethnicity

> Britain is now two entirely different worlds, and the one you inherit is determined by the colour of your skin. (Rushdie 1982)

In the article from which this quotation is taken, the author Salman Rushdie argued: 'Racism is not a side-issue in contemporary Britain; it is not a peripheral, minority affair. Britain is undergoing the critical phase of its post-colonial period.'

Many people would not agree. But to understand how far race is an issue in Britain in the 1990s and whether Britain is or is not a multicultural society, we cannot ignore its past as a colonial power, which has continued to determine both the history of immigration and the reaction to it. It was Britain that E. P. Thompson described as 'the last colony of the British empire'.

'Race' in common usage refers to any group of human beings who share a common *physiognomy* (personal appearance). Among people of European descent the distinguishing characteristic they find most worthy of note is *skin colour*, but this is not always the case in other parts of the world: the Chinese, for example, who are very close in skin colour to Europeans, refer to Europeans as 'red hairs', and the Japanese both regard and treat as an inferior 'race' a substantial group in their society, the Burukamin, who are to European eyes indistinguishable from their fellow nationals. For Europeans an additional factor is that, in the nineteenth century, the belief developed that they were superior to other peoples owing to their mastery of new technological skills. There was a mistaken attempt to apply the notion of natural selection to human societies, the doctrine called 'social Darwinism'. Hence it was then common to assume this superiority came from 'race', yet no scientific evidence has ever been found of a connection between 'race' and mental or physical achievement. The arguments of writers such as A. Jensen and H. J. Eysenck (1971) that the differences in educational attainment between Afro-Caribbean immigrant children and others were due to their genetic endowment took insufficient account of social factors (see below) and have not been supported by later research. In fact, in the last few years the technique of genetic fingerprinting has shown that all human beings are descended from one common pair of ancestors, who lived no more than 100,000 years ago, and 'around 85 per cent of total human genetic diversity comes from the differences between individuals from the same country. Individuals — not nations and not races — are the main respository of human variation' (Nigel Williams, 'Skin deep', in *The Guardian*, 13 December 1991).

For people to believe that there are significant differences between 'races', with the implication that some are superior and some inferior, is 'racialism'. If people believe that discrimination against members of specific 'races' is justified and deliberately set out to practise it, we call it 'racism', though unfortunately the two terms are not always clearly differentiated in daily use. Since the problem of discrimination stems from the use of the inadequate term 'race' in the first place, it is better to avoid it.

Modern anthropologists therefore prefer to use the term *ethnic group* (which comes from the Greek word, *ethne*, for a tribe) to designate a social group which is held together not only by common kinship, but also by culture and/or religion. Like tribes, ethnic groups can and do have procedures for incorporating new individuals from outside the group. Immigration and/or marriage are the most usual ways in which this happens.

## Historical Background

Whatever else the British may be, they certainly do not constitute a 'race'. They are the product both of many waves of immigration, and a continuous trickle of refugees or visitors from many other parts of the world. Dark-skinned Britons are by no means a new phenomenon. There were small but well-established Afro-Caribbean communities in various parts of Britain in the nineteenth century, for example in Tulse Hill, south London, following the abolition of the slave trade. But there was prejudice too, exacerbated by the myth of racial superiority which acted as a legitimating ideology for the growing Empire.

Since 1945, both push and pull factors have operated to increase immigration to the United Kingdom. Both have continued to be important but their weighting varies both by time and place. It is a truism that people emigrate in search of better economic opportunities, but in fact those who do so are often from the better-off sectors of their societies or who have a tradition of migration. In the post-colonial world, political changes sometimes made minorities unwelcome in their own countries. The expulsion of the East African Asians (see below) was an extreme case.

Given the long connection between the colonies and Britain, it was natural that many who did seek better opportunities would be attracted here, especially when in the postwar boom Britain was short of labour. Afro-Caribbeans recruited by London Transport during this period, who constituted the first wave of non-European immigration, received official help and support. The formalities of immigration were no problem, since in the days of the much maligned Empire all subjects of the Queen were legally equal and had the right to travel freely between any of her territories.

By 1955 this first wave of immigration was already tailing off, but not before it had become clear that overt racial discrimination was on the increase. Extreme right-wing organisations opposed to further immigration were already emerging, notably the so-called British National Party and the White Defence League, who organised white youths into demonstrations against Afro-Caribbeans. In 1958 demonstrations in Notting Hill, West London, and in Nottingham in the Midlands, both ended in riots. Less vocal but more significant elements in the ruling Conservative Party began to urge a change in the law. The Government was not prepared to admit it, but what their supporters really wanted was an immigration law that would exclude black people without at the same time excluding whites. In the 1962 Commonwealth Immigrants Act they achieved this, but only partially. The Act left the rights of British subjects untouched. Other Commonwealth citizens were allowed entry (other than as temporary visitors) only if they were the close families of residents or held work permits, which at that time were still fairly easy to obtain. The case against such restrictions was not helped by the fact that a number of the newly independent Commonwealth countries had already established their own immigration controls.

In the 1960s, the Indian subcontinent rather than the Caribbean became the main source of would-be immigrants. Labour had fought against the 1962 Act when in opposition, only to find that there was much sympathy for it among their working-class voters and members of trade unions. Hence in the event they did not live up to their promise to repeal the Act. Critics of the Act complained that it was not very effective — a favourite target of criticism was the number of wives who arrived as a result of arranged marriages from India and Pakistan. But the fiction was maintained that the problem (if problem there was) was not one of race, and when in 1968 a member of the Conservative shadow cabinet, Mr Enoch Powell, in a speech made in Birmingham, said that he feared 'blood' if immigration were not halted altogether, he was summarily dismissed by the Leader of the Opposition, Mr Heath.

Not long afterwards, however, British subjects of Asian descent who had been living in Kenya were expelled from their adopted countries, by African politicians who had become jealous of the roles they had performed there as entrepreneurs and businessmen. To stop them taking advantage of their rights of British citizenship and bringing these valuable talents to Britain, the Labour Government of the day rushed through Parliament the Commonwealth Immigrants Act of 1968; the first legislation to remove the rights of entry of British subjects rather than Commonwealth citizens.

With the return of the Conservatives in 1970, new legislation was devised to ensure as far as possible that future immigrants would all be white-skinned. For the Commonwealth Immigrants Act 1971, a new term, 'patrial' (from Latin *pater* = father), was coined to designate all who either had at least one British grandparent or who had been naturalised or who had lived for at least five years in Britain. Patrials and their close families and the close kin of other Commonwealth citizens legally resident in Britain before 1973 had the right to enter the country freely. The same right was, as a result of entry into the European Community, accorded to all EC citizens.

In 1978, Mrs Thatcher, the Leader of the Opposition, promised that, when the Conservatives returned to power, further immigration would be ended. Once in power, however, diplomatic considerations made it necessary to conclude a formal agreement for the return of Hong Kong to China in 1997. Hence there was a theoretical possibility that all four million British subjects in that territory might wish to come to Britain. The result was the British Nationality Act of 1981.

The new Act created three categories of British citizenship. British citizenship proper and hence rights of residence were restricted to residents of the United Kingdom or to those who have at least one British parent and were registered abroad at birth. Full British citizenship and rights of residence were removed from all citizens of British dependent territories (including Hong Kong), but as a result of a late amendment from Conservative backbenchers, not from the Falkland Islanders, whom the Prime Minister had already described as 'British people of British stock'. It also effectively removed all rights of British citizenship from those living in independent countries having no recent connection by either family or residence with Britain, though they might claim the nearly meaningless status of British overseas citizens. EC citizens, needless to say, were unaffected.

**Development of immigration controls in Britain**

**1948 British Nationality Act**

Following the independence of India and Pakistan, established for the citizens of Commonwealth countries the same rights as they had previously had as British subjects to enter Britain freely, to work and to settle permanently if they chose.

**1949 Ireland Act**

Accorded full rights of British citizenship to citizens of the new Republic of Ireland.

**1962 Commonwealth Immigrants Act**

British subjects (and citizens of the Republic of Ireland) remain free to enter country. Entry of Commonwealth citizens restricted to close relatives of existing residents and to holders of work permits and their immediate relatives.

**1968 Commonwealth Immigrants Act**

First Act to remove rights of entry of British subjects, to prevent Kenyan Asians holding British passports from exercising their rights to settle in Britain.

**1969 Immigration Appeals Act**

Removed right of would-be immigrants to appeal to the courts; established instead special tribunals; required certificate of entitlement to enter for dependants of immigrants already settled in Britain.

**1971 Immigration Act**

Right of entry further restricted to patrials (all who either had at least one British grandparent or who had been naturalised or who had lived for at least five years in Britain) and their close families; to the families of other Commonwealth citizens legally resident in Britain before 1973; and to all EC citizens.

**1981 British Nationality Act**

Restricted British citizenship proper and hence rights of residence to residents of the United Kingdom or to those who have at least one British parent and were registered abroad at birth; removed full British citizenship and rights of residence from citizens of all British dependent territories except the Falkland Islanders; removed effectively all rights of British citizenship from those living in independent countries having no recent connection by either family or residence with Britain. EC citizens unaffected.

# How Many Immigrants Were There?

Given the extraordinary trouble successive governments have gone to to restrict immigration, taking special care to exclude those such as the Ugandan Asians and Hong Kong Chinese who might be expected to bring with them special skills, it seems reasonable to ask just how much of a problem immigration was in social terms.

The first thing to note is that European (and in particular Irish) immigration has long been more significant in terms of numbers, and unlike 'new Commonwealth' immigration no effort has been made to stop it.

Secondly, by the Census of 1971 it was already clear that immigration had virtually ceased to be a significant factor in the growth of the minority group population. In that year, all racial minorities together totalled only 1.85 million people, of whom some 28 per cent had been born in Britain and were therefore British subjects by birth. Since the immigrant population was relatively young, fertility rates among immigrant groups were above average for the population as a whole. Hence even though immigration was no longer a significant factor, the minority population continued to increase, reaching 1.7 million in 1976 and 2.3 million in 1981 (4.2 per cent of the total population) (Pilkington 1984: 2−3). This figure was expected on existing trends to rise to just under 6 per cent by the year 2000. By 1986, however, over 40 per cent of all Afro-Caribbean and Asian people living in Britain were native-born and, by 1990, 64 per cent of the UK-born ethnic minority population were aged under 15 and only 4 per cent were aged over 29. Since most immigrants arrive as young adults, and hence are aged between 15 and 29, there were still as many overseas-born as UK-born in that age group, but virtually none under the age of 15 (*Social Trends*, 1990).

International comparisons on immigration are as instructive as elsewhere. There were more immigrants as a percentage of the population in Switzerland, Germany and France than in Britain in the 1960s. Far from it hindering their economic development, those countries enjoyed a faster growth in their gross domestic product in those years than Britain, and their citizens, too, were generally better off.

# Race Relations

'Discrimination' means treating a person less favourably than another person on the grounds of colour, race or ethnic or national origins. Though action against discrimination began in the context of immigration there is of course no necessary connection between the two. 'Prejudice' means being biased against a person on any ground independently of that person's actions, and is, naturally, hard either to identify or to counteract unless an overt act of discrimination can be shown to have taken place.

Table 4.2 *Ethnic minorities in Britain, 1985–7*

| Description | 000s | % |
| --- | --- | --- |
| White | 51,222 | 94.4 |
| Indian | 745 | 1.4 |
| West Indian/Guyanese | 521 | 1.0 |
| Pakistani/Bangladeshi | 415 | 0.8 |
| Chinese | 120 | 0.2 |
| African | 105 | 0.2 |
| Arab | 71 | 0.1 |
| Mixed | 255 | 0.5 |
| Other | 141 | 0.3 |
| Not stated | 570 | 1.0 |
| TOTAL | 54,736 | 100.0* |

*Source: Social Trends* 20, p. 25.

*Subtotals do not add up to 100 per cent owing to rounding.

Prejudice of employers or others against, e.g., the Jews or the Irish had existed long before the postwar wave of immigration from the New Commonwealth but no effective attempt had been made to deal with it. The Labour Government of 1964–70, concerned by the growing ethnic unrest in the United States and fearful for its possible consequences for race relations in Britain, tried to establish a new framework for improving race relations by the Race Relations Act of 1965, which:

● Established a statutory Race Relations Board with limited powers to conciliate.
● Set up Regional Conciliation Committees to consider complaints.
● Required local authorities to appoint professional Conciliation Officers with the responsibility to investigate complaints and settle cases by conciliation where possible.
● Forbade racial discrimination in certain specified public places.
● Created a new criminal charge of 'incitement to racial hatred'.

This last provision was included largely for public relations reasons, since lawyers were agreed that existing legislation (the Public Order Act of 1936, which had effectively stopped pre-war fascist disturbances) already enabled successful prosecutions and very few were brought under the new legislation. Many from the ethnic minorities believed this was because the police were a stronghold of racial prejudice and police conduct during further disturbances in the mid-1960s strengthened this impression. Home Office studies have since confirmed that young black males were more likely to be stopped and searched by the police than any other group. Blacks were more likely than other groups to be arrested, and if brought before the courts they were more likely to be punished.

The other great area of irritation was in work. Sivanandan puts a common criticism:

> racialism did not debar black people from work *per se*. It operated instead to deskill

them, to keep their wages down and to segregate them in the dirty, ill-paid jobs that white workers did not want — not on the basis of an avowed racialism but in the habit of an acceptable exploitation. (Sivanandan 1982: 3).

Although some would say this view overstates the case, research by W. Daniel in 1966–7 confirmed that there was discrimination and that it was based on colour, not on immigrant status. He took the view that prejudice was not deep-seated and that most white people in Britain were fairly unprejudiced, though some did practise acts of discrimination. These occurred, he believed, largely because immigrants were seen as unqualified and it was still felt that to act in a wholly unbiased way in assigning jobs would be unacceptable to other whites (Daniel 1968, cited in Pilkington 1984). The view that prejudice was relatively rare in Britain was supported by Rose and Deakin (1969), who argued:

> The extent of tolerance cannot be stressed too often and is indeed one of the major facts of the actual situation. . . . What is needed is not an effort to make people unprejudiced but rather to remind them that they are unprejudiced.

However, this view was not shared by many black people, and the much more spectacular manifestations of unrest in the United States were, correctly or incorrectly, interpreted by the Government as a hint of the way things might go if further action were not taken. A second Race Relations Act was therefore passed in 1968. The 1968 Act:

- Strengthened the Race Relations Board by extending its powers to cover discrimination in housing, education and employment but left it to individuals to make complaints.
- Established the Community Relations Commission with a duty to take steps to improve community relations and encourage others to do so.
- Prohibited any kind of discrimination in the provision of goods, facilities or services to the public.
- Made it unlawful to publish any kind of discriminatory notice or advertisement, whether or not covered by the Act.

In the early 1970s, a time of relatively full employment, unemployment rates among ethnic minorities were roughly the same as among whites and their housing conditions had markedly improved. The second report from Political and Economic Planning (now the Policy Studies Institute), based on research conducted in 1973–4, showed that direct discrimination against racial minorities in housing had decreased considerably since 1967, and discrimination in employment appeared to have been somewhat reduced. However, the economic position of those in work was still not as good as for whites, and the research did confirm that such differences were the result of discrimination on the grounds of colour rather than immigrant status (Smith, D. J. 1976). The Race Relations Act 1976 was a further attempt to end discrimination, especially in recruitment and employment. The Act:

- Set up the Commission for Racial Equality (CRE), empowered to conduct formal investigations and to take action before the courts for alleged cases of racial discrimination either by groups or by individuals.
- CRE took over the established network of community relations councils and was empowered to give small subsidies to minority cultural activities.
- Indirect as well as direct discrimination on racial grounds was made unlawful.

CRE found, however, that the courts were very unwilling to act on its findings, and a sense of grievance persisted. Though by 1982 there had been a further very substantial improvement in living conditions in ethnic minority households, discrimination in employment remained a major issue. Rising unemployment in 1979−81 hit all minority ethnic groups harder than whites, while there was evidence that the only reason why there were fewer represented in the lowest status jobs was that they were in fact out of work (Field 1986).

Further disturbances at the beginning of the 1980s met with no new response from the Government, though existing legislation continued in force. The sense of grievance among young blacks at police attitudes had not diminished, however, while the belief, particularly among Asians, that the police were at best indifferent to their complaints about racially motivated attacks upon them were again confirmed by Home Office research. 'The anxieties about racial attacks are justi-fied,' the report concluded. 'Racially motivated attacks, particularly on Asians, are more common than we had supposed; and there are indications that they may be on the increase' (Smith 1982).

In 1984, the *British Social Attitudes Survey* showed that 69 per cent of the population supported laws against racial discrimination. However, at the same time, it reported that 90 per cent of the people surveyed believed that there was prejudice against minority ethnic groups, and that prejudice was increasing rather than declining. More surprisingly, 35 per cent of all respondents now admitted that they themselves were racially prejudiced; the proportion ranging from 46 per cent among Conservative voters to 28 per cent for both Labour and Alliance voters. The finding that prejudice had increased since the 1970s was supported by the results of the third Policy Studies Institute survey:

> The British job market has changed little in its hostility to black workers, except that it now excludes more of them from work altogether. We are left with a rigid pattern that not only has survived through the 1970s, but also shows no signs of breaking down in the near future. (Brown, C. 1984, quoted in *New Society*, 17 January 1986)

## Perspectives on Race

There are two main perspectives on the race issue in sociology; these can be termed the *consensus* perspective and the *conflict* perspective.

*Consensus theorists* hold, with Patterson (1965), that the problems encountered by racial minorities are the product of immigrants' culture conflict, not their colour. Cultural boundaries, they argue, are part of the order of the host society. In due course immigrants will be assimilated. Time will solve any problems.

However, since problems do persist in the meantime, writing on race in Britain is dominated by *conflict theorists*. One of the earliest prominent advocates of the conflict theory of race in Britain was the Weberian John Rex (Rex 1970). In his study with Robert Moore of the Sparkbrook district of Birmingham in the 1960s (Rex and Moore 1967), Rex argued that time would not necessarily help since the effect of race is to reinforce class position, and class they saw (with both Marx and Weber) as determined by (1) the ownership of wealth, in particular the ability to buy one's own home, and (2) control over the means of production. They concluded that competition for scarce resources, such as housing and jobs, led to conflict, but the notion of assimilation was meaningless as the host society was not unitary; it too was made up of a number of groups in conflict with one another.

Robert Miles (1982) developed this thesis from an explicitly Marxist viewpoint, which emphasises the origins of postwar immigration in a labour migration. He does not regard, as earlier Marxists tended to do, racism simply as something functional to capitalism. Instead he identifies three existing interpretations of the nature of the challenge presented by the entry of black workers into the labour market, all of which he rejects (Miles 1982: 152–3).

1. 'The *unitary working class thesis*', supported by traditional Marxists, places blacks in the working class, where they share all the disadvantages of their class position (Westergaard and Resler 1975: 356–60). Empirical evidence suggests that this view is incorrect, and that the successive restraints imposed by government on immigrants mark them out as distinct (see also Phizacklea and Miles 1980).

2. 'The *divided working class thesis*' is founded on the view that migrant labour was deliberately sought by industry to fill the jobs others did not want. The division thus created in the working class, by the presence of what Marx termed a 'reserve army of labour', enabled employers to keep wages down generally, so increasing their rate of profit, while at the same time the white members of the working class came to see themselves as superior and lost their class-consciousness (Castles and Kosack 1973: 477). Miles argues that this position ignores the many other divisions that exist within the working class.

3. 'The *underclass thesis*' suggests that racial discrimination is so strong that blacks form an underclass below the working class, an argument supported by evidence that they tend to be disproportionately represented among the lowest-paid occupations as well as the unemployed, but contested both by those who reject the notion of an underclass and by those who accept it, but see it as being caused by wider social factors.

Miles' position is that 'migrant labour in Britain should be conceived of as constituting a racialised fraction of the working class' (Miles 1982: 153). The main objection to this position is that it emphasises a division between migrant labour and other members of ethnic minorities which is likely to be felt differently by different families.

# The Problem of Inequality

## Employment

The position of ethnic minorities in regard to employment is a complex one. Very different views can emerge depending on which stratum of society is studied.

Between 1974 and 1982, the proportion of Afro-Caribbean men and Asian men and women entering professional or managerial jobs increased very significantly. In the case of Asian women they had done significantly better than their white counterparts. At the other end of the scale the proportion of whites and Asians in low status jobs fell while that of Afro-Caribbean men rose slightly. However, in 1982 unemployment among Afro-Caribbean, Pakistani or Bangladeshi men was considerably higher than among whites, Indians or African-Asians (Field 1986), and there was evidence that the effect of the recession of 1979–81 had fallen disproportionately on minority groups (Brown, C. 1984).

Owing to changes in the basis of calculation, with only those entitled to claim benefit now counting as unemployed, the 1988 figures cannot be directly compared with those of 1982. In particular, Pakistani/Bangladeshi women, formerly the *largest* unemployed group, have now completely disappeared from the official figures. However, in other respects those figures show a very similar distribution to that shown in 1982 (*Social Trends*, 1990, Table 4.28).

## Housing

Given the relative poverty of their homelands, the difficulties of obtaining work, and obstruction in obtaining council housing, early black immigrants had to make do with the cheapest possible form of housing available in the private rented sector, often of very poor quality. The tendency for immigrants to settle in areas where others share their cultural background led to their being concentrated in the decaying inner city areas. Rex and Moore in the 1960s found black immigrants, as predicted by Burgess's ecological model of urban growth and decay (see Chapter 5), concentrated in the 'zone of transition' just outside the central business district.

Not only therefore was their presence disproportionately conspicuous, their living conditions were overcrowded. In 1961, nearly half (48 per cent) of immigrant households were in shared accommodation compared with 6 per cent for whites, and two-fifths of those of Afro-Caribbeans (who had arrived first) were technically overcrowded. By 1982, only 5 per cent remained in shared dwellings, as against 1 per cent for whites (Field 1986) and the standard of accommodation had improved out of all recognition. Though there were still partially segregated areas in some major cities, in respect of housing tenure at least blacks no longer appeared to be disadvantaged (Smith, D. 1977).

These changes mirrored and were the product of major changes in housing tenure patterns which affected all groups in society. In the same twenty-year period the private rented sector declined from about a third to less than 10 per cent of all households, while the proportion of council tenants and owner occupiers rose steadily. However, Afro-Caribbeans and Asians solved their housing problems in markedly different ways, the former tending to become council tenants and the latter owner-occupiers. So, while in 1961 70 per cent of Afro-Caribbeans were in private rented accommodation and only 3 per cent were council tenants, in 1982 only 6 per cent were still in private rented dwellings and 46 per cent were in council properties. At the same time, the 44 per cent of Asians who had been in private rented accommodation in 1961 had declined to 6 per cent, while the number owning their own homes had climbed from 47 per cent to 72 per cent.

Despite this very substantial progress, there are still significant differences in living conditions. Ethnic minorities have still to match the 20 per cent of white households occupying detached houses or bungalows. At the other end of the scale Bangladeshis in particular are still likely to find themselves in overcrowded living conditions. Though in 1988 9 per cent of households with a non-white head had over one person per room, as opposed to only 1 per cent for white households, only 3 per cent of Afro-Caribbean households fell in this category as opposed to 9 per cent of Indian and 32 per cent of Pakistani/Bangladeshi households (*Social Trends*, 1990).

## Education

Research in the early 1970s identified a number of possible areas of disadvantage in education. Bernard Coard (1971) suggested that Afro-Caribbean children were disproportionately represented among those sent from ordinary state schools to ESN schools (special schools). But the very small proportions (2.33 per cent of Afro-Caribbean children as against 0.68 per cent of non-immigrant children) place his statistics within the margin of error, while Asian children, on his own evidence, were *under*-represented. Other studies showed that children from the ethnic minorities were more likely to find themselves in the lower streams and found it difficult to get places in grammar schools (Townsend 1971; Townsend and Brittan 1972). The change after 1969 to comprehensive schools and the spread of mixed-ability teaching in the 1970s, however, should have done much to negate such disadvantages.

On the basis of O- and A-level GCE results, the Rampton Report concluded in 1981 that Asian children were performing at a level comparable with indigenous children but Afro-Caribbean children were not. For example, only 5 per cent of Afro-Caribbean children achieved CSE Grade 1 or O-level grades A–C in mathematics (the equivalent of GCSE grade C or better) in 1978–9, compared with 20 per cent of Asian children and 19 per cent of all other school leavers. The results for A-level were similar: only 2 per cent of Afro-Caribbeans obtained one or more passes compared with 13 per cent for Asians and 12 per cent for all others. The Rampton Report took no account of other factors such as social class and gender, and if Afro-Caribbean children were disproportionately represented in the working class, some such disparity might be expected, but it is too great to be explained simply in class terms.

Three main explanations have been given for these differences:

## Cultural background and negative self-image

Afro-Caribbean children appear to enter school with a strongly negative self-image (Milner 1975). If this were caused by racial discrimination, this self-image might be expected to be shared by other minority groups, but it is not. Two alternative causes have been suggested: a cultural background that emphasises physical punishment and one in which a large number of children grow up in one-parent families under the care of child-minders (Little 1978; Taylor 1981). The latter means that the children concerned get a poor educational start in early life and the former that discipline stunts natural curiosity.

## Ethnocentric educational values and teachers' expectations

Alternatively, minority group critics of the system have argued that it exists to perpetuate white, middle-class values, and is therefore biased against minority cultures. A further disadvantage, it has been suggested, is the remoteness of the Creole dialect from standard English (Sutcliffe 1982). Teachers see Afro-Caribbean pupils as disruptive and tend to stereotype them as less able (Brittan 1976). The report of the Swann Committee accepted that both direct and indirect racial discrimination took place in schools and saw racial discrimination in society at large as a broader cause of underachievement. However, this argument has to be accepted with caution in view of continuing evidence that Asian children do well at school despite being the targets of discrimination in society at large, and men from the Indian ethnic group and the 'other' category (including African, Arab and Chinese) were more likely than white men to hold higher qualifications. Both males and females — and especially the latter — from the Pakistani/Bangladeshi ethnic groups were not as well qualified as those from other groups (*Social Trends*, 1990: 63).

## Inadequate school community liaison

Meanwhile, the problem is being tackled by educationists themselves by an extension of methods already in use since the 1960s, namely by extending contacts between the school and parents. A weakness of this approach has been its inability as yet to secure adequate co-operation from parents and the suggestion has been made that school and parents should enter into a formal agreement (Tomlinson 1984: 117ff; see also MacBeth 1983).

## Power and politics

Despite the fact that Britain's first non-white MP was elected to Parliament (as a Liberal) as long ago as 1906, for most of the period since 1945 there have been no blacks in the House of Commons. Rex and Moore (1967), in their study of Sparkbrook, noted that in 1945, despite the fact that the sitting Conservative MP was Secretary of State for India and had held that post during the Bengal famine, race was not an issue in the election: 'not only will the Labour Party not consider running coloured candidates,' they observed, 'but ... it is extremely reluctant to take active steps to win an immigrant vote.' The seat was won nevertheless by the Labour candidate. He held it until his death in 1959, when at the General Election soon afterwards it was won by a Conservative.

Race erupted as an issue in the General Election of 1964 when Mr Peter Griffiths, who had helped the Conservatives capture control of Smethwick Borough Council on an anti-immigrant platform, was selected as Conservative candidate for the Smethwick constituency, on the outskirts of Birmingham. Shortly afterwards, most of Birmingham's Conservative MPs issued a statement inviting those opposed to immigration to vote Conservative, though two refused to do so and most later gave rather different statements of their position. Birmingham Sparkbrook was won by Mr Roy Hattersley, who has held it ever since, and is now Deputy Leader of the Labour Party. Rex and Moore note 'the dramatic change which occurred in the views of the new Labour member. Mr Hattersley made a "liberal" maiden speech on race relations, but nine months later was willing to defend the Government's policy of strict immigration control, on the grounds that Britain's social services would be overstretched' (Rex and Moore 1967: 211). Nevertheless, many immigrants and their descendants found their natural home in the Labour Party during the 1970s. Though demands by black activists in the 1980s that the party should organise special 'Black Sections' were successfully resisted, a new generation of black activists came to the fore and were selected as parliamentary candidates. Four black MPs were elected to Parliament in the 1987 election: Diane Abbot  Paul Boateng, Bernie Grant and Keith Vaz, all from the Labour Party.

The selection in 1991 of John Taylor, a black lawyer, as Conservative candidate for Cheltenham, a strongly Conservative seat, was met by overt hostility from Conservative Party activists. In the one case in which this hostility was publicly expressed in racial terms, the individual concerned was expelled from the Party, but others objected on the safer grounds that the candidate ought to be 'a local man' [*sic*].

## Law

Blacks make up only 5 per cent of the population but in 1985 they accounted for 12.5 per cent of those in prison. In 1989, the figure had actually increased to 16 per cent and, of the 48,500 prisoners in custody, 5,000 (10.3 per cent) were Afro-Caribbean and 1,300 (2.7 per cent) Asian. The disparity is even more obvious when gender is taken into account. Black women make up no less than 24 per cent of the female prison population.

Obviously, given that blacks are disproportionately likely to be deprived, and given that deprivation is related to crime, their class position could account for these disparities at least in part. The figures are consistent with the fact that Afro-Caribbeans in particular are relatively poor, more likely to live in the inner city areas, and most likely to be resentful of their poverty. However, there is consistent evidence too that they are disadvantaged by the system of justice. To begin with, the police seem particularly likely to target blacks for their investigations, especially those concerned with minor drugs offences. Secondly, there is evidence of discrimination precisely where police discretion is greatest, that is, when they have to decide whether to charge a suspect or to administer a caution; young whites are more likely to be cautioned, young blacks to be charged. Thirdly, once before the courts, blacks are more likely to be remanded in custody rather than be allowed bail. Lastly, once tried and found guilty, blacks are more likely to get custodial sentences, and whites to be put on probation or given community service.

Unhappily, the Race Relations Act does not cover either the police or the judiciary, since there is clear evidence of discrimination in some of the assumptions on which these decisions are based. Magistrates who argue that blacks are more likely to jump bail, for example, have done so explicitly on the assumption that blacks (virtually all of whom are now born in Britain) have 'somewhere else to go', and it is extremely disturbing that blacks should make up as much as 25 per cent of the female remand population.

## Comparison of the Experiences of Different Ethnic Minorities

As will be seen from the foregoing, there are in fact very substantial differences between the experiences of different ethnic groups in Britain, and there are also very marked variations within them. Thus, while Asians generally are associated with a belief in private ownership, preferring to opt even for poor-quality owner-occupation rather than reliable rented accommodation, and place a strong cultural emphasis on entrepreneurship and education as a means of social advancement, Bangladeshis are 'the most disadvantaged group on the labour market' and many of them are unemployed. The tendency towards concentration and insularity often attributed to Asians, too, is a phenomenon of immigration, and is probably just as true of the Chinese, who seldom register on the public consciousness at all, as the House of Commons Select Committee on Home Affairs noted in 1985.

Such comparisons have, however, to be made with care. Ironically, 'race' is one area of social enquiry in Britain in which international comparisons have been made as a matter of course. Since, however, they have been made with the very different social and historical pattern of the United States, they do not seem to have been particularly helpful, and indeed it is clear that fear of the sort of race riots that occurred in the principal US cities in the 1960s was a major factor in creating the present elaborate system of indirect discrimination against immigrants.

# Suggestions for Further Reading

On *gender* relations Carole Pateman (1988) deals with the key notion of *The Sexual Contract*. Firestone (1972), *The Dialectic of Sex*, argues that gender is a more important dimension of stratification than class. John H. Goldthorpe takes the opposite view — see, for example, 'Women and class analysis: in defence of the conventional view', in *Sociology* (1983), Vol. 17. Stanworth replies in Vol. 18. Britten and Heath (1983), 'Women and Social Class', argue that husband and wife can occupy a 'cross-class' position. On the role of housework in women's lives, see Ann Oakley (1974), *Housewife*, and Sallie Westwood (1984), *All Day Every Day*. The differential achievement of girls in the educational system is discussed in Sue Sharpe (1978), *Just Like a Girl: how girls learn to become women*. See also further reading for Chapters 6, 8, 10 and 11.

On *race* generally, good introductions are Andrew Pilkington (1984), *Race Relations in Britain* and John Solomos (1989), *Race and Racism in Contemporary Britain*. A. Sivanandan (1982), *A Different Hunger*, gives a view from the minority perspective. The classic study of race relations in Sparkbrook, Birmingham, John Rex and Robert Moore (1967), *Race, Community and Conflict; a study of Sparkbrook*, is still well worth reading. A. Phizacklea and Robert Miles (1980), *Racism and Political Action in Britain*, discuss the impact of the successive restraints put on immigrants by government. On the position of ethnic minorities in education, see Sally Tomlinson (1984), *Home and School in Multicultural Britain*.

# 5 Power and Politics

## Politics

The examination of political sociology at A-level is generally very narrow. The essential themes are:

- Theories of power as applied to Britain; in particular, the elitist-pluralist debate.
- Pressure groups, especially the extent of their influence.
- Factors for voting behaviour, especially the changing relationship between social class and voting behaviour. This is sometimes expressed as a question relating to the changing support base of one of the two main political parties.

Power is also relevant to the nature of organisations (discussed further in Chapter 6). Among the relevant themes are:

- Can organisations be democratic?
- The characteristics of bureaucracy and its problems, especially its inflexibility.

## Power and Politics

Politics is about the ultimate power to make decisions in society. It is a term especially associated with government, though it exists in all parts of society. The difference is that government is authoritative; if necessary, its decisions can be enforced on the rest of society through means of coercion, such as the police, law courts, prisons and other corrective institutions. In short, governments have *power*.

Power, then, is a key concept in political sociology and can be defined as *the ability to get others to do what they would not otherwise do*. Weber's definition, though old-fashioned, is clear on this point:

> In general we understand by 'power' the chance of a man or a number of men to realize their own will in a communal action even against the resistance of others who are participating in the action. (Gerth and Mills 1957: 180)

Hence power can operate on a number of levels. On a personal level, a boss may have the power to fire an employee. On an organisational level, the same boss may have the power to order a substantial reorganisation of a plant which will affect the lives and working conditions of many employees. On a national level, a government can decide to spend money on education, public health or the army; when it has decided which, it can ensure that the people in general pay the taxes necessary to pay for the changes. On an international level, a British government has to work with other governments within the European Community, and with the United Nations in the Middle East, but can fight a war in the South Atlantic or the Gulf.

When power is being exercised in many ways at the same time, the resulting confusion is sometimes difficult to disentangle, especially as there are many individuals and groups who do not have power (they cannot make a final decision on a matter) but they do have influence (they can affect the making of decisions). Lastly, the use of power involves not only the question 'Will it work?' but also the question 'What should I do?' In short, it involves moral and ethical questions about the right to use force to gain a specific result. Constructively used, power enables a community to function effectively to provide a better life for all. Selfishly used, it can make life very unpleasant indeed for many people.

**Uses and abuses of power**

| Uses | Abuses |
|---|---|
| To gain consent | To gain obedience |
| To secure agreement | To override reasoned opposition |
| To secure the general good | To push a special interest |
| To find out what people want | To tell people what they ought to want |
| To act quickly in an emergency | To use emergency powers to keep oneself in power |
| To maintain the society | To maintain the domination of a particular group. |

# Theories of Political Power

Theories of political power can broadly be divided into three categories: (1) those who believe that 'economic organisation is the key to political power' (Burnham 1945) and that the prime source of political power is the class which owns and controls the means of production (ruling class model); (2) those who believe it is located in a small, self-chosen group which is consciously aware of its own existence and role in society (ruling elite model); and (3) those who believe that, on the contrary, power is widely distributed in society and that for each centre of power there are other countervailing centres of power (pluralist model).

Political
power

| Model | Ruling class | Ruling elite | Pluralist |
|---|---|---|---|
| Source | Economic organisation | Group cohesion | Popular will |
| Bearers | Class | Elite | Competing groups |
| Conscious? | Yes | Yes | No |
| Means | Control of production | Control of information | Countervailing power |
| Why accepted | Ideological hegemony | Gratitude of the masses | Common values |

## Ruling-class model

The Marxist view is that the real centres of power are to be found in classes. For Marxists classes have a real existence. The people who compose them have a common interest and can develop a common purpose based on their common relation to the factors of production. For Marx and Engels the prime source of power in a capitalist society must be economic. The owners of the means of production constitute the ruling class, because they establish and maintain the capitalist economic market.

The ruling class, therefore:

1. Controls the state (government, police, judiciary, army, etc.) and can coerce others into obeying it.
2. Controls the processes of indoctrination (media, education system).

To those that argue that a class is much too big an entity to be self-conscious and ask *What does the ruling class do when it rules?* Göran Therborn (1978) answers:

> The answer, I think, is fairly clear. A ruling class, in a capitalist society, rules insofar as its members are able to control the state in accordance with their broad overall interest. ... In a capitalist society ... Karl Kautsky wrote in a famous phrase, the dominant class 'rules but does not govern'; instead, 'it contents itself with ruling the government'.

## Ruling-elite model

By *elite* sociologists mean a minority of people occupying the most influential and prestigious positions in a society or organisation. A political elite is one that has acquired a disproportionate share of political power. But elites can be identified wherever there is social organisation, so we can find business, scientific, artistic and religious elites also, and these may be linked to the political elite in various ways.

Elite theory originated in Italy among those pessimistic about the possibility of democracy. The term 'elite' was coined by the Italian economist Vilfredo Pareto, who became increasingly interested in sociology in his later life as he came to realise how many things economics could not explain. For Pareto logical rational action was exceedingly rare, and society evolved in a cyclical pattern in which it was invariably dominated by an elite. For him an elite was a relatively small group characterised by group cohesion or solidarity born of common perceptions, beliefs and values. Elite theorists like Pareto and his followers believe that elites are inevitable, but that if they remain in power for too long they will decay. Hence they argue that there is a tendency for elites to displace one another and indeed that a society needs a continuous 'circulation of elites' if it is to remain healthy.

A less speculative view of elites sees their power as being the natural product of the requirements of organisation. In *Political Parties* (1962), Robert Michels outlined his '*iron law of oligarchy*', which states that in any organisation (even socialist ones such as the German Social Democratic Party — SPD) the minority will come to dominate the majority: 'It is organisation which gives birth to the domination of the elected over the electors, of the mandataries over the mandators, of the delegates over the delegators. *Who says organisation says oligarchy*' (Michels 1962: 365).

Oligarchy (rule by the few) for Michels is the inevitable product of what he takes to be the basic principles of organisation:

1. *Size*. Once an organisation has grown beyond a certain size, a division of labour, specialists and delegated authority become necessary. Size leads to division of labour, which in turn leads to specialisation.
2. *Power and influence*. Specialists grow in power over their particular specialisms. They begin to take on the status of experts. Concentration of expertise leads to concentration of power and therefore:
3. *Lack of participation*. The rank-and-file have not had the necessary training, are not specialists and therefore cannot participate. The size of the organisation also means that participation is limited by the sheer physical distance between the top and the rank-and-file.
4. *Organisational facilities for power maintenance*. Provisions for the leaders to remain in power include:

    (a) Superior knowledge because of specialisms, access to files, just being there when decisions are made. Knowledge gives the power to manipulate the organisation and win any debate.
    (b) Control of the organisational media (journals, etc.). Views approved by the top are transmitted; others not.
    (c) Time, which, as highly paid, full-time organisational workers, the leaders have (together with the incentive) to prepare debates, accumulate knowledge, etc.
    (d) Political skill, needed by full-time organisational workers in order to attain power; once in power they develop this skill further and become full-time politicians.

There are also factors external to the organisation which contribute to oligarchy:

1. *The general illegitimacy of opposition.* Criticism is viewed as subversion.
2. *The economic and social gap between leaders and followers.* Leaders start developing a set of interests peculiar to their own group. These conflict with the interests of the organisation.
3. *Psychological factors.* The need for leadership, the political gratitude of the masses and the cult of veneration among the masses. The masses are politically incompetent and apathetic. They are collectively grateful for having the chores of administration lifted from them.

The Michels thesis has attracted great interest ever since it was first enunciated, since potentially it forms a major objection to liberal democracy. It was tested by the American sociologists Lipset, Trow and Coleman (1956) in *Union Democracy*, a study of the International Typographical Union in the United States and Canada. The ITU had had a democratic structure with two internally competing groups since 1815. Lipset, Trow and Coleman noted that the ITU had a large network of non-political secondary groups. Recreational groups, in particular, were much more numerous than in other organisations, and were the creation of the rank-and-file, not of the leadership, and both because of the number and because of the autonomy of these, group members spent much time in each others' company. They concluded that the occupational community tended to make men more politically active than they would be in its absence; that though the clubs were nominally non-political, and most members did not join them for political purposes, leaders were aware of their political importance.

The United States is an important test case for any theory of elites since it is so large that people who hold key positions in US politics cannot possibly all know one another and form a self-conscious group with a common purpose. Hence the US sociologist C. Wright Mills (1956) coined a new concept, 'The Power Elite'. For Mills the most powerful people in politics, the armed services and business in the United States, acted together as though they formed a single elite, even though they did not. Ironically it was the publication of this book that started the so-called *elitist/pluralist debate*, as it appeared to extend to national level the conclusions of Floyd Hunter (1953). Hunter studied the *community power structure* of Atlanta, Georgia ('Regional City'), using the *reputational method*; that is to say, he asked people whom they thought were the most important people in Atlanta. From their answers he identified some forty individuals who were repeatedly mentioned, and whom he concluded set the framework and the content of public policy. A wider conclusion was that at local level in the United States a disproportionate share of political power was in the hands of an economic elite dominated by businessmen.

## Pluralist model

The pluralist model originated wholly in the United States, a country which even Karl Marx believed might be an exception to his views on class dominance. It arose from dissatisfaction with what Robert Dahl termed 'Madisonian democracy', the view that in a democratic society every citizen has an equal chance of influencing decisions. This, the classical assumption of liberal democracy, did not take account of the fact that by forming groups, some citizens could come to have more influence or power than others.

Pluralists believe that individuals cannot command power enough to restore the balance but that groups can. Hence in a democratic society a multiplicity of groups grow up and compete to express the interests of citizens. An early statement of the view that given democratic freedom for groups as well as individuals the most powerful interests can be limited in their power is that of the economist J. K. Galbraith (1952), who in his *American Capitalism* put forward the concept of 'countervailing power' — that big business, for example, could be checked in its power by big trade unions. But the major statement of the position came from the American political scientist Robert Dahl, who coined the term *pluralism*. In his *Who Governs?* (1961), a study of New Haven, Connecticut, he examined a series of decisions that seemed to be particularly important. He found that the economic notables were only one of many groups competing with each another, and that different groups dominated city politics at different periods in history. Power, he argued, varied with the time, the place and the issue involved. Similar conclusions were reached by Suzanne Keller (1963), in *Beyond the Ruling Class*, who related the changing prominence of different 'strategic elites' to their influence over different 'issue areas'.

# Critique of the Three Models

### Ruling-class model

Marx and Engels worked and wrote in Britain and their experience of it guided many of their conclusions about the nature of capitalist society in general. The belief that Britain is dominated by a ruling class is very widespread. However, owing to the lack of definition of the key terms, the ruling-class model is very hard either to prove or to disprove. If the ruling class does not rule directly, how can it arrive at a unified view and ensure it is carried out?

Marxists argue that the model continues to be valid today, despite very different conditions from those in which Marx and Engels first elaborated it. Few dispute that in the latter half of the nineteenth century and the first half of the twentieth, however, *laissez-faire* capitalism was substantially modified, and a structure of social support created to solve what was then termed 'The Condition of England question'. In consequence, wealth was distributed far more widely in British society than Marx had anticipated and the polarisation between the bourgeoisie and the proletariat which he had predicted did not take place.

It can, of course, be argued that this was in the real interests of the ruling class, delivering a healthier workforce and acting to preserve a degree of inequality that otherwise might have led to revolution. Thus Westergaard and Resler (1975)

**Power in Britain**

Applying each of the three models in turn to modern Britain we get something like this:

### Ruling-class model

Britain is dominated by a small ruling class of capitalist employers. The state is their instrument. Party politics is a 'con' — it suggests to the propertyless working class that they do have a choice. This is not true, as all the main political parties are capitalist and have to operate the capitalist system effectively. The state depends on private industry to provide employment and tax revenue. Business interests and in particular financial institutions are extremely well organised and influential. Most government economic policy is designed to protect their interests. Most criminal and civil law relates to property.

### Ruling-elite model

In Britain only some interests are organised effectively and only some issues become political. The British political system is biased towards some groups rather than others. Most groups are controlled by small elites or 'oligarchies' which are unrepresentative of their memberships. The elites which run the key institutions in Britain (i.e. business, finance, civil service, Parliament, etc.) are recruited in the same way: white males with a public school/ 'Oxbridge' education belonging to the same London clubs; sometimes bound by ties of kinship. Big financial corporations are linked through 'interlocking directorships'.

### Pluralist model

Power is dispersed among a large number of groups and interests all seeking to influence policy. No one group is able to influence policy on a wide variety of different issues. Individuals are free to join groups and seek influence. Politics is a process of debate and negotiation. The role of the state is to uphold the rules of competition between rival interests and to implement the policy that emerges from the negotiation of those interests. There are thousands of organised groups in Britain and many more people are members of them than of political parties (although the latter are also competing interests, of course, but only a handful among the many). Most such groups are only involved in a few issues. Even very powerful groups closely involved with policy-making win some issues and lose others.

argue that:

Taxation and public welfare provision have done little to alter the broad pattern of material inequality, because the objectives and effects of public policy are limited by the needs and influence of business in an economy where private enterprise continues to play the predominant role.

For Weber, as we have seen, classes are important for the organisation of power, but so too are other types of organisation in modern society: 'Now: "classes", "status groups" and "parties" are phenomena of the distribution of power within a community' (Gerth and Mills 1957: 181). And in modern British society, even those who still hold to the notion of a ruling class recognise three things. First, the ruling class is as much defined as a status group as it is as a class. Second, other factors, especially gender and race, determine the extent to which individuals have access to political power. Third, there are at least some differences between the policies pursued by the two main political parties, Conservative and Labour. Thus in 1974 the incoming Labour Chancellor of the Exchequer, Denis Healey, was widely reported (though he denies it) to have said: 'We will squeeze the rich until the pips squeak' (Healey 1989). In fact, the proposed 'wealth tax' was not enacted, though at least until 1979 government policy maintained a strong commitment to progressive taxation. Then the incoming Conservative Chancellor, by cutting the top rate of income tax to 60 per cent (in 1987 his successor lowered it further to 40 per cent) and raising Value Added Tax from 8 per cent to 15 per cent (it was raised again, to 17.5 per cent, in 1991), began the process of eliminating the redistributive effects of the tax system.

## Ruling-elite model

The ruling-elite model has long been popular in the United Kingdom (Stanworth and Giddens 1974) because the British elite are particularly easy to identify. Virtually all of them are men. Many of them are distinguishable by accent, language and dress. A large proportion have been educated at the leading public schools and/or the Universities of Oxford and Cambridge. They share similar lifestyles and may enjoy membership of exclusive London (or provincial) clubs, where the politically powerful rub shoulders with members of the aristocracy and leading figures in business, finance or the professions. Many such people are additionally connected by directorships of e.g. the Bank of England, clearing banks, merchant banks, insurance companies, city and industrial firms. There is considerable movement of key individuals between the public and private sectors. For example, Sir John Nott, the former Defence Secretary, became head of the merchant bank Lazards.

Similar links exist in other countries, though the basis for them may be significantly different. Thus in the United States, East Coast patricians (members of the 'upper class') such as George Bush share some of these attitudes, and many will have attended one of the 'Ivy League' universities (Harvard, Yale or Princeton), studied together in law schools or worked for a time in one of the big New York law firms. In France, members of the elite will be Parisian by birth, have attended one of the prestigious lycées such as Louis-le-Grand or Janson-de-Sailly, and gained entry in a *concours* (competitive examination) to one of the *Grandes Ecoles*, from which graduation makes them a lifetime member of one of the *Grands Corps*, which administer the French state and society.

Though the institutions and terminology are different, the common factor lies in the role of education in mobilising individuals into the elite. If the elite were completely closed to outside recruitment it would not be long before severe social strains emerged, as many able individuals would be denied participation granted to less able individuals. Hence the stress laid in the Education Act of 1944 on making best use of the 'pool of ability'. Ralph Turner (1960), examining the way in which recruitment took place to social elites (see also Chapter 2 on social mobility), identified two types of mobility provided by educational systems:

1. *Sponsored mobility*. Education separates out at an early age candidates for the elite, they receive a different and better education; early *selection* (as if to a club) by the existing elite and *separation* from other members of society are key. Selection, however, is usually based on the grounds that the candidate appears to have qualities considered desirable, and this perpetuates the attitude of the elite group in the new generation of recruits.
2. *Contest mobility*. No formal *separation* takes place — all children (as in the United States) are educated together in the same kind of school and every child is encouraged to compete as long as possible so that *selection* takes place by self-selection — like a ladder up which everyone can climb until they can go no higher. The contestants strive by whatever means they can to obtain the main prizes available in a competitive society. The most competent person attains the highest goals of status and prestige.

Turner argued that contest mobility was normal in the United States. Most recent US Presidents (Nixon, Ford, Carter, Reagan) and leaders of American business, finance and the professions, have been selected in this way. However, in the United Kingdom sponsored mobility was and is the foundation of political power. Elite schools and Oxbridge remain the basis of the 'old boy network' into which other figures are integrated or from which (as in the case of such rich outsiders as 'Tiny' Rowland) they are as far as possible excluded.

Margaret Thatcher, a grocer's daughter born above a corner shop in Grantham, achieved fame as Britain's first woman prime minister, but conforms in many other respects to the normal British pattern of sponsored mobility:

1. She went to a grammar school.
2. She won a scholarship to Oxford.
3. She studied law, the norm for aspiring politicians.
4. She married Denis Thatcher, a wealthy businessman, who in 1965 sold his family firm to Burmah Oil for the equivalent of more than £3 million eighteen years later (*New Society Social Science Brief*, 6 October 1983).
5. Hence (unlike many other married women in the 1950s) she was able to employ others to look after her two young children while she was taking her first steps in politics, something that a man could have taken for granted.

Of Mrs Thatcher's first Cabinet, nineteen had been to public school, sixteen to either Oxford or Cambridge. William (now Viscount) Whitelaw, and Michael Heseltine were already both millionaires.

## Pluralist model

The pluralist model was not devised with Britain specifically in mind, but as in other liberal democracies evidence can be found which supports the pluralist thesis. For example, the French-born political scientist Jean Blondel argues that Britain contains not just one elite but several, and the power that they wield is social not political. In a 1974 study of twenty-four policy issues current between 1944 and 1964, Christopher Hewitt found a 'wide diversity of conflicting interests'. Only over the contentious issue of capital punishment did Parliament in this period go against public opinion. It is, however, fair to say that in the late 1980s both the introduction of the poll tax (the so-called 'community charge') and the privatisation of the water industry were passed by Parliament against the evidence of public opinion polls that they were each extremely unpopular.

# Who Has Power?

Whichever of the three models they adopt, most people tend to assume that the ability to wield political power is the ability to get things done. However, Bachrach and Baratz, in their work on 'The Two Faces of Power' (Bachrach 1970), demonstrated that the most crucial use of political power may often be not to get decisions made, nor even to get items on to the political agenda, but to keep them off it. What they termed 'non-decision-making' — the ability to keep issues out of the public arena — is certainly a crucial restriction on the effectiveness of pluralist debate, and much of the activity of the Green Party in the late 1980s was an attempt to bring to public awareness issues that governments had tried to keep out of the limelight.

In fact, as Steven Lukes (1974) has demonstrated, there are three faces of power. Both the power to take decisions and the power to set the agenda are underpinned by the creation of *ideology*. By ideology we refer to a systematic view of the world embodying principles and assumptions about what can and cannot be done. Antonio Gramsci, an Italian Marxist, argued that at any given time in any given society there is one such view that has attained what he termed *hegemony*. That is to say, its beliefs and tenets are so widely held that they are not seriously discussed or questioned, even by people who consciously argue other points of view.

In 1990, *The Sunday Times* (8 April 1990) was able to announce that the fifty richest persons in Britain were collectively worth some £48 billion. Wealth is obviously a useful foundation for political power, though many politicians have come from poor origins and have been successful because they had support from political parties and/or interest groups. Though the ruling-class model breaks down in that power in the boardroom cannot automatically be translated into power in Parliament, there is a two-way link between political and economic power.

The disclosure of financial interests shows that some 80−90 per cent of all Conservative MPs have business connections. From the press it is easy to see that they, and even more Cabinet ministers, can expect lucrative and not very taxing jobs on retirement or dismissal. For example, in 1990 Mr Nigel Lawson, the former Chancellor of the Exchequer, was appointed to a two-day a week part-time job with Barclays Bank, which was reported to pay at least £100,000 a year.

The power of the financial elite in Britain is so great because economic power has long since passed out of the hands of the owners of private businesses, for four reasons:

1. In modern economic conditions businesses are so big that their shareholders can no longer exercise effective control, which is exercised in their name by a small group of senior managers.
2. Within the body of shareholders a very small number of large institutional shareholders have disproportionate voting power and they are primarily concerned with profit rather than production.
3. Britain has exceptionally weak controls on takeovers, so that big money is made by buying and selling businesses regardless of the impact on those who work in them. Takeover threats mean that concern with retaining control may come before responsibility for employees; in the last analysis, if the bid is successful, the managers will receive very big payments to terminate their contracts, but employees have no say in who buys their plant.
4. Interlocking directorships weld together the power-holders in both finance and industry. However, the formal organisation representing manufacturing industry, the Confederation of British Industry (CBI), does not exercise as much influence as might be expected (see also Grant and Marsh 1977), and in recent years has complained loudly and unsuccessfully about the Government's policy of high interest rates.

## Pressure Groups

The difference between a *pressure group* (or, more correctly, *interest group*), like the CBI, and a political *party*, like the Conservative Party, however, is that a political party exists to contest for (or to retain) political *office*, while a pressure group exists to exert *influence* on decision-makers. In Britain, many more people (approximately 20 per cent of the population) are members of pressure groups than are members of political parties (approximately 3 per cent).

Pressure groups are not a new phenomenon. They arise from the fact that in every complex society there is a multiplicity of interests. Many of these are *latent*, in that the common interest (as in the case of a church) exists, but does not take a political form. But with the growth of mass participation in politics many interests have sought to exert active influence by forming pressure groups and hence the number of pressure groups has multiplied. In British politics these are usually divided into two categories: promotional groups and protectional or defensive groups:

1. *Promotional groups* are those formed to sponsor a particular cause. Generally, therefore, there is no limit to the number of members they can recruit. Membership is voluntary, and if they achieve their objectives, like the Anti-Slavery Society, they have to refocus their aims or they will lose members. Examples are:
   (a) The Campaign for Nuclear Disarmament
   (b) Friends of the Earth
   (c) Greenpeace
   (d) Royal Society for the Prevention of Cruelty to Children.
2. *Protectional groups* exist to defend the interests of their members. Their membership, therefore, is restricted to those whose interests they seek to defend. If they are successful, they may be given a privileged status in relation to government or to a specific branch of industry. In consequence, membership may be effectively compulsory. In the case of trade unions, the government has recently legislated to end the 'closed shop', but in the case of professional bodies it has been much more cautious. Examples are:
   (a) The Automobile Association
   (b) British Medical Association
   (c) The Law Society
   (d) Royal College of Nursing
   (e) Transport and General Workers Union.

How do pressure groups exert their influence? In practice, they can do so on a number of levels: by publicity aimed at the voters, by informing Parliament, by consultation with government Ministers and civil servants.

The public see mainly the public relations aspect of pressure groups when their spokespersons appear at Budget time on the television news to say what they think of government policy, when a lobby of Parliament is held or demonstrations take place in Trafalgar Square. But behind such appearances, and the news stories and paid advertisements that appear in the national press, some groups are at work much closer to the heart of government. The methods used by a group depend on the kinds of aims it has and the acceptability of those aims to those involved in the decision-making process. Some groups, such as the IRA or the Paedophile Information Exchange, have aims which challenge British law and therefore operate in clandestine (and often illegal) ways. Then there are groups such as CND which challenge widely accepted political norms and are therefore seen by governments as subversive. Lacking direct access to the centre of decision-making, they tend to use 'open market' tactics such as marches, lobbies of MPs, demonstrations, posters, badges, etc. Others, especially protectional groups, have information and co-operation to offer government. They tend to have pragmatic

Table 5.1 *How interest groups act to affect policy*

|  | | Operation | |
|  | Clandestine/illegal | Ideological/open market | Pragmatic/'insider' |
| --- | --- | --- | --- |
| Promotional Groups | IRA<br>Animal Liberation Front | CND<br>Anti-Poll Tax Union | RSPCA |
| Protectional Groups | PIE | NUM during the miners' strike | BMA |

approaches to their aims and are often given limited access to the decision-making process. They negotiate on the inside of Government, with the Departments where Parliament's 'skeleton legislation' is fleshed out.

For some groups, their influence over MPs begins at election time, when they try to secure the return of MPs favourable to their cause. A substantial group of Labour MPs are sponsored by trade unions — a custom which dates back to the days before MPs were paid. Many Conservative MPs combine an active role in business or the financial world with their work as an MP. Many members of both main parties are barristers. Others become effectively lobbyists for special interests. If they accept payment of any kind for this, they have to declare it in the Register of Members' Interests; this is a very recent development. On most issues, however, MPs are not specialists, so information from pressure groups has become an important part of the way in which they make up their minds.

To make the task of government easier, ministers often recognise the value of consulting with representatives of interests before formulating policy or embarking on legislation. They are not always pleased to be told that their ideas will not work or are unpopular, but as the events of 1989−90 demonstrated, ministers who try to impose unpopular taxes, dictate new terms to the professionals of the Health Service or try to give solicitors the right to plead cases in the higher courts can find themselves in trouble. As in the case of the British Medical Association (BMA) and the Department of Health, some interest groups have won a legal right to be consulted, and when they are consulted they expect to have their views taken into account. The BMA is a particularly useful group to government for two reasons. On the one hand, medicine is a highly emotive subject which arouses strong feelings in the electorate and the co-operation of Britain's doctors is essential. On the other hand, it is an area in which 'expert' opinion is especially strongly valued. Hence the BMA, which was closely involved in the setting-up of the NHS, has hitherto invariably been consulted over any changes involving it.

In a similar way, reflecting the close relationship that has grown up between government and some interest groups, some government committees and QUANGOs (Quasi-Autonomous Non-Governmental Organisations) contain representatives of interest groups as a matter of course. This situation appears to support the pluralist model of politics and to be desirable, in that a multiplicity of interests are being represented. But the process is highly selective. In the words of Schattschneider (1961) 'the flaw in the pluralist heaven is that probably 90% of the people cannot even get into the system.'

International comparisons strengthen reservations about the uncritical acceptance of the pluralist view. The growth of special interest groups in the United States in the 1980s has increased concern about the effect of their negative impact on the process of choice. They may not have been able to secure victory for their chosen candidates, but they have been able to destroy the chances of their opponents. The systematic destruction of the Democratic candidate for the Presidency in 1988, Michael Dukakis, by a combination of invective and innuendo, merely replicated what had already become the norm at state and local level.

Quasi-federal status has come to Britain too with its entry into the European Community. However, special interest groups in Britain have still much to learn of the process of decision-making in Europe, where the bureaucratic structure of the Commission in Brussels and the retention of ultimate decision-making power in the hands of individual country ministers makes systematic lobbying an absolute necessity. French farmers, who are widely distributed and exercise great power on French decision-making, have been a major influence on the shaping of the Common Agricultural Policy, for example, the main beneficiaries of which (apart from the French) have been smaller states such as Ireland and Denmark. Despite, or perhaps because of their traditional links with the Conservatives, British farmers have not been so successful in defending their interests.

## Bureaucracy

Strictly speaking, *'bureaucracy'* means simply 'government by officials'. Sociologists, following Max Weber, use it to refer to a specific form of systematic administration through rules applied by an orderly hierarchy of paid officials appointed for their qualifications: 'In public and lawful government these three elements constitute "bureaucratic authority". In private economic domination, they constitute bureaucratic "management"' (Gerth and Mills 1957: 196). So 'bureaucracy' is a term that no longer simply applies to government, but to organisations generally. And in popular use, it has by extension become a common term of criticism, implying that decisions are made in a rigid, unbending way which takes no account of individual needs (Albrow 1970).

Max Weber held that organisations are administered in a bureaucratic way because it is the most rational way yet devised of organising resources to obtain the desired goals. For this reason bureaucracy replaced the older systems under monarchies or other forms of traditional authority, in which places in government were held by relatives, friends or clients (those who have put themselves under the protection of a patron). Bureaucracy may not be ideal, but these systems are worse.

Summarising the characteristics of bureaucracy listed by Weber, we get the following standard pattern (or 'ideal type'):

1. Each official has a clearly defined area of responsibility and complex tasks are broken down into specialist areas.
2. Officials form part of a hierarchy; every lower office is under the supervision and control of a higher one.
3. Organisational behaviour is directed by a set of abstract rules which lay down the procedure to be followed in all likely cases. Officials must apply the rules in a formal and impersonal way.
4. Officials are not elected. They are appointed, specifically because of their knowledge and expertise. Their work forms a career. Promotion is by seniority or achievement or a combination of the two.
5. Private and official spheres are rigidly separated. Officials cannot own parts of the organisation and may not use it for their private gain. Conversely, they are accountable only for their official actions (Weber 1965: 333–4).

In Britain a professional civil service was established in 1857 by the so-called Northcote–Trevelyan reforms. Entrance to the Foreign Service and to the highest reaches of the home civil service was to be, as Weber notes, by competitive examination, resulting in the almost exclusive success of candidates from public schools and Oxford and Cambridge. Since 1945 there have been attempts to broaden the social base of entrance and to permit a greater degree of equality to women. Though few of the many reforms proposed have been implemented, those that were did include provision for easier promotion from lower ranks to senior positions (the 'First Division').

Though Weber himself regarded bureaucracy as technically superior to the system that had preceded it, he did not fail to note disadvantages. Not only did the system limit the personal freedom of people to act in a way that they might have considered desirable, it also generally limited spontaneity, creativity and personal initiative. Or as Michels put it:

> Bureaucracy is the sworn enemy of individual liberty, and of all bold initiative in matters of internal policy ... We may even say that the more conspicuously a bureaucracy is distinguished by its zeal, by its sense of duty, and by its devotion, the more it will show itself to be petty, narrow, rigid and illiberal. (Michels 1962: 191–2)

Bureaucracy is essential to modern industrial society, but it is also a threat because it makes the controller of the bureaucratic apparatus supremely powerful. Control should not be left to the bureaucrats themselves because:

1. Bureaucrats follow orders and deal with routine situations; they cannot take policy decisions or deal with crises.
2. They will be pressured to fit their administrative practices to the wishes of the dominant interests in society. Politicians must have overall charge but Weber (who was a politician himself) wrote: 'The "political master" always

finds himself, *vis-à-vis* the trained official, in the position of the "dilettante" who stands opposite the "expert", facing the trained official who stands within the management of administration' (Weber, in Gerth and Mills 1957: 232).

Lipset (1950), in *Agrarian Socialism*, cites the case of the Co-operative Commonwealth Federation being thwarted by Canadian local government bureaucracy. Similar criticisms were voiced by the functionalist R. K. Merton (1952), in an article entitled 'Bureaucratic Structure and Personality'. For him the dysfunctional aspects of bureaucracy limit the adaptive capacity of bureaucrats. Adherence to rules can lead to 'goal displacement'. The rules ('red tape') become an end in themselves. Impersonal relationships with clients may cause friction: 'The very elements which conduce towards efficiency in general produce inefficiency in specific instances.'

Peter Blau (1963) argues that ritualistic behaviour by officials is caused by the insecurity of the established social relationships within the bureaucracy and not from over-identification with the rules. The more unforeseen and disruptive the occurrences, however, the less effective the rules are in meeting it. In his study of a federal law enforcement agency he found that information and expertise were regularly pooled by rank-and-file members despite the rules of confidentiality which prohibited this practice. This had an unexpected consequence: 'Unofficial practices which are explicitly prohibited by official regulations sometimes further the achievement of organisational objectives.' In the New York City Welfare Department, Blau found that officials showed a systematic tendency to bend the rules where possible in favour of the client. He recognises organisations as necessary for the existence of large-scale democracy but also sees them as undermining it. The main concern of organisations is for their own goals not for society as a whole. 'The concentration of organisational power in the hands of a few men shielded from public surveillance and control poses a serious threat to democracy,' he concludes (Blau 1963, 1974).

Guy Peters (1978) suggests that mechanisms exist for public participation and influence in public organisations, but that apathy constitutes the greatest threat to democracy (see also Gouldner 1954; Burns and Stalker 1966). This argument received strong confirmation from the consequences of the Fulton Committee report on the British civil service of 1968. Leslie Chapman, in *Your Disobedient Servant* (1978) describes how Whitehall put into effect all the recommendations that resulted in more top jobs, better pay and pensions for civil servants, while shelving ideas on tighter civil service management and more control on bureaucrats' powers. The widely popular comedy television series *Yes Minister* showed the same process, illustrating the way in which senior civil servants can and do use a variety of methods to frustrate the wishes of elected representatives. Such methods of 'non-decision-making' include overloading the minister's agenda and reading, restricting the choice of options considered and making use of informal networks of power to initiate objections from other government departments or even outside interests. The programme was said to be extremely popular with the Prime Minister of the day, Mrs Thatcher, who asserted, however, that none of this had ever happened to her.

## Voting Behaviour

Most (80 per cent) of the British population lives in England, and is heavily concentrated in the south-east and major conurbations such as the West Midlands, Merseyside and Strathclyde. Though heavy concentrations of this kind are common in the Third World, Blondel notes that 'No industrial country has such a large proportion of its population concentrated in so few urban areas' (Blondel 1975). Two-fifths of the population live in the seven major conurbations. Many of those outside are commuters into the conurbations. Only 2 per cent of the workforce work on the land and, unlike France, for example, there is no independent peasant class with its own traditions. So Britain has a very concentrated population in which social class forms the main division between the political parties.

This is historically a fairly recent development. Political parties emerged in England as factions in Parliament between 1678 and 1682, long before there was any substantial popular participation in elections. It was not until after the Reform Act of 1832 that first the Liberals (formerly the Whigs) and then the Conservatives (still called Tories) established national organisations to fight parliamentary elections. After 1884, the enfranchisement of working-class males led to demands for a new political party to represent their interests. Out of this emerged the Labour Party (1906), which displaced the Liberals after the First World War and formed its first government in 1924. Since women found the new party much more sympathetic to their cause than the Liberals had been, many became Labour activists, although in time women came also to be very significant as workers for the Conservative Party.

Such a process is not peculiar to Britain; a similar pattern of the extension of the franchise and the emergence of new parties was followed in most other European countries. However, the results were very different. In most other European countries (e.g. France, The Netherlands) religion is as important a division in politics as social class and there are many more political parties. Only in Britain was the unrepresentative 'first past the post' voting system retained, effectively ensuring the domination of the Conservative Party for most of the period since. In 1951 the Labour Party secured the largest percentage of the popular vote for any political party since the Second World War, but the Conservatives secured a majority of seventeen seats. Only in Britain did a Conservative Party survive as an independent political force.

## Stable Two-Party Voting

Certainly class, in the sense of an explicit difference between socio-economic groups, has long been regarded as the major factor in determining British voting, and neither gender nor racial differences have significantly altered this pattern in the long term. Between 1935 and 1970 a stable pattern of two-party voting was established. The overwhelming majority of the electorate voted for either the Conservative or the Labour Party, which together took 97 per cent of the votes in 1951. And four factors indicated the strength of partisan alignment: party membership was high relative to other European countries, most people identified with the party for which they voted and supported its policies, and relatively few people changed their votes between elections, though it was these changes, in a limited number of 'marginal seats', which displaced old governments and created new ones. If the working class had voted Labour and the middle class had voted Conservative the Conservative Party would never have held office. However, even during this classical period of alignment, some 30−5 per cent of the manual working class consistently voted for the Conservatives.

This apparent anomaly was explained in many ways, none of which was adequate on its own. Among these explanations were:

*False consciousness*

Marxists explained working-class Conservatism as a delusion inculcated by education, the Church and other agencies, which sought to disguise the 'real' class interest of the working class. Runciman's (1966) suggestion that members of the working class would tend to vote Conservative if they saw themselves as middle class made sense in the late 1950s when the working class were becoming more affluent, but it did not explain the historic tendency.

*Deference*

As early as the nineteenth century, Walter Bagehot in *The English Constitution* (1872) argued that the British prefer to be governed by their 'social superiors', whom they believe are born to rule and will do so most effectively. Nordlinger

Table 5.2   *Social class and voting patterns in 1950*

Percentages, United Kingdom

|  | Proportion of the population | C. | Lab. | Other |
|---|---|---|---|---|
| Solid middle class | 15 | 85 | 10 | 5 |
| Lower middle class | 20 | 70 | 25 | 5 |
| Upper working class | 30 | 35 | 60 | 5 |
| Solid working class | 35 | 30 | 65 | 5 |
|  | 100 |  |  |  |

*Source:* Blondel (1975), p. 55, after Abrams (1958).

(1967) found that working-class Conservatism decreased with increased affluence but increased with economic satisfaction. He argues that a Conservative preference goes hand in hand with low economic aspirations. Thus he falls broadly into a deferential explanation of working-class Conservatism. McKenzie and Silver (1968) suggest that many members of the working class vote Conservative because they regard the party as better fitted to rule; though others are 'secular' and vote 'instrumentally', i.e. in what they see as their own self-interest. It does not explain why people go on voting, as in 1959 and 1987, for governments that are manifestly acting against their interests.

*Generational voting*

Butler and Stokes (1974) suggested (in line with similar theories in the United States) that people tended to retain the voting patterns prevailing at the time they first became politically conscious and that by the time they were in their thirties their preferences had stabilised. Hence different 'age cohorts' had different voting patterns and tended to retain them throughout life. They believed that working-class Conservatism was a product of political socialisation that would decline with time.

These theories are all characterised by the same assumption, that the working class 'ought' to vote Labour. However Hindess's (1987) study of Liverpool, *The Decline of Working Class Politics*, suggests that the Labour Party was not in fact class-based, either in personnel or in policies. No less significant than the one-third of the working class that habitually voted Conservative was the one-fifth of the middle class that normally voted for Labour. The reason was ideological. But Butler and Stokes found that many middle-class electors voted Conservative because they saw the Conservative Party as being more representative of the

Table 5.3   *Electoral support for the Conservative and Labour parties, 1945–87*

Percentages, United Kingdom

| Election | C. | Lab. | C. & Lab. | Other |
|----------|------|------|-----------|-------|
| 1945 | 39.8 | 47.9 | 87.6 | 12.4 |
| 1950 | 43.5 | 46.1 | 89.6 | 10.4 |
| 1951 | 48.0 | 48.8 | 96.8 | 3.2 |
| 1955 | 49.7 | 46.4 | 96.1 | 3.9 |
| 1959 | 49.3 | 43.9 | 93.2 | 6.8 |
| 1964 | 43.4 | 44.1 | 87.5 | 12.5 |
| 1966 | 41.9 | 48.1 | 90.0 | 10.0 |
| 1970 | 46.4 | 43.1 | 89.5 | 10.5 |
| 1974 Feb. | 37.8 | 37.1 | 74.9 | 25.1 |
| 1974 Oct. | 35.8 | 39.1 | 75.1 | 24.9 |
| 1979 | 43.9 | 37.0 | 80.9 | 19.1 |
| 1983 | 43.4 | 27.6 | 70.0 | 30.0 |
| 1987 | 43.3 | 31.5 | 74.8 | 23.1 |

*Source: Times Guide to the House of Commons* (London, Times Newspapers, various dates).

general interests of the British people, not just those of the middle class. So the Conservative Party, too, acted as a 'catch-all' rather than as a class party. When Butler and Stokes looked at age cohorts and their voting behaviour, they found that people were much less consistent than had been assumed from the overall figures. Many people transferred their votes from one of the two parties to the other.

These findings are consistent with Frank Parkin's *dominant-value theory* (Parkin 1972). He suggests that British society is based on a dominant set of values and norms which are favourable to Conservative voting. Labour voting is thus deviant behaviour and it is this that has to be explained. Where protective processes (e.g. unionisation) operate, working-class Labour voting will be greater. This is also the explanation that most adequately fits the tendency for voting to be relatively constant across gender and ethnic differences.

# Partisan Dealignment, 1974−87

In the 1970s two-party dominance rapidly crumbled (Table 5.3 above). Two general elections in 1974 failed to give Labour a good working majority, though it was able to retain power as a minority government because of the divisions of its opponents. Though the Liberal Party failed repeatedly to make a significant breakthrough, it secured a series of gains at by-elections and consolidated these. In Scotland and to a lesser extent Wales the Nationalists emerged as a significant force. Northern Ireland was plunged into virtual civil war. When the Conservatives returned to power in 1979 it was with the support of only some 44 per cent of the votes cast, though the 'first past the post' system gave them an unassailable majority in Parliament.

However, a split in the Labour Party led to the secession of some of its activists to form a Social Democratic Party (SDP). The formation of an Alliance between them and the Liberals followed. The 1983 General Election took place in the worst economic recession since the 1930s. Unemployment and inflation had both increased spectacularly since the Thatcher Government had been elected in May 1979. Yet the Conservatives, who at the beginning of 1982 had been lagging badly in the polls, secured a majority of 144.

These trends, which could be documented well back into the 1970s (Sarlvik and Crewe 1983) were termed *partisan dealignment*. They had four characteristics:

1. An increase in the 'volatility' of the electorate.
2. A decline in the number of people identifying with the political party for which they voted (see also Table 5.4).
3. A marked decline in party membership, especially in that of the Labour Party.
4. Labour supporters found themselves less and less sympathetic to the policies advocated by the Labour Party, which were perceived as more 'extreme' after the formation of the Alliance. Some argued that this meant there had been a clear shift to the right, but this was not supported by other researchers.

**Stereotypes
don't fit**

> The working class have abandoned Labour in droves. Labour no
> longer has a majority even among semi- or unskilled workers, nor
> among trade unionists. Within the working class, home ownership
> is strikingly reflected in voting. In 1983, home owners split roughly
> 50:25 Conservative against Labour, while council tenants did just
> the opposite; the Alliance picked up about 25 per cent from both.
> The 1983 election, in contrast, confirmed the old truth that the
> Tories win far the largest share (60 per cent plus) of professional
> and managerial votes, although well over half the Tory vote comes
> from lower down the scale. The Alliance . . . won close to 25 per
> cent of the vote in all classes. . . . Labour could once count on
> more than its fair share of new voters: 42 per cent in October 1974,
> against the Conservatives' 24 per cent. No longer: the two were
> neck and neck in 1979, the Tories 42:33 ahead in 1983. (*The
> Economist*, 15 October 1983)

Traditional explanations of voting behaviour in terms of class alignments found
it difficult to account for this change. Some of it could certainly be explained
by long-term social changes, such as the movement out of the inner cities, the
drift to the south-east and the increased proportion of white-collar to blue-collar
workers. Declining Labour Party membership was partly a product of Britain's
industrial decline between 1979 and 1981 and the sharp fall in trade union
membership that accompanied it. But evidence rapidly accumulated that there
had also been a marked change in policy preferences, and that this change was
having more effect on voting patterns than traditional social cleavages (Whiteley
1983). Issues on which Labour voters no longer supported their party included
nationalisation, the trade unions and comprehensive schools. Conservative success
in 1979 came because many traditional Labour voters stayed at home: the same
percentage of the electorate, 38 per cent, regarded themselves as supporters of
each of the two main political parties (Crewe 1984).

By 1983 the schism in the Labour Party, and the formation of the Alliance,
offered voters a third choice. Just over a quarter of the voters (26 per cent) voted
for the Alliance, the strongest showing for a third party since the 'realigning'
election of 1923. Significantly, support fell for both Conservative and Labour
during the course of the campaign and a BBC exit poll showed that another 16 per
cent seriously considered voting Alliance. Most did not because they did not think

Table 5.4  *Strength of identification with the three main parties, 1964–79*

| Alignment very strong | Election | | | | | |
|---|---|---|---|---|---|---|
| | **1964** | **1966** | **1970** | **1974 Feb.** | **1974 Oct.** | **1979** |
| Conservative | 19 | 17 | 20 | 11 | 9 | 9 |
| Labour | 21 | 22 | 20 | 16 | 14 | 10 |
| Liberal | 4 | 3 | 2 | 2 | 2 | 2 |

*Source:* David McKie, 'Charting a dealignment decade', *The Guardian*, 3 June 1983.

the party had a chance; if they had, such is the lottery of the British electoral system, the Alliance could have won (see also Curtice and Steed 1986).

The Labour Party lost a quarter of its support in 1979 and polled little more than the Alliance, only 27.6 per cent of the vote, its worst result since 1918. The substantial decline in electoral support for Labour and the rise in third-party voting masked the continuing weakness of electoral support for the Conservatives. Though the Conservatives gained a landslide in terms of seats, the largest majority since 1935, their vote had actually fallen since 1979 and only two governments this century had been elected on as low a percentage of the votes cast. For the first time since the 1930s, fewer women than men voted Conservative. And in class terms unemployment failed to polarise the electorate: the Conservative vote among the middle class fell and, while the commercial middle class (as might be expected) moved towards the Conservatives, professionals voted for the Alliance (Heath, Jowell and Curtice 1985). On the other hand, the working-class vote for the Conservatives rose while that for Labour failed to turn out except in unemployment blackspots. The strength (or, as it was to prove, weakness) of the Alliance was that its support was fairly evenly spread across the social classes (Table 5.5).

Three political factors were also widely believed to have affected the outcome of the 1983 election. The first was 'the Falklands factor'. Support for the Conservatives rose by some 15 points between the outbreak of war with Argentina and the successful recapture of the Falkland Islands (Malvinas). Although there is evidence that the movement began before the crisis, there is no doubt that the war helped consolidate it. What counted was not the Falklands issue itself, but its symbolic value as a metaphor for the government's domestic policies. It enhanced the images of both the Conservative Party and its leader. Secondly, Michael Foot's leadership of the Labour Party was widely, if unfairly, seen as fumbling and incompetent, but this was just part of an image of disunity and extremism which had led to the secession of the SDP in the first place. A third belief, that huge spending by the Conservatives on election propaganda helped tip the scales, appears not to have been correct. The party that spent the least on advertising, the Alliance, gained the most impact; the others very little.

By the 1987 election a new Labour leader had been chosen, and the Falklands

Table 5.5  *Class and Party, 1974–83*

| | Percentage support by group, United Kingdom | | | | | | | | |
| | skilled manual | | | semi/unskilled | | | trade unionists | | |
| | C. | Lab. | L/A | C. | Lab. | L/A | C. | Lab. | L/A |
|---|---|---|---|---|---|---|---|---|---|
| 1974 Oct. | 26 | 49 | 20 | 22 | 57 | 16 | 23 | 55 | 16 |
| 1979 May | 41 | 41 | 15 | 34 | 49 | 13 | 33 | 50 | 13 |
| 1983 June | 40 | 32 | 26 | 33 | 41 | 24 | 31 | 39 | 29 |

*Source:* MORI.

crisis had faded even further into myth. But the result, though better for Labour, was still defeat, with the Conservative Government being returned for an unprecedented third time under the same leader with a majority over all other parties of 102 seats. The Alliance held on to its support very well, even if (given the electoral system and the very even spread of their support) the result in terms of seats was most disappointing for them, confirming that 1983 had not been the great 'realigning' election for which they had hoped. Once again, therefore, the chief beneficiary of a divided opposition was the Conservative Party.

Conservatives, perhaps naturally, attributed their success to the attractiveness of their policies, and some observers thought that the sale of council houses, the sale of shares in privatised industries and the effects of the pre-election boom engineered by the Chancellor of the Exchequer, Nigel Lawson, had all played a part. Certainly, exit polls showed that 47 per cent of home-owners, 22 per cent of council tenants, 55 per cent of the new shareholders and 36 per cent of those who had *not* bought privatisation issues all voted Conservative. But there was no evidence that these changes had actually caused people to shift their votes and other polls showed that since 1983 an ideological shift had set in away from the Conservatives, whose proportion of the vote overall was actually fractionally less than in 1983. A consistent finding was a high level of support for the structure of the welfare state and particularly for the National Health Service, against Conservative policies intended to cut taxes, reduce welfare 'dependence' and privatise health care (Curtice 1986, 1987). Despite this, the same negative views of Labour's electoral potential were to remain.

## Class Warfare: A Return to Traditional Values?

The Alliance had fought the 1983 election under one leader, Roy Jenkins, who had failed to hold his seat. In 1987 they had a divided leadership, the leader of the Social Democrats, Dr David Owen, often contradicting both the leader of the Liberals, David Steel, and the agreed Alliance platform. The logical course was to merge the two parties, but this Dr Owen refused to accept. So when the majority of his own party voted for merger he and a small group of followers decided to fight on under the SDP label. The sudden collapse of the Alliance vote that followed was virtually inevitable, given the 'softness' of their support and the degree of confusion engendered in voters' minds.

The Liberal Democrats have retained substantial representation in local councils and have continued to run ahead of the polls. The polls suggest that they cannot count on even the level of support the Liberals on their own commanded in the 1970s. The rump of the SDP retained for several months a level of poll support far in excess of its ability to field candidates, but in the Bootle by-election of May 1990 they were roundly beaten by the Monster Raving Loony Party and its leader, Screaming Lord Sutch, wittily offered Dr Owen a merger. With the writing on the wall, the SDP was abruptly wound up.

Meanwhile the Lawson boom of 1987 had collapsed. Inflation rose; high mortgage interest rates and the poll tax (the so-called 'community charge') had begun to bite on different sectors of the electorate. It was not so much the collapse of the political centre as the evaporation of the Tory 'good times' which produced a massive surge in Labour support in late 1989 and early 1990. The Conservatives had ceased to do well what the electorate had believed they could do best, namely manage the economy. Despite the fall of Mrs Thatcher in 1990, the succession of John Major as prime minister and a wide-ranging review of many of the policies of the previous decade, polls continue to show that this perception remained, though an interesting discrepancy persisted between public opinion polls and the way in which people actually voted in local elections (see Figure 5.1) and in the General Election of 1992, won by the Conservatives, to the surprise of the pundits.

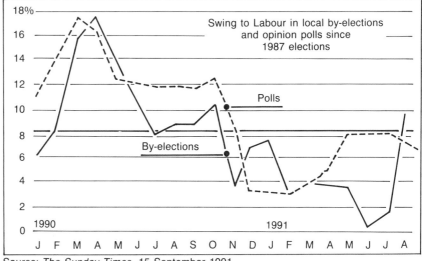

Source: *The Sunday Times*, 15 September 1991.

Figure 5.1   *Local election swings and public opinion polls, 1990–91*

# Suggestions for Further Reading

Steven Lukes (1974) is not easy reading but is central to the discussion of *Power*. On the 'iron law of oligarchy', see Robert Michels (1962), *Political Parties*; on *The Power Elite* C. Wright Mills (1956); on pluralism Robert Dahl (1961), *Who governs?* Philip Stanworth and Anthony Giddens (eds) (1974) discuss *Elites and Power in British Society*. Leslie Chapman, *Your Disobedient Servant* (1978) discusses British bureaucracy. On voting behaviour, see Anthony Heath, Roger Jowell and John Curtice (1985), *How Britain Votes* and its sequel (1991), *Understanding Political Change*; and Frank Parkin (1972), *Class Inequality and Political Order*, for the conservative effect of Britain's dominant-value system. A good general introduction to this area is Denver (1989), *Elections and Voting Behaviour in Britain*.

# 6 Work and Organisations

## Work and Organisations

Some frequently examined themes in these syllabus areas are:

- The changing nature of British industry, especially the decline of manufacturing. This may be related to the declining size and changing nature of the traditional working class, or alternatively to the growth of the white-collar sector (including white-collar unions).
- The centrality of economic relations to any society. Sometimes this theme is examined at an individual level by questioning the relationship between work and other aspects of a person's life. (A variation is the relationship between work and leisure, for which see Chapter 10.)
- Similar questions may be asked about the converse — unemployment: the importance of unemployment as a source of social division and the concept of an underclass. The changing structure of unemployment — differences in rates by region, class, race and gender. The effects of unemployment on family life.
- Technology and work satisfaction, the extent of deskilling.
- Sociological explanations of industrial conflict. Changing patterns: the decline of trade unions, variations by organisational size, etc.
- What are the 'professions'? Do teaching and nursing fit? How do professional associations and trade unions differ?
- The theory of total institutions and the extent to which it helps us understand behaviour in prisons, mental hospitals, etc.

## What is Work?

What is work? One definition is that it is an instrument for acquiring resources to satisfy basic needs. In modern complex societies, in most families, at least one person achieves this through having an *occupation*. An occupation or employment is a contractual arrangement to work for someone else, an employer, and it usually characterised by the facts that:

1. It is separate from the home geographically.
2. It occurs in periods of time separate from other activities.

3. It forms a source of income.
4. It gives identity and status within society.

However, many women of child-bearing age in our society work very hard but do not have an occupation. The confusion between work and occupation has many consequences. The use of an occupation in social identification explains its use in class stratification, but it also creates problems of identity for those who are engaged exclusively in housework, who are 'out of work' or who are retired. People who do not have a formal occupation may work extremely hard, but they do not always get credit for their efforts in a society that tends to assume that *paid* work is a good thing and that those who are not in formal employment are idle. These attitudes are already internalised by teenage girls such as those studied by Griffin: '*Real* work was paid, it took place outside of [*sic*] the home, and it conjured up images of hard manual labour, "men's work". Even when women were employed as childminders, this seldom reached the status of *real* work' (Griffin 1985: 37).

Why is this? Why work? Marx regarded work as the basis of human life because of its economic importance, but it seems that individuals need to work not just to satisfy economic but also social and psychological needs. Certainly, at its best work can be co-operative and creative, a sound basis for a harmonious and prosperous society. But it can also be a duty which is not wholly welcome. Long before Marx, the French Protestant theologian Jean Calvin held that work was a moral and economic necessity, and the moral virtue attributed to working diligently in any station of life is embodied in the couplet from the Victorian hymn: 'Who sweeps a room as in Thy sight/ Makes that and th' action fine.'

# Working Population

The 'working' population or *workforce* is defined as all those over the age of fifteen who are employed or are registered as being available for employment, including persons serving in the armed forces.

Table 6.1   *Workforce and unemployed, 1931–89 (millions)*

|      | Workforce | | | Employment | |
|------|-----|-------|-------|------|-------|
|      | Men | Women | Total | Emp  | Unemp |
| 1931 | 14.9 | 6.3  | 21.0  |      | 2.5   |
| 1960 | 16.3 | 8.3  | 24.6  | 24.5 | 0.35  |
| 1989 | 15.8 | 11.8 | 27.6  | 25.9 | *1.77 |

* Basis of calculation changed.

Source: *Social Trends*, 20, p. 25.

# Types of Industrial Production

For purposes of economic analysis, industrial production is divided into three *sectors*, depending on the nearness of the activity to the beginning of the process of production:

1. *Primary sector*, which includes agriculture, mining and oil production, all of them industries which extract resources directly from the environment.
2. *Secondary sector*, which turns raw materials into goods, including both the manufacturing of goods and the processing of agricultural and other raw materials into finished products.
3. *Tertiary sector*, which provides services such as transport and distribution. All professional and many clerical workers can be found in this sector, but others can be found working for firms in either of the other two sectors.

As the British economy has matured, the proportions of people employed in each sector have changed. In 1931 primary industry accounted for 12 per cent of employment, secondary for 39 per cent and tertiary for 47 per cent. By 1961 the proportion in primary industry had been halved to 6 per cent. Since then the biggest decline in employment has again been recorded in the primary sector, with an accelerating decline in secondary manufacturing industry and a further growth in the tertiary sector.

# Location of Industry

The location of industry is of great social importance. It has been influenced primarily by:

## Resources

There are obvious economic reasons why heavy industries in particular have grown up on or near large deposits of natural resources; in fact, the proximity of coal and iron ore is the major reason why the Industrial Revolution began in Britain and began specifically in Shropshire. Today, factories and power plants are still

Table 6.2  *British economy by sector, 1931–89*

| Sector | Percentage of workforce in selected years | | | | |
|---|---|---|---|---|---|
| | 1931 | 1961 | 1971 | 1981 | 1989 |
| Primary | 12 | 5.9 | 5.6 | 4.9 | 3.4 |
| Manufacturing | 39 | 39.3 | 36.4 | 28.4 | 23.1 |
| Services | 47 | — | 52.5 | 61.5 | 68.7 |

Sources: *Social Trends*, 3, 1972, Table 17, p. 72; 20, Table 4.11, p. 73.

located near the Durham and South Wales coalfields, and the iron works at Consett uses iron ore from local deposits.

### Transport

Since the 1960s major growth has occurred in new industries along the so-called 'M4 corridor' and in the area around Cambridge, and other new roads have been planned to link ports like Liverpool and Southampton to the industrial centres that supply them in the expectation that they will contribute to economic growth.

### Personnel

Unskilled labour was freely available for older factories and was utilised by deskilling jobs. Modern industrial production requires far fewer workers, but they need to be skilled, especially for the new 'sunrise' industries located south of the M4 corridor in a rough quadrilateral bounded by Portsmouth and Poole.

### Markets

London's industry has always been largely centred on satisfying demand for consumer goods and services. As mobility has increased since 1945 it has accelerated the 'drift to the south-east'. At the same time, the decline of the older extraction and manufacturing centres of the North, Midlands, Central Scotland and South Wales, has been very marked. Deliberate attempts were made between 1934 and 1979 to persuade industries to locate in poorer regions, but these policies have since been abandoned in England. Wales and Northern Ireland continue with European Community help to implement policies of regional development.

## Ownership of Industry

A major political issue in Britain (unlike other European countries) has been the question of who should own industry. It is true that Marx argued that private ownership of the means of production was exploitative and this view was subsequently put into effect in the Soviet Union, though doing so merely changed the source of exploitation. However, even Western European socialists have not accepted this argument uncritically, and many major state-owned plants, such as Renault in France, owe their nationalisation to wartime needs and not to any political dogma.

The main choices in Britain have been between:

### Public ownership

This has taken three forms:

| Forms of ownership | *Public ownership* | *Example* |
|---|---|---|

| | | |
|---|---|---|
| State owned | British Rail |
| Municipally owned | Hull telephones |
| Public corporation | BBC |
| | |
| *Co-operative ownership* | |
| Retail co-ops | Co-operative Wholesale Society |
| Producer co-ops | Les producteurs de Mont Tauch |
| Mutual associations | Halifax Building Society |
| Co-partnership | John Lewis Partnership |
| | |
| *Private ownership* | |
| Small businesses | corner shop |
| Joint Stock Companies | ICI, Unilever |

*State-owned*

The postwar Labour Government (1945–51) adopted a policy of bringing what were described as 'the commanding heights of the economy' into state ownership, and coal, steel, gas, water and electricity, rail and bus transport were all nationalised. These industries too were placed under the direct responsibility of Ministers and their Departments. Many of them (steel, gas, water and bus transport) passed out of public ownership through the privatisations of the 1980s.

*Municipally owned*

Most public utilities were originally run by local authorities for the benefit of their citizens: tramways, buses, water supply, harbour and docks, even banks and theatres. The councils of the local authorities were responsible for them to the people who elected them. Many of these services, e.g. gas, were nationalised in the postwar period (1945–51), though Hull still runs its own telephone service.

*Public corporation*

Public corporations were established in Britain to provide public services on a national basis without involving the Government in day-to-day control of their activities, starting in 1926 with the Central Electricity Board (later, on nationalisation, to become the Central Electricity Generating Board). In 1927 the British Broadcasting Corporation (BBC) was formed to guard against political bias in its programmes.

## Co-operative ownership

*Retail co-operatives*

Voluntary organisations owned by those who use them, to whom any profit is redistributed in proportion to their use. In England and Wales in 1958 there were

1,015 Co-operative Societies with a membership of 12.5 million. Producer co-operatives are marketing organisations, mainly in agriculture, such as the French winegrowers co-operative Les producteurs de Mont Tauch, makers of Fitou. They have no connection with retail co-operatives.

Similar organisations include:

*Building societies (with the exception of the privatised Abbey National Building Society)*

*Mutual associations* owned by their depositors, who receive interest on their deposits which being very numerous can then be used to finance mortgages.

### *The John Lewis Partnership*

A rare example of an enterprise owned collectively by its workers, who are termed 'partners' and share democratically in its management.

## Private ownership

### *'Small businesses'*

Most business enterprises in Britain have been built up in the first instance by individuals, and they, their family or their descendants retain ownership of many of them. Since 1979 it has been official government policy to encourage the growth of small businesses. However, there has been and continues to be a very heavy failure rate among small businesses, especially when high interest rates prevail.

### *Joint stock companies*

In its original form the term 'joint stock company' only meant that two or more people took joint liability for a business. The invention of 'limited liability' meant that each shareholder was only liable for the amount that shareholder put in, that is, if the business went bankrupt he could not be required to pay any more. Conversely, each drew rewards (dividends) in proportion to their stake in the company. The main advantage of limited liability is that it enables funds to be raised from a large number of people each of whom has only a very small degree of risk. Under the Companies Act of 1861, which established proper standards of accounting and management, it was the basis of the rapid growth of capitalism in Britain and the world in the later nineteenth century.

Sociologists and others have, however, pointed out that private ownership of public companies in this way also has certain problems.

1. Ownership of the company is divorced from control. Shareholders are numerous, so most can no longer exercise effective influence on decisions. The largest shareholders may themselves be corporate bodies, often trusts, insurance companies and pension funds, who have no interest in the company except in the maximisation of profit (Stokman, Ziegler and Scott 1985).

2. Actual control of policy in such firms tends to be concentrated in the hands of a few professional managers (Scott 1977). These often have a large stake in the company and thus a degree of ownership, but they may well own only nominal shareholdings and be to all intents and purposes employees of the company.
3. Companies can be (and are) subject to changes of ownership when 'takeover' bids succeed. Such changes can have drastic effects on both management and employees and can in the extreme case suddenly put them all out of work.

## Industrial Society in Britain

How far industrial society is still the basis of Britain's economy is itself a disputed question. No one doubts that Britain's industrialisation in the eighteenth and nineteenth centuries is the most important factor in creating its present social structure. As usual with social development, however, traces of earlier stages have yet to disappear.

1. Pre-industrial society (before *c.* 1730). This was marked by *traditional action* within communities and primary groups. Economically production was an individual matter and there was little if any separation between home and work.
2. Industrial society (*c.* 1730–1960) was distinguished by *rational action*, if the term 'rational' is used in the narrow economic sense. In 1776 the economist Adam Smith argued that division of labour gives greater *efficiency* (Smith, D. J. 1976). As Durkheim (1964) noted, social production became standard, creating new forms of organisations (companies) and workplaces (factories). But the concentration of work in specific places had other social consequences as well.
   (a) *Domestic divisions* were created between members of a family, as *either* the father went out to work and the mother stayed at home at least intermittently while giving birth and looking after the children, *or* both went out to work but worked in different areas of the same factory. It was the late nineteenth-century, and initially middle-class assumption that women of childbearing age would stay at home that led to the emergence of the concept of *housework*, which economists today believe still accounts for some 25 per cent of GDP in the United Kingdom. The gender differences established at this time continue to structure women's occupational inferiority to men through the persistence of a number of distinctive conditions of women's employment which make them available as a *secondary labour force* (Barker and Allen 1976: 22, 47ff).
   (b) *Class divisions* were created between employer and employee and between employees engaged on different tasks. These added to but did not necessarily replace older divisions between *estates* (see Chapter 3).
3. Today some argue that we are moving into *post-industrial society* (Gershuny and Miles 1973). Fewer and fewer people are concerned with primary or

secondary industry, the basis of industrial society. Such production is already heavily mechanised and soon may be almost entirely performed by robots. With the growth of the services sector, the distinction between home and workplace itself is being eroded in some respects. *Supersession theory* is a term used by those sociologists who argue that Europe and the United States have reached a stage beyond that of industrial capitalism, which has been superseded.

# Sociology of Industry — Conflict vs. Consensus

The question of whether or not there is an identity of interest between employer and employee and, if so, how far it goes, is fundamental to the sociology of industry. Some authors see a deep and irreconcilable division between their interests, leading to a fundamental *conflict* of interests, resolvable only by placing the control of industry in the hands of those who work in it. Others believe that industry could not function at all were there not a high degree of *consensus*.

*Conflict theorists* believe that there is an irreconcilable conflict of interest between management and workers. Marx argued that this conflict stemmed from the fact that the capitalist was exploiting the worker by taking as profit what the worker had produced over and above the amount needed to make the article produced.

Traditional management notions of consensus are 'unitary' (Fox 1966). Unitary consensus theorists believe that both workers and employers have an interest in production, but that it is for management and management alone to define that interest. 'Management must be free to manage,' they claim. Hence, they see no legitimate role for any other form of organisation within the factory, including trade unions.

Other consensus theorists are 'pluralist'. The pluralist approach does see conflict as existing within certain accepted limits in Britain. No procedure for arbitration could exist without the acknowledgement of both employers and employees of the legitimate interests of the other group. Yet such procedures have been devised and institutionalised in a number of forms, notably that of the Arbitration and Conciliation Service (ACAS), an independent agency established by government to find ways of ending industrial conflicts by agreement between the contending parties. Thus pluralist sociologists believe that class and class conflict have declined and enabled industrial conflict to be institutionalised and so controlled.

# Corporations and Power

The historical base for the distinction between management and workforce is to be found in the way that industrial production developed. No provision was made for the participation of the workers in the ownership of the enterprise and they were treated merely as a resource to be obtained at the lowest possible cost. As early as 1795 the idea of mass production, the making of many units built of interchangeable parts, was put to work in the production of muskets for the US Army. At the beginning of the twentieth century this was to result in two further developments: Fordism and Taylorism. At his automobile plant at Dearborn, Michigan, Henry Ford Sr became the first to introduce assembly-line production. By moving the assembly line instead of the workforce, the reorganisation of tasks originally proposed by Babbage could be made a reality. Each worker would perform, repetitively, one simple task or operation. 'Time and motion study', first proposed by Frederick W. Taylor (1856–1915), in his *Principles of Scientific Management* (Taylor 1911), made it easier to break down operations into their component parts and make them suitable for less skilled operatives. It also made it possible to do them more quickly so that the assembly line could move faster. With the 'speed-up' the business became ever more profitable, but the degree of interest and job satisfaction in the workforce fell, and in times of economic crisis they lost their jobs altogether. These three factors are the foundation of modern industrial society.

# Post-Industrial Society

The concept of 'post-industrial society' originated with the economist John Kenneth Galbraith, in *The New Industrial State* (1967), though the term achieved prominence in the work of Daniel Bell, *The Coming of Post-Industrial Society* (1973). Galbraith noted that technology caused increased division of labour and required increased specialisation and expertise, and additional numbers of co-ordinators and planners. Meanwhile the quest for profits and efficiency resulted in large-scale production and mass distribution, which in turn led to large-scale organisations and bureaucracy.

These characteristics of modern industry had therefore promoted increased state involvement because:

1. Industry requires some services that cannot be provided privately for profit, e.g. commuter rail services.
2. The state has many advantages in speculative industry, e.g. it can afford huge losses, has a certain market for a product, and can ensure the necessary skills are available through state education.

Hence, Galbraith argued, market forces are superseded by state planning in post-capitalism. In contrast to *laissez-faire* capitalism, post-capitalist society is also called the 'new corporatism'. As these processes are generally applicable, supersession theorists expect there to be a tendency for post-capitalist societies to converge and to become more like one another. Kerr *et al.*, in *Industrialism and Industrial Man* (1962), argued that industrialism led to similar problems in all societies that were at that stage of development, leading to similar institutional adaptations. Similar societies emerged characterised by:

- Geographical mobility.
- Occupational mobility.
- Flexibility.
- Individualism.
- Meritocracy.

The French political scientist Raymond Aron (1967) argued that differences in ownership in capitalist and communist systems were incidental. The problems of industrialism relating to planning and economic growth were the same in both and the differences would disappear as industrial development occurs. Similar prestige and status hierarchies emerge in different industrial countries for the same reasons (Banton 1987). Supersession theorists were keen to show that Marxist analysis was no longer applicable to Europe and the United States. Their ideas have acquired a new relevance with the dramatic changes in Eastern Europe in 1989 and the revival of interest there in the Western concept of the market economy.

## Critique of Supersession Theory — The Neo-Marxists

Recent neo-Marxist theories are largely a backlash against supersession theory. They emphasise the impact of economic, political and ideological forces on work, mainly within capitalist societies. Esland, Salaman and Speakman (1975) asserted work was central to modern capitalist society because it maintains capitalism. Political and ideological influences contribute to capitalist society, but work is the key. Technology exists as a result of social relations — it is not an independent determining variable. Like Marx, such writers hold that ownership or non-ownership of the means of production is the determining factor that affects social position and therefore all aspects of a person's life. The kind of society created by profit, they argue, is quite different from that created by planning for need (Davis and Scase 1985). Fundamental conflict inevitably exists in capitalist society between those who own and those who do not. The level of technology employed cannot alter the essential nature of that society, it only contributes to it.

Braverman (1975) argues that it is capitalism's need to increase efficiency to reduce prices for competition and to ensure mass markets which gives rise to technological development. Modern capitalism ensures that small companies disappear — they cannot afford the investment in technology. Technology reduces the need for labour but increases the need for investment. Hence large, capital-intensive organisations dominate production and distribution. Ownership therefore concentrates in fewer hands. This is known as the 'monopoly capital' stage of capitalist development. Cartels ensure that capitalists can control prices, production and market conditions in their own interests. Free market competition declines.

Monopoly capitalism requires more supervisory workers, hence manual occupations have declined in numbers and non-manual occupations have increased.

## Other Criticisms

Criticism of supersession theory from the New Right has been of a very different kind. Their insistence on the market being the only practicable way to distribute resources in society has often ignored the fact that markets themselves are social constructs. Without the protection of law markets cannot function; the question is not whether regulation is necessary, but how far should it go.

Perhaps the most powerful criticism of theories suggesting that industrial capitalism is followed by a post-industrial phase is the simple commonsense one that such a model depends on a predictable future. Its assumption is that development is unilinear, whereas in fact there are many important variations amongst advanced industrial countries and still more when less developed nations are taken into account. It is true that some recent developments in Europe might suggest the globalisation of Western post-industrial capitalism, but others, such as ethnic unrest, do not. The emergence of fundamentalist Islam as an ideological challenge to the West should serve to remind us that we live in a multicultural world. Likewise, growing concern for our environment may eventually force us to reconsider the high levels of energy consumption on which the post-industrial model rests.

## The Managerial Revolution

A different view is presented by the German liberal Ralf Dahrendorf. In *Class and Class Conflict in Industrial Society* (1959), Dahrendorf argues that controllers (managers as opposed to workers) are now closer to workers than under the industrial capitalist system, but owners are more remote; the gap is wider between owners and workers than before. Some neo-Marxist writers have claimed that the economic interests of management are the same as those of owners, and Dahrendorf accepts that management are still closer to owners than they are to labour. Dahrendorf describes as 'the decomposition of capital' the fact that ownership is now more widely spread and 'the decomposition of labour' the observation that manual jobs are declining in favour of non-manual ones. For him, society is now meritocratic, specialist expertise is more important than capital and the social base of traditional leftist politics is in decline.

The latest trend in corporate management has so far received little attention from sociologists, but is clearly of great significance. This is the decentralising of power in large corporations into a large number of separate divisions. The parent company leaves the vast majority of decisions in these divisions to their own managers, over which, through the use of computers, they retain only financial control. If a division fails to make the profits expected, it can be sold off or even shut down without affecting the rest of the corporate structure.

# Inequality in Work

Jack Nobbs, in *Sociology in Context* writes:

> It is at the workplace that social class differences are most marked. Generally, the middle class undertake non-manual occupations where they enjoy relatively high pay, job security, autonomy, responsibility and interesting work. The working class undertake manual occupations where they are likely to suffer less pay, insecurity, close supervision and boring, repetitive work. The middle class enjoy fringe benefits, longer holidays and good working conditions. The working class have few 'perks' (apart from illegal ones), shorter holidays and working conditions which are frequently noisy and dirty. (Nobbs 1983: 103–4)

Dorothy Wedderburn's (1970) survey of males in manufacturing industry (the gender divisions in industry mean that the position of working-class women is even less favourable) found that the comforting middle-class view that executives worked longer hours than junior office staff or factory workers was not well founded. She found that most machine operators and foremen worked the longer hours and were more likely to be working shifts. Many of the other differences she identified also remain, including:

1. Physical segregation of non-manual and manual workers both while working and during meal-breaks, etc.
2. Stricter supervision of timekeeping for manual workers.
3. Less paid time off and shorter holidays for manual workers.
4. The tendency for manual workers to be paid weekly, often in cash; not to receive annual increments reflecting increased skill and experience and to achieve an early earnings peak rather than a slow progression towards a much higher salary.
5. The tendency for manual workers not to enjoy adequate company pension provision.

Wedderburn emphasised how workers felt. She used an *interactionist* perspective. She recognised that differential conditions at work produce different behaviour in non-work life-chances.

## Accidents at work

Every year about a quarter of a million workers are injured in accidents at work badly enough for them to be absent from work for three days or more. In 1988, 481 workers were killed in fatal accidents at work. Nearly all the fatal accidents occur in manual occupations, but some occupations are much more dangerous than others; by the late 1980s agricultural work accounted for by far the largest share of non-fatal industrial accidents, with construction work second. But construction accounted for the largest share of fatal accidents (*Social Trends 1990*, p. 119); by May 1990, six people had already been killed working on the British end of the Channel Tunnel, for example, and one at the French end.

## Sickness

Social classes IV and V have more days off work through sickness. There are many reasons for this, not least that these classes tend to be the lowest paid and therefore tend to have the poorest diets and to live in the worst housing conditions. But some occupations are well recognised to cause illness. Miners are liable to the chest complaint pneumoconiosis, and people who do a lot of lifting are prone to backache. Backache is in fact the most common cause of absence from work, with respiratory ailments the second most common cause.

## Sick pay

Wedderburn's survey showed that 43 per cent of the firms studied did not supplement national insurance sickness benefit for manual workers while no less than 98 per cent of non-manual workers enjoyed such provision. This situation remains although certification for short illnesses has become easier, and even manual workers who are in a sick pay scheme are at a relative disadvantage because such schemes calculate sickness benefits according to basic, not actual rates of pay, and do not take account of the production/attendance bonuses and overtime with which many manual workers have to supplement their earnings.

## Unemployment

Unemployment, too, varies with occupation. Unskilled manual workers have the highest unemployment rate. One reason is that it is customary for manual workers to be laid off if there is no work for them to do. In 1990 Ford workers at Southampton agreed to accept a pay deal offered by management; then were laid off because other plants had held out for more money. In this sense Marx's description of the unemployed as the 'reserve army of labour' is still true of Britain in the 1990s. Those laid off are much more vulnerable than management staff who are dismissed when companies fall upon hard times, since the latter are usually entitled to some compensation.

There is little evidence that these differences between management and workers encourage efficiency, an argument often used in favour of the status quo. In this respect British industry, which in Europe is regarded as inefficient, contrasts strikingly with Japanese, which is regarded as extremely efficient.

Japanese industry is characterised by:

1. A family organisation which accepts the responsibility of the firm for the employee who has a job for life. Work is a career for all workers, not just for the management. Every worker is encouraged to contribute to making the product better and the company more successful.
2. The absence of distinctions between management and workforce. As at the Nissan factory at Washington, Co. Durham, all wear identical work clothes and eat together.
3. A collective pride in the firm. The firm is central to the life of all Japanese workers, and a major factor in their socialisation and that of their families.

# Alienation

The division of labour which is one of the main foundations of modern complex societies leads in turn to specialised tasks and hence to *alienation*. The creation of factories and workshops has been accompanied by the emergence and development of the separate workplace. This separation of work and home sharpens the sense of alienation of the factory worker. Alienation reduces the job to a chore, and erodes the self-esteem of the worker:

> It's the most boring job in the world. If I had a chance to move I'd leave straight away. It's the conditions here. Ford class you more as machines than men. They're on top of you all the time. They expect you to work every minute of the day. The atmosphere you get in here is so completely false. Everyone is fed up. You can't even talk about football. You end up doing stupid things. Childish things — playing tricks on each other. (Ford car worker quoted in Beynon, *Working for Ford*, 1973)

Blauner (1964) tried to operationalise Marx's notion of alienation by identifying *variations* in the degree of alienation. The organisational requirements of different levels of technology determine the forms of the tasks undertaken by workers. The nature of such tasks causes variations in feelings of 'powerlessness', 'meaninglessness', 'isolation' and 'self-estrangement' experienced by workers. Alienation is the product of technology and not necessarily the result of relations of production in a capitalist society. He sees levels of alienation rising with time as labour becomes mechanised, reaching a peak in the assembly-line style of production. He believes that alienation will be reduced again by automation, as he found in the process-production techniques of the chemical industry, where work is primarily supervisory.

Later writers have made a number of criticisms of Blauner's work. Except for his work on the chemical industry, Blauner's data is all taken from a 1947 Government survey of industry. This information was prepared for different purposes and may be incomplete for the purpose to which Blauner puts it. Blauner's empirical research into the chemical industry was based on interviews with only twenty-one operatives. Other studies of process workers in France and Britain (Gallie 1978) do not support his findings. Blauner ses technology as the independent variable and ignores other possible factors, such as individual expectations, which may affect a person's degree of alienation. He wrongly assumes that there is a clear relationship between industry and type of technology.

Marxists have some additional complaints. They protest that Blauner's concept of alienation is in fact narrower than that of Marx, because of his separation of the concept of alienation from that of the division of labour, which for Marxists is in turn based on the mode of production. All the plants studied were operating under capitalism, so the research is not a test of Marx's ideas. But the Marxists have their own critics. Bertell Ollman (1971), for example, defines alienation only as the absence of unalienation, which for him is the state that exists under communism. Few factory workers in Eastern Europe would agree, as has been demonstrated by the history of Solidarity in Poland and emigration from the German Democratic Republic. The emergence of strikes among the workers in the Donbas merely confirms that alienation is a phenomenon of male workers' experiences in the former USSR also.

Joan Woodward (1980) predicted that better relations between workers and management could be expected as the result of specialisation under process production. However, Nichols and Beynon (1977), in their study of 'Riverside', found that on six out of the seven sites visited, 'process production' involved two different kinds of work: the 'scientific' work of the control-room operatives, who were a minority of the workforce and the 'donkey work' of four-fifths of the male workforce, which included maintaining the chemical plants, driving the lorries and carrying hundredweight bags of chemicals or shovelling muck. They gave a very different view from Blauner. Chemical workers, they concluded, saw themselves as manual workers and were very alienated from their work, militant in their trade unions and highly class-conscious: 'What we came up against time and time again during the time we were at ChemCo is the immense waste of human potential that is locked up within capitalist factory production.'

Other writers have not emphasised alienation, and suggest an overall satisfaction with their situation even among industrial workers. Goldthorpe *et al.*, in *The Affluent Worker* studies (1968a), write: 'workers are disposed to define their relationship with their firm more as one of reciprocity and mutual accommodation rather than one of coercion and exploitation'. Their attitude towards their employment can be entirely instrumental, meaning that they are interested only in earning income, not in obtaining job satisfaction. But Goldthorpe and Lockwood acknowledge that instrumentalism may be a product of alienation, that because their work cannot be fulfilling workers have lowered or changed their expectations of it. Hence they sought to identify three contrasting attitudes to work.

## 'Affluent' worker — instrumental orientation

The primary meaning of work is as a means to an end or ends, external to the work situation; that is, work is regarded as a means of acquiring the income necessary to support a valued way of life of which work itself is not seen as an integral part. Work is therefore experienced as 'labour'. Workers act as expected by the 'economic man' assumption, seeking to minimise effort and maximise rewards, but the latter is the dominant motive. Workers therefore have a low intensity of involvement with work, their job is not a central part of their life interest and hence workers' lives are sharply divided between work and non-work.

## Salaried employee — bureaucratic orientation

The primary meaning of work is as service to an organisation in return for a steadily increasing income and social status (a career) and for long-term security. Economic rewards are regarded not just as payments for particular amounts of work done but as emoluments appropriate to a particular grade or length of service. Hence the employee accepts a moral commitment to the organisation, and if it is felt this commitment is not being reciprocated, involvement can be strongly negative. Work is a central life interest and 'position and prospects' are significant components of social identity. Workers' lives cannot be sharply dichotomised.

## Traditional worker — solidaristic orientation

Work is not just a means to an end but also a group activity. Economic returns from work may therefore be sacrificed if they would offend group norms and threaten group solidarity. If the workers identify with the firm as a whole, then their involvement will be moral and positive; if with a 'shop' within a larger enterprise, it is likely to be in some degree alienative. Ego-involvement in work is strong and work is a central life-interest because it fulfils expressive and affective needs as well as instrumental ones. Work and non-work are likely, therefore, to form related parts of a whole way of life.

There are different interpretations of how the manual/non-manual divide has been institutionalised. Silverman (1970) takes a social action approach, seeing the division in phenomenological terms as the product of people acting on their environment and rejecting both the managerial approach and functionalism. Taking a similar approach, Paul Willis, in *Learning to Labour* (1977), finds that working-class boys destined for manual jobs do not feel second-best. Hard manual labour is seen as a sign of masculinity and toughness, and working hard for qualifications as effeminate (a view expressed in literary form by writers such as Jack London in *The Sea Wolf*). Anti-school behaviour, Willis argues, is a good preparation for unskilled work — shop floor and wage packet mean escape from school. The future shop floor worker adopts the behaviour appropriate to what will be expected of him. As Erving Goffman says in *Encounters* (1977): 'A judge is supposed to be deliberate and sober, a pilot in a cockpit cool, a book-keeper to be accurate and neat.'

Christine Griffin's *Typical Girls?* is a valuable contrast 'because it focused on young *women's* lives and was carried out by a *female* researcher' (Griffin 1985: 5). Most of the fifth formers interviewed were eager to leave school and 40 per cent of the sixth form students interviewed already had part-time jobs. But middle-class sixth formers found it much easier to get jobs than working-class ones, and only 13 per cent of young black working-class women had jobs compared with 50 per cent of white working-class women. The work involved was 'boring, menial, poorly paid and *hard*' (Griffin 1985: 86). Once they left school most young women were employed in traditional female factory jobs, such as clothing manufacture or assembly-line production in light engineering plants. Not surprisingly, they were not interested in poorly paid jobs with minimal training and limited prospects. They valued the social comfort of a good working group. But they recognised that the range of choice open to them as women was limited by the structure of the secondary labour market and the expectation that they would have to make an economic contribution to the household, both before and after maternity. Both expectations operate even more forcefully in the case of women from ethnic minorities (Westwood and Bhachu 1988).

# White-collar Workers

In Britain in the 1980s white-collar workers came for the first time to outnumber blue-collar workers. Between 1973 and 1983 non-manual jobs rose from 43 per cent to 52 per cent of all jobs. Braverman (1975) emphasises the deskilling and proletarianisation of much routine white-collar work. In support of Braverman's arguments, in the United Kingdom, following the unionisation of many white-collar workers in the 1970s and the decline of blue-collar membership in the 1980s, the National Association of Local Government Operatives (NALGO) is now the fourth largest in the Trades Union Congress (TUC), the general federation of trade unions in England and Wales.

If we apply Blauner's (1964) ideas to clerical work we do find that technological advances have altered the nature of clerical work as they earlier did manual work. First the printing press, then the mimeograph and the typewriter, caused a dramatic expansion in the ability to communicate. The telephone and the dictaphone separated the boss from the worker and removed management from the shop floor to its own suite of offices. But modern clerical workers are now often concentrated in a 'typing pool' in a large, open plan office. From the 1960s on, the introduction of calculators, electric typewriters, word processors and fax machines have made the individual clerical worker much more 'efficient', i.e. they increase the volume of work handled. This 'efficiency' is achieved at the cost of separation from meaning of overall operation. However, although clerical workers, like shop floor workers before them, have been undergoing a process of industrialisation in which the main factor has been technological change, it is not at all clear that its effect has been to 'deskill' clerical work, as the technology itself requires a considerable degree of understanding to use effectively.

Certainly, there are still significant class barriers between clerical and shop floor workers. As Lockwood (1958) argued, many clerical workers simply do not see themselves as working class. Braverman has been taken to task by Wood

(1982) for attaching too much importance to the formal structures of administration and not enough to the way it works in practice. An interplay of employer pressure and worker resistance, Wood argues, has left the middle classes still relatively unaffected by deskilling. The validity of this argument is much strengthened by the historical studies of Littler (1982), who uses comparative material from other countries to show that the Bedeaux system (the British equivalent of Taylorism) was applied mainly where the craft system had never applied or was in decline. In fact, the system was consistently opposed by the foremen and supervisory staff who were able to delay or soften its introduction. Similar resistance by senior white-collar staff has mitigated much of the logic of the industrialisation of clerical work. However, gender remains a barrier to the promotion of many clerical workers to administrative positions for which they would appear well qualified.

# Organisations

The expanding variety and content of work roles has resulted in increasing problems of co-ordination. Durkheim, in *The Division of Labour in Society* (1893), suggested that in modern complex societies consensus has been replaced by *organic* integration (that is, society remains together not so much because of fundamental agreement but because of the dependence of one part on another). Rapid social change since then has caused change in turn in the nature and structure of organisations of all kinds, but in the workplace there has been a consistent trend to increase the administrative/productive ratio, owing to the automation of production and the increased need for co-ordination of tasks.

Presthus (1962) complained: 'Organisations have come to control man, rather than the reverse' — a trend forecast at the beginning of the century by Michels' Iron Law of Oligarchy (see Chapter 4). Etzioni (1964) defines organisations as 'social units which are predominantly oriented to the attainment of specific goals'. He identifies the following characteristics of organisations:

1. Division of labour, power and communication responsibilities. This division is designed to achieve certain fixed goals (however, the sociologist must distinguish between formal goals and real goals!).
2. The presence of centres of power and co-ordination, designed to increase efficiency.
3. The substitution of personnel.

# Management

Most work on organisations has been done from the point of view of management and results in what Mouzelis (1967) called 'the managerial tradition'. The first theoretical analysis of management activities is generally accepted to have been that of the Frenchman Henri Fayol (Fayol 1930), who identified five functions of management:

- Forecasting and planning.
- Organising.
- Commanding.
- Co-ordinating.
- Controlling.

Fayol laid down a number of basic rules of good management, which have been generally accepted since. For example, authority and responsibility should go together, and each employee should have only one boss. Meanwhile, Elton Mayo's (1933) studies of the Hawthorne plant of the Western Electric Company showed, quite unexpectedly, that workers' productivity rose simply because they were being studied. Hence later work in what has become known as the Human Relations School, for example, Roethlisberger and Dickson's study (1939), concentrated much more on the informal social relationships within the organisation, and emphasised that social factors, not organisational factors, were the main cause of increased productivity. The Human Relations School in turn was criticised by Marxists for not finding conflict, and for ignoring influences from outside work; by interactionists, whose contention is that institutions can only be understood from the inside and observers cannot know their 'real' meaning to the worker; and by feminists, who criticise the way in which their 'unisex' view of industry has pervaded mainstream industrial sociology (Barker and Allen 1976: 24–6). The negative features of boredom and conformity were shown in William H. Whyte's *Organization Man* (1956), which was of prime interest to writers in social action and Marxist perspectives.

Since then, the main interest has tended to be upon the relationship between the organisation and its environment, and much of the work has taken a *structural-functional perspective*, specifying the self-regulating mechanisms which systems have to satisfy their needs for survival and adjustment (Parsons 1964; Etzioni 1964; see also Scott 1977). Although most of the work was conducted in the United States, the difficulties Scottish firms found in adapting to electronics led Burns and Stalker (1966) to distinguish:

1. *Mechanistic management system:* Characteristics — specialised differentiation of functional tasks, the specification of what will be done by whom, precise definition of responsibility, emphasis on rights, obligations and work-methods, hierarchical structure, insistence on loyalty.
2. *Organic management system:* contribution from various specialists to a common task, adjustment and continual re-definition of tasks, shedding of responsibility, the spread of commitment, a network structure, commitment valued more highly than loyalty and obedience.

Modern ideas of a mechanistic system are well expressed by Urwick and Brech (1948–9), who believe that a 'logical structure is better for efficiency and morale than one allowed to develop around personalities'. Maximum specialisation gave rise to three kinds of formal relations: (1) Line, (2) Functional, and (3) Staff. Line managers pass instructions down the hierarchy. There should be a clear line of authority, which is known and recognised. Staff subordinates should be used to help with the detailed work of co-ordination. Duties, responsibility and authority of each position should be defined in writing and made known to all interested parties. Authority should be commensurate with responsibility in each position. Any one manager should only be directly in charge of some five or six sub-ordinates, whose work should be interlocking. Leaders should take primary responsibility for their subordinates' actions but delegation is a primary necessity at all times.

Burns and Stalker, on the other hand, found that mechanistic organisation was hampered by departmentalism. Total loyalty to the organisation was demanded and hence any chance of change to organic management was forestalled. Under stress of changing conditions problems were referred up the hierarchy and the top became overburdened. Some effort was made to add to the formal structures creating branches to the hierarchy, but this in acute cases led to the appearance of the 'mechanistic jungle'. Burns and Stalker reject the basic premise of structural-functional analysis, the technological-determinism argument, and show that alternative forms of organisation are, in fact, always possible.

The key to good organisation is the involvement of all in a common purpose (Barnard 1938). Communication links the common purpose with the co-operators. Large organisations, Barnard points out, are invariably made up of smaller groups of 2–15 people. Their exact size depends on their complexity of purpose and the technology available, but they cannot grow further because of the need for intercommunication between their members. An informal organisation exists within the formal organisation and regulates members' activity. Executive work, therefore, is 'the specialised work of maintaining the organisation in operation' by:

1. Maintenance of communication.
2. Securing essential services from individuals.
3. Formulation of purpose and objectives.

These ideas were taken a stage further by Mary Follett Parker (1941), whose idea of organisation as an 'integrative unity' openly conflicts with many traditional notions of power, responsibility and leadership. Parker talks of 'joint responsibility' and 'multiple leadership'. She sees power as 'power with' not 'power over'. A good manager will be able 'to create a group power rather than express a personal power'. However, as Elliot Jacques (1978) and the Glacier investigations demonstrated, democracy in itself can easily become a management strategy — he terms this the problem of pseudo-democracy. Even if it does not, Kenneth Boulding, the inventor of the phrase 'the Organizational Revolution', argues that there is always likely to be a collision between the values of management and the routine expectations of a democratic society (Boulding 1970).

A third view is that originating with Herbert Simon (1976), who equates management with decision-making. There are three stages of decision-making: intelligence, design and choice. Executing policy is the same as making more detailed policy. Decisions are not purely rational, they are not made on the grounds of the best possible course of action, but because the course chosen is satisfactory, hence the term '*satisficing*'. As human beings are less efficient at unplanned than planned decision-making, organisations try to programme as many decisions as possible, resulting not only in individual habit but in *standard operating procedures* and a system of common expectations for the firm as a whole.

However, Peter Blau found that the higher the qualifications of the personnel, the greater the ratio of managers. Extra managers are required to deal with the decentralised nature of a department of autonomous professionals, but do so, not by command and supervision, but by consultation and communication. He writes: 'What is inappropriate for an organisation staffed by experts is a hierarchy in which official authority is centralised in the hands of a few managers' (Blau 1974). In post-industrial society, therefore, there is a growing tendency to seek new forms of diffuse and decentralised relationships, which are different from those of traditional organisations.

# Professions

The study of the present day alone cannot explain the nature and significance of professions — they can only be understood in historical context. The so-called *classical* professions, such as the Church, law and medicine, were *self-regulating* and were originally organised in guilds (small-scale estates) having special privileges. In the classic pattern professionals:

1. Have special skills of recognised social value.
2. Cannot practise until they have passed examinations and been accepted by their fellows.
3. Are subject to a governing body of practitioners.
4. Are paid by fees for their services.

In the nineteenth century new professions emerged or were formally recognised: for example, surgeons, nurses, architects. These conformed to the classical pattern in that each required specific skills and was able to establish a degree of independent self-regulation. Conversely, since the special knowledge which is the stock-in-trade of professionals has to be seen to be 'true', the status of the Church has fallen, and universities, formerly part of the Church, have assumed independent professional status (Abercrombie *et al.* 1988).

Another recurrent theme, first voiced by Durkheim, is the notion of service to the community. Not all sociologists, however, would go as far as Parsons, who argues that the high rewards given to professionals reflect the high regard society has of them because they are seen to be driven by a desire to engage in public service rather than a desire to make money. Nurses, for example, are highly regarded but poorly rewarded!

Nor is there agreement among those who try to determine the nature of professions empirically. Millerson (1964) identified six traits:

1. A skill based on theoretical knowledge.
2. An extensive period of education and training.
3. The testing of competence before admission to the profession.
4. The existence of a code of conduct.
5. A theme of public service and altruism.
6. The freedom of the profession to regulate itself.

Today, however, in the United Kingdom most doctors work for the NHS and many lawyers for companies, building societies, etc. 'The concept of a profession is not very precise ... and it has a curiously old-fashioned air about it' (King and Raynor 1981).

What seems to be most important is that:

1. Professionals *think* of themselves as a profession: Becker *et al.* (1961) emphasise the importance of the process of initiation of young medical students in creating a sense of self-consciousness of professional responsibility.
2. Professions are largely self-recruiting: Malcolm Johnson (1983), in a study of 497 doctors from five medical schools, confirmed that entry to medical school — and thus to the profession — was largely determined by family and hence by class influences. Similarly, John Griffiths (1977) shows that 80 per cent of the judiciary is drawn from public schools, Oxbridge and the upper middle classes, not least because judges up to now have been appointed from among the ranks of barristers, who because of the nature of their work find it hard to survive their first few years in the profession without private means.

## Professionalism as a Strategy

Another view, exemplified by Wilensky (1964) sees professionalisation as a collective occupational *strategy* with five stages:

1. Emergence of a full-time occupation.
2. Institutionalisation of specialist training.
3. The establishment of a professional association.
4. Recourse to legislation to secure the recognition and protection of the association.
5. Formulation of a code of professional conduct.

Parry and Parry (*The Rise of the Medical Profession*, 1976), in the same way, argue that for the classical profession of medicine itself professionalisation was a social strategy — 'collective social mobility' — the key stages being: restriction of entry into the profession, formation of an association to control entry into the profession and creation of a monopoly in the provision of particular services.

Doctors achieved the second when they formed the British Medical Association (in 1832) and obtained the first and third when Parliament established the General Medical Council (1858). Teachers, they suggest, were less successful in obtaining full professional recognition, not least because universities long controlled both main routes into the profession. With their numbers enormously increased by the spread of state education, they were in the end to adopt the alternative strategy of unionisation.

Though the term 'professional' is now very loosely used to imply possessing a skill and being paid for it, the main new groups since the nineteenth century where professionalisation is recognised are:

● Health and social services.
● Engineers, scientists and technologists.
● Accountants.

However, any differences between 'old' and 'new' professions are hard to draw and the Registrar General's categories of 'higher' and 'lower' professions confuse the issue further, since they essentially are based on income, which also acts to divide people within individual professions. Some describe teaching and nursing, which lack many of the classical 'traits', as 'semi-professions'. But that is a term that is quite understandably resented, especially since a significant common factor which has both restricted acceptance of autonomy and resulted in very poor economic rewards is gender — the classical professions are patriarchal, and nursing and teaching are both badly paid because so many women work in them.

## The Attack on the Professions

Terence Johnson, in *Professions and Power* (1972), questions both the professionals' claim to superior knowledge and their altruism. John Griffiths (1977), a lawyer himself, shows that the legal profession is primarily used by the rich and powerful to protect their own interests. The limited nature of Legal Aid means that most people cannot afford to have much to do with lawyers. Ivan Illich (1971), as part of a general attack on the professions, has specifically attacked both education (1973) as a closing off of possibilities of awareness and development, and the medical establishment (1977) as 'a major threat to health' concentrating on technical repair. In his 1980 Reith Lecture, Ian Kennedy (1981) said that society gave too much power to doctors (see also Jacques 1978).

Society has not been slow to respond. Under the Thatcher Government the war on monopolies has been extended to the professions, whose members in the past have so often given active support to the Conservative Party. Solicitors have lost their lucrative monopoly on conveyancing (a move which, in fact, began with a Private Member's Bill introduced by a Labour MP, Austin Mitchell, in October 1983) but have yet to make good on the Lord Chancellor's promise to allow them to appear in the High Court, thereby breaching the monopoly interests of barristers.

University teachers have been deprived of the tenure which protected them from political interference in their teaching. A new contract system requires universities to 'bid' for courses with the aim of driving down the cost of higher education. All other teachers have had their negotiating rights removed and have been forced to accept what they see as poorer pay and conditions. In addition, they have had the control of the curriculum taken out of their hands. Nurses have been exploited through their commitment to service to accept abysmally low pay, and doctors have been forced (since 1990) to accept new NHS contracts which means continuous monitoring and financial control. Ambulance workers, who, as paramedics, had been following the traditional path of professionalisation described above until a protracted strike in 1989–90, have been denied professional status.

# Trade Unions

## Why trade unions?

Trade unions are voluntary organisations formed by workers to maximise their bargaining power with their employers. The right to belong to a union and to engage in industrial action is recognised both by the United Nations and by the European Declaration on Human Rights as fundamental.

## Development of unions

Guilds, which were associations of both employers and employees in specified trades, had existed since the Middle Ages and were given the power to regulate apprenticeship and similar matters. However, early attempts to form trade unions were strongly resisted by employers. The government of Lord Liverpool (1812–27) passed the Six Acts, which made all such attempts illegal, but public reaction brought a change of attitudes and in 1824 trade unions were legalised. During the next fifty years many new unions came into existence and they, together with the older craft unions (the former guilds), formed the Trades Union Congress (TUC) in 1868.

Towards the end of the century labour began to get direct representation in Parliament, culminating in the formation of the Labour Party in 1906. Legislation enacted by the Liberal Government was passed to remove corporate liability by unions for the actions of their members during industrial disputes. This cleared the way for unions to negotiate effectively for improved pay and conditions, using the ultimate threat of withdrawal of labour to gain concessions. However, an attempt by miners and rail workers to mount a General Strike in 1926 was defeated by the Conservative Government using middle-class volunteers to maintain essential services. The 1945 Labour Government legislated to protect the 'closed shop' (an agreement between a union and an employer that membership of that union will be a condition of employment) and the 1974 Labour Government

Table 6.3   *Trade union membership, 1901–87*

|  | 1901 | 1911 | 1921 | 1931 | 1941 | 1951 | 1961 | 1971 | 1981 | 1987 |
|---|---|---|---|---|---|---|---|---|---|---|
| Members (million) | 2.0 | 2.6 | 8.2 | 4.6 | 6.6 | 9.5 | 9.9 | 11.1 | 12.1 | 10.5 |

Source: *Social Trends*, 20, table 11.1, p. 163; table 11.17, p. 171.

introduced the Dock Labour Scheme, giving dockers security of employment in most of Britain's major ports.

Regular annual meetings of the TUC have been held since 1871, and between 1945 and 1979 it became normal for it to be directly represented in government discussions on economic questions, and nominate representatives to the National Economic Development Corporation ('Neddy') and similar bodies. Nevertheless, it remains a federation with no power over its member unions except that of suspension or expulsion. In 1979 there were 13.5 million members of unions in Great Britain, but since then union membership has fallen steeply. The number of unions has also fallen from 414 in 1981 to 330 in 1987, with more than 80 per cent of members in unions with more than 100,000 members (*Social Trends 20*, Tables 11.1, 11.17).

## Organisation of unions

Union members pay dues and have the right to elect union officials according to the constitution of their unions. Until 1985 much of the business of unions was transacted in large public meetings which were often poorly attended and open to manipulation by union officers. Since that time unions have been required to hold secret ballots on strike action, but this gives only limited protection to the union if a firm makes use of the legal procedure of injunction to try to head off a strike. Today, British unions are widely seen (even by their members) as lacking 'muscle', and this seems to be confirmed by the finding that the estimated percentage of extra earnings that members gain as a result of union membership in Britain is only 8 per cent. This is only slightly above the 7 per cent estimated for West Germany, and compares badly with 13 per cent for Australia and 26 per cent for the United States. However, 51 per cent of men and 41 per cent of women (i.e. 47 per cent) of the workforce in Britain are members of unions as compared with only 21 per cent of men and 12 per cent of women (17 per cent) in the United States (Blanchflower and Oswald, in Jowell, Witherspoon and Brook 1989: 26, 22).

# Strikes

The belief dies hard that in the 1970s Britain was a country particularly prone to strikes. In the early 1980s public perception, encouraged by the Conservative-

**Table 6.4**  *Number of strikes, workers taking part and work days lost, selected years, 1971–90*

|      | No. of stoppages | '000 workers taking part | Days lost '000 |
|------|------------------|--------------------------|----------------|
| 1971 | 2,228            | 1,178.2                  | 13,551         |
| 1976 | 2,016            | 668                      | 3,284          |
| 1981 | 1,338            | 1,512.5                  | 4,266          |
| 1986 | 1,074            | 720.2                    | 1,920          |
| 1990 | 598              | 290.5                    | 1,890          |

Source: *Yearbook of Labour Statistics*, 1981, Table 28A, p. 611; 1991, Table 31A, p. 1047.

owned press, was that Britain's record of strikes under the previous Labour Government had led to poor economic growth. There are three commonly used measures of strikes: the number of strikes that actually take place in a year, the proportion of the workforce that takes part in them, and the number of working days lost as a result. In fact, between 1973 and 1977 Canada, Italy, India, Denmark, the United States and Ireland all had more strikes than Britain, and in 1977 only 10.4 million working days were lost in Britain because of strikes, compared with 310 million for sickness. In the 1980s Italy and Canada have continued to be particularly subject to strikes, and Britain, as in the 1970s, is about average among the OECD countries. In addition, there is no correlation between strike levels and national economic performance.

Nevertheless, the 1979 government believed that there was and legislated to control strikes. Similar legislation passed by the 1970–74 Conservative Government had been ineffective, not least because 95 per cent of strikes were and are unofficial, conducted by workers dissatisfied both with the Government and their own unions (Thompson 1989). Until the miners' strike of 1984, therefore, the legislation passed was cautious and not very effective.

Department of Employment statistics for the period show that the most strike-prone industries in Britain at that time were the docks, coal mining and motor car manufacturing. Figures for strikes among agricultural workers, those employed in public utilities (e.g. gas, electricity, telephones) and workers in the (enlarged) public sector were low. This British pattern was in fact close to that described internationally by Kerr *et al.* (1962) who suggested that dockers, miners and seamen are the most militant of workers because they live in close-knit communities, relatively isolated from other occupational groups. This caused them to be more aware of common occupational interests and more insulated from disapproval of their actions by other sectors of society. But Kerr ignored the extent to which a strike may be *effective* as an industrial strategy in securing better conditions of work or reward.

An example of the effectiveness of strikes in a technologically advanced industry is the British motor car industry. A small strike in a car plant can stop the whole production line. Also, assembly-line production may lead to high levels of alienation among workers. But technological explanations are inadequate on their own, as they cannot account for international variations in strike rates within the same industry. For example, car workers in Britain have historically been more likely to strike than their counterparts in Germany and Japan, and, further, the strike rates vary very much from firm to firm (see also Hyman 1972, 1975).

Pay is often not the 'real' issue, but emerges because there has to be something to negotiate about. Most disputes are resolved locally by negotiation between management and shop stewards and never lead to strikes. As Lane and Roberts (1971) comment in *Strike at Pilkingtons*, 'workers can be drawn into a strike without being conscious of an exceptionally wide range of grievances and without being subject to unusual stress on the shop floor'.

The miners strike of 1984—5 was consistent with these findings. However, since it seemed to confirm the need to curb trade union power, it resulted in the Conservative Government implementing its anti-trade union strategy. The strike was called by the President of the National Union of Mineworkers, Arthur Scargill, who claimed that the Coal Board planned to shut down pits and dismiss miners. Generally such moves were regarded by management as necessary rationalisation under pressure from the Government to cut subsidies to the industry. Despite the fact that no specific moves had been announced, miners saw the possibility as a threat to their jobs, and felt a particular sense of betrayal after management agreement in the early 1980s on *Plan for Coal*, which envisaged the expansion of the industry. They accepted the interpretation that management had not been telling the truth about their plans. The Government saw the ill-timed strike call as an opportunity to break the power of a major trade union, and did not intervene.

The union leadership, who may have been lulled into a false sense of their own strength because of the success of an earlier strike in 1981, chose the worst possible moment to call the strike, which began in the spring, when substantial stocks of coal had been built up and demand was dropping. After a long and bitter struggle in which large-scale unrest occurred outside pits and a taxi driver was killed, the union split. The Nottinghamshire miners seceded to form their own union and the strike collapsed. The consequences were severe. Many more pits than Scargill had originally stated were closed, and the decline of the coal industry accelerated. The fact is that the strike weapon is not a good way to save jobs, and can only work where the firm concerned really does have the resources to meet the demands. In 1990, without further legislation, the number of workers on strike was the lowest since 1962.

# Employment and Unemployment

A good account of occupational change in the first eight decades of twentieth-century Britain is Routh (1980). Trends in employment and unemployment since that time, however, are not only significant but politically controversial. The problem of assessing them is not helped, to say the least, by the statistical problems of comparability mentioned in Chapter 2. Before 1982 the definition of 'unemployed' included all who were registered for work at Job Centres. From 1982 they consisted only of those out of work and claiming unemployment benefit. Those available for work but ineligible for benefit (e.g. many married women) were no longer counted, removing some 250,000 from the official totals quoted in the press and on television. In March 1983 men over 60 who had previously been claiming long-term supplementary benefit no longer had to claim benefit, so they too, totalling some 200,000, ceased to be counted as unemployed even though they were. Also excluded from the official tally were those eligible for the newly instituted Youth Opportunities Programme, removing at a stroke all school leavers, another 495,000 in all. Paradoxes abound, so that retired people who have ceased to be economically active do not count as unemployed, while people who have only limited part-time work count as employed (Sinclair 1987). Whether or not these changes were desirable in themselves, the fact that the former series of figures was immediately discontinued, so that no direct comparisons could be made, was justifiably criticised.

By the beginning of 1990 the new figures had steadily fallen for some six years but still remained much higher than they would have been in 1979. Hence government spokespersons often preferred to emphasise that there was a record number of people *in* work. For in the 1980s there were more people entering work, especially married women, so the true number in work in 1990 was at a record level, but unemployment was still very high and constituted a major social problem. Being out of paid work not only means that the person concerned is short of money (which can be bad enough). It also means that they have much less to do, lack an ordered rhythm to their day, and have narrower social horizons with much less opportunity to make social contacts (Fryer and McKenna 1987).

Assessing trends is made more difficult by the fact that unemployment goes up in the winter and falls in the summer. 'Seasonally adjusted' figures allow for such regular changes, and may give a very different impression of underlying

Table 6.5  *Unemployment, 1971–90*

|      | Total  | %    | Men    | %    | Women | %   |
|------|--------|------|--------|------|-------|-----|
| 1971 | 792.1  | 3.5  | 665.9  | 4.6  | 126.2 | 1.5 |
| 1975 | 977.6  | 4.1  | 517.9  | 3.7  | 102.6 | 1.1 |
| 1979 | 1390.5 | 5.7  | 963.9  | 6.7  | 426.5 | 4.3 |
| 1983 | 3104.7 | 11.7 | 2218.6 | 13.8 | 886.0 | 8.4 |
| 1987 | 2953.4 | 10.6 | 2045.8 | 12.5 | 907.6 | 7.8 |
| 1990 | 1664.5 | 5.9  | 1232.3 | 7.9  | 432.2 | 3.6 |

Source: *Yearbook of Labour Statistics*, 1981, Table 9A, p. 327; 1991, Table 3A, p. 381.
N.B. definition change 1982 — see text.

trends from the raw figures. At any one time the figures are also swollen by a significant number of people moving *between* jobs. Such changes are known as *frictional* unemployment, and account for between 180,000 and 350,000 a month appearing on the register for less than four weeks.

Nothing is more unlovely than the sight of well-to-do members of the middle class dismissing unemployment as the product of 'shirkers'. Fraudulent claims for unemployment benefit had a high political profile in the early 1980s, but all the evidence now suggests that they account for less than 1 per cent of all claims. In fact, many times the number do not claim benefits to which they are entitled. As for the suggestion that the unemployed are 'idle', in 1984, after the rules had been changed to exclude anyone who did not accept a job without 'good cause' only 12,000 refused to accept an offer of a job without good cause, and only 7,000 lost benefit in consequence. As for those that are unemployable for reasons of physical or mental disability, the best estimate is that at most they number some 135,000, and many of these people would welcome an offer of work suitable for them.

Those worst hit by high levels of unemployment are:

1. Young people under 20. They lack the necessary skills and training; when employed, they are 'last in, first out'.
2. Long-term male unemployed. Long-term unemployment is defined as those without work for more than twelve months. Two-thirds are over 35, an age beyond which many firms refuse to accept applications. Being older they often lack the training for new skills and may also be ill.
3. Blacks tend to be disproportionately represented because they are young, untrained or live in areas of high unemployment.
4. Regional blackspots for unemployment are those of the older 'smokestack' industries, above all Northern Ireland, the North-East, Merseyside.

Among the social consequences of being out of work are:

1. Poverty is almost inevitable, and dependence on welfare accentuates its effects through the 'poverty trap'.
2. Marital breakdown is more likely, either through the effects of relative poverty or through the effects of enforced proximity on a couple who are used to leading separate working lives.
3. The effects of poverty are to a limited extent offset by the existence of the 'informal economy' by which those who are out of work help one another. However, this creates additional social problems.

# The Future of Work

As noted above, British management structures are very old-fashioned, and recent trends have been to accentuate the 'top-down' structures. Yet the future of work

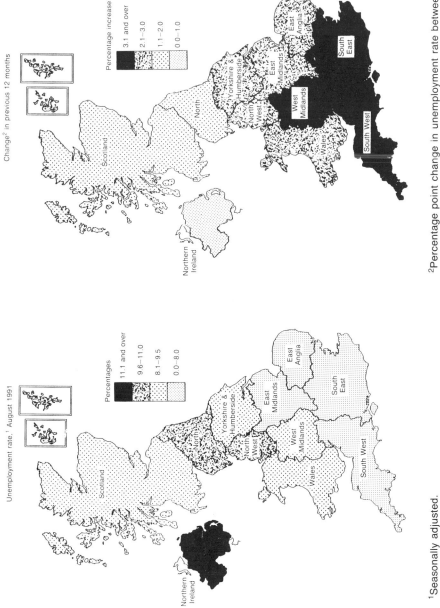

*United Kingdom*

Unemployment rate,[1] August 1991

Change[2] in previous 12 months

[1]Seasonally adjusted.

Source: Employment Department

[2]Percentage point change in unemployment rate between August 1990 and August 1991.

Source: *Social Trends 22*, Table 4.27, p. 81.

Figure 6.1   *Unemployment by region*

clearly involves a number of changes which require an educated workforce capable of and so allowed to take its own decisions.

1. *Homeworking* (see also Chapter 4) is likely to become increasingly common as transport difficulties increase, costs rise and corporations seek to shed responsibility for their workers.
2. Group production has been successfully applied in the Volvo factory in Sweden, replacing the drudgery of the assembly-line by a team approach in which each worker performs a range of tasks.
3. Industrial democracy is already far more developed on the Continent than it is in Britain. German law, for example, requires the presence of worker-directors on the board, something that has been strenuously resisted in Britain.
4. The role of the European Community (EC) in facilitating the free movement of capital and labour is therefore likely, after 1992, to lead to a drive to democratise working practices throughout the Community. The 'right to work' enshrined in the UN Charter is consistent with the proposals of the Delors Plan for a Community-wide system of social security, which is likely to be generally accepted by other states. If Britain does not come into line, many more skilled workers will migrate.

## Suggestions for Further Reading

Much of the traditional literature on work focuses on the experiences of men. Christine Griffin (1985), *Typical Girls? Young Women from School to the Job Market*, discusses teenagers' expectations. Diana Leonard Barker and Sheila Allen (eds) (1976) bring together a number of contributions on women's *Dependence and Exploitation in Work and Marriage*. Paul Willis (1977), *Learning to Labour*, gives insight into the hopes and aspirations of working-class boys. Routh (1980) gives a good account of occupational change over the first eight decades of the century. The problems of unemployment are dealt with in Marie Jahoda (1982), *Employment and Unemployment*. For a general introduction to work, see Grint (1991), *The Sociology of Work*.

On supersession theory, see the classic by Daniel Bell (1973), *The Coming of Post Industrial Society*, and Jonathan Gershuny and Ian Miles (1983), *The New Service Economy; The Transformation of Employment in Industrial Societies*. T. Burns and G. M. Stalker (1966) investigate *The Management of Innovation*. The best introduction to the professions is Raynor (1969), and a critique can be found in Terence Johnson (1972), *Professions and Power*. A most useful overview of the area is S. R. Parker *et al.* (1983), *The Sociology of Industry*.

# 7 Community, Urbanisation and Development

## Community, Urbanisation and Development

Some themes which have formed the bases of questions in this part of the syllabus have been:

- The differences between rural and urban societies and whether there can be said to be a distinctive urban way of life.
- The conflicts and problem areas associated with cities. Sociological explanations of such phenomena. Class segregation.
- The loss of community in Western societies.
- The major perspectives on economic development/underdevelopment. Critiques of the theories.
- Is there a single path to development? Are industrial nations becoming increasingly alike?

## Society or Community?

We often hear about people living in communities. What do we mean by community? Certainly it is not as broad a concept as 'society'. A good definition is: 'Any circle of people who live together so that they share, not this or that particular interest, but a whole set of interests wide enough and complex enough to include their lives' (McIver and Page 1931).

Thus communities share particular territories, but also exhibit common *values*. Such values include a mutual sense of dependence, identity of interests, a sense of belonging and of an expected pattern of behaviour. The important thing about communities is that people should feel they 'belong'. They are more likely to do so if:

- The locality in which they live is compact, with a clear boundary and good internal communications.

- They live in a tightly-knit society with extensive networks of family relationships binding them together.
- There are few major divisions between them that make for conflict; they have numerous interests in common, and agreement on basic values maintains stability without the repeated need for the intervention of the agencies of social control.

The process by which people have come to live in cities explains the nature of the societies they have created there, and it was precisely the fact that they felt the spirit of community had been lost, or seriously damaged, that made the process of industrialisation and its impact on the way people lived a matter of special concern to earlier sociologists.

**Alternative views of rural vs. urban divide**

| AUTHOR | Rural | Urban |
|--------|-------|-------|
| Toennies | Gemeinschaft | Gesellschaft |
| Durkheim | Mechanical | Organic |
| MacIver | Community | Association |
| Redfield | Folk | Urban |
| Weber | Traditional | Rational |
| Becker | Sacred | Secular |

Many sociologists have distinguished between *rural* and *urban* society, and there is a strong tendency to assume that community is something particularly applicable to rural society and now lost. In fact, different writers have taken different views of the rural/urban divide, though their categories do have basic features in common. All later distinctions tend to rely heavily on the work of Toennies (1955), a German sociologist whose distinction between societies based on *Gemeinschaft* (community) and those based on *Gesellschaft* (association, also the normal German word for a company) is fundamental. Durkheim drew a similar distinction between the *mechanical* and the *organic*. However, it is important once again to note that these are 'ideal-types'. Hence they need not (and probably do not) exist in pure form in the real world, and since there is no way of measuring accurately how people feel about the nature of the societies in which they live, it is difficult if not impossible to tell whether they exist, still less whether they correspond to a real difference *between* town and country or can be found as differences *within* towns (or countryside).

# Urbanisation

Urbanisation is the process by which people have moved from the country (*rural* areas) and become *concentrated* in towns or cities (*urban* areas). Sociologically a city is not just an agglomeration of housing. Louis Wirth (1938) defined a city for sociological purposes as:

---

Community or mechanical society

1. Relationships are close, based on face-to-face contacts.
2. Status is *ascribed* but personal behaviour is also important.
3. People *identify* with the community of which they are part.

Association or organic society

1. Relationships are *impersonal* and formal.
2. Status is *achieved*.
3. People stress their individuality; they do not identify with the community.
4. People often divide into groups or subcultures based on race, class, age, etc.

---

a relatively large, dense and permanent settlement of heterogeneous individuals. The three variables — number, density of settlement, and degree of homogeneity — explain the characteristics of urban life and . . . account for the differences between cities of various sizes and types.

1. *Size*: Towns and cities, unlike villages, cover a large geographical area. As a result they need public transport and good roads. The size of towns prevents all people from knowing one another. Urban areas are often divided into different zones by class or race.
2. *Density of population*: Towns have a higher density of population than rural areas. This results in problems such as housing shortages, traffic congestion and pollution. But it does make it worth while for traders to provide all sorts of amenities, e.g. shopping precincts, pubs, cafés, cinemas, clubs, dance halls, amusement arcades.
3. *Social heterogeneity*: In urban areas, many different sorts of people (different classes, different races) all live close to one another. This can create problems as different groups may be hostile to each other, but it can also be seen as creating a richer, more diverse environment. Modern literature would be unimaginable without the culture of the city.

Britain is the most heavily urbanised of all industrial nations (if city-states such as Singapore are disregarded). In 1801 about 17 per cent of the population lived in towns and cities. By 1851 this figure had increased to 50 per cent and in 1951 it reached a peak at 81 per cent. Since about 1960 the trend has reversed and people have been moving out of the big cities into new developments in the former countryside. In 1990 about 78 per cent of the population were living in large towns and cities.

The most important historical reasons for urbanisation were:

1. *The agricultural revolution*. The number of people needed to work in agriculture has declined. Only 2 per cent of the British population now work on the land.

Table 7.1 *Percentage population in urban areas, United Kingdom, selected years, 1851–1990*

| Year | % urban |
| --- | --- |
| 1851 | 50 |
| 1891 | 72 |
| 1911 | 78 |
| 1931 | 80 |
| 1951 | 81 |
| 1990 (est.) | 78 |

2. *Industrialisation*. From about 1750 onwards the new factories needed large workforces living nearby and such population centres then attracted retail services. Later, for fear of social unrest, central government acted to set up systems of local government for the new towns and cities. Then systems of mass transport were devised which enabled them to spread over much larger areas.

The urban way of life with all the characteristics of associational society has spread to most parts of Britain. The differences between rural and urban areas in terms of culture and social structure have almost disappeared. Many people who live in the country now commute to urban areas to work, and those who do not have been subject to 'urbanism' as a result of transport and the media. The government expects a million new houses to be built in the 1990s to accommodate an increase in population of some two million, many of whom are now living in smaller family groups. Most of these will be in the crowded south-east, further eroding the tenuous difference between town and country there.

## The Decline of Community?

Already in the early postwar period sociologists were beginning to question the ideas of Toennies and Durkheim. Young and Willmott (1957) found a strong sense of community among East Enders in the 1950s, a feature still echoed among residents of 'Albert Square' in the TV soap opera *East Enders*. When much of East London was redeveloped and the East Enders were re-housed it took a long time for them to develop a new sense of community. Pahl (1970), in *Patterns of Urban Life*, reported research in urban Swansea on neighbourhoods which exhibited the features of community rather than association. It appears, therefore, that the distinction between community and association is not identical with that between town and country. There has, however, been considerable debate among sociologists not only as to how far the spirit of community existed in urban areas at all, but (given that most now think that it did) how far it has survived the depopulation of the inner cities and the expansion of the suburbs.

The classic pattern of a traditional community in an inner-city urban area, Bethnal Green, is that described by Young and Willmott (1957). They emphasise especially how 'Mum' figures are at the centre of local interactions, functioning as combined information exchanges and transit depots. The key link in the traditional working-class extended family is the relationship between mother and daughter. This continues when the daughter is married because of the likelihood that the newly married couple will live close to the female's family of origin. Traditionally men spent much of their leisure separately from women in pubs and Working Men's or Labour Clubs. Such general segregation has long been breaking down, though there are still public bars in some areas where 'respectable' women would not drink, even in male company. The traditional working-class community survives, woven in a 'web of talk and gossip' and in the passing of time together in ways more or less amusing or practically useful. There are reserved areas of personal and family privacy and strict rules dividing the private from the open and collective.

**Community in Bethnal Green**

In a place like Bethnal Green you can find several generations of families and their relatives. They may live, work and spend their leisure together.

'I've got my drinking friends', he said, 'that's my brothers-in-law mostly. We're a proper mixing family. I see the wife's mother at least once every day and most of her sisters and my brothers-in-law too. All the brothers-in-law go out together — mix in the same company, use the same pubs, have the same activities, follow the same sports. At the week-ends we all take our wives along when we can, so it's a real family gathering round the pub — us two and the wife's sisters and all their husbands and the wife's mother and father. Annie's eldest girl — she's thirteen — she usually gives eye to our two and comes up and tells us if they wake up.'

Young and Willmott (1957: 53).

Significantly, however, Bethnal Green was an area in economic decline. Its traditional relationships and the feeling of unity among its inhabitants survived largely because there was no longer any significant migration into the area. Young and Willmott themselves noted how family links, and with it the sense of community, was broken, as when a daughter living on a new estate some 20 miles away was no longer able to maintain this close contact and had to integrate in a new pattern locally. Their conclusion was that the decline of community, where it occurred, was caused at least in part by the very policies of urban renewal that were supposed to be socially beneficial.

This view seemed to be confirmed by other studies, notably Coates and Silburn's (1970) study of the impoverished working-class St Ann's district of Nottingham. Frankenberg (1969), in his *Communities in Britain*, accepted the idea of a 'retreat from community' in Britain, but summarised a range of studies to show that many communal societies did then still exist in specific types of area, as indeed most if not all still do. On the other hand, Konig (1968) argued that community is basic to human organisation. Hence it would remain despite industrialisation and urbanisation.

What has been termed the 'liberal' view of urban sociology has been that it is for politicians and town planners to use resources in such a way as to enhance this sense of community, to make people feel at home in the 'artificial' environment of the city. The outbreak of racial unrest in the decaying city centres of the United States in the early 1960s, and the 'events' of 1968 in Paris, brought a belated recognition of how far the processes of urban growth in Europe also had outpaced the sense of community and allowed dangerous tensions to develop. However projections about British cities based on US experience must always be approached with considerable caution, in view of the very substantial differences between the two countries.

The decline of 'community' has assumed a new meaning in the 1980s, emerging as a theme associated with the critique of Thatcherite values (Hoover and Plant 1989: 290−1). It was made explicit in Mrs Thatcher's statement to *Woman's Own* magazine (31 October 1987): 'There is no such thing as society, only individuals and their families.' However, despite the individualist orientation of government in the 1980s, Jacobs and Worcester (1990) found no retreat from the collectivist values that lent support to community-based structures.

## How Urbanisation Occurred in Britain

Unlike the US cities studied by Ernest W. Burgess and Robert E. Park (Park 1915; Park, Burgess and McKenzie, 1967) and the Chicago School of sociologists, British cities emerged in a countryside that was already densely settled and pocketed with towns and villages, many of them of great age. The rapid growth of towns in the early nineteenth century led to drastic changes. Small towns such as Manchester, running into neighbouring Salford, became great cities, and villages became towns, as in the Potteries. It was left to speculative builders to provide the rows and rows of 'back-to-back' houses for the new urban working class, and only after repeated outbreaks of diseases such as cholera and typhoid were by-laws passed enforcing a minimum standard of construction. This is the housing familiar to millions thoughout the world through the television serial *Coronation Street* — in fact, there are many people in, say, New Zealand who believe that most British people still live in such areas.

Though at first the size of such industrial cities was limited by horse transport, the railway was already linking such communities together, and with the introduction of the electric tram (1886) cities developed on a web pattern linked by fixed lines of transport which in many cases are still clearly recognisable. The irregular pattern of development means that it is hard to see in Britain the neat pattern of concentric zones identified by the Chicago School, in which the central business district is surrounded in turn by a transition zone, an area of working-

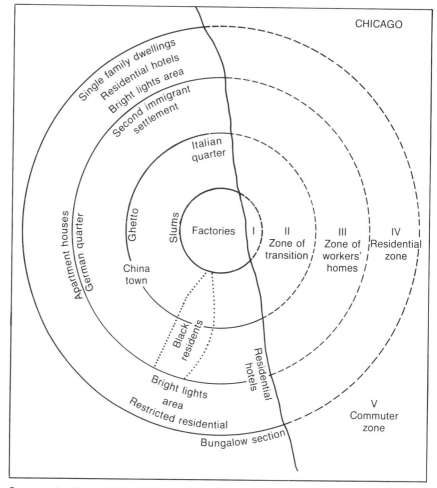

Source: after Robert E. Park, Ernest W. Burgess and Roderick D. McKenzie (1925), *The City*, Chicago: University of Chicago Press.

Figure 7.1   *Inner city zones*

class residence, an area of middle-class residence, and, on the outside, the commuter belt. However the problems associated with the invasion, succession and dominance of the transition zone have been identified in Britain, as by Rex and Moore (1967) in the Sparkbrook district of Birmingham.

By the late nineteenth century the early industrial housing was overcrowded and falling into decay. Some philanthropists tried to provide a better substitute — as with the '1024 Improved Industrial Dwellings' backing on to the railway at Bethnal Green — but such efforts had only a limited effect. In 1909 the first Housing and Town Planning Act gave local authorities power to clear the 'slums'. But soldiers returning from the First World War found little changed. Even though the Prime Minister, David Lloyd George, had promised them 'homes fit for heroes' there was little money available and houses built by private enterprise, e.g. at Peacehaven in Sussex, were too expensive for most people. The Wheatley Housing Act, passed by the first Labour Government in 1924, gave subsidies to local authorities to build houses to rent to working-class families, and throughout the rest of the inter-war period and down to the 1970s council house estates became a major feature of urban expansion. Being large and located on the outskirts of existing cities they lacked the urban feel their inhabitants had been used to, and their advantages were offset by the increased cost of travel to work and having to rely on small local shops. Many such estates may seem unattractive in the 1990s, reflecting both their low-cost construction and the poor architectural period during which they were built, but they remain magnificent in terms of both the accommodation they offer and their visual impact compared with public housing in the United States, for example.

The arrival of the motor car, however, was also to lead to the unplanned 'sprawl' of private speculative housing. Large estates grew up catering for middle-class house buyers. Though supposed to be of a higher standard than council housing, such areas had many of the same disadvantages of remoteness from work and lack of facilities. Through lack of planning, building was allowed to spread unchecked along the main roads out of and between cities ('ribbon development'). This eroded the distinction between town and country, and in due course was to prove self-defeating as the roads became congested, creating the demand for by-passes and a new system of roads. It created a new sort of environment that was neither town nor country, the 'suburbs', from which people travelled to work and to which they returned only to sleep ('dormitory suburbs').

The Town and Country Planning Act of 1947 was intended to put an end to this unchecked growth. 'Green belts' were to be established around existing urban areas. However, this occurred too late to prevent urban areas in the London region, the Midlands, Merseyside, etc. spreading into one another, forming what in the United States had come to be known as a 'conurbation'. As envisaged in Patrick Abercrombie's Greater London Plan (1944), the whole area of greater London was to be redeveloped on the Chicago model of a pattern of concentric zones linked by a web of urban communications. To achieve containment without urban sprawl, it would be surrounded by a green belt some 10 miles deep in which further building would be severely restricted. Up to a million of the overcrowded population of the inner zone would be dispersed in eight new 'overspill' towns: Harlow, Stevenage, Basildon, Bracknell, Crawley, Hatfield, Hemel Hempstead and Welwyn. Overspill was also relocated to existing towns, notably Slough and Basingstoke. The Housing Repairs and Rents Act 1954 accelerated the drive to demolish the slums. In England and Wales more than three million people were moved as a result between 1955 and 1974.

The original inhabitants were moved out to new estates often miles away from their former homes, and when the new housing was completed it was too expensive for them and a new generation of middle-class urban dwellers took their place.

In this process, close communities within cities were destroyed and replaced with inhabitants conforming much more closely to Wirth's model of impersonal urban relationships. With the 1969 Housing Act attention was therefore switched to a system of housing improvement grants to encourage the upgrading of existing urban neighbourhoods, local authorities being empowered in 1974 to designate Housing Action Areas and Priority Neighbourhoods for this purpose.

As in the inter-war period, new factories and workshops were planned for new *industrial estates* on 'green field sites' on the outskirts of existing urban areas. Separate residential areas were developed for people to live in. However, the separation of housing and industrial estates broke the link between industry and workforce, and at a more basic level meant the end of many opportunities for unskilled workers.

# New Towns

Some enlightened employers had always recognised that good living conditions were essential for a contented workforce. An early example, still standing, was Saltaire, commissioned by Sir Titus Salt, and built over about 20 years on a 'green-field' site near Bradford. But modern town planning in Britain is usually taken as beginning in 1879 when the Cadburys, the Quaker chocolate-manufacturing family, started building at Bournville near Birmingham. In 1888 their example was followed by the Lever brothers at Port Sunlight on the Wirral Peninsula opposite Liverpool, and shortly afterwards by Joseph Rowntree at New Earswick near York. Planned towns made possible a better balance between built-up areas and open space, and the advocacy of Ebenezer Howard of planned 'garden cities' was first put into practice at Letchworth in Hertfordshire in 1903, and at Welwyn Garden City in 1920. Such 'New Towns' were intended to be complete communities in which people would both live and work and enjoy themselves. They were not just large residential estates.

The New Towns Act of 1946 had the urgent purpose of stopping the endless outward growth of London. The Minister of Housing and Local Government was given the power to designate certain areas as sites for new towns, which would then be built by a development corporation specially established for the purpose. Though slow to get started, during the 1950s the eight London new towns were built. Outside the London area Aycliffe, Corby, Cwmbran and Glenrothes had also been designated, as were East Kilbride and Cumbernauld in the Clyde Valley in Scotland.

In the second wave, new towns were again planned to relieve pressure in specific conurbations. For the East Midlands, Milton Keynes, Peterborough and Northampton; for the West Midlands, Redditch and Telford (originally called Dawley); for Merseyside, Runcorn, Skelmersdale and Warrington; for Central Lancashire, New Town; for Tyneside, Washington; for Wales, Newtown; for Clydeside, Irvine; for Edinburgh, Livingston; and for Belfast, Craigavon. By

1979 thirty-four new towns had been designated in this way. Since 1979 their special status has been ended in line with a general policy of relaxing government control over planning as far as possible.

Though the new towns are generally seen as having been successful, in that they achieved the goals for which they were established, they are criticised on two grounds. First of all, they have only played a limited part in solving the overall need for housing and resources devoted to them have been achieved at the cost of more support for the inner cities themselves. Secondly, the emphasis of their supporters on self-government is considered by some to be more apparent than real. The policy of 'social balance' — drawing on different classes roughly in proportion to their numbers in society at large — Ruth Glass (1960) considers as 'a device for securing middle-class control under the guise of leadership'.

# Migration, Emigration and Immigration

## Migration

Towns and cities, therefore, were formed by a process of migration. The bulk of the migration was on a small scale and went on over a long period, typically several generations. But the mass migration after 1846 of Irish people fleeing the famine has left a permanent mark on the social structure of Glasgow and Liverpool (Celtic and Rangers, Liverpool and Everton). As the folk song 'Paddy Works on the Railway' commemorates, Irish workers provided the workforce that helped join the towns together, and many still work for the giant motorway construction contractors such as Sir Alfred McAlpine ('McAlpine's Fusiliers').

Since the 1960 Census the direction of migration seems to have reversed, in line with trends in other industrialised nations. People are no longer moving *into* cities, as they have been doing for so long; now they are moving *out*. Between 1979 and 1988 the number moving between Wales, Scotland, Northern Ireland, and standard regions of England, went up by some 22 per cent (*Social Trends*, 20, Table 1.7, p. 27). Migration is not a social fact which happens regardless of circumstances. Both push and pull factors operate.

Businesses are pushed out of older cities by the cost of premises, for example. People also move to get away from unattractive environments, when cities decay and their jobs cease to exist. Greater London alone lost 472,000, or about 6 per cent of its population, between 1971 and 1977. At the same time, the population of the south-east *outside* London rose by 3 per cent or some 300,000 people. East Anglia and the south-west both gained as much; lesser gains were recorded in the Midlands (other than the West Midlands conurbation), Wales, and rural Yorkshire and Humberside. Scotland and the major English urban areas lost population, Merseyside most of all.

People are *pulled* by the lure of jobs, of economic opportunities or of more attractive living conditions. During the same period, 1971–7, the fastest growth was recorded in small towns such as Loughborough, Taunton, Thetford or Yeovil. When Margaret Stacey returned to Banbury in the late 1960s, it was to find that the town had grown out of all recognition (Stacey *et al*. 1975).

## Emigration

During the late eighteenth and nineteenth centuries vast numbers of British subjects left these islands altogether to seek new lives abroad. Family ties remain strong with the so-called 'old Commonwealth' countries, Canada, Australia, New Zealand as well as with some newer states such as Zimbabwe (formerly Rhodesia), with former British colonies such as the United States, Israel or South Africa, and even with some countries which have never been under British rule, notably Argentina.

A revival of emigration in the 1980s is the clearest proof of social dissatisfaction. In 1984−8 more people entered the United Kingdom than left it, but in 1988 itself more people left than entered. However, in each of the three five-year periods since 1974 there has been a net outflow of British citizens from the United Kingdom and many of the British citizens entering the United Kingdom are from non-Commonwealth countries. In 1988 itself there was a net loss of British citizens by migration of 34,000 (*Social Trends 20*, 1990: 30−1).

## Immigration

Even in the eighteenth and nineteenth centuries port cities were distinguished by small-scale immigrant communities from a variety of ethnic origins. But in the late nineteenth century and the 1930s the main impetus to immigration came in the form of Jews and other refugees from central Europe fleeing persecution in Russia and Germany.

Then in the years of relative prosperity in Britain after the war, to 1973 substantial numbers of people from the New Commonwealth countries migrated to Britain in search of work. Initially as British subjects and fellow citizens of the British Empire there was no obstacle to their doing so. Indeed in the 1950s London Transport advertised in the West Indies for workers who were prepared to take the jobs that British-born workers preferred not to do, and they settled in the decaying areas where housing was cheap and the British-born preferred not to live. West Indian immigration peaked before 1960, and by that time immigration from the Indian subcontinent had already begun and was to peak in the mid-1960s.

As the number of black immigrants has grown, regrettably, so has racial prejudice coupled with educational disadvantage to keep them out of better jobs and better homes, and their British-born children soon found they suffered from the same prejudices (see Chapter 4). From 1962 onwards legislation progressively deprived citizens of the former Empire of the right to live or work in Britain by the introduction of quotas, and in the early 1980s the concept of 'patriality' was introduced effectively limiting the right of entry to the British born or those with British parents. Today about 6 per cent of the British population is non-white, of which about half were born in Britain. In 1988, 49,000 people subject to immigration controls were accepted for settlement in the United Kingdom.

# Town and Countryside

People are moving out of the inner cities and into the suburbs; those who can afford it are going even further afield, into the countryside, creating a new kind of social phenomenon, the picture-book Dorset or Cotswold village with stone walls and thatched roofs, inhabited by well-to-do members of the middle classes who commute to work in nearby towns. But in such *commuter villages* there is a culture clash, as R. E. Pahl discusses in *Urbs in Rure* ('The city in the countryside', 1965) between indigenous village inhabitants and the commuter

**Community in the Cotswolds**

> It might seem odd, then, that one of the chief concerns of the Cotswold District Council is a topic known to sociologists — and increasingly to politicians who seek the country vote — as rural deprivation. Who is being deprived and of what? The short answers are (a) the poorer sections of the native population, and (b) houses, mobility, schools, telephone boxes, shops. Technology and money are to blame. For every hundred men who worked the Cotswold land at the turn of the century, five may now be employed. Families quit their tied houses, which were bought as retirement homes or weekend retreats. The incomers had cars and telephones and shopped elsewhere, buses grew emptier, trade fell away at the coin-box and the local store. Many incomers did not have children. Desks at the local school went unoccupied.
>
> For a time none of this seemed to matter too much. And, then, in the seventies, came the balancing of the books. The Department of Education decided that a school with fewer than twenty pupils was not a viable proposition. Transport authorities looked with alarm at a bus which took two women, six miles, twice a day. The GPO decided that a telephone kiosk that collected under £145 a year did not pay for itself in maintenance costs. The storekeeper became despondent at a weekly turnover of fifteen Mars Bars and six small tins of Spaghetti Hoops. Schools and stores closed, buses vanished, telephone kiosks stayed vandalised.
>
> Meanwhile — and quite perversely — the prices of humble village houses reached heights which put them well outside the buying power of the people who needed to live there. Today the Cotswolds' population is actually rising, but that simple statistic (62,000 people ten years ago, 68,000 now) disguises an important social change. The poor are moving out and the rich are moving in.
>
> (Jack 1988: 155–6.)

families, and in extreme cases those who would formerly have worked on the land can no longer afford to live there at all. Pahl's study of 'Dormersdell', a commuter village in Hertfordshire, showed deep social cleavages between the commuters and the remaining locals. The locals resented the newcomers and certainly did not accept them as a substitute for the old gentry; the irony being that in their search for community commuters have helped destroy the very thing that they were looking for.

But they have not done so unaided. What they were looking for was a nostalgic picture of an idealised countryside. But as W. M. Williams' (1963) study of 'Ashworthy', an agricultural community in Devon, documents, time has been steadily moving on since 1949 and the country has undergone social change as great as has the town. Town and country are linked in a national process of change. Howard Newby (1980) points out, and the television 'soap opera' *Emmerdale* increasingly reflects, the key role of *intensive farming* in bringing about profound changes in the countryside which strike at the very foundation of the old division between town and country. The large farmer of today is an 'agri-businessman' for whom the computer is more important than the combine harvester and EC subsidies balance the books that crop and livestock sales fail to keep up. Other country people are better off than ever before but they lack mobility and so they lack opportunities the urban dweller takes for granted. The real division is between the 'haves' and the 'have-nots'. Worst off are the remaining rural workers, who have been schooled to be 'deferential', and whose poor pay offers them no hope of ever becoming landowners in their own right (Newby 1977).

## Problems of the Inner City

At the same time the inner city, or the inner city ring (area around the business centre), has come in most cases to be inhabited by low-income groups, as predicted by the Chicago School model of Park and his colleagues. Once thriving manufacturing areas were hit by the decline of stable industries, such as the docks, shipbuilding, traditional manufacturing and textiles. In addition, advanced technology made the craft industries and other small-scale production units in areas like the East End of London obsolete and uncompetitive. People moved out. Between 1961 and 1971 almost 100,000 people left the London Borough of Tower Hamlets. Those who remained were drawn, disproportionately, from the old, socially disadvantaged, unskilled and semi-skilled workers. It was into these areas that the New Commonwealth immigrants of the 1950s and 1960s moved in search of housing at affordable prices.

Where possible, the centre and inner city zones were redeveloped as office and service areas. Comprehensive redevelopment of this kind favoured the creation of huge new estates for the former residents, and these centred on 'high rise' blocks which had previously been thought technically impossible. But the architects' and planners' dream of 'living in the sky' proved to be a mirage, and after the partial collapse in 1968 of Ronan Point, a 22-storey system-built block in Newham, 'tower blocks' went out of fashion and no more were constructed. By then it had already been learnt that high rise blocks made a sense of community virtually impossible, since they were quite unsuitable for small children who could not play safely outside unsupervised. Even such an apparently small detail as the fact that youngsters were too small to reach the top buttons on the lift control panel was a problem, since it meant they had to rely on the co-operation of unknown adults to get back 'home'.

The medium-height cliff-like structures that replaced them were also criticised for the lack of community spirit, which was blamed for the prevalence of vandalism. Certainly, the new housing was generally an improvement in the material, if not the aesthetic sense. But other factors contributed to the outbreak of riots in Brixton and elsewhere in 1981, and though Broadwater Farm and similar estates were later recognised to have dark corners and overhead walkways which facilitated crime, they did not necessarily lack a sense of community.

## The Crisis in the Cities

The new interest in urban sociology in the 1960s in the United States was closely associated with this phase of large-scale state intervention in urban areas to redress what the planners saw as generations of neglect. Backed by substantial financial resources, the planners could direct resources towards some groups and away from others, and urban sociologists (among others) sought to analyse how and why this happened. As disillusion grew and resources were diverted into the Vietnam War, political attention shifted to the ways in which politicians determined priorities, while urban sociologists increasingly focused on how communities responded to the shortage of resources in individual localities. These trends were followed (at a respectful distance) by sociologists in Britain. There, however, the state had always been much more powerful and its central role in determining urban policy taken for granted.

Many were therefore receptive to the argument of the Spanish Marxist writer Manuel Castells (1977) in which we can see both the influence of the French Marxist philosopher Louis Althusser and the events of 1968. Castells rejected the explanation of urban life based on individuals, groups and their interaction, in favour of a *structuralist* explanation. He argued that cities were not significant sociological entities which could be studied in isolation from the study of capitalism as a whole. They were important, but that was because they had a fundamental role to play in capitalism as *spatial units of collective consumption*. For Castells, the city was the vehicle by which the state provided the labour-power required by private industry. Since it was becoming increasingly expensive to do this, governments were trying to reduce their commitments and the result would be the radicalisation of large sections of the urban population.

In fact, of course, the crisis of government revenue in the mid-1970s was the direct result of an external event, the first oil shock of 1973, and the consequence in Britain was not radicalisation, but a marked shift to the right in political support. More traditional Marxist critics pointed out that cities were not just units of consumption but places of production. Even socialist societies would have to have cities, and indeed Eastern Europe was (as it later turned out) already experiencing many of the same problems of over-concentration of population as had earlier been experienced in the West. Non-Marxists rejected the claim that their thinking was 'ideological' and pointed out that there was and could be no evidence for Castells' structuralist view. By 1983 Castells had rejected his own earlier position (Castells 1983).

Certainly in the 1990s the expected polarisation of rich and poor in the city has not yet occurred. What has happened is that there has emerged a small but distinct *underclass* (see Chapter 12) of the very disadvantaged, concentrated mainly in the cities. But this group has little bargaining power and has been largely ignored by government policy. Meanwhile the crisis of the cities has been overlaid in public consciousness by a feeling of being better off generated in large part by the sale of council houses, continued tax incentives for owner occupiers and the substantial inflation in house prices which averaged between 11 and 15 per cent annually between 1965 and 1979 (Farmer and Barrell 1981) and was further fuelled by the free market policies of the mid-1980s. Home-ownership brings with it not only marked financial advantages, including the ability to borrow for improvements, but also an important if intangible sense of one's own worth.

However cross-national surveys show that British respondents still strongly support welfare measures and are much less attracted to the idea that social differences are necessary for economic growth than, say, Americans or Australians (Smith, in Jowell *et al.* 1989). And in fact, the 1980s have seen growing concern on the part of the Church about social conditions in the inner cities, and the Prince of Wales (1989) has called for architects to put community needs and aspirations first.

## Demographic Patterns in the 1990s

The population of the United Kingdom grew steadily from 50.3 million in 1951 to 55.9 million in 1971. The birth-rate peaked in 1965 and by the mid-1970s Britain's birth rate (like that of France in the inter-war period) had dropped to the point at which the population was actually falling. The popularity of smaller families was so marked elsewhere too that a former French Prime Minister, Jacques Chirac, remarked: 'In demographic terms, Europe is vanishing' (*The Guardian*, 15 November 1989). The expected impact of the fall was used as the reason for substantial cuts in education and other age-related services. However, by the mid-1980s the situation looked very different, and in 1988 the UK population, estimated at 57.1 million, was projected to grow to some 60 million by 2011, as the youngsters born around the new peak in the early 1980s grow up and have families of their own (see also *Social Trends*, 1990: 14).

United Kingdom

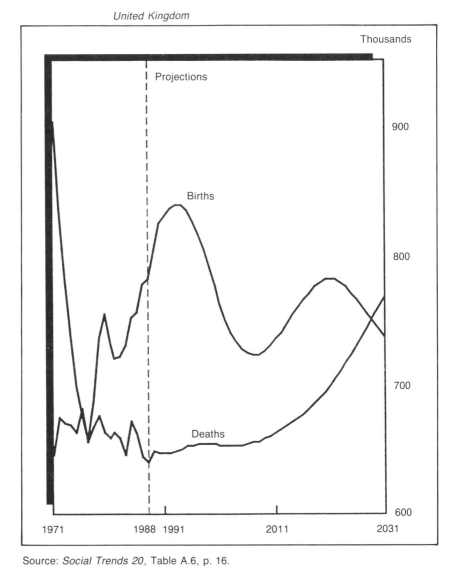

Source: *Social Trends 20*, Table A.6, p. 16.

Figure 7.2   *Births and deaths, 1971–2031*

The proportions of different age-groups in the population are also changing and are set to change further in the foreseeable future. By 1988 there was a smaller proportion aged under 16 in the population and a higher proportion aged 65–79. There has been a steady trend towards an older population since 1961 and this trend is continuing. The younger working population (16–39) is expected to decline gradually after the early 1990s while the older working population (40–64) continues to increase. This in itself would not be a cause for concern were it not for the fact that the number of people of pensionable age is also growing and can be expected to grow more quickly after the turn of the century (see also Chapter 12).

Hence employers, who often supported the drastic cuts in taxation and educational provision in the 1980s, are already complaining about the shortage of skilled youngsters as the low birthrate of the late 1970s shows up in fewer people going into higher education and coming into the labour market. At the same time, pressure for more places for the elderly is already emerging as a major challenge facing the National Health Service, alongside the capacity to recruit youngsters for nursing training to take care of them.

One early effect of the decline in the number of school-leavers has been to spur a new interest among employers in recruiting women. Since 40 per cent of women with dependent children (and 80 per cent of single mothers with children under five) do not take paid employment, they are also taking a fresh look at the need to provide childcare facilities to enable them to continue in work. Thus far tax concessions (introduced in 1989) have only extended to workplace nurseries and then under fairly stringent conditions (see also Chapter 4).

## Problems of an Ageing Population

Britain has by no means the best life expectancy in the world, but in 1988 a female child at birth could be expected to live to 77.5 years and a male child to 71.7. Depite the uncertain prospect presented by the AIDS epidemic, these figures were projected to rise to 80 and 75 by 2011 after which they were expected to level off at about 81 and 76. These are conservative estimates: in 1988 the expectation of life at birth in Japan had already reached 80.5 and 74.8 respectively, and in the United States 78.2 and 71.2. On the other hand, the average life expectancy at birth for a child born in Sierra Leone in West Africa was only 42 years.

The social effects of an ageing population are far-reaching. A fundamental problem is that as the proportion of people of pensionable age increases relative to the working population they have to be supported by taxing fewer and fewer people who are in work. Allowing people to work longer would be one possible solution, and elderly congressmen have already argued successfully for that in the United States. But in Britain the prospect is rather of more and more people having to take early retirement as the long-term decline of British industry continues.

Looking further ahead, the growing problem of caring for some elderly people is going to increase disproportionately. In 1988 there were nearly half as many people again in the over-80 age-group as in 1961, and the proportion had grown from 2 to 3.5 per cent of the population. Of course, those that are fortunate may well continue for many years yet to enjoy a good standard of life, but quality of life is very much class-related, especially so in retirement when company pensions become so important, and generally age does bring the increased risk of chronic disease and debilitating accidents. It also sadly brings another problem,

Table 7.2 *Life expectancy, selected countries, 1985–90*

| Country | Both sexes | Males | Females |
|---------|------------|-------|---------|
| Sierra Leone | 41.0 | 39.4 | 42.6 |
| Afghanistan | 41.5 | 41.0 | 42.0 |
| Ethiopia | 44.0 | 42.4 | 45.6 |
| India | 57.9 | 57.8 | 57.9 |
| Iraq | 63.9 | 63.0 | 64.8 |
| Mexico | 68.9 | 65.7 | 72.3 |
| USSR | 70.0 | 65.0 | 74.2 |
| Sri Lanka | 70.3 | 68.3 | 72.5 |
| Argentina | 70.6 | 67.3 | 74.0 |
| Israel | 74.5 | 73.6 | 77.2 |
| *United Kingdom* | 75.3 | 72.4 | 78.1 |
| United States | 75.9 | 71.9 | 79.0 |
| Switzerland | 77.1 | 73.8 | 80.4 |
| Japan | 78.3 | 75.4 | 81.1 |

Source: *World Population Prospects, 1990*, United Nations Department of International Economic and Social Affairs, New York, 1991.

the problem that relatives who earlier would have been glad to volunteer to look after their elderly parents or relatives may by then have died, or if still alive be no longer physically capable of doing so.

Quite a number of people move home when they retire, and this tendency has been growing in the past decade, despite growing evidence that the additional trauma of moving at what is, for men in particular, a very stressful time can have a serious effect on their health.

# Regional Differences: the North/South Divide

The drift to the south-east, such a marked feature of the 1980s, was expected to continue in the 1990s. The population of Greater London, Scotland, Wales and the North of England outside the metropolitan areas is, therefore, expected to remain static, while an increase of over 0.5 per cent a year is expected to take place in East Anglia, the south-west and the south-east outside Greater London. The effect of the opening of the Channel Tunnel in 1993 is only likely to make matters worse, the more so since the rail link will not be ready until 1998 at the earliest. Already concern is being expressed in parts of rural Hampshire and Dorset as to the probable impact of the estimated one million new houses the government hopes to see built in this region in the coming decade. However the recession of 1989 has hit the south-east harder than other areas and may delay, though it will hardly stop, the rising pressure on housing in the region.

The upgrading of Islington and Limehouse in the 1970s and the London Docklands Development in the 1980s in very different ways show how urban areas can be made attractive and encourage people to return to the inner cities.

These facts, like the New Town story, support Brian Berry's (1976) thesis that people move, when they can, in search of what he calls *amenity-rich environments*. So too does the success, which is even more remarkable, of strife-torn Northern Ireland, where the population increased overall throughout the 1980s, in attracting executives and new businesses since 1969. However, the pressures on the south-east, in the view of those who live there, are significantly degrading the environment which they came to seek. The top British city in a survey (1990) of the world's 100 largest metropolitan areas by an American environmental organisation was Manchester, rated 8th, well ahead of London (28th), which ranked behind Birmingham, Paris, Madrid, Berlin and New York. Indicators taken into account in this calculation included housing density, water and power supply, drainage, communications, education, public health, traffic flow and noise levels, and public safety (Population Crisis Committee, *Life in the world's 100 largest metropolitan areas*, reported in *The Guardian*, 29 December 1990).

## Economic differences

Analysis by social classes shows how many regional differences reflect long-standing patterns of inequality, rooted in differential economic conditions.

Particularly significant in the discussion of the regional divide is the impact of government economic policy, which in the early postwar years was deliberately targeted to try to improve conditions in the poorer regions of the country. However, the issue was complicated by the apparent inability of successive governments to cope adequately with the crisis of the inner cities. The 1974–9 Labour governments accepted not only that postwar planning policies had not helped, but also the far more sweeping generalisation that they were the actual *cause* of the crisis (Rees and Lambert 1985). With the return of the Conservatives in 1979, therefore, the use of planning as a tool to counteract unfavourable social trends was largely abandoned, and with it most of the effort that previous governments had put into promoting economic growth in the more peripheral regions of England, such as the south-west and the north-east. Northern Ireland, for security reasons, remained a notable exception, and Wales and Scotland continued to benefit from development money from the regional fund of the European Community. There emerged a clear North–South divide, along a line drawn from Bristol to the Wash, and in the mid-1980s the most rapid development of the new 'sunrise' industries took place in a quadrilateral south of the M4 corridor taking in Poole and Portsmouth and in Cambridgeshire. Only towards the end of the decade did the North begin to share in the boom years, though when recession came, ironically it had a far greater *proportionate* effect on the relatively prosperous South.

Geographers warn, however, that very significant changes are taking place within regions, which must not be overlooked. The deindustrialisation of the great northern conurbations hit many smaller industrial centres also. But a significant

Table 7.3   *Head of household by social class and region (percentages)*

| Region | Social Class | | | | | |
|---|---|---|---|---|---|---|
| | I | II | IIN | IIIM | IV | V |
| N. Ireland | 3.2 | 18.8 | 7.7 | 23.6 | 10.6 | 4.8 |
| Wales | 3.7 | 16.6 | 7.5 | 26.6 | 11.8 | 4.5 |
| Scotland | 4.2 | 16.4 | 8.4 | 27.3 | 13.2 | 5.0 |
| North | 3.5 | 14.6 | 7.6 | 29.8 | 13.0 | 5.3 |
| North-West | 4.1 | 16.8 | 8.7 | 26.7 | 13.5 | 5.0 |
| Yorks & Humberside | 3.3 | 16.9 | 8.0 | 28.8 | 13.2 | 4.4 |
| West Midlands | 3.8 | 17.4 | 7.8 | 29.4 | 14.2 | 2.3 |
| East Midlands | 3.8 | 18.1 | 8.1 | 29.9 | 13.2 | 3.6 |
| East Anglia | 4.4 | 19.6 | 8.3 | 25.6 | 12.5 | 3.5 |
| South-East | 5.8 | 22.2 | 11.1 | 23.0 | 10.5 | 2.5 |
| South-West | 4.7 | 19.9 | 9.2 | 23.8 | 10.9 | 3.1 |

Source: *Regional Trends*, 20, 1985.

number of smaller centres in the North and in Scotland were able to benefit from the partial recovery of the 1980s, while many places in the South — such as Great Yarmouth, Southend, the Medway towns, Deal and Thanet — have experienced only a prolonged period of stagnation and high unemployment.

## Social deprivation

In Chapter 6 it was noted that there are considerable differences in unemployment rates between the regions. Thus in 1985 the average rate of unemployment for the whole of the United Kingdom was 13.5 per cent, but regional figures ranged from 9.9 per cent in the south-east to 21.0 per cent for Northern Ireland (see Table 6.6).

Mass unemployment is associated with poor housing conditions and other forms of social deprivation. Scotland has the worst child accident rate in Western Europe and the rate is highest in areas such as Easterhouse, a large Glasgow housing estate, where the level of poverty can be gauged from the fact that more than 65 per cent of the children receive clothing grants. In such depressed areas many flats stand empty and fires started by vandals can spread rapidly to neighbouring apartments. Homes are overcrowded and children have little or no alternative but to play on the streets. Government restrictions on council spending have effectively ended the provision of new playgrounds and the one community centre has been burnt down. Many children are killed in street accidents while running, skateboarding or playing. They share the streets not only with motorists but with packs of large dogs and many get bitten or are the victims of assaults or gang violence (Bob Holman, 'Heirs to years of living dangerously', *The Guardian*, 27 November 1991).

## Health

Retirement is only one of a number of factors leading people to move, but it is one which most clearly shows the tendency to move towards the warmer parts of these islands and away from the cooler ones. A daytime maximum of 18°C may be seen by weather forecasters as a nice warm day in Belfast, but it would be regarded as chilly in Bournemouth. However, there are many other reasons why health considerations would suggest a move.

The epidemiology of heart disease, for example, shows that the incidence of premature deaths from this cause in both men and women in the industrial North is more than twice that in the South. Measured by the standard mortality rate (SMR), the highest mortality in England and Wales is to be found in Lancashire, Yorkshire and Durham. For the age group 15−64, the SMR is highest in north Manchester (148) and lowest in north-west Surrey (59) (Health Education Authority 1990). Of all the major regions of the United Kingdom, SMR is highest in Northern Ireland. This is not because of violence — half as many again crimes of violence are recorded in the East Midlands — but a prime cause among men is undoubtedly the very high consumption of animal fat, and especially the famous Ulster breakfast, fried in generous quantities of lard, which locally has been described as 'a heart-attack on a plate'.

Sociological factors explain much of the variance in the incidence of heart disease. Causes include smoking, exercise and diet, all of which are theoretically under the control of the individual concerned. But what people eat, whether or not they smoke, and how much exercise they take are conditioned by the societies in which they have been brought up and live, and hence by the economic and social histories of the respective communities. Occupational hazards also play a part — stressed Surrey executives may think they are having a bad time, but statistically manual labourers are at much greater risk. Hence the higher the proportion of manual labourers, the greater the incidence of heart disease.

Consumption of alcohol contributes significantly to health problems and here too there are vast regional differences. In the North and Wales over 30 per cent of the male population can be described as 'heavier drinkers'; in East Anglia less than 15 per cent. Heavy drinking is associated not with wealth but with poverty. In turn drunkenness on the streets, fuelled by reports in the local press of street fighting and violence, leads to a perception of town centres as dangerous and hence unattractive, and leads to a further deterioration of the environment.

The impact of industrial factors is reflected, too, in the regional figures for cancer. The male SMR for lung and throat cancer for the North is 129 compared with 79 in the south-west. The discrepancy for women is even greater, from 141 to 82, reflecting the steep increase in smoking among working-class women in recent years. Such discrepancies, however, also reflect the availability and efficiency of medical treatment, and here too there are important differences. In fact, regional variations in the waiting time for NHS operations have been a major target of government criticism. Since there are also great differences between areas in the same region, the 'market' system is intended to even them out.

# National Differences — Theories of Development

The less-developed countries (LDCs) make up most of Africa, Asia and Latin America. They contain 70 per cent of the world's population but receive only 17 per cent of its income. Older theories of national differences in terms of economic development are based on a *unilinear* model of societies moving slowly from traditional to modern structures. As modernity, mainly in the form of technology, industry and capital investment, is diffused to the less-developed countries, they will, it is argued, develop greater economic capacity, become more socially differentiated, more rational and so on, rather in the way that Toennies would have predicted. For W. W. Rostow (an early theorist of economic modernisation — 1960, 1971), this process accelerates into self-sustaining growth after a certain stage of development (the take-off point) has been reached.

Talcott Parsons (1964) exemplifies for sociology the corresponding functionalist perspective on development in describing the stages a society goes through on its way to modernity:

1. Primitive society, e.g. Australian aborigines.
2. Archaic society, e.g. Ancient Egypt.
3. Historic society, e.g. India.
4. Seedbed society, e.g. Ancient Greece.
5. Modern society, e.g. United Kingdom, United States, France, etc.

As societies move towards modernity, Parsons argues, they display increased social mobility and division of labour; they throw up more voluntary associations such as trade unions; they are increasingly secular, have developed educational systems and nuclear family patterns. In fact, they increasingly conform to the model of the industrialised West. In apparent confirmation of modernisation theory, the transfer of Western capital and technology has produced a developmental spurt in the so-called newly industrialising countries (NICs) of South-East Asia.

Such theories have been challenged as many nations fail to develop in the manner expected. As a glaring example of economic failure, Argentina would be hard to beat. It is a sophisticated nation with many of the traits associated with a complex modern society. It reached what Rostow believed was its take-off point in the 1920s and was at that stage among the half-dozen richest nations in the world. Today it ranks 80th (*Buenos Aires Herald*, 15 July 1990). It is no coincidence that poor economic performance in Argentina and some other countries of Latin America where economic development was expected by some modernisation theorists has been accompanied by the proposal of alternative models of development.

Among Marxist critics of the functionalist model, André Gunder Frank (1978) argued that capitalism had become global, so that the rich Western nations were now the global 'bourgeoisie' exploiting the Third World 'proletariat'. Capitalism, he says, is *causing* underdevelopment, both on a global scale and within underdeveloped countries. It promotes uneven growth in the form of both national and regional polarisation. Funds flow, not from the rich nations to the poor as aid agencies would like, but rather from the poor nations to the rich, as they pay for expensive imported manufactured goods and the multinational corporations (MNCs) who operate on their territory repatriate their profits. In the 1970s this Marxist model of *dependent development* was refined into *dependency theory*.

The MNCs are the link between the rich and the poor economies. The largest 500 MNCs account for some 80 per cent of all foreign investment. Most of the largest MNCs are American and they also tend to be oil companies, e.g. Exxon (formerly Standard Oil of New Jersey), Mobil and Texaco. The top seven oil companies control more than two-thirds of the world's oil and gas.

Of course MNCs can and do raise money in the capital-rich developed world and use it to sink wells, build factories or create mines and plantations in the labour-rich LDCs. But these developments typically involve the large-scale exploitation of minerals or export crops which have a low value on the world market, while the local inhabitants increasingly find themselves buying high-value goods imported from the rich manufacturing countries. In this way the MNCs often come to be seen as milking the poorest of the world's peoples for the benefit of the rich. In Honduras (Central America) the United Fruit Company (later United Brands) of Boston created a true 'banana republic'. Their plantations on the north coast formed an *enclave economy*, which paid only modest export taxes to the government of the country in which they operated. In 1975 the President of Honduras was overthrown in a military coup after it was disclosed that United Brands had offered him $1.5 million dollars to lower the export tax on bananas by 25 cents a box (Lapper 1985). In neighbouring Guatemala, land formerly used to grow food has been converted to growing cotton for export — it will be spun and woven and made into clothes elsewhere and then reimported in the form of high-value finished goods, while a growing population goes hungry. In both cases, few people benefit in the countries concerned but the government and a handful of the ruling elite.

In Central America generally the MNCs are accused of 'cultural imperialism' ('Coca-colonisation') — raising expectations of material goods beyond the means of the society to fulfil, as advertising creates a demand for expensive consumer products, which the local inhabitants cannot afford. Worse still, some of the products may actually be harmful. Time and again MNCs have been detected selling goods in LDCs which are banned in their own countries. Perhaps the most blatant example of the unscrupulous exploitation of consumer markets in LDCs has been by the large tobacco companies, who when citizens of the rich countries of the United States and Europe gave up smoking following government health warnings, concentrated their efforts instead on poor Africans and Latin Americans, using the very same sales techniques that the rich countries had outlawed.

# Convergence

The theme espoused by modernisation theorists, that all societies tend to move from more traditional forms of organisation towards a single, more modern form, is also found in the work of Marx, Weber and Durkheim. For Marx, societies were scattered at various stages along the road leading to socialism, but all were moving at greater or lesser speed towards the same place, a place where satisfaction of material needs would rest on the large-scale production associated with industrialisation. For Weber, the tendency towards the complexity of mass industrial society increasingly required societies to move from traditional and charismatic forms of authority towards legal-rational authority and bureaucratic organisation. Durkheim saw modern society as increasingly characterised by a division of labour and interdependence. These themes are all in evidence in *convergence theory*.

Convergence suggests that all societies are *en route* to industrialisation and subsequently to post-industrial society; that similar class-structures rating professionals and technicians of various kinds above those who perform manual tasks are emerging; that similar Western-style democratic political systems will displace authoritarian and state-socialist arrangements. The emerging societies will reflect the 'logic' (or needs) of industrialism, including urbanisation, advanced technology, well-developed communications, enhanced educational opportunities and high social mobility. Increased economic interdependence and increasing cultural similarity will reduce conflict between states and make the world a more stable and peaceful place.

Of course, there are arguments that can be raised against the convergence model. There are many societies in the world that it would be difficult to see as moving towards industrialisation. Many parts of the world — Africa south of the Sahara, for example — have so little infrastructure (good roads, railways, adequate power supplies, etc.) and so many social problems (not least, feeding their populations) that industrial development must be very limited for the foreseeable future. Industrial development itself, in any case, takes many forms, and the oil-producing states of the Middle East vary markedly in social structure from the 'high-tech', manufacturing states of the Far East, such as Taiwan and South Korea. Both are different, again, from older industrialised nations. The professional and technical experts accorded most respect in any hierarchy of occupations varies a good deal too, as does the degree of status attached to education. Education is often least valued in the most industrialised nations and the convergence model does not explain this. Authoritarian and personalist rulers remain, and only when they openly and flagrantly violate international law, as in the case of the 1990 Iraqi invasion of Kuwait, do they attract much attention from the world community. The emergence of fundamentalist Islamic regimes in countries such as Iran and the Sudan has also provided evidence against the convergence hypothesis.

The convergence hypothesis depends on the assumption, first formulated in the 1950s by Rostow, that all economies are in turn capable of reaching the stage of sustainable growth. It is contradicted by the *dependency* thesis, which holds that, far from being destined to follow the same pattern of development as the industrialised countries, the LDCs are the victims of the world economic system. Their lack of development is not something natural; it is actually caused by the existence of the developed economies, which has ensured that they remain suppliers of the primary raw materials the developed economies need. Only through a major change in the balance of power in the world system and a radical shift in the terms of trade in their favour can they be enabled to break out of this condition of dependence.

However in 1973 the Organisation of Petroleum Exporting Countries (OPEC) tried to engineer just such a change by restricting production and forcing up the price of crude on the world market. Though this brought about a brief recession in Western Europe and the United States, both this first 'oil shock' and the second that followed in 1979, had a much more serious effect on the majority of Third World economies, which did not have petroleum. By 1990, despite a failure to implement effective conservation measures, the advanced industrial countries had become much less dependent on imported petroleum, and the collapse of the world coffee and sugar agreements, which had existed since the 1930s, demonstrated that similar attempts to maintain prices in other commodities were even less likely to be successful. On the other hand, the so-called 'tiger' economies of Singapore, Thailand, Taiwan and South Korea, developed in co-operation with the advanced industrialised countries on the basis of low-cost production, had brought about very rapid rates of economic growth and a substantial degree of prosperity for the peoples of those countries.

Certainly, economic development depends on a number of preconditions, and the variety of the world's states means that no one pattern is likely to be applicable to all. On the other hand, the pessimism of the dependency theorists appears to be misplaced. It is possible for states in the Third World to develop. However, in the meanwhile, for most of their inhabitants the gap between their living conditions and those of the inhabitants of the advanced industrialised countries is continuing to widen.

## Suggestions for Further Reading

Young and Willmott (1957), *Family and Kinship in East London*, is a classic study of an urban community. The transformation of Britain between 1955 and 1970 is a theme of Stacey *et al.* (1975), *Power, Persistence and Change*. Howard Newby's (1980), *Green and Pleasant Land*, discusses the real and the fictional countryside. On the significance of community, see Raymond Plant, 'Democratic socialism and equality', in D. Leonard and D. Lipsey (1981), *The Socialist Agenda: Crosland's Legacy*.

On *theories of development* see W. W. Rostow (1971), *Politics and the Stages of Growth: a non-communist manifesto*. A. G. Frank (1978), *Dependent*

*Accumulation and Underdevelopment*, puts the argument for the 'development of underdevelopment'. Not until the Club of Rome's *The Limits to Growth* (1972), however, was the aspiration to Western-style growth questioned. For an excellent and readable overview of the theoretical alternatives, try A. M. M. Hoogvelt (1976), *The Sociology of Developing Societies*, and for a thematic approach, covering key aspects of Third World development, Caroline Thomas (1987), *In Search of Security*. Other introductory books include Hulme and Turner (1990), *Sociology and Development*. and Andrew Webster (1990), *Introduction to the Sociology of Development*, 2nd edn.

# 8 Family

## Family

Many examination questions on the family deal with the nature of the modern family and how it came about:

- The origins of the nuclear family. Is it a cause or a consequence of industrialisation?
- The advantages and disadvantages of the nuclear family — a question which may sometimes be related to a comparison of two theoretical analyses, i.e. the functionalist and the Marxist interpretations of the family.
- The decline of conjugal role segregation.

Others take up the central theme of whether the institution is in decline, though different reasons for this supposed decline may be stressed, e.g.:

- Is the family now simply a unit of consumption?
- To what extent has the welfare state undermined the functions of the family?
- Consider the various factors for the rising divorce rate and/or its consequences for women and children.

## The Nuclear Family

The *family* is such a basic part of our social experience that we tend to accept uncritically the pattern with which we ourselves grew up. For many people in British society this means ourselves, our parents and our brothers and sisters. Beyond this, most of us also have another image of the 'ideal' family, the 'cereal packet family' as it is often known, consisting of a mother, a father and two children, one of either sex. This idealisation, systematised in the popular card game 'Happy Families', conceals certain assumptions, among which is one about the desirability of what sociologists term the *nuclear family*. But families are not always happy. Every family is a social construct, and this model of the 'typical' family conceals the very real diversity of experience. In fact, the supposedly 'typical' family is not only not the dominant form in our society, it is not even very common. Families consisting of a working man with non-working wife and two children account for just 8 per cent of all families. Twenty-eight per cent of all families are headed by a married couple, with or without children, and together families with no children and families whose children have reached independence account for more family groups than those with children.

Probably the attraction that the nuclear family has is that it demonstrates in the clearest possible way why families exist. The nuclear family is created in two ways: by a contract (formal or informal) between a man and a woman, which in turn gives a special meaning to the kinship ties which arise from the process of reproduction. Whereas the contractual basis of the family, the choice of spouse, is voluntary, kinship is not (Allan 1985). The expectations of kinship differ widely from society to society. Kinship is the most basic form of social security; it establishes a bond of trust and reciprocal obligations to care for one's relatives. But as the institutions of marriage and adoption show, the obligations of kinship can equally well be created by contract as by tradition and custom, and can indeed be more clearly stated.

New families, therefore, are most often created by the formal institution of *marriage*. In all known societies there are clear rules determining who may marry and who may not. In addition there are both taboos and legal sanctions against *incest*, sexual relations between close relatives. Though what constitutes an incestuous relationship is socially determined and may, and indeed does, change over time, there is general agreement that it is forbidden because sexual relations within the family group would give rise to insupportable strains. In Britain as in other formally Christian societies polygamy is also forbidden, though polygamous marriages contracted abroad by non-British citizens (e.g. in Islamic states) are tolerated.

In most societies marriage is a major *rite of passage* and is marked by elaborate ceremonies. The custom in Britain that the bride's father pays for the wedding reception is a survival of the elaborate formal exchanges of economic resources which in patriarchal societies mark the transfer of the bride from her *family of origin* to her *family of procreation*.

A new set of relationships is created when one or other of the original partners to a marriage dies leaving children and the surviving partner remarries, and increasingly when a couple divorce and either or both of the former partners remarries. In this case the children of the former marriage may have to adapt to *step-parents*, who may well have children of their own.

## Perspectives on the Family

The family has long been seen by *functionalists* as a biological necessity. In theory, it fulfils four main functions: sexual, reproductive, socialisation and economic. It enables sexual drives to be satisfied within the framework of a stable relationship. It provides for the birth and rearing of children. Even though extensive provision

Perspectives
on the family

| |
|---|
| **Functionalist**<br><br>Family is a biological necessity.<br>Four functions: sexual, reproductive, socialisation, economic.<br>Transmits culture of society to new generation.<br><br>**Marxist**<br><br>Family stems from institution of private property.<br>One function: to ensure that men can leave 'their' property to 'their' offspring.<br>Reproduces forms of capitalist society.<br><br>**Feminist**<br><br>Family is an instrument for the exploitation of women.<br>One function, the sexual division of labour: makes women responsible for housework, parenting, care of sick and old people.<br>Transmits gender differences in home to work sphere. |

is made for education outside the home, it plays a key role in fitting children for existence in a complex society, and, in so doing, establishes its members in a certain status or position in society. And even where as in modern urban society it is not normally a unit of production (as it would be in a rural, agrarian society), it nurtures the labour force, provides for the physical needs of all its members on a shared basis, and acts as a basic unit of consumption (Allan 1985; Allan and Crow 1989).

Other functions of families in traditional rural societies also exist in Britain, but the main responsibility for these has passed at various times to other institutions. Among these are care of the very sick, the provision of education and the administration of justice (social control). Religion and recreation, however, remain important adjuncts to the main functions of the family for many British households.

The *Marxist view* asserts the primacy of the economic function of the family to the exclusion of all other functions. Engels (1972) argued that the family was the result of the acquisition of private property, it was a social construct created by the growth of male dominance and the desire of men to ensure they could leave 'their' property to their heirs.

For Marx, marriage was a form of 'exclusive private property'. Hence immediately after 1917 there was a rejection of the conventional family in Russia. Though in the 1930s the Soviet Union under Stalin reasserted the identity of the family and importance of motherhood, the biological family is clearly not necessary either as a device for childrearing or as an economic unit. Israeli kibbutzim have successfully solved some of the problems of communal childrearing as well as the communal management of economic processes (Spiro 1968). On the other hand, the attempted abolition of the contractual aspect of the family did not eliminate the notion of ties of kinship.

For modern Marxists the most important thing about the family is the way in which it acts as the prime vehicle for the reproduction of the forms of capitalist society. It is central to the transmission of class as well as of gender differences.

*Feminist perspectives* on the family take up Engels' theme of subjection, and explore the wide-ranging consequences of the fundamental inequality between husband and wife. This inequality stems from traditional differences in what men and women are expected to do, or *conjugal role separation*. Whether or not these differences are narrowing, there remain four problems that are clearly directly related to them:

## Housework

Women continue to do most if not all of the housework. Even in the former Soviet Union, where women have long had the expectation of full-time employment and equal pay, when they return home it is they who do the cooking and cleaning. In England the sexual division of labour noted by Engels continues to be the norm, not only among working-class households but also in middle-class ones, which are often assumed to be more 'enlightened' (Edgell 1980; Finch and Groves 1983). Moreover, because it is *unpaid labour*, housework, however hard, boring and repetitious, is undervalued in social terms and disregarded in the calculation of the gross national product.

> The characteristic features of the housewife role in modern industrialised society are (1) its *exclusive allocation to women*, rather than to adults of both sexes; (2) its association with *economic dependence*, i.e. with the dependent role of the woman in modern marriage; (3) its status as *non-work* — or its opposition to 'real', i.e. economically productive, work; and (4) its *primacy* to women, that is, its priority over other roles. (Oakley 1974)

## Home and work

Home and workplace are related and interdependent spheres. But not only is the relationship between them a complex one, it also continues to be fundamentally different for men and women. Men and single women are expected to go out to work; married women are not necessarily expected to do so, though many have to do so from economic necessity. But when women do go out to work, and most do, their earnings are usually lower and, if they are married, seen as additional to the basic support of the household (Hunt 1980; Cunnison 1983). At work, women remain primarily concerned with home and family in a way that men apparently are not (Westwood 1984). Some feminists argue, therefore, that gender differences at work are the direct product of gender differences in the home, and that the family bears the prime responsibility for creating them (Delphy 1984).

## Parenting

Prime responsibility for parenting, with all the hard work round the clock that it entails, remains with the mother, not with the father. Fathers who engage in parenting are seen as giving 'help' rather than being engaged in a social duty. However, even then, in 23 of 50 households surveyed in the London area Boulton (1983) found that the husband's 'help' was 'minimal'. Parenting takes up a very significant period of a woman's life, the first four years or so of each infant's life, which for the average family means 8 to 10 years altogether. Since these are the crucial years in which men establish their career patterns, women who return to work after child rearing are placed at a serious economic and social disadvantage.

## Social services

Women have long been expected in addition to care for the elderly and sick, a task only partly taken over by the welfare state. With an ageing population, determination of the Government to save money by a policy of 'care in the community' looks increasingly like deliberate exploitation of women.

It has been said that women are the only social group that actively co-operate in their own oppression, and many women have ambiguous feelings about child care. They may obtain great satisfaction from parenting and housework, and they may at the same time find it exhausting, exasperating and boring. However critics of the conventional division of labour have to accept that for many women it fulfils their social expectations of reassurance and stability. The numerous small and apparently trivial transactions of everyday life in the family reflect this sense of stability and continuity, which is what family life is really 'about' for men too.

# The Nuclear Family in Britain

Nevertheless the view is widespread that the family is in crisis. Given the apparent centrality of the nuclear family to modern society, a major debate centres on the nature and desirability of the nuclear family itself.

The typical nuclear family in Britain is created by the marriage of husband and wife at a fairly young age. During the 1970s the average age of marriage for men was 23 and for women 21; in the 1980s it rose slightly. The general expectation is that a newly married couple will establish a household of their own. In the past this might well have been a property rented either from the local council or from a private landlord, but in the 1980s there was a steep rise in the proportion of home-ownership and in the expectation that the family would 'pay its own way'. Husband and wife are ideally regarded as partners. They often discuss family matters together and make joint decisions. Given the increase in home-ownership the economic contribution of the wife has been increasing in importance and in many households it is now essential if the present standard of living is to be maintained. However, traditional assumptions persist in some respects, notably that the husband has a right to recreation, and may well make important decisions without consultation.

Children are where possible 'planned for', with couples choosing to limit the number of children they have to maximise the opportunities open to them and to their children. The family is 'child-centred'. It is generally accepted that the child's needs come first. And as the average family now has two or three children compared with six in 1871 or between 3 and 4 in 1900 their welfare is a major concern of the household as a family unit.

The American sociologist Talcott Parsons identified the 'isolated nuclear family' — that is to say, husband, wife and children living together in a separate household — as the characteristic unit of 'modern' society as found in the United States. He claims that it is the product of the theoretical model of 'structural differentiation' by which the family ceases to be a fundamental unit of economic production. He argues that the 'isolated nuclear family' is the form best adapted to industrial societies since it best fulfils the four basic requirements Parsons ascribes to modern industrial society. For him society's main characteristic is that it is *achievement oriented*; hence the individual is hired for his or her competence. Standards of promotion are *universalistic*. Hence industrial society is an *open class system* with mobility between classes. Therefore there must be *geographical mobility* so that each individual may move to where job prospects are best.

The isolated nuclear family's emphasis on the relationship between husband and wife, he believes, also helps avoid the collisions between values inherent in more traditional patterns of the extended family. With the move towards meritocracy, the preference for kin characteristic of the extended family would be incompatible. Hence originating with the middle-class, for whom mobility was a prime requirement, it has spread to American families generally.

Clearly, Parsons assumes that family and household are the same thing, as well as that there is in fact a sharp contrast with the 'extended family' — a larger household including one or more grandparents and perhaps unmarried siblings — of pre-industrial societies. But in Britain Young and Willmott (1957) undercut this assumption by showing that what Litwak (1960a, b) calls the 'modified extended family', an extended family living close together but not necessarily under one roof, was widespread in Bethnal Green. Their findings have been confirmed by Rosser and Harris (1965) and Bell (1968) in Swansea, as well as in studies in such diverse locations as Wolverhampton, Liverpool, Acton and Banbury. In other countries functionalists have to accept that other forms of family (polygamous, polyandrous) may be 'functional' for their particular societies. And from the United States, Sussman and Burchinal (1971) argue that the 'modified extended family' is in fact the typical form of modern societies.

In fact, the distinction between the nuclear and the extended family is in many respects unrealistic. Willmott (1988) points out that though distances between relatives may have increased, the evidence is that contacts between them have also increased, aided by improved mobility and the spread of the telephone. Hence he distinguishes further between the 'local extended family', for whom proximity is the main factor in maintaining contact, and which he believes still applies to about one-eighth of the adult population; the 'dispersed extended family', among whom contacts are less frequent but still regular (once every week or two weeks), and which is probably typical of about half the adult population, and the 'attenuated extended family', for whom kinship is less important still, but for whom it has not disappeared altogether.

The specific disadvantages of the nuclear family have also been stressed. The anthropologist Edmund Leach regarded the nuclear family's role in socialisation as essentially anti-social: 'Far from being the basis of the good society, the family, with its narrow privacy and tawdry secrets is the source of all our discontents' (Leach 1957). Specifically, it has been argued, through emphasis on hierarchy the nuclear family exists mainly to fit children to the needs of capitalist society. 'The child is not taught how to survive in society but how to submit to it' (*ibid.*; see also *New Society*, 10 October 1986). The nuclear family is also criticised especially, but not exclusively, by feminists, who see it as an instrument for both the exploitation and oppression of women (Gardiner 1976). The 1980s have certainly witnessed a highlighting of the dark side of family life in Britain, including the isolation and loneliness of women and the elderly, attacks by husbands on their wives and children, and child sexual abuse. The isolation of the nuclear family is clearly a major contributing factor to each of these social problems.

## Change in the Family

Can the nuclear family be reformed without being abolished? Possibly, but the evidence is mixed. Given the assumptions of British society, perfect equality between the partners (even if wanted by both of them) is hard to attain.

Michael Young and Peter Willmott (1975) in *The Symmetrical Family* suggest that the dominant modern form of the family in Britain is home-centred, relatively isolated from wider kinship networks and has considerably desegregated conjugal roles. They see this desegregation of roles as the most important feature and therefore term this new family pattern *symmetrical*. Some role differences do remain, but the husband and wife relationship is more equal than previously was the case.

Young and Willmott see the symmetrical family as the highest form of family evolution. It is made possible by the process of industrialisation and is more common among the higher social strata, though it is spreading down the class hierarchy according to what they term the principle of *stratified diffusion*.

Their findings were based on interviews in communities in the London area. The most dramatic changes they found, they believed, were among the working class, which they saw as changing from extended family forms to nuclear patterns.

However, though many wives have jobs outside the home in modern working-class families, Young and Willmott's own evidence suggests that they still perform most domestic functions, and feminist writers such as Ann Oakley (1972, 1974; see also Davidoff 1976) have emphasised that women still bear the burden of domestic work, are expected and indeed constrained to do so as a matter of priority over other tasks, and get little formal credit for it. On the other hand, conjugal roles have changed. More women have entered the labour market as the service sector of industry has expanded, as the birth rate has fallen and as the home has become increasingly mechanised. The shorter working week and relatively higher wages have also combined to make men more 'home-centred'.

## The 'New Man'

The media in the 1980s talked enthusiastically of the 'new man' who shared domestic duties and participated in the bringing up of the children. Not only did the 'new man' exist, but he was 'a caring, considerate and sensitive soul less interested in macho pursuits and more inclined to stay at home,' claimed the market analysts Mintel (reported in *The Guardian*, 7 February 1990). 'On the work front, women are likely to have an easier time than men' and with women accounting for 43 per cent of the workforce, 34 per cent of households in 1990 had a 'working wife'. However, Young and Willmott's prediction that the form of nuclear family in which the husband and wife are equal and share responsibilities would become the norm has not been borne out so far by later research. Martin and Roberts (1984) found that 54 per cent of all working wives did all or nearly all the housework, findings confirmed by the *Inside the Family* (1988) report. And Hunt (1980) concluded that despite the formal structure of equality pay and equal opportunities legislation, the basic principle underlying social policy in Britain as elsewhere was that men were the chief 'providers' and women principally responsible for the maintenance of the household.

## One-parent Families

Increasingly common, too, are one-parent families, persons (usually elderly) living on their own, and fictive 'families' of pairs or groups of individuals choosing to live together although not bound by blood ties. There has been much political concern at the increase in the number of one-parent families. This concern, however, does not reflect the actual importance of an increase in one-parent families (since because of mortality, unstable cohabitation and illegitimacy, one-parent families were common also in Victorian times and, indeed, throughout history; see Laslett 1979) but a well-organised political campaign for the recognition of the problems of single parents. However, since the formation of the National Council for One-Parent Families in 1973 and the Finer Report (1974),

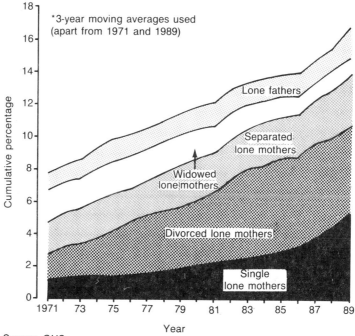

Source: *GHS*

Figure 8.1   *Percentage of all families with dependent children headed by lone mothers (by their marital status) and by lone fathers, 1971–89,\* Great Britain*

the political debate has become polarised and some recent contributions to it have been less than helpful.

The term 'one-parent family', despite its apparent clarity, is in fact an umbrella term covering a wide range of experiences (see Jackson 1982; Robertson 1986; and Hardey and Crow 1991). In 1971 only 8 per cent of all families with dependent children had a single parent. By 1988 this figure had almost doubled, to 15 per cent. The vast majority of these single parents were women: 5 per cent being single mothers, 1 per cent widowed mothers, 6 per cent divorced mothers, and 3 per cent separated mothers.

The common assumption was that this was a bad thing. In 1974 Sir Keith Joseph explicitly adopted the view, widely shared by others on the Right, that the one-parent family was inferior. He claimed: 'The balance of our population, our human stock is threatened . . . by inadequate parents, very frequently young unmarried women from social classes 4 and 5,' and argued that their children would be 'problem children, future unmarried mothers, delinquents, denizens of our borstals, subnormal educational establishments, prisons, hostels for drifters' (reported in *The Guardian*, 21 October 1974). In 1990 these ideas were revived by the then Chairman of the Conservative Party, Kenneth Baker, who, though he was careful to say 'I am not in any way trying to suggest that single parents are incapable of rearing children', blamed the rise in reported crime on the breakdown of family life, and that in turn on 'the undermining of the family by the permissive Sixties and Seventies' (Paul Barker, in *The Guardian*, 13 May 1990).

But there is no evidence at all for a simple association between single parenthood and social class, intelligence or deviance. Nor is there any evidence that children from single-parent families (and 12 per cent of all children are in single-parent families) do any worse at school than comparable children from a similar social background (Pheonix 1988). Nor did a Home Office research study in 1985 demonstrate any link between single parenthood and crime. Certainly, single-parent families are more likely to be poor, and it is their relative poverty that places them at a disadvantage. However, despite claims from the government to be supporting the family, changes in the social security system in 1988 reinforced the 'poverty trap' for single parent families. 'A lone parent has to earn a considerable sum to lift herself above the dependency on means-tested benefits' (NACAB 1989). Yet in 1990 the right-wing Centre for Policy Studies was reported to be considering the abolition of child benefit for the 8.4 million children aged between 5 and 16. At the same time, in what was heralded as a major speech by the Prime Minister, Mrs Margaret Thatcher, she complained that too many single-parent families were living on income support and laid the blame on the failure of absentee fathers to maintain their children. Subsequently, despite the obvious social problems involved, legislation was introduced to compel women to name the fathers of their children and to punish fathers if they failed to pay.

The fact is that the problems of single-parent families can more revealingly be regarded as an extreme case of a more widespread phenomenon, the unequal opportunities and the unequal returns open to women in the job market (see Chapter 4). Some 40 per cent of all women with dependent children do not have paid employment. For mothers of under-fives the position is especially difficult: only 9 per cent work full-time and 25 per cent part-time. But the employment situation for single mothers is markedly worse: 58 per cent of all single mothers have no paid employment; 80 per cent of those with children under five.

The problem begins with what Oakley (1979) terms 'the myth of motherhood'. She draws a distinction between the biological (childbearing) and the social (motherhood). Childbearing is an essential function of society, but it does not follow that those who give birth have as a result to spend a very substantial part of their lives looking after their offspring; yet this is in fact what usually happens because traditionally once begun motherhood became a full-time occupation and the full-time mother had no job to return to.

Mothers share the general expectations of society that they will look after their own children. It is therefore interesting to recall the words of Margaret Thatcher in 1954:

> There are certain factors which are essential if this dual role is to be successful. For a woman with a family there is, firstly, having trusted and competent help with

the children. Without this it would be impossible to go out with an easy mind. (quoted in *The Guardian*, 21 March 1990)

Mrs Thatcher was fortunate to be able to afford to hire a nanny, but even in the 1990s domestic help is still available to only a very small proportion of the British population. In fact, public day care for small children in the United Kingdom even today is virtually non-existent, and public and private nursery schools combined cover only 2 per cent of the nursery age group. Hence most mothers can only go out to work part-time, and the 20 per cent of single mothers who can work do so only as a result of family or other voluntary support. In 1987 it was estimated in a report to the Equal Opportunities Commission that as many as 467,000 mothers of pre-school children would return to work or work longer hours if suitable childcare facilities were available (*The Guardian*, 1 March 1990). However the most comprehensive study of its kind yet, conducted in the United Kingdom by the pressure group Kids Club Network, showed in 1990 that 'childcare for working parents in Britain is the worst in Western Europe' and there are virtually no publicly funded facilities for looking after children of primary school age out of school. In Britain only 1 child in 500 attends an out-of-school club, compared with 1 in 5 in Denmark (age 7 – 10) (*The Sunday Times*, 11 March 1990). A tax on workplace nurseries introduced in the 1984 budget was scrapped in 1990 (*The Guardian*, 20, 21 March 1990) but the government continued to take the view that such provision was a matter not for the state but for the employer. No tax relief is available to working mothers on the costs of the private child care, which enables them to work.

This situation has proved to be disadvantageous for employers also. The Midland Bank, for example, which has a largely female workforce, reported in 1990 that it cost some £14 million a year to pay for the 70 per cent of trained women staff who go on maternity leave and never return. However 90 per cent of women in the United Kingdom do eventually return to paid work at some time. Hence a number of employers (Barclays and NatWest, for example) have introduced formal career-break schemes, which will allow employees to interrupt their career for five years (or two periods totalling five years) and return with no loss of seniority or status. Such schemes usually operate on a retainer basis and involve at least two weeks' paid relief work at the company each year and refresher courses. Other employers allow extended periods of voluntary reduced time or part-time working, or arrange for 'time off' during school holidays (*The Sunday Times*, 18 February 1990; see also Cooper and Lewis 1990).

## Childhood, Adolescence and Adulthood

Like the notion of the family, the concepts of *childhood*, adolescence and adulthood are social constructs. In pre-industrial societies children took part in the work of the community as soon as they were able. 'Childhood' was an invention of the Victorians; 'adolescence' an even more recent development, originating in the United States. Both 'stages' in an individual's development are not fixed, universal reference points, but the relatively modern product of the invention of universal education. Though universal education is an essential preparation for modern industrial society, it has the unwanted effect (to the child) of retaining children in dependence on parents and teachers much longer than previously.

It is this dependence and the need for socialisation and education that is the main characteristic of childhood. Obviously the small scale of the 'cereal-packet family' presents problems for the children as well as the parents. The family may be a microcosm of society (though many would not agree); what is certain is that it is not all of society. 'Going to school', the process of leaving the home, is made much easier if it occurs in easy stages. During the school years the child's time is divided between school and the home and s/he continues to be influenced to a large extent by family expectations and values.

*Adolescence* is a term associated with rebellion against the culture of home and school and has attracted much attention from sociologists. Much work has focused on the culture of groups of young men, and the experience of the 'gang' has been the subject of a large literature (e.g. Willis 1977; see also Chapter 11). Women have different social experiences of adolescence and the way in which they form groups is significantly different from that of men (Griffin 1985). The realisation of sexuality, regarded as the norm for men, has long been and in many respects is still regarded as deviant for women, despite the fact that it is what distinguishes adolescence from childhood.

# Old Age

Just as the notions of childhood and adolescence are socially determined, so is *old age*. Prehistoric human beings rarely, if ever, lived beyond the age of thirty, and today in some Third World countries both women and men are old by their forties, if they have been lucky enough to survive to that age. However today, men in Britain may reasonably hope to enjoy some ten or fifteen years of healthy and active life after the statutory retiring age and women even more. At present the normal age of retirement for women is 60 as against 65 for men. Britain is to come into line with European Community legislation requiring equality between men and women but no decision has yet been taken on how this can be achieved.

Again, gender differences are important. As with parenting, 'caring' for the sick and the elderly (and the very elderly are often both) is seen as a duty for women rather than men. However, since women live on average longer than men, this means that what has been termed the traditional 'tricycle of care' involves three stages: 'first babies, then elderly parents, then ageing husband' (Hardyment 1990). But there is no guarantee that they will, in fact, be able to cope with the problems presented by sickness and old age. The partially paralysed, for example, have to be moved regularly if they are to avoid bedsores. In hospital this task is done by at least two nurses, but in the home it is often the responsibility of one woman, who may herself be elderly and infirm. Care of the mentally ill in the community, too, though obviously desirable in principle, can mean a wife locking herself into her bedroom at night for fear she may be attacked by her sick husband. Certainly the 'respite care' (giving time-off to carers who need a break), necessary if the community is to help share the burden of looking after the sick and the old, is rarely available.

# Marriage

Despite repeated predictions that as a social institution it is on its way out, marriage is still very popular. In 1987 Britain (and Portugal) had the highest rate of marriage within the European Community: 7.0 marriages per 1,000 eligible population, compared with 6.3 for West Germany, 5.3 for Spain and 4.7 for France (*Social Trends* 20, 2.14). By the age of 40 95 per cent of women and 91 per cent of men have married. The proportion of first marriages of men and women under the age of 29 has fallen since the beginning of the 1970s. After this age, the proportion of married people has remained steady or risen slightly. It appears that the trend towards earlier marriage which began before the Second World War has gone into reverse.

However, it is important when studying marriage, and even more when contemplating marriage on one's own account, to remember that although to the individuals concerned it is an agreement to share their lives and interests, in the eyes of the law it is very definitely a property contract. In the event of an opposed divorce marriage can have serious effects on one or other of the parties concerned. Contrary to popular belief, there are really no fixed rules as to the share-out of property on divorce and courts can do very much what they like.

Table 8.1    *Trends in marriage and re-marriage, 1961–79, United Kingdom*

| | Marriages (000s) | | | | |
|---|---|---|---|---|---|
| | **1961** | **1971** | **1981** | **1986** | **1989** |
| Total marriages | 397 | 459 | 398 | 394 | 392 |
| First for both partners | 340 | 369 | 263 | 254 | 252 |
| First for one partner | 36 | 54 | 74 | 76 | 77 |
| Second (or subsequent) for both partners | 21 | 36 | 61 | 63 | 64 |

Source: *Social Trends*, 20, 21: Chart 2.10, p. 39.

# Cohabitation and Illegitimacy

Not until 1981 was there any hard data on the number of people cohabiting. In the census of that year about 330,000 couples were reported as cohabiting outside marriage. By 1987, the General Household Survey reported 900,000 women, 17 per cent of women aged between 18 and 49, were living with a man outside marriage. In 1988 there was a further sharp rise: 21 per cent of all single women were cohabiting, as were 38 per cent of divorced men and 27 per cent of divorced women. More significantly for the future, more than half the couples marrying in 1987 had lived together first. *Social Trends* 20 (p. 46) reported in 1990:

> During the past 30 years the percentage of births outside marriage has risen steeply, stabilising only for a brief period in the 1960s, and by 1988 it had reached 25 per cent of all births. At the same time there has been an increase in the proportion of births outside marriage registered by both parents, from 45 per cent of births outside marriage in England and Wales in 1971 to 70 per cent in 1988 . . . Further, it is known that in 71 per cent of these joint registrations in 1988, the mother and father gave the same address as their usual place of residence. These figures suggest that at least half the children born outside marriage in 1988 had parents who were living together and were likely to be bringing up the child within a stable non-marital union.

Cohabitation is quite normal in other countries — largely for financial reasons, more than half of all Mexican couples, for example, are not formally married. But in Britain such relationships present two problems. First, for the cohabitees, their relationship has no legal standing, and the courts have as yet to rule on the legality of 'cohabitation contracts', so there is no clear right of support from one to the other. (On the other hand, it is this very lack of legal ties that for some people makes cohabitation an attractive option.)

Secondly, until 1990 the children of the union were technically illegitimate. Many countries have no concept of illegitimacy for a child. Though it is hard to see why a child should ever have been blamed for its parents' actions, at least it can be said that today in Britain little if any stigma now attaches. In 1981 only one child in eight was born outside marriage, in 1990 one in four. With marriage no longer an economic necessity no direct impact should occur on the child, but research still suggests that the 'illegitimate' child suffers educational disadvantages.

In 1990 Kathleen Kiernan and Malcolm Wicks, in a report published for the Joseph Rowntree Memorial Trust, predicted that by the year 2000 one in two children could be living in alternatives to the 'conventional' family (*The Guardian*, 25 June 1990).

# Separation and Divorce

A marked increase in the number of divorces has followed each liberalisation of the law. How much truth is there in the alarmist statements of the press that

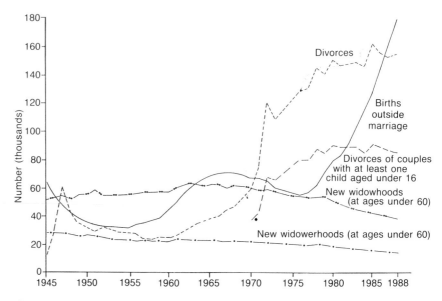

Source: Michael Hardey and Graham Crow (eds), *Lone Parenthood* (Toronto, University of Toronto Press, 1991), p. 20.

Figure 8.2 *Trends in divorce, births outside marriage and widow(er)hoods, 1945–89, England and Wales*

the overall trend represents a spectacular general increase in family breakdown?

In 1988 72 per cent of all petitions were granted to wives, over half on the grounds of 'unreasonable behaviour', a term which in the case of unopposed divorces may be very liberally construed but in the case of opposed ones may not be. When men petition for divorce, on the other hand, it is most often on the grounds of adultery. Of the marriages dissolved in 1988, 9.5 per cent had lasted under two years, 13.4 per cent 3 or 4 years, 28.0 per cent between 5 and 9 years, and 17.5 per cent between 10 and 14 years. A quarter of all divorces involved at least one partner who had previously been divorced. It is often stated on the evidence of such figures that one-third of current marriages will end in divorce. But such is not necessarily the case, and in any case divorce is not a permanent state and more than 70 per cent of divorcees remarry; men rather more quickly than women.

Why do people divorce? Personal considerations of course are important and it is certainly significant that today people live much longer than their ancestors. Since 1851 average life expectancy in Britain for men has risen from 40 to 70 years and for women from 42 to 76 years. Marriages therefore can last much longer, and a significant number break up when children leave home and partners realise that they have nothing left in common. This is reflected in the second divorce peak after 21 years of marriage. It is often forgotten that in earlier times

**The Law and divorce**

1. Before 1937 *adultery* (sexual relations between a married person and a third party of the opposite sex) was the only ground for divorce and, in the case of a woman, before 1923 she had also to prove other grounds *in addition*. The **Matrimonial Causes Act 1937** established wider grounds for divorce, but before the **Legal Aid and Advice Act 1949** divorce remained very difficult for people without financial means. The result was that many marriages remained formally in existence and could not be legally ended.

2. The rate of divorce rose sharply after passage of the **Divorce Reform Act 1969** which introduced 'no-fault' divorce. This was, in practice, a misnomer since the one *cause*, 'the irretrievable breakdown of marriage', could only be proved by one of five '*facts*', of which, e.g. adultery or unreasonable behaviour, seemed still to be held to imply 'fault'. However a divorce could be granted on the grounds of separation after *two* years with the consent of both spouses and after five without this consent. The Act when it came into effect in 1971 was followed by a peak in the number of divorces granted on basis of separation for five years or desertion. Both have since fallen back to much lower levels, though the overall number of divorces granted remained much greater than before the Act. Moreover, the government survey *Family Formation* (1976) showed divorce statistics reveal only about half of all 'broken' marriages. Of women in this survey married between 1961 and 1965 11 per cent were separated and 6 per cent divorced ten years later.

3. After the **Matrimonial and Family Proceedings Act 1984** couples were allowed to petition for divorce after only one year of marriage, compared with at least two previously. This too was followed by a record 191,000 divorce petitions in 1985, but the number of petitions granted fell back to the 1984 level the following year.

many marriages were terminated by the early death of either of the partners and that one-parent families and orphans were as numerous as they still are in many countries of the Third World. Economic independence and greater equality at work, improved birth control and smaller families, higher expectations of marital relationships, and the isolation of the nuclear family are all seen as factors which have contributed to the rise in the number of women seeking a divorce.

However there is a highly significant relationship between divorce and social class:

> Divorce rates are four times higher in social class V than among professional groups, and highest of all among the unemployed. It is impossible to contemplate such variations without acknowledging that, however 'private' the marital relationship has become, marriage in its institutional guise remains connected to the broader structures of the employment and housing markets, and indeed to the network of health and social services. (Clark 1987)

Richard Lampard, in a study of some 5,000 people in Aberdeen, Kirkcaldy, Northampton, Coventry, Rochdale and Swindon, commissioned by the ESRC, demonstrated that an unemployed married person would be 130 per cent more likely to suffer a separation in the following calendar year than would a person who had never been unemployed. Someone who had been unemployed in the past, even if now in work, is 40 per cent more likely to separate than someone who has never been unemployed. Overall, unemployment caused a 70 per cent increase in the chance of a marriage break-up in the following year (reported in *The Guardian*, 1 June 1990).

What effect does divorce have on the children of the family? Dr Penelope Leach monitored the progress of some 12,000 children born in one week in 1970 at roughly five-yearly intervals. At the age of 16, 70 per cent of them were living with both their natural parents. Of the 30 per cent who were living with only one parent, half had a stepfather or stepmother in residence. Dr Leach found no marked differences between 'disrupted' families and others — children, it seems, can be as depressed and as delinquent in nuclear families with overstressed working parents as in families that have separated. Dr Leach concludes: 'We can do much more to prevent divorces by looking at the needs of all children in society rather than by manipulating the endgame of divorce itself' (Hardyment 1990). This is consistent with the view of Martin Richards and others that divorce does affect children, but that it is the processes happening before and after separation, rather than the fact of divorce itself that are harmful (Richards, Burgoyne and Ormrod 1987).

## Is the Family in Decline?

Both the rise in cohabitation and in divorce have led some people to believe that the family itself is in decline as an institution. As has already been noted, marriage and the family are not by any means the same thing, and here, as with all other sociological debates, it is important to distinguish between the arguments and the evidence on which they are based.

The two main areas of debate are the following:

1. Whether or not people respect the family as an institution and accept the obligation to maintain it.
2. Whether or not since the state has taken over many of its functions the modern family can still socialise its members adequately and provide a secure moral and social upbringing for children.

The evidence for the view that the family is in decline is that: fewer people are recorded as formal religious believers, divorce rates are rising, marriage is no longer seen as a contract for life, partnerships in which both partners go out to work are under particular strain, more couples are living together outside marriage, and there are more births outside marriage and more abortions (Harris 1983).

Those who say that the death of the family has been much exaggerated say that: formal religious belief has been on the decline for a long time but the rise in divorce is relatively recent, divorce rates merely reflect the real rate of the breakdown of marriage more closely than in the past; a higher proportion of the population get married than ever before and most marriages do not end in divorce, the separation of partners at the workplace is equally true of the traditional family group, the majority of couples living together outside marriage have stable long-term relationships, there are more births outside marriage but in many cases the parents subsequently marry, and while the true rate of illegal abortions before 1957 can never be known it was undoubtedly very high and frequently resulted in death or permanent injury. The balance of the argument appears to be in favour of the family retaining its pre-eminence as a social institution.

# Suggestions for Further Reading

For an historical analysis of changing family patterns see Peter Laslett (1979), *The World We Have Lost*. On the family generally, see Graham Allan (1985), *Family Life: domestic roles and social organisation*; and C. Harris (1983), *The Family and Industrial Society*. S. Edgell (1980) deals with conjugal role separation among *Middle-Class Couples*. The continuing significance of home and family to women is dealt with by Sallie Westwood (1984), *All Day Every Day*; and Ann Oakley (1974) deals with the central role of *Housewife*.

C. Delphy (1984), *Close to Home*, argues that the family is directly responsible for gender differences at work, discussed further in Barker and Allen (1976), *Dependence and Exploitation in Work and Marriage*. Empirical studies of modern family life in Britain include Michael Young and Peter Willmott, (1975), *The Symmetrical Family*; the important 1988 report *Inside the Family*; and Cary L. Cooper and Suzan Lewis (1990), *Career couples* (compare Rapoport 1971). On *Lone Parenthood*, see Michael Hardey and Graham Crow (1991); and on divorce Martin Richards, Jacqueline Burgoyne and Roger Ormrod (1987), *Divorce Matters*.

# 9 Education and Belief Systems

## Education

Questions take a variety of forms, but for the most part centre on two main themes:

- Inequality and educational success, especially *class* as a source of differential achievement, but also *gender* and *race*. Students may be asked to evaluate the relative importance of the various means by which inequalities are replicated in academic success or failure; e.g. the school, the teacher, linguistic codes, etc. Occasionally, a specific example of inequality of opportunity is presented for examination; for example, social class differences in access to higher education.
- The relative importance of the various 'functions' of education, often with particular references to the transmission of cultural values. Sometimes such questions specifically identify a 'hidden curriculum'.

## Belief Systems

The main examinable areas relating to religion are:

- The functions of religion, a question which could be related to the class structure; i.e., does religious belief fulfil different needs in different sections of the population?
- The relationship between religion and social change.
- The meaning of the term '*secularisation*' has constituted a major debate and the question may be asked in the form whether secularisation has actually occurred, especially in urban Britain.
- Related to the assumed decline of mainstream religion is the growth of alternative or 'fringe' religions (*sects*)

# Socialisation

Education is part of *socialisation*, that is, the process by which children learn the values, norms, etc. of society and are incorporated in its dominant culture. Hence society's influences begin long before the start of formal education and go on long after it. However the education system remains central, for it is the means by which society consciously sets out to transmit its values and norms to a new generation.

# Brief Historical Background

Before the Reformation, education was the domain of the Church, and both *schools* and *universities* were religious foundations.

In England, schools founded in this period, such as Winchester (1382) and Eton (1440), educated the sons of the upper class as well as scholars destined for the clergy, and both went on to the Universities of Oxford and Cambridge. After the dissolution of the monasteries, especially in the reign of Edward VI, some of the proceeds went into the new *grammar schools* (so-called originally because they taught basic literacy, the grammar of the learned language of the day, Latin). Membership of the established Church, however, remained necessary for entry to the Universities of Oxford and Cambridge.

With the Industrial Revolution came the expansion of education to cater for the children of the new middle classes. Old schools were expanded and new ones, such as Marlborough and Haileybury, founded to educate the rulers of the Empire. Various Dissenting sects, such as the Quakers and the Methodists, established their own schools and academies, the curriculum of which was often more innovative and more in tune with the changing times. New Universities began to appear, free from the old requirement that all teachers be members of the Church of England; University College London (1828) was planned from the beginning as a secular organisation. But the education that was available to the poorer classes was still voluntary and limited by their ability to pay, despite the fact that in the United States free, universal public education had been established as long ago as 1777.

It was not until 1870 that *Forster's Education Act* set up a system of public elementary education in England and Wales supported by local taxation and administered by School Boards. Even then, it has been argued, the object was the 'gentling' of the masses rather than their education. Governments of the day saw education as a means of combating the high crime rate and instilling the discipline of work. But it was costly, and for the next thirty years debate continued about whether education should be controlled by local or central government. This debate is still not resolved and has recently resurfaced (see below).

The solution of the 1902 *Balfour Education Act* was to place control of education in the hands of Local Education Authorities (LEAs) but to support it with central

**Principal education Acts, 1870–1988**

| | |
|---|---|
| 1870 | Forster's Education Act<br>Established free public elementary education in England and Wales, administered by school boards supported by local taxation. |
| 1902 | Balfour Education Act<br>Local Education Authorities (LEAs) control education supported by central government grants. |
| 1918 | Fisher Education Act<br>School leaving age raised to 14<br>Voluntary schools controlled. |
| 1944 | Butler Education Act<br>National system of education, locally administered.<br>School leaving age raised to 15; nursery and secondary education brought into system; grants for higher education available. Tripartite system.<br>Ministry of Education established. |
| 1976 | Education Act (Williams)<br>School leaving age raised to 16.<br>Fully comprehensive secondary system envisaged. |
| 1988 | Education Reform Act (Baker)<br>National curriculum established.<br>Principle of 'parental choice' enunciated.<br>Local Management of Schools (LMS) and 'opting out' takes selected schools out of LEA control and places them under central government funding.<br>Central control of universities and polytechnics. |

government grants. As with so many other things, the First World War made the limitations of the existing system more obvious. In 1918 the *Fisher Education Act* cleared away the old voluntary schools and raised the school-leaving age to 14. The Second World War, with its emphasis on technological progress, raised expectations further. Following the Beveridge Report of 1943, which for the first time spoke of education as a right, the *Butler Education Act* of 1944 adopted a new, well-defined philosophy of education and set out a plan to achieve it.

The intention of the new Act was to establish a national system of education, locally administered, founded on 'equality of opportunity and parity of esteem', within which children would have the opportunity to develop their talents. Not only did it envisage a national system of secondary education (and raise the school-leaving age to 15) but it also made provision for LEAs to establish nursery schools and set up a system of grants to enable selected children to go on to higher education (over 18). The principle of selection by aptitude was central: at secondary level there were to be two main types of schools, 'grammar schools' for the more academic, and 'technical schools' and 'secondary modern' schools for the more technically minded. Selection was by test at age 11 or higher (the '11 +'). The effect of this was to consolidate and extend a pattern of 'sponsored' social mobility which was already well established.

On the administrative side, the 1944 Act replaced the old national Board of Education with a Ministry, which had powers and duties to co-ordinate the work of the LEAs. The number of LEAs was also reduced, the job of providing education going to county councils and county boroughs (the largest urban areas only). The London County Council formed the major concentration of expertise in the country and pioneered many developments. With the reorganisation of local government in the capital after 1964 the powers of the old LCC were transferred to a special-purpose Inner London Education Authority (ILEA), and with the disappearance of county boroughs in 1973 the counties remained the only direct providers of education.

The 'equality of opportunity and parity of esteem' proposed by the 1944 Education Act failed to materialise, however. Richard Rose (1969) remarks that the education system, far from promoting the meritocratic ideal, has not encouraged mobility and acts instead as a conservative force preserving existing social divisions when it 'implicitly transmits cultural norms concerning inequality'. The hallmark of academic 'success' was represented by the old grammar schools and both middle-class parents and middle-class children tended to treat 'failure' in the 11+ as a sign of 'failure' overall. This feeling was reinforced by the tendency of the secondary modern schools to adopt a grammar-school 'style', reinforcing the feeling that they were at best a second-rate alternative and at worst a dumping ground for unwanted children until they could be removed from the system altogether at the school-leaving age. The fact that working-class children were under-represented in the grammar schools was thought in part to be caused by the nature of the 11+ itself — being a test of verbal and numerical reasoning it tended to favour middle-class children.

Concentration in the primary schools on preparation for the 11+ distorted the curriculum; the top stream were taught to pass it. But the rigid criterion of performance at 11+ was unfair to those children who were late developers, or who for one reason or another had been under performing, since, once they had been sent to a separate school, they found it difficult if not impossible to regain entry to the grammar stream. This led to pressures for change to a *non-selective system* (Ford, Julienne 1960; Jackson and Marsden 1962; Douglas 1964).

First pioneered in Leicestershire (hence 'the Leicestershire plan') the new system was known as *comprehensive education* and was based on large, multi-purpose 'comprehensive schools' at secondary level. Entry to these was automatic at the appropriate age. Thereafter pupils could in theory pursue an individual route suited to their particular talents. In 1965 the incoming Labour Government, through Department of Education and Science circular 10/65, ordered LEAs to prepare plans to replace their existing system with one that was fully comprehensive. The process took a long time and was interrupted on more than one occasion by political changes at Westminster. The 1976 Education Act made it compulsory for LEAs to reorganise their provision of schools on a fully comprehensive basis, but many of the old grammar schools left the state system altogether (Lodge and Blackstone 1982).

The changeover was still incomplete when the Thatcher Government took office in 1979. Since then areas such as South Bucks and Bournemouth have been able to retain their grammar schools. On the other, hand more grammar schools have disappeared since 1979 than under the previous Labour Government. Before discussing these and other more recent developments, it will be helpful to consider what education does and what the main sociological perspectives on it are.

# Perspectives on Education

## Functionalist

In a functionalist perspective, education serves a number of *functions* in society, the balance varying from one society to another.

**Perspectives on education**

---

### Functionalist

- Socialisation — teaches how society works.
- Social control — establishes norms of good behaviour
- Economic — trains for work.
- Selection/mobility — selects for different opportunities.

### Marxist

- Economic — reproduces capitalist society.
- Social control — teaches hierarchy, the division of labour and subordination/superordination.
- Selection/mobility — social closure excludes contenders for power
- Socialisation — teaches official ideology; for dominant class establishes 'banks' of cultural 'capital'.

---

### *Socialisation*

Education is the formal part, but only part, of the process of *socialisation*; the way in which culture (in the sociological sense) and social values are transmitted from one generation to another. By this process 'understanding' of the society in which one lives is established.

### *Social control*

There is, however, also a 'hidden curriculum'. The understanding of society transmitted by education is the 'official version' of the way in which that society works. It has the specific function of establishing norms of good behaviour and obedience to *authority*, and the wider function of creating a *framework of ideas* which make this acceptance of authority easier. This framework, termed *ideology*, is central to Marxist interpretations of education (see below).

The realisation that existing education systems act in this way has led some educationists, notably Ivan Illich and the Brazilian Paulo Freire, to argue that such systems should be reshaped or replaced by ones that will encourage a more critical attitude to the world. Ivan Illich (1973) focused his criticism on the central institution of education, the school. His well-known call for the 'deschooling' of society reflects his argument that the school defines what is knowledge. It does not, therefore, allow the student free range to explore the real nature of the society of which it forms a key part. To understand society, and to learn how to make use of education, one must first break free from the influence of the school. Freire (1974) calls this process, by which the child or adult is led to develop a critical awareness of the social order and of the world, *conscientisation* — an awkward word, which is only marginally more pronounceable in Freire's native Portuguese. Freire's work has had a great impact on education in Third World countries, particularly in the development of literacy programmes for adults, for whom standard primary school reading texts have little relevance.

### Economic

Obedience to authority is in turn closely related to the function of education to prepare children for economic life. Central to this task is *training* of children in specific skills (reading, writing, numeracy, computer literacy, design, craft, etc.), which are required by existing jobs in industry. However *education* goes beyond mere training; in a world in which industrial processes are rapidly changing and new skills emerging, education must provide the child with the ability to *respond to changing circumstances*. The problem is that this may, and does, involve potential challenges to established work-practices and existing patterns of authority, both in the school and in the workplace. Once established, patterns of education can be very difficult to change. Though the relationship between education and socio-economic development is by no means clear-cut, in Third World countries at least education is highly valued because of its association with economic progress, even though only developed countries can afford advanced educational systems.

It is not necessarily an easy matter, however, to determine what a society really 'needs' in the way of education. The more rapid the change, the harder it is to predict, and those entering working life today may expect to have to retrain and/or to change course on one or more occasions before their retirement. Following themes originally developed by Max Weber, however, it has been the working assumption of British education since 1944 that a modern, bureaucratic society 'needs' meritocratic, vocationally orientated, mass education.

### Selection/Mobility

By 'meritocratic', as we have already seen, is meant a system in which all children have the opportunity to obtain qualifications appropriate to their ability and (which is not necessarily the same thing) to use those qualifications to obtain jobs appropriate to their skills. Talcott Parsons regards a major function of the education system, therefore, as being to allocate roles in society (see also Davis and Moore 1945).

Critics of these assumptions say that such qualifications tend to become an end in themselves and are not necessarily related to work needs. Thus knowledge of Latin, a necessary requirement to those training for careers in the Church in the middle ages, was still a requirement for entry to science courses at Cambridge in the 1960s. Conversely, students may choose programmes of study, not because of their real importance to society at large, but because they offer prospects of high social standing or substantial economic gain. Thus in many Third World countries able students among the elite gravitate to the study of law rather than to chemistry, engineering, medicine or veterinary science, even though the latter skills are often in critically short supply.

## Marxist

Marxist interpretations of education stress the centrality of power relationships in education. The school is a hierarchical organisation, like the society of which it forms a part, and the teacher—pupil relationship is a model for the relations of power and superordination/subordination in society at large, backed as it is by the support of other teachers, school organisation and the law.

Durkheim like Marx recognised the need for society to pass on dominant values in this way. However Marx himself, living in the mid-nineteenth century, saw religion rather than education as the main vehicle for socialisation. Only after the development of modern systems of education did later Marxists recognise their importance as vehicles for the reproduction of capitalist society. For example, the system of competitive examination so characteristic of French education reflects the individualistic and competitive values of a capitalist society. In the United States Bowles and Gintis (1975) used the Marxist idea of alienation to define the role of the school in preparing children for capitalist society. The power relations students encounter in school, they argue, are a reflection of and a preparation for the social relations of work that they will find when they leave school. Pupils come into contact for the first time with the concepts of *hierarchy* and the *division of labour*. Both form essential features of the organisation of modern capitalist enterprises.

The French Marxist philosopher Louis Althusser centres his analysis on the concept of *ideology*. To survive, he argues, the authorities must either resort to repression through the use of force or they must establish and/or control the ideological state apparatuses (ISAs) which teach people to accept the existing order of things. The ISAs do this by establishing the framework of class relations, which, once incorporated in the student's thought, acts as framework of reference in interpreting the possibilities and limitations of society. Since this acceptance is (or becomes) 'voluntary', it is highly effective.

The French educational theorist Pierre Bourdieu (see Bourdieu and Passeron 1974) develops the theme of schools in capitalist France serving the interests of the bourgeoisie. For him, schools are, as it were, banks of 'cultural capital' — information, skills and techniques which enable the individual to make use of the institutions of capitalist society. Children of the middle classes, with cultural capital, he argues, do well in the system. However, the examinations which serve as markers of educational attainment also become part of strategies of social closure by which the middle classes assert their cultural dominance and exclude potential challengers for social or political power.

His concept of the 'cooling out' of students who do badly at school, and the notion of 'learned ignorance' as the process by which schooling defines the working class and confirms its subordination, finds its echo in Britain in Paul Willis's *Learning to Labour* (1977), which combines Marxist and phenomenological perspectives, was extremely influential in educational thought in the early 1980s and remains a key text.

## Other Perspectives

In recent years there has been increasing criticism of the fact that neither the traditional functionalist perspective, nor most Marxist writing, treated women in education as anything other than as a subset of men, and often failed to observe their existence at all (Acker 1981). *Feminist* perspectives emphasise not only the differences between the sort of education men and women receive, but the way in which education reinforces the differences between the sexes and acts to reproduce gender relations in society as a whole. Education has more easily, perhaps, been recognised by politicians and others to be an integral aspect of *race relations*, and this aspect has already been considered in Chapter 4.

# The Sociology of Knowledge

The conflicting views of the nature of society exemplified by the positivist and phenomenological perspectives again confront each other on the question of what constitutes knowledge. Indeed the question of whether there can be objective social facts susceptible to scientific investigation is the core issue in the sociology of knowledge. A key element in the positivist approach is that the social scientist is objective and relies on empirical evidence. The sociology of knowledge questions the status of social facts, whether they can ever be more than interpretations.

In sociology, the questioning of the nature of knowledge has derived from a variety of sources and developed in several different ways. For both Durkheim and Marx, there was an area of scientific knowledge superior to beliefs and ideologies, which could be identified and used to explain human society. But even for them, social structure was a source of human ideas and knowledge. Both contribute to the sociology of knowledge, Durkheim through stressing the transmission of culture in the process of socialisation, though it is Marx' work which was a major source of developments in this field. Marx held that knowledge was distorted into ideology which could then be used to justify the prevailing economic structure. In other words, in a capitalist society, the dominant ideas would be those sympathetic to the capitalist system. The exception to this distortion of knowledge was 'scientific socialism', which did not need ideology because there were no class interests to express.

Weber's contribution to the sociology of knowledge again reflects the complexity of Weberian thought. He at once had sympathies with those who sought to make social science objective, but he could not accept that a social scientist could ever achieve this ideal. He saw all social knowledge as reflecting particular points of view and social scientists who claimed otherwise were deceiving themselves. It was this naive self-deception which was dangerous to social science.

Phenomenology has also provided strands of thought from which this school has developed. George Herbert Mead's (1934) idea that primary socialisation causes a child to see the society around him at that time as an objective reality, at least until he is older and comes into contact with other societies, provides an important theme. The child accepts the subjective definitions imposed on him as objective and develops his identity from them. He assumes the rules with which he is presented are objective because they are external to him. He cannot have an understanding of the compromises between individuals which produced the tentative and temporary rules presented to him.

For Mead and for the symbolic interactionists who followed him, the instrument for the transmission of what is seen as knowledge was language. Linguistic symbols enable each generation to obtain the knowledge already acquired by society without having to rediscover it all. Hence each generation has a base from which to go on to discover new knowledge, it need not waste its time on that which someone else has discovered previously. Significant others (those around him who socialise the child) are the audience which encourages or discourages action according to the rules of subjective reality. They set limits on the creation of new knowledge. It is the emphasis on the subjectivity of reality and the development of knowledge within small groups of significant others which sets the phenomenological contribution to the sociology of knowledge apart from that of the positivists.

Marx's work was taken up and extended by Karl Mannheim (1893–1947) working at the Universities of Heidelberg and Frankfurt until the rise of Hitler led him to seek refuge in Britain. Mannheim did not believe with Marx that it was possible to strip away the class bias of ideology through scientific socialism to get to the base of social knowledge. Only some 'pure' sciences such as mathematics could be seen as free from their social context. For Mannheim, in *Ideology and Utopia* (1948), all other knowledge is a product of its social setting, but this does not make it a distortion of the truth. All members of society have their own perspectives dependent on their social positions and the role of the free-booting intellectual is to rise above these social attachments and seek to identify their respective perspectives.

Mannheim reflects Weberian as well as Marxist thought and the same is true of subsequent work in the area. Jürgen Habermas, for example, emphasises the importance of the individual in suggesting that external reality could be compared with and evaluated against personal standards of what is true and good (Habermas 1972).

Also within the Marxist tradition but reflecting the influence of phenomenology is Michael Young (*Knowledge and Control* 1971) whose work on knowledge has contributed much to the sociology of education. Young stresses that knowledge is socially determined, transmitted and evaluated. Thoughts and beliefs, both conscious and unconscious, are related to the social structure. People actively construct their own way of experiencing life. Their knowledge is subjective and will vary over time. Knowledge cannot be objective as it is not static, it is a negotiated process. For Young knowledge and social power go together. Knowledge is controlled, both in terms of what is defined as knowledge and by limiting access to that knowledge. Control over knowledge leads to social power. Social power and control over knowledge are reflected in the class structure of society. A changing class structure is accompanied by changes in the nature of knowledge. It could be argued within this framework that the enhanced status of scientific, technical and business knowledge and the declining status of the classics and literature reflect the rise of the technical/commercial middle class and the relative decline in power of aristocratic interests in Britain in the 1970s and 1980s. Young's argument that the chief function of the education system is the determination of what is thought of as knowledge would appear to be borne out at least in part by the introduction of the new national curriculum.

Much other primary Marxist-inspired work on the nature and control of knowledge has been done in the sphere of education. As shown above, Pierre Bourdieu has reached similar conclusions regarding the use of the education system to maintain the dominance of certain social groups in France, and Bowles and Gintis find the same in the United States. Illich recognises similar features of education in developing societies. Likewise it has been the Marxist strand of the sociology of knowledge with phenomenological overtones which has tended to dominate the most interesting work in the sphere of deviance (see Chapter 9). The same has been true in the area of media studies, where the work of the Glasgow University Media Group (1976, 1980, 1982) and Hall (1980) have been of particular interest.

What is most obvious about the theoretical influences which have contributed to the development of the sociology of knowledge is that they cannot be clearly separated and defined. Where sociology is at its most philosophical and esoteric it is extremely difficult to disentangle the various perspectives which comprise the discipline. Perhaps the most important lesson to learn from the interconnectedness of the approaches within the sociology of knowledge is that each is interesting in it own right and should not be set aside in favour of some other narrow interpretation. Studying society blinkered by one theoretical perspective may replicate the problem illustrated in the well-known story of the blind men who seek to describe an elephant. One caught hold of it by its leg and said: 'An elephant is like a tree.' Another touched the ear and said: 'An elephant is like a sheet.' A third stroked the trunk and said: 'An elephant is like a snake.'

Each of them was partly right. But, even though it was the same elephant they were describing, none of them made sense to the others.

# Inequalities of Opportunity and Outcome

## Opportunity

The 1944 Education Act called for 'equality of opportunity and parity of esteem', and the Oxford Social Mobility Survey, reported in Halsey, Heath and Ridge (1980), showed that for those born between 1914 and 1972 there was remarkable progress for the population as a whole. 'The State selective schools, i.e. technical and grammar schools, are doing far more than merely reproducing cultural capital, they are creating it too. They are bringing an academic or technical training to a very substantial number of boys from homes that are not in any formal sense educated,' the report claimed. Many respondents — working-class sons of working-class fathers — did not see themselves as prisoners in a rigid class system. Compared with their fathers they were enjoying greatly improved pay and conditions and generally a much higher standard of living.

However the 'service class' (I & II on the 7-point Hope-Goldthorpe scale described in Chapter 3) had roughly three times as much chance of obtaining some kind of selective secondary schooling as working-class children (VI, VII). The relative chances of a working-class child staying on at school until 18 and going into higher education had actually decreased; the number of working-class entrants to university increased by only 2 per cent despite a massive increase in university places.

Why was this so?

1. There were demographic changes. The birth rate increase in the 1940s affected all social classes so that the relative size of the middle class also increased. Thus new places were filled by middle-class children.
2. The expansion of grammar schools was at the expense of technical schools. What the working class gained by the expansion of grammar schools, they lost by the contraction of technical schools. The changes merely relocated the most able working-class children.

Halsey, Heath and Ridge concluded: 'The Education Act of 1944 brought Britain no nearer meritocracy or equality of opportunity.' In fact, privileged groups have made greater absolute gains from educational expansion. Heath, in his *Social Mobility* (1981), shows that in this same period a child of the elite had a 1-in-5 chance of getting into *Who's Who*. The comparable ratio for children of higher professional/managerial parents was 1 in 200, for other white-collar parents 1 in 500 and for working-class parents 1 in 1,500. 'Silver spoons', they remarked, 'continue to be distributed' (Halsey, Heath and Ridge 1980).

## Outcome

It has to be recognised, however, that equality of opportunity, even if it existed, would not necessarily lead to equality as an end-state. *Class, gender* and *race* all influence the outcome of education as far as the individual child is concerned, and their effects are cumulative.

### Class

The problem begins at the pre-school stage. Because of the virtual absence of childcare facilities for working-class mothers, their children enter school less well prepared and throughout their school career they will continue to be at a disadvantage in material terms. At school the working-class values of the peer group work often against the dominant values of school. Anti-school attitudes are part of a social structure which provides the manual workers the capitalist economic system needs (Willis 1977). There will be strong pressure for the child to leave school at the earliest possible opportunity, in order to earn money and contribute to the family income (Bowles and Gintis 1975; Halsey, Heath and Ridge 1980). The possibility of going on to higher education is unlikely to receive very positive responses from hard-pressed families.

### Gender

Girls and boys have traditionally been directed towards a different range of school subjects, each a reflection of stereotypes of their future role in society. The problem begins with the *labelling* of girls in infancy as passive, compliant and non-aggressive, and the assumption that their main role in life will be to marry and have children. Well into the 1960s the school curriculum still reflected this distinction, with classes in domestic economy and needlework being available only to girls. The 1975 Sex Discrimination Act made it illegal to offer different subjects to boys and girls. However, both family influences and peer group pressure combine to perpetuate different outcomes, and girls are still much less likely than boys to specialise in mathematics, physics or technological subjects.

This in turn affects the take-up of places in higher education, though the overall picture has steadily improved. In 1970 women took up only 33 per cent of all full- and part-time places available in higher education; by 1987−8 the number of places in both full- and part-time higher education had increased and women accounted for 43 per cent of the total (*Social Trends 1990*, p. 59).

### Race

The Swann Report 1985 showed that black underachievement was only partly accounted for by class position. However, as discussed earlier in Chapter 4, the performance of Asian and Chinese children is comparable with that of indigenous groups, suggesting that the relatively poor performance of Afro-Caribbean children

**Mixed progress for girls in science**

The research, by Alan Smither and Pamela Robinson, shows that a sample of 595 boys on mixed [A-level] courses had 207 different subject combinations between them, and among 596 girls there were 345 variations. The sexes proved to have very different subject preferences. While maths, physics and geography were among the five front-runners for boys, biology, geography and English had that status for the girls. However, boys and girls alike most frequently chose maths.

The big divide comes with physics — taken by 27 per cent of boys on mixed courses, but a mere 6 per cent of girls. This finding supports previous research which demonstrates that physics is the least popular science among girls. One reason given is that physics is not taught in a manner sympathetic to girls' perceptions, by omitting human and social factors.

The Manchester research also shows that mixed courses have gathered momentum since the advent of economics as a A level subject. Boys in particular often take economics with physics and maths as an alternative to geography. Girls are far more likely to cross the arts/sciences divide. About half the girls on mixed courses study biology and a third English, compared with a fifth and a tenth, respectively, among boys.

Jan Harding, an equal opportunities consultant . . . received the research findings with qualified optimism. She welcomed the fact that more sixth formers were being taught to think scientifically. But her fear is that biology, particularly human biology, is often taught descriptively — leaving out the 'scientific processes' involved. This led one school inspector to call it an 'anti-science'. . . . She uses subjects chosen by boys as a litmus test for those which hold the best career prospects; boys dropped biology when there were no jobs in that field and biology now has a reputation as a 'soft science'. By contrast, in the US — where the most prestigious research is in genetic engineering — biology qualifications are at a premium, and therefore popular with the boys. Perhaps we are catching up slowly.

(Adrian Caudrey, 'Mixed progress for girls in science', *New Society*, 22 August 1986).

results from factors external to the school, such as home and family influences, as well as teacher expectations.

## The School

Few of the children of the elite in England enter the state school system. For those who can afford it, or whose children can obtain scholarships or bursaries, their choice is likely to be private education, and gender as well as class will determine their choice. In 1988 there were 2,600 independent schools in Britain with 582,000 pupils, some 7 per cent of all pupils. Though for all ages there was only a slight disparity between the proportion of boys and the proportion of girls in independent schools, after the age of 16 the difference increased and there were significantly more boys — 19 per cent as against 15 per cent (*Social Trends 1990*, p. 54).

The so-called 'public schools' are an even more select group, being usually defined as those schools whose headmasters are members of the Headmasters' Conference. Though they include older and more famous schools (Eton, Harrow, Winchester), the majority are nineteenth-century foundations. As well as boarding schools (Marlborough, Charterhouse) they include some old established day schools (Westminster, St Paul's, Manchester Grammar School) and the direct grant grammar schools which resumed their independent status after the 1976 Act. Almost all were intended originally for boys, but many have in recent years opened their sixth forms to girls, thus entering into direct competition with the small number of girls' public schools founded by the pioneers of women's education in the nineteenth century, such as Roedean and Cheltenham Ladies' College.

The continuing demand for public school places despite the cost (at the time of writing it costs just under £10,000 a year to keep a boy at Eton) reflects the value placed by the parents on social status and advancement. Segregation of pupils from those of other social classes (or economic groups) identifies them as children of the elite. The ethos of the institution gives them a common learning experience which further sets them apart. And the intensive nature of the education experience as *total institutions* make them very effective in shaping the values and assumptions of their pupils, though some retreat and a few rebel.

The term *total institution* was first applied by Goffman (1961) in his pioneering interactionist study of a mental hospital in Washington, DC. The term also applied to other closed organisations such as the military units, orphanages and prisons. They are 'the forcing houses for changing persons; each is a natural experiment on what can be done to the self'.

The authority of the institution is established from the beginning by breaking down the self and depriving the inmate of individuality. Devices for this purpose include cutting their hair, putting them in uniforms and giving them a number instead of their own name, while requiring them to accept unconditionally the authority of those set over them. A new 'self' is then rebuilt using a series of rewards and punishments designed to create submissive and manageable behaviour. The inmate may react in five different ways, ranging from 'situational withdrawal' to 'intransigence', which, however, given the range and severity of punishments available is generally short-lived. Most inmates adopt a strategy of staying out of trouble ('playing it cool'); some come to find the institution essential to them and to be unable to survive without it ('colonization') and may go so far as to adopt the ideals of the staff as their own and to become enthusiastic advocates of them ('conversion').

Critics of Goffman's ideas argue that insufficient attention has been given to people's experiences *before* undergoing total immersion (Irwin 1970), but since in the case of boarding schools they form part of a coherent view of society and their inmates pass through them before reaching maturity, their effect is likely to be strengthened rather than otherwise.

At present the special atmosphere of an individual secondary school in the state system depends mainly on social composition of the catchment area from which it draws its pupils (see also Ball 1981). Those in the better off areas will be particularly affected by the general tendency for the abler children of middle-class parents to be 'creamed off' by the private sector, or in some cases by a parallel stream of the state sector. However, there are also important differences between schools. Michael Rutter (1979) and his colleagues, in their study *15,000 Hours*, showed that 'secondary schools in inner London differed markedly in the behaviour and attainments shown by their pupils' (Rutter 1979: 178). More controversially, they ascribed these to the *dominant ethos* of the individual school; that is to say, the way in which the school was organised. However, the study was criticised as methodologically unsound on the grounds that its authors had failed to make a clear separation between home and school in their selection of variables. The cumulative effect, therefore, was to underestimate the effect of background characteristics and to overestimate the effect of the school (Hargreaves 1980: 214).

## The Teacher

The teacher is middle-class no matter what his/her social origins may be and perceives middle-class children as more 'educable'. Nell Keddie's (1973) study of a comprehensive school found that teachers consistently though subtly treated pupils differently, according to whether they were of high or low ability. She suggested that it was the very fact that middle-class children did not challenge authority that led to them being perceived as successful.

Today's teachers are more careful to avoid gender discrimination than their predecessors, though even now they tend to use gender differences as an organising principle to inculcate rivalry between boys and girls (Clarricoates 1980). However, their task is not made easier by the pupils themselves. Observation of teacher—pupil behaviour in a primary school shows that girls tend to sit in an orderly block in the centre of the classroom; boys to take up much more visible positions on the outside, from which they command a disproportionate share of the teacher's attention (French 1986). In the secondary school boys have learnt to dominate the mixed classroom, and girls have learnt to accept a lower proportion of the teacher's attention (Spender and Sarah 1980). Michelle Stanworth argues that it is for the teacher to be aware of and to seek to counteract such gender differences by, for example, given more attention to the quieter pupils, who are often girls (Stanworth 1981). A more radical view is taken by Dale Spender and Elizabeth Sarah (1982), who argue that women's education has to be made by women for women, and effectively argue for the return of segregation between the sexes in secondary schools. Though this view has some following among feminists, there is still too little evidence about the effects of pre-school socialisation or even mixed education in primary schools to be clear to judge if this drastic remedy would work even for the limited purpose of equalising educational attainment. Moreover it might well create social problems which would disadvantage women even more. Single-sex schools for *boys* have not evidently helped the cause of equality between the sexes.

# The Curriculum

All learning takes place through the medium of language. However language itself is not a constant. The work of Basil Bernstein (1961, 1973) on linguistic codes has drawn attention to the way in which education helps perpetuate the use of a *restricted code* by working-class children, which is less fitted to the expectations of school than the speech of middle-class pupils. Not only are middle-class pupils, he argues, encouraged to develop a wider vocabulary and one less closely fitted to the limited expectations of working-class employment, but their speech will therefore approximate more closely to the *elaborated code* used by those who exercise power in society.

Bernstein's argument is a structuralist one and is close to that of Pierre Bourdieu, though he has specifically rejected the idea of cultural deprivation. He has been attacked by the American William Labov (1973) for seeming to suggest that middle-class language is superior to that of the working class. But this he has denied, and in any case it is not the point of his argument.

Not only does the working-class child (especially when from certain ethnic minority groups) encounter linguistic problems, but the emphasis of the curriculum on acquiring the skills valued by higher education creates a sense of alienation from the world of school. At worst, school is seen as a tiresome irrelevance, which has to be endured before entering upon the real world of work, rather than a preparation in skills that will be of use in later life. The problem is, of course, that the curriculum — that body of knowledge with which an 'educated' person should be equipped — is not value neutral, but (being only a small selection from all the knowledge that is available) is itself determined by certain assumptions about the nature and stability of existing social patterns and transmits those values to the pupils.

# Access to Higher Education

## Grants and places

Britain is still unusual among European countries in spending a substantial proportion of its education budget on grants for students in higher education, spending £739 per head per year compared with £195 in France and £54 in Germany (1991). In England and Wales (as opposed to Scotland or Northern

Ireland) very few full-time students study in their home towns, and some travel considerable distances to do so.

This system is the creation of the 1944 Education Act, but for the first twenty years or so the numbers entering higher education were still modest. The Robbins Report in 1963 called for higher education to be made available to everyone who could benefit from it. As a result existing universities were much expanded and new ones founded. At the same time, however, the Labour Government of 1964 established a new kind of higher education institution, the *polytechnic*. Polytechnics would concentrate on preparing students for careers in science and technology and would be funded and supported by local authorities. Unlike universities they would not have the power to award their own degrees; this would be done by a central body, the Council for National Academic Awards (CNAA). By 1970, when the new system was fully operational, there were 456,800 students in full-time higher education. During the 1970s, it was estimated that there would be a sharp fall in demand for teachers. In consequence many former teachers' training colleges began to offer Arts degree programmes, and by 1980–1 the total in higher education had risen to 534,900.

Despite cuts in public expenditure, the number of students in full-time higher education continued to rise during the 1980s, reaching 627,000 in 1987–8, when a Government White Paper on *Access to Higher Education* called for a further increase. In 1991 government spokespersons were claiming that 'one way or another' over a million people were now engaged in higher education (Open University, 'Open Forum', 23 March 1991). Only a small proportion of this expansion, however, has taken place in the universities, who until 1991 remained strictly bound by quotas imposed by the government-controlled UFC. The polytechnics and colleges, which offered much less choice of courses and whose costs per student were therefore less, were simultaneously encouraged to recruit as many as they could to drive down the 'unit of resource' across higher education as a whole, and in 1990 the universities were made to bid for student numbers at unit prices not exceeding the lowest previously measured for the country as a whole.

## Differential Access

Access to higher education, therefore, has to some extent been artificially restricted. However changes in governmental policy do not account for the extent to which the higher social classes are overrepresented and the lower ones underrepresented in universities (see Table 9.1).

A. H. Halsey's longitudinal study of 8529 boys educated in England and Wales in the 1950s and 1960s showed that the Robbins expansion had benefited the middle class more than the working class. In fact, since 1963 there had been a fall of about one-third in the number of students coming from working-class homes, though over the same period there had also been a relative fall in the size of the

Table 9.1 *University entrants and the 18-year-old population, 1990 (percentages)*

| Social class | 18-year-old population | University entrants |
|---|---|---|
| I | 7.0 | 23.9 |
| II | 22.0 | 49.0 |
| IIIN | 10.0 | 9.1 |
| IIIM | 38.0 | 12.2 |
| IV | 18.0 | 4.9 |
| V | 6.0 | 0.9 |
| Total | 100.0 | 100.0 |

Source: Association of University Teachers, *AUT Bulletin*, 1991.

working class itself. Whereas compared with their parents, the proportion of working-class boys entering university increased by 2 per cent (as shown above), the proportion of boys from the 'service class' increased by 19 per cent (Halsey, Heath and Ridge 1980).

From an educational point of view the traditional pattern of three years' full-time education, normally away from home, between 18 to 21 has great advantages. The English system is both selective and intensive and hence highly efficient in two respects: very few students, once admitted to courses, fail to complete them, and they graduate in less time, three years, than in the United States or other European countries, where four, five or even six years is quite normal. Both universities and polytechnics have long offered 'sandwich courses' which incorporate both study and work experience, training in language and computational skills, and a wide range of optional paths. However working-class children are likely to encounter both family and peer group pressures to enter work early, and as student grants have fallen in real terms and in part been replaced by loans they have less and less incentive to want to study away from home.

Awareness of the limitations of the traditional pattern has led to increasing emphasis on 'non-traditional' routes into higher education. The Open University itself is a world pioneer of 'distance learning'. It offers people a chance to study in their own homes at times convenient to them without the need for formal entrance requirements. But even it has found that the majority of its entrants come from the middle classes, in particular from teachers wanting to upgrade their qualifications. And though the fees are not high compared with full-time education, the fact that they (and other costs) have to be borne by the student is an obvious disincentive. The same problems apply to other routes into higher education: mature entry, work-experience and access courses.

## Compensatory Education?

'Compensatory education' was a term coined in the United States following research which appeared to show that working-class and ethnic minority underachievement was caused by 'cultural deprivation'. The Johnson Administration (1963–9) funded a series of programmes, notably 'Operation Headstart', designed to give American blacks additional education to compensate for what they lacked. If this were to be fully effective, they argued, it must take effect as early in the child's life as possible. One of the consequences of this therefore was the children's TV programme *Sesame Street*, in which the Muppets first appeared.

Following the Plowden Report (1967), 'Educational Priority Areas' (EPAs) were set up in Britain, in London and three major provincial areas. The concept on which they were based, however, was challenged, when the American Arthur Jensen (1969) produced figures suggesting that 'intelligence' as measured by IQ was 80 per cent inherited, and used this as the basis for arguing that compensatory education had failed. Though this view was supported by the British psychologist, Hans Eysenck (1971), among others, Jensen's conclusions were criticised on the grounds that the very test on which he relied, that of IQ, was itself culturally biased in favour of white, middle-class Americans (Labov 1973). Ironically, Bernstein also criticised the idea of compensatory education on the grounds that no such programme could make up for the deficiencies of society.

# The Great Educational Debate

In a key speech in 1976, the prime minister of the day, James Callaghan, who had himself left school at the age of 14, called for a 'Great Debate' on the aims of education and the success of the education system in meeting them. It was an open invitation to identify a 'crisis' in the school system and to put forward ways of coping with it.

The debate soon came to be dominated by theorists of the so-called 'New Right'. The assumption on which their arguments were based was that there had been a *decline in standards* in British education. This 'decline', they argued, stemmed from one or other of three main causes. The change to comprehensive education, they argued, was destroying 'quality' schools, i.e. the old grammar schools. At the same time, a move away from the traditional curriculum ought to be focused on technical skills of use in the market place, and instead the introduction of new subjects (such as sociology!), was, they thought, making education increasingly 'irrelevant'. Thirdly, teachers, who had borne the brunt of heavy cuts in local government finance and resorted to strikes in defence of their position, were regarded as trouble-makers who were politically motivated and ought to be disciplined.

The remedies proposed were: (1) to increase central government control over education and lay down requirements for a national curriculum; (2) to link education more closely to the needs of industry; (3) to deprive teachers of the right to negotiate their pay and conditions and to impose a new contract on them; and (4) to allow parents greater freedom of choice as with buying any other product in the marketplace.

Table 9.2   *Total government spending on education, 1970–1 to 1988–9, United Kingdom*

| Years | £million, actual | | |
|---|---|---|---|
| | 1970–1 | 1980–1 | 1988–9 |
| Current expenditure | 2,331 | 12,171 | 21,406 |
| Capital expenditure | 409 | 768 | 911 |
| Total | 2,470 | 12,940 | 22,317 |
| of which LAs | 2,318 | 11,160 | 19,123 |
| Expenditure as % GDP | 5.1 | 5.5 | 5.1 |

Source: *Social Trends*, 1991, Table 3.34, p. 62.

These remedies were, of course, incompatible with one another. However, the dispute over how and when they should be applied tended to overshadow the fact that the basic assumption that the system was 'failing' had never been proved. There was to begin with no agreement on when the system had been better and when it had begun to decline. Comparisons were repeatedly made between the performance in examinations in different schools, as though these could be separated from consideration of the socio-economic background of the pupils and the areas from which they came. Comprehensives were criticised for not being more like grammar schools, but were not given credit for their success in developing the very technical skills for which they had been designed and equipped. Nor was it appreciated how far teachers had been used to working on a voluntary basis well beyond the terms that any contract could stipulate. Lastly, no allowance was made for the fact that the amount of money made available to the system had been falling in real terms throughout the decade. In 1982 capital spending on schools, for example, was £355 million; in 1990 it was £352 million, but allowing for inflation this represented a drop in real terms of a third. Total spending fell from 5.85 per cent of GDP in 1981 to 5.06 per cent in 1989 (*The Guardian*, 11 February 1991).

## Education and Training

However, despite their official opposition to comprehensives, by the early 1980s many Conservative LEAs had in practice become reconciled to the comprehensive system, if only on the pragmatic grounds that large, purpose-built schools were much more economical both to build and to run. Hence though the incoming government ended the compulsion to change, they left the system essentially unchanged for several years, while the general emphasis on limiting public expenditure precluded experimentation.

Meanwhile a number of initiatives were taken. Some were taken independently of the Department of Education, by the Department of Employment, in a clear attempt to bypass the existing educational system. All emphasised vocational training in job skills rather than broader educational perspectives. The Technical and Vocational Education Initiative (TVEI) of 1982 was funded by the Manpower Services Commission to provide vocationally orientated courses within comprehensive schools on the basis of a contract between the school and the Commission, and proved attractive to schools at a time of sharp cuts in normal educational funding. The Youth Opportunities Scheme (YOPS), and later the Youth Training Scheme (YTS), sponsored by the Department of Employment, then offered a further year of 'on the job' training for school-leavers, which in a time of high youth unemployment they could not forgo without forfeiting any right to state benefits. Millions were poured by the Department of Education itself into City Technology Colleges (CTCs) which were supposed to be sponsored and paid for by industry and to be closely linked to their personnel needs.

The Education Reform Bill that was published in 1987 and eventually became law as the Education Reform Act of 1988 fundamentally altered the 1944 system. Though it left intact (for the time being) the principle that education was 'a national service, locally delivered', it gave the Secretary of State more than 400 additional powers, enabling him to intervene in almost every aspect of the work of the LEAs and extending central government control over polytechnics (previously under LEA control) and universities (previously independent, but receiving most of their funds through the independent University Grants Commission or UGC). The main provisions of the Act were:

1. *The national curriculum*: For the first time, a national curriculum was to be required of all state schools (though not, curiously enough, of independent schools). Children would be tested on their knowledge of it at 7, 11 and 14.
2. *Parental choice*: Parents could no longer be required to send their children to their neighbourhood school and could instead choose any other school within the local area.
3. *Local management of schools* (LMS): Schools were to be given independent budgets and head teachers given freedom to manage them within the limits of the resources made available to them and subject to the overall approval of their Boards of Governors. The structure of boards of governors was revised to eliminate the majority of representatives of local authorities and of teachers and to increase business and parental representation.
4. *Opting out*: Schools that wanted to 'opt out' of local authority control altogether were encouraged to do so. By doing so, however, they would come directly under the control of national government, from which they would receive their funding. The Inner London Education Authority was abolished and responsibility for education in their area transferred to the inner London boroughs.
5. *Central control of universities and polytechnics*: The University Grants

Committee (UGC) was replaced by a new Universities Fundi
with powers to direct expenditure towards specific areas and
Elaborate systems of performance review were set up and t
to bid annually for funds for specific student numbers. Cor
was taken away from local government and transferred to the ⌐⌐
since been allowed to adopt the title 'University' and most, if not all, have
chosen to do so.

It is still too early to forecast the social consequences of so many far-reaching changes. However in 1990 a European survey showed that in one respect at least the government had been all too successful. Only 37 per cent of Britons expressed their confidence in the educational system of their country, the lowest rate in Western Europe, and 69 per cent of pupils left school by the age of 17, the same proportion as Spain and more than in any other European country. In West Germany only 15 per cent of pupils left school before 17 and more than 70 per cent of the population expressed their confidence in their system (Gallup, May— June 1990, reported in *The Guardian*, 12 February 1991).

# What is Religion?

Though religious education, as we have seen, forms part of education, in general *education* is concerned with the learning of ideas about those aspects of the world

Perspectives
on religion

**Marx**

All phenomena explicable in materialist terms.
Religion originates from primitive myths.
Becomes a device for social control.
In capitalist society, helps domination of bourgeoisie; will disappear
in socialist society.

**Durkheim**

Arises from society — a social construct.
Set of symbols expressing social reality.
Forms basis for other social values.
Contributes to social solidarity.

**Weber**

Originates with charismatic individual; routinised in organisation.
Influences social structure.
In some forms, facilitated capitalist development.
Tends towards rationality.

the correctness of which can be demonstrated by reasoning, observation, experiment or calculation. *Religion*, on the other hand, concerns itself with those aspects of life which are beyond proof, and involves a commitment of faith that a certain view of things is true.

Religion can be defined in either of two ways. Some define it in *exclusive* terms, as requiring belief in certain specific things, usually the existence of a supernatural being, a God. Christianity, Hinduism, Islam are all religions according to this definition. However Buddhism, a system of belief which does not require belief in a supernatural being, would be excluded. So others define a religion in *inclusive* terms as any unified system of belief, a definition which, as well as Buddhism, might include humanism and Marxism.

The importance of religion in determining and regulating social behaviour has made it a subject of great interest from the time of the earliest sociologists, and Marx, Durkheim and Weber all wrote on the subject.

# Perspectives on Religion

## Marx

Marx considered himself to be a *materialist*. He did not believe in a supernatural being or beings, and regarded religion simply as a device for social control, a method by which the ruling class stopped those less well off from fighting for social justice. 'Religion is the sigh of the oppressed creature . . . ,' he wrote, 'the opium of the people' (Marx and Engels 1955). Engels said that the parson went hand in hand with the landlord to maintain the existing social structure.

For Marx, religious belief came into existence when 'primitive' human beings constructed myths to explain things that they did not understand, such as why the sun rose in the morning or disease destroyed their crops. It ceased to be necessary with the advance of scientific understanding, which enabled human beings not only to understand but also to control the forces of nature. Meanwhile in any society the nature of religion would be determined by the underlying economic realities of power.

Ironically, in the hands of his followers Marxism itself became a sort of secular religion (cf. Zaehner 1971). For many decades citizens of the former Soviet Union worked in the belief that they were building a better society for the future which their efforts were scientifically certain to achieve. With the collapse of this hope, significant numbers, as in Poland and Lithuania, have turned back to older forms of religion.

## Durkheim

Durkheim too was interested in the origins of religion. However, his *The Elementary Forms of Religious Life* (1964) deals with only one 'primitive' society, and in this respect has been superseded by many later works. Still useful, on the other hand, is his use of the distinction between the *sacred* and the *profane* to develop a sociology of religion.

For Durkheim religion arises out of society and is therefore a social construct, which acts to help preserve the society which constructs it, protects its traditions and strengthens the collective consciousness of society. For Durkheim, therefore, religion consists of a set of symbols expressing social reality. It provides a systematic basis for social values, which determine the way people behave in society. And its ceremony and rituals contribute to social solidarity.

Many modern complex societies, however, have more than one religion. Religion does not always act as a unifying principle in such societies, and in a number of societies religion identifies members of warring communities, such as Catholics and Protestants in Northern Ireland, Hindus and Muslims in India, Buddhists and Hindus in Sri Lanka or Christians and Muslims in the Lebanon. Where religion is seen as deeply divisive, as in Mexico or the early USSR, governments have tried to ban the teaching of religious doctrines and the public observance of religions altogether, though in both cases these laws were later relaxed. And in such societies, the secular creed of nationalism is often promoted instead as a unifying system of ideas, so that it, too, may be regarded as a religion of a sort.

## Weber

Weber, too, was brought up in a Christian society and attached great importance to religion, and it was from the religious sphere that he borrowed his secular concept of *charisma*. Charisma, the 'gift of grace', had for Christianity been transmitted by Jesus to Peter, and in turn from Peter to his successors, the popes. In the process it had been rationalised and systematised, and had become routine. His hypothesis was that other religions too would become increasingly rational over time.

Using once more his concept of the 'ideal-type', he derived from this a typology of religions. As with other 'ideal-types', these are not found in their unmixed form in the real world, but are used to point up the most salient features of a specific set of ideas.

Unlike Marx, Weber did not see religion as invariably static and conservative of existing systems. For both Marx and Durkheim, it was the underlying social structure that generated religious expression. For Weber, on the other hand, religion could also influence social structure, and could, indeed, be a potent force for social change.

In his *The Protestant Ethic and the Spirit of Capitalism* Weber argued that a specific form of Christianity, puritan protestantism, found in Northern Europe, had proved particularly favourable for the economic development of that region (Weber 1974). The argument is a complex one, but the fundamental point about it was the suggestion that the puritans, lacking the assurance of revelation and

**Weber's typology of religions**

|  | world-accepting | world-rejecting |
|---|---|---|
| ascetic | Puritanism |  |
| mystic |  | Buddhism |

hierarchy saw material success in this world as a sign of fitness for the next. Though within Europe, the hypothesis has support from the historical evidence, its converse is not necessarily true, and Catholic societies such as those of Western Germany, Italy and France have in recent years been outstripping Northern Europe in economic development. Japan, too, has enjoyed accelerated capitalist development, but not being a Christian country, this can hardly be attributed to the puritan ethic, or at least not in Weber's original sense of the phrase (see also Marshall 1982).

# Secularisation

The founder of sociology, Auguste Comte, believed that in time science would displace metaphysics, which he believed had already displaced theology as the centre of human thought.

*Secularisation* is the process of religious thinking, practice and institutions losing their social significance (Wilson 1966, 1982). In Western Europe it appears that the dominant trend over the past century has been for religion to lose its central place in thought, and for those who continue to engage in formal religious observance to do so in an increasingly perfunctory way. Thus, for example, Christmas has largely ceased to be a religious occasion of deep spiritual significance, and instead to be seen as an occasion for having a good time, eating and drinking rather too much and spending a great deal of money. In 1979, for the first time, more people married in civil ceremonies than in churches.

Not surprisingly, however, it is quite difficult to measure trends accurately when they concern anything as intimate and personal as religious belief. Comparison between survey responses and objective observation of individual behaviour strongly suggests that people when asked about their religious views tend to claim to be more 'religious' than they actually are.

Church membership is an unreliable guide, as different denominations define membership in different ways. In England, the Church of England is the 'established' religion, and so enjoys a special position. Yet even in 1851 only

40 per cent of the population attended church services every week — the corresponding figure today is less than 10 per cent. Nor do we know for sure why they did so. Church attendance may have been a sign of religious affirmation, but it may equally, as David Martin (1967) argues, simply have been a social requirement for respectability. Today most of the many people who are nominally Anglicans seldom, if ever, attend church or engage in collective religious activity, and many others attend Anglican services occasionally, whether they are practising Christians or not. So church attendance is not necessarily a good guide to religious belief either. People may attend church purely for social reasons or not at all, but still have religious beliefs. Religious beliefs do not have to be collectively expressed. Though almost all Christians regard at least some degree of collective participation as necessary to membership, in some other faiths religion is quite personal and there is no formal requirement to engage in collective acts of worship.

The evidence is, however, that the old are more likely to be believers than the young, but the young (except in the Church of England itself) are more likely to be church attenders. The young, if they are practising Christians, are more likely than the old to belong to one of the newer, smaller groupings or *sects*. Women are more likely to be active believers than men. Contrary to what Marx might seem to imply, however, the well-to-do are more likely to be active church members than the poor, and the middle class are more likely to be members of the old-established denominations than the new. But there is a great deal of variation by region. Methodism, derived from a fundamentalist schism within the Anglican Church, is strongly entrenched in Wales and the West Country.

Although the established Church exists and forms part of the state, since 1689 the principle of religious *toleration* has existed in England, Wales and Scotland at least in some degree and today the state officially tolerates all faiths and their members provided they do not break the secular laws of the country (e.g. by practising human sacrifice, or slaughtering animals in an inhumane manner). The Church of England, as custodian of the state religion, does enjoy special privileges. It is directly represented in Parliament by those bishops who are members of the House of Lords. It conducts the ceremonies of state. The religious ideas which are disseminated more widely than ever before are predominantly those of the established Church, and its interpretations and ritual form the basis for the compulsory religious instruction which must be given in all schools, though this is tempered by the requirement on schools to take due note also of the views of other faiths.

The question of how far British society is becoming more secular also involves consideration of what is meant by 'secular'. It is possible to argue that recent changes in the Soviet Union have made it *more* secular, in that people appear to have lost faith in the beliefs and doctrines of the Communist Party. But many would probably argue it is becoming *less* secular, as some of those who have lost faith in materialist philosophy have turned back to the Russian Orthodox Church and some have chosen to embrace other Christian sects. There has also been a significant increase in Islamic consciousness in the Central Asian republics, influenced by the growth of Islamic fundamentalism in Iran.

The ecumenical movement, the trend within Christian denominations to work together and to try to seek common ground, with a view to possible eventual reunification, can similarly be regarded, as Wilson (1982) suggests, as a sign of weakening faith, or as its proponents claim, as a means of securing revival.

# Fundamentalism

The Islamic revolution of 1979 in Iran, which led to a theocratic state (one ruled by religious leaders) dominated until his death by the Ayatollah Khomeini, was, however, only the most spectacular instance of the revival of religious *fundamentalism* within Islam. In Muslim states as far apart as Pakistan and the Sudan power has also for longer or shorter periods passed into the hands of rulers bent on creating an avowedly 'Islamic' state and making the Quran (or their interpretation of it) the sole basis of secular as well as religious law. And the rise of Islamic fundamentalism has led to major internal and international conflicts with grave social consequences: the civil war in the Lebanon, the outbreak of the eight-year war between Iran and Iraq, Iraq's subsequent invasion of Kuwait in August 1990, and the Gulf War that followed.

The 1970s and 1980s, too, saw a significant increase in religious fundamentalism within Christianity. In the United States Jimmy Carter (President 1977–81) became the first Baptist to reach his country's highest office, and Ronald Reagan (President 1981–9) the first to do so as a member of one of the new sects, the Christian Church of California. In Britain there has been, as we have seen, a steady decline in church attendance among members of the principal denominations during the twentieth century. In recent years a major exception has been the emergence of the pentecostal movement and the rapid growth of new sects, notably, though not exclusively, those of the Afro-Caribbean community.

# New Religions

Weber was the first sociologist to make a distinction within Christianity between *churches* and *sects*, and in this he was followed by the influential work of Ernst Troeltsch (1931).

For both of them, *churches* are broad, inclusive groupings. *Sects* are smaller, defined by opposition to established groups, and can demand 'higher standards' of their members. People are usually born into churches. They are often not born into sects — they are attracted to them by their conviction and their zeal to make converts, and frequently undergo some kind of mystical experience at the point of conversion. (However a Gallup survey in 1986 showed that such mystical experiences were, perhaps surprisingly, common — some 48 per cent of respondents believed that they had experienced some kind of religious/mystical event.) Churches accept the world as it is and adjust to its harsh realities. Sects may reject the world if it fails to live up to their standards. In rare cases this rejection can be total, such as the mass suicide of the 900 members of the People's Temple cult in Jonestown, Guyana in November 1978. The People's Temple had formed under the leadership of a single, charismatic leader, the Rev. Jim Jones, who had previously been a Unitarian, a Methodist and a Disciple of Christ before founding his own sect.

Howard Becker (1950) expanded the work of Troeltsch, distinguishing not only between church and sect, but introducing two new categories: the *denomination*, between church and sect, and the *cult*, which for him lacked formal organisation. The category of churches he also divided according to whether they were *international*, like the Roman Catholic Church, or *national*, like the Church of England. However, all such typologies have weaknesses in that assigning groups to a category is very subjective, and there are many overlaps. Thus in England the term 'denomination' is commonly used to designate what Weber would have called a 'church', and the Anglican communion is — thanks to the former British Empire — widely spread throughout the world, with bishops and the formal organisation of a church in places as far apart as Buenos Aires and Seoul.

Roy Wallis (1984, 1985) sees the division between 'world-rejecting' or 'world-affirming' as existing not just between churches and sects, but between sects.

- 'World-rejecting' sects, like the People's Temple, the Children of God or the Unification Church ('Moonies'), affirm the infinite superiority of a God, reject the modern world and its contamination, and are often highly authoritarian.
- 'World-affirming' sects, such as scientology and transcendental meditation, regard God as a spirit active in the modern world and offer a path through which that world can be more successfully negotiated. However, both of the latter have been significantly modified by the changing nature of that contact.

## Summary

Belief systems are influenced by social structure and play a significant part in determining the social behaviour of individuals. Some systems of ideas may be more favourable than others for encouraging initiative and enterprise. However, capitalist development in Britain owes much more to the availability of natural resources and power than it does to social structure or beliefs. In Britain as in Western Europe generally public observance of religion appears to have been steadily losing its significance for many decades, but religious beliefs do not have to be publicly expressed and there is a clear tendency for young people interested in religion to belong to one of the newer sects. In both Christianity and in Islam, now a significant minority belief in Britain, the rise of religious fundamentalism has had significant social consequences. 'World-affirming' sects are more likely to be compatible with modern democratic societies than 'world-rejecting' ones, but only so long as they continue to accept the well-established social value of toleration.

# Suggestions for Further Reading

A good overview of the more long-standing controversies is R. Meighan (1981), *Sociology of Educating*. A radical critique of the school and its methods comes from Ivan Illich (1973), *Deschooling Society*; Paulo Freire (1974), *Education, the practice of freedom*; and, in Britain, Willis (1977), *Learning to Labour*. Nell Keddie (1973), *Tinker, Tailor . . . The Myth of Cultural Deprivation*, discusses the unconscious prejudices of teachers. Rutter (1979) is concerned with the contribution of school organisation to academic success. On social mobility and the role of education see especially Halsey, Heath and Ridge (1980), *Origins and Destinations*. Comparisons with the United States are always dangerous, but S. Bowles and H. Gintis (1975), *Schooling in Capitalist America*, is thought-provoking.

On the sociology of knowledge a good introduction is Michael Young (1971), *Knowledge and Control*. Stuart Hall and Tony Jefferson (1976), *Resistance through Rituals*, deals with modern approaches to youth culture. Theodore Roszak (1970), *The making of a Counter-culture*, deals with wider philosophical issues.

On religion, Durkheim's *The Elementary Forms of Religious Life* (first published 1915) and Weber's *The Protestant Ethic and the Spirit of Capitalism* remain key texts, though the latter should be supplemented by G. Marshall (1982), *In Search of the Spirit of Capitalism*. On secularisation, see Bryan Wilson (1966), *Religion in a Secular Society*. David Martin (1978), *The Dilemmas of Contemporary Religion* deals with the inherent conflict between modern society and religion. Roy Wallis (1984), *The Elementary Forms of the New Religious Life*, assesses the importance of the new sects.

# 10 Culture, Communications and Leisure

## Mass Media

The main themes are as follows:

- The relationship between ownership, control and production in the media, especially in so far as this determines content. The question of accuracy and impartiality, particularly with regard to political issues.
- The effects of the mass media (often, the impact of television violence) on children.
- Whether the mass media, especially television, are a source for the development of mass culture.

## Culture and Community

The term 'culture' has many meanings. To a sociologist, culture refers to the entire pattern of behaviour of a society. Marxists (in particular, those of the former Soviet Union) have in the past often argued for a rather simple economic determinism, in which culture forms only part of the superstructure of society, resting upon the dominant economic base. However, even before the collapse of communist regimes in Eastern Europe, many Western Marxists had independently come to accept that the culture of a society (in the sociological sense) also affects and shapes its capacity for economic production, an idea which has long seemed obvious to non-Marxists.

Confusion arises from the fact that the word 'culture' is much more commonly and widely used to designate the evidences of specialised forms of self-expression, such as art, music, literature, etc. Culture in this sense, sometimes termed 'high culture', is generally seen as being the particular province of middle-class intellectuals. However although this may to a considerable extent be true of Britain, the existence of the mass media makes this 'culture' available to a much wider public than would have been possible half a century ago.

In Chapter 7 we examined the evidence for and against the notion of a decline of community in Britain. One of the reasons why those who believe community has declined is that Britain has in the twentieth century developed a mass national culture in which at times regional and local differences have seemed to be completely swallowed up. Whether or not the sense of community has declined, it is certainly through the agency of the *mass media* that this national culture has become so all-pervasive.

# Mass Media

Mass media are agencies by which the same message can be transmitted simultaneously to a large number of people, who may live far apart and come from all social strata. The mass media form only one of the agencies of socialisation in modern society. They are, however, fundamental to all other areas of social life, since they are increasingly the main means of access to the knowledge on which other activities are based. Their relative novelty, their impact and their all-pervading nature lead them to be regarded with particular respect (or suspicion).

Best established of the mass media is the *press*. In a very restricted form newspapers date back to the early eighteenth century, and the oldest daily paper, *The Times*, was founded (as *The Daily Universal Register*) in 1785 (Times Newspapers 1985). The institution of universal free primary education created a need for new, cheap, mass-produced papers and books, which was first felt in the United States and met by the application of steam to rotary printing towards the end of the nineteenth century. Today, although less than one newspaper per household is purchased daily, 70 per cent of men and 64 per cent of women read a daily newspaper, and Britons remain among the world's most avid newspaper readers.

Visual images (illustrations) in nineteenth-century newspapers and magazines still had to be supplied by the slow process of line engraving. In the 1890s the *cinema* became a practical proposition, and for the first time the public could easily recognise important public figures and share in the excitement of public occasions. Cinema attendance peaked in 1955 at 23 visits per person, but had declined to just under one by 1984 but since then has been rising slightly (*Social Trends, 1990*, 10.9).

*Radio* arrived after the First World War, in 1920, when it had been belatedly realised that radio's greatest disadvantage for military purposes, the fact that everyone who had a receiver could hear it, made it ideal for entertainment, news and propaganda. It reached a peak of social importance between 1939 and 1945, when it played a major part in holding together a country under the pressures of war. Though long in decline in the face of competition from television, in recent years radio listening has been increasing once more. In the course of an average week some 73 per cent of the population listen to the radio for an average in 1988 of 9 hours 12 minutes.

Britain was the first country to have regular, scheduled *television* programmes, starting in 1936, but the service was suspended on the outbreak of war and not resumed until 1948. It was in the 1950s that television began its rapid rise to become the most successful of the media clamouring for consumer attention, but for three decades the number of channels available was restricted. In the 1980s the spread of satellite and (perhaps more importantly) cable TV not only increased dramatically the number of channels available but also created the possibility (available to radio listeners since the 1920s) of receiving programmes directly from overseas countries. In 1988 94 per cent of the population watched television at some stage of the week and did so on an average for 25 hours and 21 minutes — more than one day in every seven!

# Functions

Within their general function of communication, the mass media perform a number of more specific functions.

## Educational

The media transmit information about what is going on in the home society and in other societies. This information can form the basis either for individual action, as in the case of gardening or cookery programmes, or for social action, as in the case of people who join pressure groups devoted to ecological or similar causes. Programmes may form small parts of formal courses of instruction, as with Schools Television, or complete courses in themselves, as with Open University broadcasts.

## Socialisation

The media communicate social attitudes, opinions, fashions and tastes to their mass audience. They do this both consciously, through the deliberate selection of material deemed to be of cultural or artistic value, and unconsciously, in that those who work in the media tend to choose material which they regard as having 'correct' social attitudes. Further, the media present what current social *attitudes* are perceived to be, whether 'correct' or not, and thus may harden such attitudes by confirming their widespread existence.

## Economic

Those media, such as the press and commercial television, that rely on advertisements to make them pay overtly promote the consumption of a wide range of goods, ranging from beer and tea to expensive overseas holidays. However, in a wider sense the media also promote consumption by publicising the consumption patterns and tastes of the rich and famous, or, as in the case of disc jockeys, playing certain records rather than others.

Table 10.1  *Ownership of the British press, 1991*

| Firm & Title | Circulation Av. July–Dec. 1990 |
|---|---|
| *Apollo Ltd* | |
| *Sunday Sport* | 401,911 |
| | |
| *Associated Newspapers Holdings Ltd.* | |
| Chairman: The Viscount Rothermere | |
| *Daily Mail* | 1,708,280 |
| *Mail on Sunday* | 1,902,706 |
| *Evening Standard* | 501,624 |
| many regional newspapers | |
| | |
| *The Daily Telegraph plc* | |
| Chairman: C.M. Black | |
| *The Daily Telegraph* | 1,075,980 |
| *Sunday Telegraph* | 594,223 |
| *The Spectator* | |
| | |
| *The Economist Newspaper Ltd* | |
| Chairman: Sir John Harvey-Jones | |
| *The Economist* | |
| | |
| *Financial Times Group Ltd* | |
| Chairman: Lord Blakenham | |
| *Financial Times* | 289,726 |
| | |
| *The Guardian & Manchester Evening News plc* | |
| Chairman: H.J. Roche | |
| *The Guardian* | 424,124 |
| *Manchester Evening News* | |
| | |
| *Mirror Group Newspapers* | |
| Publisher: Robert Maxwell, MC* | |
| *Daily Mirror* | 3,082,943 |
| *The People* | 2,565,287 |
| *Sunday Mirror* | 2,893,868 |
| *Sunday Mail* | |
| *Scottish Daily Record* | 777,879 |
| *The Sporting Life* | 80,962 |
| | |
| *Morning Star Co-operative Society Ltd* | |
| *Morning Star* | 8,500 |

## Political

The media convey a stylised picture of the political order. State ceremonies such as the Trooping of the Colour glamorise the dry business of government. Elections, represented as 'horse races' between rival political leaders, are presented as the product of informed democratic choice. News and current affairs programmes offer information pre-packaged in the form of politically 'balanced' debates between two or three persons.

Table 10.1  *Ownership of the British press, 1991*

| Firm & Title | Circulation Av. July–Dec. 1990 |
|---|---|
| *News International plc* K.R. Murdoch (director) News Group Newspapers Ltd | |
| *The News of the World* | 5,056,315 |
| *The Sun* | 3,854,694 |
| Times Newspapers Ltd Chairman: K.R. Murdoch | |
| *The Times* | 420,127 |
| *The Sunday Times* | 1,165,474 |
| The Times Supplements Ltd *The Times Literary Supplement* *The Times Educational Supplement* *The Times Higher Education Supplement* | |
| *Newspaper Publishing plc* | |
| *The Independent* | 411,378 |
| *Independent on Sunday* | 352,335 |
| *The Observer Ltd* Chairman: R.W. Rowland | |
| *The Observer* | 551,475 |
| *The Thomson Corporation plc* Lord Thomson of Fleet *Evening News* *The Scotsman* many regional newspapers | |
| *United Newspapers plc* Executive Chairman: Lord Stevens of Ludgate | |
| *Daily Express* | 1,585,495 |
| *Daily Star* | 911,761 |
| *Sunday Express* | 1,663,922 |
| *Scottish Daily Express* | |

Source: *Benn's Media Directory* 1991, Tonbridge, Kent, Benn Business Information Services, 1991.
* Died November 1991.

## Cathartic

Television is much more effective in transmitting emotions and attitudes than it is in conveying information. Though game shows and other forms of entertainment tend to carry the subliminal message that consumption is good, the prime purpose of the programmes that fill by far the largest share of air time is simply to entertain and to amuse. Providing relaxation after work makes people more willing to accept the existing order of things.

# Ownership and control

The press in Britain has always been in private ownership, and the experience of those countries where a state-controlled press has been created tends to confirm the view that a 'free' press (i.e., one that is owned by private individuals), is necessary if a liberal-democratic society is to operate.

However, the *ownership* of the British press is in fact heavily concentrated in the hands of five major syndicates, and hence of only a few individuals. This tendency towards concentration has not been substantially affected by the emergence of a number of new titles in the 1980s, since most of which, like the *Sunday Correspondent*, failed to survive. These groups are in turn linked to one another and to television and other media companies by an elaborate structure of *interlocking directorships* (Trowler, in Trowler and Riley 1984).

A surprising number of these individuals have in the past century come from overseas. Thus Rupert Murdoch, owner of the 'top people's' *The Times* as well as the down-market *Sun*, was an Australian who chose to become an American citizen because he would not otherwise be allowed to own American television franchises. The fact that he is also the major shareholder in British Sky Broadcasting illustrates the fact that (apart from the BBC) ownership of television is mainly in the same hands as the press. ITV franchises were reallocated in 1991. Officially, they were supposed to go to the highest bidder, provided only that the company concerned had passed a vaguely defined 'quality threshold'; however, in the actual allocation two companies, TVS and TSW, were passed over because it was believed that they could not afford the cost of the bid.

The British press is heavily (up to 90 per cent) pro-Conservative, particularly when the politics of local as well as national newspapers is taken into account. Of the national daily press, only the *Daily Mirror* supports Labour. Opinion polls consistently show that *The Sun* is also regarded by most people as being Labour because its main readership is working-class, even though it is in fact very Conservative. *The Times*, nominally independent, has in recent years expressed far more 'Thatcherite' views even than *The Daily Telegraph*, which is and always has been a committed Conservative journal. In fact, surveys show that just over half the readers of *The Times* vote Labour. In general, the press tends to accept Conservative Party policy and, especially when the Conservatives are in government, to take a pro-Conservative stance on current political issues.

It is an interesting fact that many reporters on Conservative newspapers are in fact Labour voters. However, all this indicates is that they do not have a say in editorial policy. All editors say that their proprietors exercise no day-to-day influence on what they choose to put in their pages, but few can fail to be aware that the proprietor's tolerance depends on their continuing to sell newspapers and make a profit. Consequently with few exceptions newspapers devote a great deal of their time to reporting sensational news, freak events, court cases (particularly with violence and/or sex), sport and entertainment-related items (the doings of showbusiness personalities or pop stars) — an extreme example of most of these tendencies being the idiosyncratic *Sunday Sport*. This in itself, of course, conveys a certain view of the world which cannot but influence the attitudes of newspaper readers.

Television, on the other hand, is constrained by the Charters both of the BBC and the IBA to be politically neutral, in so far as this is possible. This is met by a policy of 'balance' by which in the course of a week the time apportioned to known representatives of the major political parties is roughly equal and so too is the time allocated to each side in coverage of political events like by-elections. However, there has been criticism that this policy makes it difficult for minority groups and those holding unpopular views to make themselves heard. ITV's *Channel 4* was set up therefore with precisely these sorts of minority interests in mind. An exception to the rule of balance is any area designated by the government as involving national security. TV channels need not, and indeed must not, give equal weight to the views of the government and the Provisional IRA. In addition, a specific government instruction means that at present the voices of IRA spokespersons cannot be heard on British radio or television. The official reason for this is 'to deprive them of the oxygen of publicity', though they are, needless to say, heard and seen by everyone else in Europe.

However, in other respects television companies have become increasingly influenced by the *multi-media groups* that dominate the European electronic media. These groups have been the main actors in promoting new forms of television provision, satellite and cable, which, because they transcend national boundaries, escape many of the constraints traditionally imposed by governments on national public service television. In Britain the most important actor is Thorn-EMI, an electronics, music and software conglomerate, which owns 46 per cent of the shares of Thames TV, and three satellite TV channels. Yet, output even in the satellite–cable field is dominated by two large US consortia with which, for marketing reasons, the European companies have to work. US influence on television output in Britain, therefore, is very marked (McQuail and Siune 1986).

# The Influence of Television on Behaviour

Virtually everything that happens in the modern world which people dislike is blamed in some way on television. The influence of television on people's *behaviour* is, for many people, proved whenever someone commits a crime similar to one that has recently been shown on television. This was seen as a problem even in the days of the press or the cinema. The film *The Manchurian Candidate* was put on general release in the United States just before the assassination of President Kennedy (in 1963), and the fact that there were strong resemblances between it and the assassination led to the film being immediately withdrawn. However, there is no evidence that the President's assassin had in fact seen the film.

Obviously there is a risk that tips on, for example, how to commit a burglary can be 'learnt' from television, and for this reason programmes such as *Crimewatch UK* are carefully vetted to ensure they do not give away such details. But when it comes to violent acts there are in fact only a limited number of ways in which they can take place, and a resemblance between the act and the programme is not necessary proof that the programme 'caused' the act.

Greatest concern is voiced at the possibility that children's behaviour might be influenced adversely by what they see on television. In particular there is concern that they might be stimulated to commit acts of violence — or, perhaps no less seriously, desensitised to the consequences of violent acts in a way that makes them seem more appealing. Both pyschologists and sociologists have undertaken research to try to find out if the hypothesis that television programmes 'cause' violence is supported by the evidence.

A number of laboratory experiments to try to determine the effects of watching violence on children seem to show that the children do imitate what they see on the screen. However, there are a number of problems which in the nature of things cannot be easily resolved. First of all, the very fact that the children are taking part in an 'experiment' may influence them to behave in a way that they think adults expect. Secondly, it is not at all clear that such imitation leads to *real* violence — children mimic in play all sorts of violent acts but they seldom do each other any real damage. Thirdly, there are many other ways in which children can react.

In her study of children in the first year of watching television, Himmelweit *et al.* (1958) found no evidence of increased propensity to violence among the children studied, although she did find that after scenes of violence children did tend to be more anxious and find it difficult to sleep.

Laboratory studies are generally suspect as they create an artificial situation in which other influences do not register. In these and similar studies subjects will stay rather than simply go off and do something else. Studies based on depth interview techniques, on the other hand, encounter other problems: the limitations of the respondents' memory (particularly where childhood is concerned), the difficulty of ensuring that all respondents have a common definition of 'violence', and the tendency of teenage boys in particular to exaggerate the daring and danger of their own actions. Thus L. D. Eron's research on information supplied by the parents and classmates of 875 children aged 8–9 showed only a very weak relationship between reported viewing habits and propensity to violence, and then only in boys. Though a later study of some of the same children ten years later showed a slightly stronger correlation between earlier viewing habits and later violence, critics noted that those who later said they had been interested in TV violence were not always the same as those whose parents had said they were interested earlier (Eron 1963; Eron *et al.* 1972).

Halloran, Brown and Chaney (1970) arranged for probation officers to interview a sample of probationers (281 male, 53 female) aged betwen 10 and 20 and compared their responses with those of a matched sample of working-class adolescents. As regards violence their findings were inconclusive.

Reviewing twenty years of media studies, F. S. Anderson (1977) reported that most (three-quarters) of such studies showed some association between the media and child aggression; 20 per cent showed no association and a very small proportion (3 per cent) showed a negative association.

William Belson's *Television Violence and the Adolescent Boy* (1978), based on interviews with more than 1,500 London boys aged between 12 and 17, claimed that his findings showed that boys who have watched a great deal of TV violence were more likely to commit 'serious' acts of violence themselves. It was criticised on each of the above grounds by Murdock and McCron (1978), who pointed out that, in leaving out the social context in which the acts occurred, they had lost almost all their individual meaning and that the definition of what was 'serious' was so broad as to include breaking into a parking meter or snapping off a car aerial. Their own study of 300 teenagers in 'a large Midlands city' (Leicester), they said, confirmed the findings of all other postwar studies of group violence, namely that it formed part of:

> a male leisure culture, centred on the search for laughs and excitement, on the values of toughness and, above all, on fighting ability. Fighting is central to this 'delinquescent' (not always actually *delinquent*) street culture. It is the prime means of expressing values, confirming reputations and cementing group identities.

Television *might*, they suggested, contribute to teenage violence. However if it did, it was less likely to be the effect of overtly violent programmes, but that of 'give-away' shows (such as *Going for Gold* or *The Generation Game*), which by pointing up the contrast between the consumer society and the lives most people actually led, could well 'generate feelings of frustration and resentment that feed into acts of violence, vandalism and theft' (Murdock and McCron 1978). If television does influence violence, therefore, its influence is likely to be indirect. In other words, it does not influence *behaviour* but *attitudes*.

# Influence on Attitudes

Halloran, Brown and Chaney (1970) drew attention to a number of mediating factors influencing the effects of television on the individual.

## Individual predispositions

The individual selects the degree of exposure to television — it is not a one-way process. In addition people vary widely in their *perception* of what they see and their capacity for *retention* — whether or not they remember it. The same message means different things to different people. New knowledge is absorbed and made use of, not just simply catalogued.

In general, in adults strong existing attitudes lead to selective perceptions and to reinforcement of existing ideas. However, this is less likely to be the case where existing attitudes are weak or non-existent, hence it does appear that concern about the effects of children's viewing on their *attitudes* is justified. The Annan Report (1977) supported this view that television had more influence on unformed opinions and attitudes, and hence on children.

## Group membership and group norms

Groups, notably families, tend to agree. They filter out and use what they accept and ignore what they reject. Primary groups establish their own norms and attitudes which harden when opposed from outside the group. Hence the content of TV programmes is *selectively disseminated* among their audiences. Not only are there striking individual differences in the effects of television, but age, class and educational status all affect the way in which the TV message is received.

## Opinion leaders

As in other aspects of social life, it appears that *opinion leaders* are of great importance in determining the degree of acceptance given to media stories. People check what they see against the views of those to whom they are accustomed to look for guidance. Where television is particularly important, however, is that TV personalities are also opinion leaders. People believe what they see rather than what they read, and Halloran *et al.* argue that people now use television as their main source of evidence for social attitudes, etc. Television reinforces existing stereotypes, though it can also demolish them, as, for example, when a personality who normally projects a warm, 'caring' image loses their temper in front of the camera.

Recent research suggests that the first careless acceptance of television is long since over, and with changing attitudes its place in the scheme of things has to be re-evaluated. The most obvious point is that television is on much more than it is watched. People do other things. The average TV set is switched on for some 5–6 hours per day. But studies using two-way screens show it is certainly not watched for all that time. The amount of actual watching varies with social class, but overall average British adults only watch about 3 hours a day. They also do an amazing variety of things at the same time as they are 'watching', some of which (such as making love, a very popular alternative) should — if done properly — leave little attention free for the TV set or its programme.

## Advertising

It would be impossible adequately to evaluate the impact of television without some consideration of *advertising*. Advertising is in itself a major 'service' industry and one which, along with banking and financial services, underwent a boom in the Thatcher years. It has also become increasingly identified with the mass media. Television now has about a third of advertising spending, which in 1981 totalled some £2,800 million and rose steadily to the end of the decade.

There is considerable debate about the true impact of advertising. However, both government and the political parties make use of advertising and pay particular attention to the use of TV. They must think it works.

Supporters of advertising claim for it two main social functions:

1. *Providing information*: The most usual justification of advertising by those who work in it is that it promotes public awareness, both about some social problems (public service advertising) and what products are available.
2. *Encouraging consumption*: To their clients, advertising agencies emphasise the role that advertising plays in promoting consumption and increasing the demand for products. Manufacturers' consumer advertising in the 1980s accounted for between 33 and 40 per cent of total advertising spending. There is in fact little difference between many such products (which can be, and indeed often are, made specifically to be advertised).

Critics of advertising accept that advertising promotes consumption, but many of them disapprove both of this and of its consequences. Three main criticisms are made:

1. By promoting consumption advertising plays a leading part in promoting *materialism* and materialist values.
2. *Manipulation and exploitation*: Since there is little real difference between many competing products, advertisers use various psychological tricks to associate them with desirable qualities and/or achievements. Some of these methods were first exposed as long ago as the 1950s by Vance Packard's *The Hidden Persuaders* (1981). In recent years the feminist critique that too many things are sold by exploitation of images of naked or scantily clad women's (rarely men's) bodies, whether relevant (e.g. bath foam) or not (e.g. motor cars), has been strenuously argued and some modification of advertising practice has taken place. The ecological critique, first voiced in John Kenneth Galbraith's *The Affluent Society* (1958), that too many things are being sold which are not needed, gained fresh attention in the 1980s with the spread of the Green Movement. These critics argue that in promoting mass production of consumer items, advertising actively causes waste and can in fact be harmful to the environment (e.g. by promoting the sale of aerosols containing CFCs — see also Meadows *et al*. 1972).
3. *Social control*: Marxists are not the only critics who see a more sinister purpose in advertising. Concentration on the trivia of consumption keeps people's attention off more serious matters, they argue, such as who is making the huge profits from the big companies who make the goods. However, it also irritates those who are badly off. The overt use of advertising to promote health awareness, discourage smoking, etc., is both more widely recognised and more favourably received.

### Control of advertising

The danger that advertising claims may be fraudulent or harmful, especially to vulnerable groups such as children and the elderly, has been met to some extent by government legislation. Blatant misuse is checked by the Advertising Standards Authority, which has power to order advertisements to be withdrawn and to impose penalties. What constitutes misuse is established by law. Claims for a product have to be capable of being substantiated, for example. Hence up to now advertisements for religious groups have not been accepted. There are also certain 'no-go' areas — a product cannot, for example, be promoted as a *cure* for something, and cigarettes cannot be advertised on television at all. Making paid advertisements look like news items is also banned, though a feature writer can still 'talk up' ('puff') a specific product.

Political advertising is an exception to the general principle that advertising must be based on verifiable claims. In 1978—79, for example, the Conservatives attacked the then Labour Government's employment record in a poster campaign with the slogan 'Labour isn't working'. They won, and within two years unemployment figures had nearly tripled. There is also no effective control over the use or abuse of party time on television. Political advertising as such is not allowed in the United Kingdom. Instead, political appeals are confined to so-called 'Party Political' broadcasts in which the main parties each get a fixed allotment of time which they can fill much as they choose.

In the United States TV advertising is much more pervasive, and many programmes have long been 'sponsored' by an advertiser, whose name is thus wholly associated with the show. Long banned in the United Kingdom, sponsored programmes are now permitted but do not yet constitute much of output. Moreover in the United Kingdom advertising is still limited to 6 minutes per hour of television. The figures in the United States are much higher: US series are made with much more frequent breaks and interruptions are longer. Something of an extreme is reached in Argentina, where Canal Once (Channel 11) only occasionally interrupts its advertising to show part of a programme — which makes for rather less than gripping viewing.

# How News is Selected

Good journalism has long distinguished between *news items*, which are supposed to be factual, and *opinion* as expressed in the newspaper's 'leading articles' ('leaders' or 'editorials'). Unfortunately, the distinction is not always preserved in practice. A more subtle problem arises with the presentation of news on television, particularly given the apparently 'authoritative' nature of the TV picture.

Thus in 1991 British viewers were presented with a sustained picture over several weeks of British troops rolling to victory in the Gulf War (with a little help from the United States). Little attention was given to the role of Saudi Arabian troops and, it could be argued, none to the anomaly of fighting to restore the rule of the Al-Sabah family in Kuwait, who had suspended their only attempt at a degree of democratisation six years before. As Murdock and Golding (1973) point out, the media habitually emphasise certain core values, such as patriotism, the national consensus and support for government decisions. Socially, this tendency serves the cause of conformity and excludes outsiders and their criticisms. War merely accentuates this general tendency.

Interestingly, the Prime Minister, John Major, took a different view of the role of the media in the conflict from that of his predecessor. During the Falklands War, Margaret Thatcher displayed public anger at the attempts of BBC speakers to present a balanced view of the conflict, and especially at the use by the broadcaster John Snow of the term 'British' troops — she wanted 'our' troops. Major took the view that the BBC was heard all over the world and not just in Britain; it must therefore be 'seen' to be impartial. His view received unexpected support later in 1991 after the attempted coup in the Soviet Union, when President Gorbachev testified that in his Black Sea isolation he had got his best information from the BBC World Service.

However, this does *not* mean that British viewers get a representative selection of all the possible 'news' that is happening at any one time. It has long been recognised that the British media can be said to have a 'catastrophic' approach towards the rest of the world. Indeed, there was once a competition among journalists on *The Times* for the most boring headline — the prize went to 'Small earthquake in Chile — not many hurt'. Generally, bad news gets attention, good does not. On the other hand, the nearer to the reader the scene of the bad news the greater its coverage. Hence a road accident in the Home Counties may get headlines if more than a few people (or even one public figure) is involved; abroad the extent of the catastrophe determines its newsworthiness, and an earthquake in Chile could notch up many dead without making page 7. Bizarre or unusual incidents get quite disproportionate coverage. Coverage of the first ever Royal Visit to Belize in Central America was reduced (by *The Daily Mirror*) to a culinary curiosity under the banner headline: 'The Queen Eats a Rat'.

The Glasgow University Media Group, starting with their aptly named *Bad News* (1976, see also 1980, 1982), made a systematic study of the social processes which result in the TV news bulletins we all see. Their study was based on a careful content analysis of six months of news programmes between January and June 1975.

At that time strikes dominated the news. They observed that some strikes were consistently given more coverage than others, especially those that occurred in the car industry. They noted that managers and experts not only were given more coverage than trade unionists and members of the public, but they received more favourable treatment in the setting and tone of their interviews. However, reporting consistently emphasised the supposed effects of the strikes on the public rather than the pay and conditions of the workers, and accepted uncritically the Labour

Government's claim that wage demands were inflationary, without any mention of other inflationary pressures, such as the steep rise in oil prices after 1973. Criticism of management was muted and in some cases (as in reports of a speech by the then Prime Minister, James Callaghan) left out altogether.

Despite their own left-wing views, the group based their argument clearly on the evidence of their sample. They believed that the outcome was consistently 'slanted' news, but they did not regard this as the product of a conscious conspiracy, nor did they accept the argument of the journalists themselves that news is the product of a kind of 'market' in which stories compete for attention and audience demand determines which are selected. Rather, they saw it as the outcome of three processes:

1. Selection for news value.
2. Simplification of issues.
3. Sensationalisation to add to news value.

All of these routine processes create distortion in the finished product, without 'slanting' for editorial reasons. Despite the controversy these studies have engendered, the work of the Group has continued and has focused lately on issues of war and peace (Broadbent 1985).

## Conformity and Deviance in the Media

In 1976 — and not for the last time — press obsession with 'welfare scroungers' developed from the reporting of a number of individual cases of welfare fraud into a full-scale campaign against the structure of the welfare state, backed by some very dubious statistics. A committee, the Co-ordinating Committee on Social Security Abuse, was set up by the Government and reported in 1977 that fraud accounted for only about 3 pence in every £100 correctly paid. But this did not stop the campaign. The *Daily Express* argued (18 December 1977): 'It is the official figure based upon frauds which have been found out. Nobody knows how much larger the figure would be if we could take into account the undiscovered fiddlers and thieves.' Of course, the *fact* was that *nobody* knew, and therefore there might *not* be any undiscovered fraud (Golding and Middleton 1976). There was no comparable 'moral panic' over the extent of tax evasion; no attempt to level blame at those who ask their plumber, electrician, bricklayer or gardener whether there is any reduction in price for payment in cash.

## Leisure

Historically, the rigid division between work and leisure did not exist. Apart from the requirement to attend church, in the early modern world Sunday was much like any other day on the farm. Cows had to be milked and the chickens fed.

The notion of *permanent* leisure, a distinction which previously had only been enjoyed by a few, emerged in the later nineteenth century among the new manufacturing classes of the United States and was attacked by Thorstein Veblen in *Theory of the Leisure Classes* (1912). On the other hand, leisure in both Britain and the United States was more generally seen as a mark of civilisation, and called into existence facilities for sport, reading and entertainment for a much wider number. In the nineteenth century humanitarian pressures brought the introduction of the Saturday afternoon off (still known in Argentina as 'the English Saturday') and the promotion of organised games. Such games were considered as preparation of body and mind for more work, so the two concepts of work and leisure remained closely related. The notion of an annual holiday also emerged, though in the industrial North and Midlands it could only be achieved by shutting down the factories themselves for two weeks at a fixed time of year. The railways made annual holidays available to the new middle classes and created the 'English seaside holiday' and with it the many resorts of the South Coast and the 'Cornish Riviera', which enjoyed their heyday in the inter-war period. Outwardly, the biggest change in British leisure patterns since 1945 has been the extension of the paid annual holiday from two weeks to four, five or six, and the growth in availability of package tours which has made Spain Britons' principal holiday destination. In 1961 97 per cent of employees were entitled to only two weeks' annual holiday; in 1988 99 per cent were entitled to four weeks or more (*Social Trends 20*, Table 10.2). But otherwise increasing demands on time from travel to work and overtime have meant that a shorter working week has not been directly reflected in extra time available for leisure activities. In fact, between 1938 and 1955 hours available for leisure activities fell (*New Society*, 29 November 1979; see also Parker, S. 1976; Roberts 1979).

Such leisure activities are characteristically shared with *friends* and play a significant role in establishing the network of personal links which we term 'friendship' (Allan 1989a, b), the wider social significance of which can hardly be overstated. Though the sociology of friendship remains relatively underdeveloped as compared with, for example, the sociology of the family, two facts stand out. Men tend in general to have a wide circle of male acquaintances, and in the maintenance of this circle shared leisure patterns are predominant. But they have relatively few friends. Women, on the other hand, tend to have a smaller circle of friends who, in addition to their shared leisure interests form a valuable extension of the family in helping to cope with unexpected demands or crisis situations.

Within the home the major influence has been the impact of television on patterns of leisure. Surveys showed that households were averaging 19–20 hours television viewing a week when the whole country had been covered in the 1970s, though lower socio-economic groups were watching up to one-third more than higher. In 1988 average television viewing for all age groups was 25 hours 21 minutes a week, with 77 per cent watching every day and 94 per cent watching at least once every week. People aged 65 and over watched half as much again as the average viewer (*Social Trends 20*, p. 153). Leisure activities in the home are very much more popular than any other form of leisure activity, as Table 10.2 shows.

Mass education in Britain means that 21 per cent of the population read for recreational purposes daily — more than in any other European country. Visiting/entertaining, going out for a meal or for a drink, listening to records and cassettes, reading books, DIY and gardening are also major activities. Less probably, Britain in the mid-1980s had more home computers per head of population than any other country in the world. And a distinctive feature of Britain, the product of fortunate climatic patterns, are the very numerous gardens. That this is a distinctive feature of British life in the cultural sense also is shown by the fact that the pattern spread with British cultural influences. (For example, gardening for enjoyment rather than profit can also be seen in Sierra Leone, a former British colony in West Africa, despite its poverty and in spite of climatic problems, but it is much less evident in France.) And on a summer Sunday, 18 million people (40 per cent of the population), visit the countryside for recreation (*New Society*, 27 February 1987).

Apart from DIY and needlework the differences between male and female leisure activities are not very great, but there is a marked difference in the amount of time devoted to them. Retired men have the most leisure time — 92 hours a week. Women in full-time employment have the least — 31 hours a week against 48 hours for men, even though women work fewer paid hours per week on average (*Social Trends 20*, p. 152). Until recently women's leisure activities have been relatively little studied by sociologists, but evidence exists that they are less likely than men to have either the time and space for extended periods of leisure and their leisure activities tend to be short-term, of the kind that can be combined with the demands of housework (Deem 1986, 1990; see also Smith, J. 1987; Allan 1989a).

Leisure activities are clearly distinguished by age as well as by gender. It is during leisure time that youth most distinctly asserts its difference from adult society (see Chapter 11). Not surprisingly, the time between leaving school and establishing a new family is marked by more active leisure pursuits which generally take place outside the home (Appleton 1975).

## Tourism

With the decline of British manufacturing industry since 1979, tourism is now a mainstay of the British economy. There are, however, two problems with it, one economic and one social. The economic problem is that much of the revenue raised from visitors coming to Britain is offset by the fact that most British people prefer to take their own holidays overseas. The social problem is that the industry is heavily concentrated on a few key attractions in a limited number of places: London, Oxford, Stratford-on-Avon, Edinburgh, etc.

Table 10.2 *Spare-time activities, by gender, 1979, 1986 (%)*

| Spare-time activities | 1979 | | 1986 | |
|---|---|---|---|---|
| | Men | Women | Men | Women |
| Visiting/entertaining relatives and friends | 89 | 93 | | |
| Dancing | 14 | 16 | 9 | 12 |
| Visiting historic sites | | | 9 | 10 |
| Going to the cinema | | | 8 | 8 |
| Going out for a meal | 71 | 57 | 47 | 47 |
| Going out for a drink | | | 65 | 47 |
| Listening to records/tapes | 64 | 60 | 69 | 65 |
| Reading books | 52 | 57 | 52 | 64 |
| Do-it-Yourself | 51 | 22 | 54 | 27 |
| Needlework etc. | NA | 51 | 3 | 48 |
| Gardening | 49 | 35 | 47 | 39 |

Sources: General Household Survey 1977 in *Society Today* 29 November 1979 and *Social Trends 20*, Table 10.3.

Among those tourist attractions that are free, the most popular has for many years been Blackpool pleasure beach, with 6.5 million visitors. The British Museum in London attracts just over half that number — 3.8 million in 1988 (*Social Trends, 1990*, 159). The introduction of admission charges in 1987 halved the number of visitors to London's outstanding Natural History Museum, a special favourite of children. The most popular attraction charging admission in 1988 was Madame Tussaud's waxwork museum (2.7 million visitors), followed by Alton Towers, an amusement park (2.5 million) and the Tower of London (2.2 million). During the 1980s several significant new developments have taken place aiming to attract visitors to other places outside London such as Bristol (the *Great Britain*), Portsmouth (the *Mary Rose* and HMS *Warrior*), and York (the Jorvik Viking exhibition). Sociologically the interesting thing about these developments is the way in which the promoters have sought to recreate the sense of actually being in a different age and a different society, aided by many of the devices of modern media presentation. For the future we may expect the construction of an increasing number of elaborate *leisure complexes*, which offer a complete range of leisure activities on one site.

Tourism requires an extensive infrastructure. Overseas visitors, like natives, have been increasingly critical in the 1980s of Britain's overstretched public transport systems. They also complain about the high prices charged by British hotels. The 1991 *Which Hotel* guide reported that prices were in many cases double those charged by comparable hotels elsewhere in Western Europe and that service often left much to be desired. British class divisions are perhaps perpetuated in the surly way in which complaints are often reported to have been received — in the United States and in other European countries service to the customer is seen as being part of the job.

# Suggestions for Further Reading

A starting point for the connection between television and violence is William Belson (1978), *Television Violence and the Adolescent Boy*. A broader view is put by Halloran, Brown and Chaney (1970), *Television and Delinquency*. On the selectivity of news see Glasgow University Media Group, *Bad News* (1976).

General treatments of the sociology of leisure include S. Parker (1976), *The Sociology of Leisure* and Ken Roberts (1979), *Contemporary Society and the Growth of Leisure*. Rosemary Deem (1986), in *All Work and No Play: the sociology of women and leisure*, gives new insights.

# 11 Social Control

## Deviance

Questions on deviance often examine the following areas:

- The sociological explanations of differential rates of deviance by class, age and gender, and between urban and rural areas. The importance of relative deprivation may be specified.
- The social construction of deviance.
- The comparison of theoretical explanations. Sometimes the contribution of two specified examples, such as labelling theory and media amplification.
- The relative effectiveness of formal as against informal controls.

## Youth

- Whether youth constitutes a class, conscious of itself, with interests in opposition to those of adult society.
- Other variations questioning the term 'youth subculture', in particular as a means to resist the dominant order or as an expression of class or gender.
- The influence of adolescent subcultures on educational achievement.

## Order and Deviance

In complex modern societies there is a 'need' for order. This is mainly achieved without overt coercion, because within any society norms are upheld informally by social disapproval of those who transgress unwritten rules of acceptable behaviour. Individuals who infringe these informal rules are regarded as *deviant*.

Such rules vary from time to time and place to place. Today, for example, it is quite acceptable not to have formal religious beliefs, but as recently as the nineteenth century Charles Bradlaugh, an early advocate of accessible birth control for the masses, was banned from membership of the House of Commons and persecuted for not accepting Christianity. People adhere to norms in the main however not because of the threat of punishment but because their socialisation has made adherence habitual. Hence they have come to believe in their rightness, or at least usefulness, and do not challenge received ideas.

Only when the formal rules of society are broken is coercion used and sanctions applied. We call these formal rules 'laws' and the breaking of these laws is termed 'crime'. But crime is only one form of deviance.

## Perspectives on Deviance

The earliest 'explanations' of deviance are not explanations at all, in that they rely on the concept of 'wickedness' which is itself defined as the propensity to break rules. The idea that there is such a being as the 'criminal', who is 'a particular type of person, apart from the rest of society and with a special predisposition towards criminal behaviour' (Marsh, in Marsh, Rosser and Harré 1978: 15) is, of course, very comforting to all those who do not see themselves as 'criminals'. It lies at the root both of biological theories of deviance and of many psychological theories. There is no good reason to suppose that it is true.

*Biological theories* of deviant behaviour were popular in the mid-nineteenth century and still reappear despite being comprehensively discredited. The Italian Cesare Lombroso in the 1860s believed that he could identify a 'criminal type' from facial characteristics of quite surprising ugliness which he claimed to have determined by measuring the faces of people in prison. However not only do the same facial characteristics also appear on people of blameless life, but even in nineteenth-century Italy there was, of course, no guarantee that everyone who committed a crime would actually be caught and sent to jail. The same problems recur with more modern studies such as that of Glueck and Glueck (1964). They found that institutionalised delinquents whom they examined were much more likely to be mesomorphs (short, squat and muscular) than the general population. However again the direction of the relationship, if any, is not clear. People kept on a prison diet and made to work hard at breaking stones, etc. are likely to become squat and muscular, whether or not they were to begin with. Further, they are characteristics that would be likely to be more common among the poorer sections of any community.

*Psychological theories* similarly began with the notion that there is a 'criminal type'. Research has not confirmed this view. A more sophisticated position is that certain personality characteristics make a person more likely to be deviant. Thus Eysenck, finding that a disproportionate number of criminals showed extrovert characteristics, argued that the extrovert was more likely than the introvert to break the rules of society. However, they are also more likely to become politicians, military leaders or captains of industry. In fact, they are more likely to get themselves noticed in whatever they do. A third possibility is that abnormal personal experiences, whether in childhood or beyond, might distort the personality so as to increase the possibility of deviant behaviour. But again

many people with seriously damaged personalities do not engage in anti-soci.
behaviour, while the range of deviance is so great that it seems unlikely that the
same complex of circumstances can account for all possible cases.

From time to time those who believe in psychological theories of deviance claim
to be able to identify 'potential criminals', and in 1991 it was reported that the
Home Office had plans to target children as young as five and six to 'stop them
drifting into lawlessness in later life' (*The Sunday Times*, 15 September 1991).
The list of factors they claimed were relevant were: criminal history in the child's
family, unhappy family background, inconsistent behaviour by parents, large
family size, a record of truancy and failure to do well at school. However, as
will be seen later, this list does not include many of the well-established sociological
factors, and so is at best worthless and at worst an excuse for Orwellian state
intervention.

## Sociological theories

Durkheim, in keeping with his time, identified one class of possible deviants whom
he terms 'biological deviants'; those who for physical or psychological reasons
find deviant behaviour 'normal'. But modern sociologists argue that deviance is
not a property of the individual but is *socially defined*. It is measured by reference
to the social norms of the society in which it occurs and must therefore be explained
by reference to the structure of that society. Moreover within each society deviance
is much more prevalent in some social groups than others.

*Functionalists* see deviance as both functional and dysfunctional.

Deviance is *functional* in two ways. On the one hand, like Durkheim's
'functional rebel', there are some individuals who challenge the prevailing morality

**Perspectives on deviance**

**Functionalist**

- Deviance is the product of poor socialisation and social disadvantage.
- Punishment reinforces social norms.

**Marxist**

- Deviance is defined by the power-holders.
- Laws criminalise those who threaten the existing power structure.

**Interactionist**

- Deviance is what is labelled as such by society
- Law is selectively applied against threatening groups. Periodic 'moral panics' occur.

of society and so bring about its reform. On the other, society's response to everyday deviance reminds the rest of us what our values and norms are and the punishment visited on deviants serves as a warning to others. Hence the rituals by which we confirm our disapproval, trials, are very significant events and are given extensive media coverage.

Alternatively, when there is something wrong with society itself, deviance is *dysfunctional*. When it occurs something has gone wrong, as when a cancerous cell appears in an organism. The conventional wisdom is that deviance is the product of poor socialisation, caused by poverty, social deprivation and lack of education. The state establishes the educational system for precisely this reason, to facilitate the task of social control.

Explaining just *how* such factors result in deviance is more problematic. The American sociologist Robert K. Merton (1968) saw the problem as lying in *anomie*, or alienation. This results in turn from the gap between goals and the means to achieve them which he saw as the natural result of the emphasis of American society on individual success. The assumption is that every member of a society absorbs the same goals and will seek to achieve those goals before failure leads them to seek other means. Of the many possible adaptations to the problem of reconciling goals and means, some will be deviant. Merton identifies five categories:

1. *Conformism* is the acceptance of both goals and means and is the most common response.
2. *Innovation* involves acceptance of the goals but rejection of the means. Many are able to do this in a way that is socially acceptable, by striving for success in a particular way, such as 'pop' singers. A small but significant proportion of such people are able to apply their talents for innovation in a way that is not only socially acceptable but makes them wealthy and/or famous. Many of Britain's millionaires — Alan Sugar is a well-known example — are 'self-made' and left school at the earliest possible age. Those who are at the lower end of the social pyramid, however, will feel the strongest pressure to 'innovate' but because of social deprivation and lack of education they are the least likely to be able to do so.
3. *Ritualism* involves either rejection of the goals of society or disbelief in them coupled with a maintenance of the means by which they are to be achieved. Merton sees this as a characteristic of the lower middle-class individual who has reached a peak of advancement but continues to believe in the importance of 'getting on'.
4. *Retreatism* is one possible way towards the rejection of both goals and means. It is the least common response since it involves the acceptance of outcast status. Some who respond in this way, such as tramps and chronic drinkers, are deviant but probably not criminal. Drug addicts, on the other hand, are trapped in a pattern of behaviour which will inevitably lead to them breaking the law and almost certainly lead to them being caught and labelled as criminals.

5. *Rebellion* involves rejecting both goals and means, and proposing alternatives. If successful, the rebel is a hero; if unsuccessful, a villain.

However, Merton is open to the criticism that he looks at society as a whole and does not stress that some specific groups within society are more likely to encounter problems than others. Marxists have been particularly critical that there seems no clear relationship between class position and response, although in this respect they are not necessarily on strong ground, since deviance is widely distributed, if not as easily identified, throughout society and criminal behaviour is not confined to the poor. Hence more recent functionalist approaches have focused on subcultures within society, which for one reason or another seem disadvantaged relative to society as a whole. Cloward and Ohlin (1961) argue that members of the working class have less chance of achieving their goals by legitimate means owing to their relative lack of resources. The theory can even be applied to relatively small sub-groups, as, for example, when Albert Cohen (1955) identifies deviance among adolescent boys with *status frustration*. Such boys may achieve status within a delinquent subculture that they are unable to attain in society as a whole.

*Marxists* argue that deviance, and especially crime, is related to the power structure. It is those with power who make laws and criminalise those who threaten their interests. Hence most laws relate to the protection of private property. Private property is a hegemonic value. That is to say, it is one so powerful that for the most part it is not questioned, but assumed to be natural, derived from the dominant capitalist ideology. Likewise criminal activities are seen as more prevalent and more threatening in some social sectors than others. The classic example is the disproportionate moral outrage expressed by politicians and the media over social security 'fiddling' as compared with the far more costly problem of tax evasion. Further the law is seen by Marxists as being more vigorously applied against some groups rather than others.

*Interactionists* also see the power structure as important. It is a process set in motion by the establishment of rules, the breaking of which may constitute deviance if the rest of society labels it as such. The *reactions* of others are as important in creating deviance as are the intentions of the actor when performing the deviant action. Interactionists recognise that society exhibits a plurality of subcultures whose values may conflict with one another. Only some people who break rules are 'found out' and only some of those are then subsequently labelled as deviant. Once a label has been attached, the wearer may live up to it. Hence much interactionist work on deviance is subsumed under the title *labelling theory* (Becker 1973).

For interactionists, as for Marxists, the law is selectively applied, most harshly against those social groups perceived as the greater threat. Cicourel (1968) found that black working-class youths were most likely to be labelled as delinquents and to be charged with offences by US police. White middle-class youths were far more likely to be handed over to their parents, whom officers saw as responsible citizens who could deal with any problems themselves. Similar evidence has been found in Great Britain (see below).

Interactionists have further been interested in the way in which small problems become amplified by the media. 'Folk devils' are created, a 'moral panic' (Cohen, S. 1980) occurs, a *deviancy amplification spiral* is set up (Wilkins 1964) and the process runs out of control as the media seize on the issue to make 'good copy' (Young, J. 1971). Recent examples of such issues in Britain have been 'mugging', 'football hooliganism' and 'child abuse'.

Though bearing a new American name, 'mugging' is in fact an old British custom, for Victorian gentlemen carried 'life preservers' to protect themselves from attack on the gas-lit streets of London.

'Football hooliganism' is as common on the Continent of Europe as in Britain, and in South America pitches are surrounded by fences and moats to protect the players and most particularly the referee. But following the Heysel stadium disaster the issue was used by government to argue for repressive legislation which would impose strict controls on (mostly young and working-class) football supporters, most of whom behave themselves most of the time. In the words of Stuart Hall (Hall *et al.*, 1978: 34) the effect of the panic is that 'the tendency is increased to deal with any problem, first by simplifying its causes, second by stigmatising those involved, third by whipping up public feeling and fourth by stamping on it hard from above'. The irony is that the stricter application of the law creates its own 'justification' by criminalising new groups, thus in turn increasing the figures for reported crime.

More recently publicity given to cases of child abuse, which has given rise to a national campaign on television to search out more cases, was followed by several spectacular 'disclosures' in different parts of the country of groups said to have been engaged in systematic child abuse. In the course of the panic the media entirely lost sight of the distinction between *abuse in general*, e.g. beating, and *sexual abuse*. The two were repeatedly confused in debate, creating the impression that sexual abuse of children was very common. Simple neglect remains by far the most frequent and dangerous form of child abuse, but parental incapacity does not sell as many newspapers.

## Explanations of the Growth in 'Crime' in the 1980s

The central paradox of the 1980s was that under a government that repeatedly claimed to be committed to 'law and order' policies, official crime statistics showed a strong upward trend. In 1974 there were 89,599 recorded crimes of violence, in 1984 the figure had almost doubled, to 154,000. But the figures concealed very considerable nationwide variations. The murder rate had remained almost constant, rising by only 3 per cent over the decade to 620 in 1984. Yet woundings and assaults had doubled; robberies tripled. And although sexual assaults had fallen, from 17,000 to 15,000, the most serious of these, the relatively small number of reported rapes, had increased from 1,050 in 1974 to 1,430 ten years later. In the latter years of the decade the figures for recorded rape climbed even more steeply.

Government explanations included:

1. *The 'permissive society'* of the 1960s and its effects on the upbringing of children. This is very unlikely to be an explanation of the figures given above, however, for two reasons. First, the *rate of increase* in reported crime in the 1970s was almost identical with that in the 1950s, before the advent of 'permissiveness'. Second, 'permissiveness' is largely a feature of middle-class upbringing, and has had less impact on working-class families. Hence it cannot be invoked as an adequate explanation of increased crime amongst the working classes.

2. *Inadequate policing.* The Thatcher Government of 1979—83 increased both the numbers and the pay of the police and the Public Order Act 1986 substantially increased their powers of detention, etc. Crime figures continued to rise.

3. *Inadequate punishment.* Backbenchers and police spokesmen alike stressed the need for sharp punishment of offenders as an example to others. The problem with this is, of course, to catch the offender. Successive Conservative Home Secretaries, however, took a number of initiatives (notably the Criminal Justice Act of 1987) designed to increase the certainty and severity of punishment, including introducing mandatory minimum sentences for certain crimes, extending custodial sentences (imprisonment), and providing harsher alternatives to non-custodial sentences. The figures continued to climb and the prisons became so overcrowded that a major prison-building and

Table 11.1 *Number of offences recorded by the police: England and Wales*

| Year | Number of offences | No. per 100,000 pop |
|------|--------------------|---------------------|
| 1977 | 2,636,500 | 5368 |
| 1978 | 2,561,500 | 5215 |
| 1979 | 2,536,700 | 5159 |
| 1980 | 2,688,200 | 5459 |
| 1981 | 2,963,800 | 5971 |
| 1982 | 3,262,400 | 6577 |
| 1983 | 3,247,000 | 6546 |
| 1984 | 3,499,100 | 7047 |
| 1985 | 3,611,900 | 7258 |
| 1986 | 3,847,400 | 7331 |
| 1987 | 3,892,200 | 7773 |
| 1988 | 3,715,800 | 7396 |
| 1989 | 3,870,100 | 7681 |
| 1990 | 4,363,600 | |

Source: *Criminal Statistics for England and Wales, 1986*, p. 27, HMSO, cited by Smith, D., 1988.

refurbishment programme had to be undertaken. In 1990 a new White Paper, *Crime, Justice and Protecting the Public*, called for measures to divert less serious offenders from prison, provided their offences had been non-violent. It later appeared that recorded crime had risen by 15 per cent in the first quarter of the year — the sharpest rise since records began in 1857 (*The Guardian*, 29 June 1990).

4. *Public co-operation*. The need for the public to co-operate in crime prevention. 'Neighbourhood watch' schemes were therefore encouraged and individuals encouraged to fit more locks and other security devices in their homes — at their own expense, of course. The effect of these was often to make people feel *less* safe (Smith, D. 1988).

## The Statistical Problem

Official figures on the incidence of crime refer only to *recorded crime*, that is to say, crimes that have been reported to the police and have been recorded as such. Media reports of such figures often do refer to this fact, but the distinction is often lost in what follows.

Crimes are not recorded if:

1. They are unknown to the police. Many incidents of rape are still not reported to the police because the victims fear that they will have to undergo the further suffering involved in appearing in court and defending themselves against defence lawyers' accusations that they had invited the attack.
2. They are known to the police but not defined by the police as being crimes. When police officers stop a speeding motorist they have the option either of prosecuting or of giving the motorist a verbal warning. In the former case the incident becomes a crime; in the latter it does not.
3. The police do not regard the activity concerned as being of sufficient importance to warrant the use of police time and effort and so do not bother to find out if it is going on or not. Homosexual importuning is a classic case of an activity which is legally criminal but which may or may not be 'noticed' by the statistics according to the policy of the Chief Constable of the force concerned.
4. The police lack the facilities to determine whether or not a crime has been committed. This is true of much of what is now often termed 'white-collar crime' — 'crime committed by persons of respectability and high social status in the course of their occupations' (Sutherland 1949; see below, p. 255) — such as embezzlement or tax evasion.

Criminal statistics are therefore an uncertain guide to the actual incidence of crime. At one extreme, a very high proportion of murders, probably over 90 per cent, are recorded as such, though it does not follow, of course, that the murderers will actually be caught. At the other, breaches of factory safety legislation, though potentially fatal, are rarely successfully prosecuted. When they are, the punishment for the firm concerned is usually trivial. These and other 'white collar' crimes account for significant numbers of fatalities and mammoth losses by big corporations but are rarely successfully prosecuted, strengthening the impression that the only 'real' crime is working-class crime.

Crime statistics are therefore not 'objective' facts, as the early positivists would have seen them (it is only fair to say that few modern researchers would), but the product of three processes:

1. Social ideas about which of many deviant actions are to be considered criminal (labelling theory).
2. Social reactions to specific categories of acts (social reaction theory).
3. A process of negotiation within the control agencies by which certain individuals are selected as criminals (ethnomethodology).

This process of selection is, as Jock Young (1971) showed in his study of drug control in Notting Hill, strongly influenced by the segregated position of the police in society. He argued that a quarter of London police officers lived in groups of six or more police, and three-quarters of them believed that their job adversely affected their social life. They had little knowledge of ordinary people, especially middle-class youth, outside the arrest situation and were therefore particularly vulnerable to the effects of media distortion. They lacked the contact with deviants which would be necessary in order to understand their motivations, and hence acted in such a way that deviance was amplified, as for example by 'planting' drugs on known pot-smokers. They were more concerned to catch the 'pusher' than the smoker and did not recognise that the dynamics of the situation means that the two were often synonymous. In court the smoker kept up the pretence that the pusher was someone else in order to get a minimum sentence, thus in turn reinforcing the police image of the situation.

If these interactionist arguments are correct, then we should find that:

> some societies, for some reason, find it necessary to treat deviance with great intolerance, and others are able to accommodate greater degrees of tolerance, and, as a result of such tolerance, experience less serious deviance (Wilkins 1964).

The evidence is that this is indeed the case. Unfortunately moral panics serve a useful purpose to those who for one reason or other wish to create a more repressive society.

# The Impact of Crime on the Public

Despite these reservations as to whether there was a real rise in crime during the 1980s, there is clear evidence that in the inner city areas crime was seen as an important problem by the majority of residents. In Islington, Jones and Young (1986) found that a third of all households had been affected by *serious* crime in the previous twelve months:

> Crime shaped people's lives to a remarkable degree. A quarter of all people *always* avoided going out after dark, specifically because of fear of crime, and 28 per cent felt unsafe in their own homes. There is a virtual curfew on a substantial section of the female population. Over half of the women never or seldom went out after dark, because of their fear of crime.

This finding seems at first sight to contradict the contemporary evidence of the British Crime Survey, which showed that the average person could expect to be burgled only every 40 years and robbed every 500 years. But residents of Islington, and especially women, were shown not only to be much more at risk from robbery than the global figures would suggest, but their experience of other more serious crimes was even more alarming. Over half had experienced some form of sexual harassment and a fifth knew someone who had been sexually assaulted or molested in the previous year. The experiences were not evenly spread across racial and age groups. Effectively whites over 45 lived in 'a totally different universe' from younger people. White women in the 16–24 age-group were thirty times more likely to be sexually attacked than those over 45. The groups most at risk were not consistent: the risk of attack was greatest for Afro-Caribbean women aged between 15 and 44, and for Asians over 45. But all agreed with a remarkable degree of consistency which crimes were the most serious and believed it was the duty of the police to enforce those standards across the board.

> Young blacks think the police should give most attention to (i) racist attacks; (ii) sexual attacks on women; (iii) robberies in the street; (iv) use of heroin; (v) burglary; (vi) drunken driving. These are exactly the same top six crimes given priority by the population as a whole. The only difference in ordering is the understandable exception that racist attacks move into first place and that, in common with all young people, sexual attacks on women are seen as a somewhat higher category of assault. (*New Society*, 24 January 1986).

Comparisons with other European countries show that all portions of the United Kingdom have lower crime rates than the European average, and especially low rates for violence and sexual assaults.

## Deviant Groups

The anti-sociological currents in Britain in the 1980s were reflected in the dusting-off, revival and indeed development of the oldest 'explanation' of deviance, that it constitutes a simple choice between good and evil. This view, revived in the 1970s in the United States, was expressed publicly by such prominent people as the Chief Constable of Greater Manchester, who claimed to be directly inspired by God, and the Governor of Strangeways Prison, who saw the rebellion of 1990 as 'an explosion of evil'.

In this view crime is seen as a deliberate action based on calculations of gain and chances of escaping punishment. It specifically rejects the 'dominant liberal' view of deviance as a reaction to problems of poor upbringing, deprivation etc.

Even allowing for differential opportunity, it is hard to see how this theory can explain the marked prevalence of deviance among some social groups.

In April 1990 a large demonstration against the newly imposed 'poll tax' was held in Trafalgar Square. A small group broke away from the main demonstration and advanced on the new gates installed by Mrs Thatcher on the Whitehall end of Downing Street. Their way was barred by police. Suddenly a bottle and other missiles were thrown and without warning the situation erupted into violence. The police drove them back towards Trafalgar Square, believing that in the larger crowd they would be neutralised. Instead, the police were pelted with masonry and scaffolding from a building site, and what had been a peaceful demonstration became a major riot. When it was over, several hours later, 600 had been injured and 341 people had been arrested on charges ranging from arson to criminal damage and looting.

The riot shocked middle-class opinion and caused a 'moral panic'. The breakaway group were immediately labelled 'a new, seemingly mindless, group of street fighters' (*The Sunday Times*, 8 April 1990). Yet there was nothing unexpected about the social profile of those charged. Their *average* age was 22. Their other main distinguishing characteristic was that they were poor and/or working-class: 'Many were recorded as of no fixed abode. The majority said they were jobless. Two came to court shoeless.'

**Deviant groups**

| | |
|---|---|
| Those labelled as 'deviant' by society are *more likely* to be: | |
| *Social class* | Working-class |
| *Gender* | Male |
| *Race* | Black |
| *Age* | Young |
| *Area* | Urban |

## Social class

Recorded crime is overwhelmingly working-class. Part of this is almost certainly the product of social interpretation. 'White-collar' crime is not only difficult to detect but is quite likely not even to be reported to the police. It is clear that companies often do 'deals' with erring employees, who if they return the missing funds are then simply dismissed, allowed to resign or even permitted to retire. The directors are unwilling to prosecute for fear of loss of shareholders' or bankers' confidence in their ability to manage, and the treatment of firms who do prosecute seems in some cases to confirm their fears.

Second, *it is middle-class values that define what is deviant*. The social order based not on consensus (as is asserted by ruling elites and accepted by functionalists) but on control by the middle class. What the middle classes do, then, becomes normal; 'crime' is what is done by the working class.

Third, *what is crime is what has led to a conviction*. The middle classes present an image of respectability both to the police and in court, which strengthens their claim to be innocent. The more well-to-do among them can afford the high fees charged by lawyers. Ironically, this advantage is shared to a limited extent not by members of the working class in regular employment but by the very poor with no resources. The British legal aid system hits middle-income groups hardest, as they neither get help nor do they have the funds to pay the fees.

The police reflect the dominant values of society, which are middle-class values. They are therefore less willing than sociologists to draw a distinction between what is legal and what is normal. As Willmott (1966) has shown, stealing may be an aspect of 'normal' behaviour in some urban working-class areas. Those areas will therefore gain a reputation for housing 'criminal' elements and be policed accordingly. The middle-class person who steals in the same fashion is less likely to be caught and more likely to escape severe punishment on a first offence.

Beyond this, following Durkheim and Marx, many commentators still see the rest of the explanation of working-class crime in the concept of anomie. The working class, they argue, have in general fewer chances to achieve the same goals as members of the middle class. Crime offers a possible, if risky, alternative route to wealth. However, it remains a question whether in fact the same goals are internalised. Most appear to recognise all too well the limitations of their socio-economic position. We have to explain therefore not only why some should feel differently, but why they should turn to crime, for middle-class expectations often exceed achievements too.

Pyle (1987) demonstrated a strong link between crime levels and the rate of unemployment — a link strenuously denied by government spokespersons at the time. He argued that the effects of the increase of unemployment after 1979 had in effect 'blanketed' any fall in crime rates resulting from more effective policing and harsher sentences.

## Gender

It seems to be true, not just for the United Kingdom in the 1990s, but for all known societies, for all historical periods, for all age groups and for all but a few crimes (the most important exception being cruelty to children), that women *commit* fewer crimes than men. Despite dark suggestions that women have a greater opportunity to conceal their crimes (e.g. poisoning), the probability that their role as accomplices in crime is under-reported, and the evidence that they are more likely than men to be cautioned as opposed to charged, there is no reason to suppose that the degree of under-reporting of female crime is really very much greater than that of male. If men make the laws, it seems, it is also men who break them.

So why do women commit fewer crimes than men?

1. The simplest answer, but almost certainly an incorrect one, is that owing to traditional restrictions on their role in society women have less *opportunity*

to commit crimes. However, for most crimes the differences are so marked that this can hardly be the explanation. It is true that 40 per cent of those convicted for shoplifting are women, but given the number of hours that women spend shopping compared with men this figure is less impressive than it looks. Moreover, the move towards equality for women in the twentieth century for some fifty years was not reflected in any change in the crime statistics, and the rise in female crime since the 1960s has almost exactly paralleled the rise in male crime.

2. The second possibility is that women do not through lack of strength or otherwise have the *ability* to commit as many crimes as men. However, since they do not seem to commit those crimes which they could commit (which is almost everything), this does not seem to be a very good argument.

3. The third possibility might be that *women express their deviance differently*, and what women do is not made criminal by the law. However though this is undoubtedly true in some rather special instances, e.g. lesbianism, for those actions which are most universally regarded as crimes, e.g. murder, the law makes no distinction.

4. Sociologists and psychologists concur, however, that there could be some connection between the propensity to commit crimes and the fact that men and women undergo *different socialisation processes*. Will, Self and Datar (1976) found that this process began with the newborn child. Babysitters treated the same child differently depending on which gender they believed it to be. Boys were encouraged to be adventurous and aggressive, and their toys, comics and TV heroes reflect these assumptions. Girls were encouraged to co-operate with one another, and to be non-violent and docile. In their teens they have less tendency to form large friendship groups (gangs). They tend to have a single role model, to become a mother, which is both practical and restrictive, while boys are encouraged to aim for a career which they may well not attain and which can leave them bitter and dissatisfied.

## Race

The steep rise in unemployment between 1979 and 1981 was accompanied by outbreaks of urban violence in England on a level not previously seen in modern times. The first occurred in April 1980 in the St Paul's district of Bristol when police raided a café frequented by blacks. The much bigger riots in Brixton, South London, the following year (1981) were triggered by a police 'stop and search' operation, and in July of the same year riots occurred in over thirty cities and towns. After that there was a lull until 1985, when again two major outbreaks took place in Handsworth in Birmingham and on the Broadwater Farm Estate in Tottenham, London. In the latter instance firearms were used and in the course of the running battle with police an officer was hacked to death.

In the course of the enquiry that followed, chaired by Lord Scarman, attention focused on two issues: the sense of disadvantage felt by some ethnic groups and the lack of citizenship rights they felt. Once again the problem was the *interaction* between the police and ethnic minorities. The police felt that they were simply doing their job; the ethnic minorities perceived the police as aggressive and hostile (Scarman 1982).

The Scarman Report showed that blacks were more likely to come under suspicion from the police than whites. While the police saw black youths as especially likely to be associated with crime, many young people in Brixton had become suspicious of everything the police did. They particularly resented their use of the 'stop and search' powers, which the Metropolitan Police had under an Act of 1824 which entitled them to stop people on suspicion of being involved in crime.

In fact, from the 1960s onwards there had been major changes in the strategy and tactics of policing in the metropolitan area. The 'bobby on the beat' had been replaced by patrols in 'panda cars' (from the black-and-white stripes which distinguished them), and the police, increasingly preoccupied with 'serious' crimes, had been distanced from the public. Recruitment to the force had become increasingly difficult and among its overwhelmingly white membership there were many who openly held and expressed racist views (Coleman and Gorman 1982; Policy Studies Institute 1983). Hardly surprisingly, few members of the racial minorities joined. In fact, the feeling of dissension among West Indian youths had characteristically led them to take refuge in a 'counter-culture', some elements of which, such as the habit of smoking ganja (marijuana), helped legitimise the unwelcome attention of which they complained (Pryce 1979; Rex 1982).

## Age

Some of the earliest sociological studies of youth focused on delinquents, notably W. F. Whyte's *Street Corner Society* (1956), the pioneering study utilising participant observation, and Thrasher, *The Gang* (1927). At this stage delinquency was seen mainly as something relatively mild, which occurred outside school. However, since the 1950s deviance in Britain has been highest in the latter half of the teens but with its origins related to the process of formal education. It could be because social maturity, responsibility and fear of being caught are later developments, or because teenagers, especially boys, near the age of adult responsibility become more conscious of their growing experience and become over confident about their ability to get away with acts they know to be criminal. This seems to be confirmed by the statistics for motoring offences, which are most likely to be committed by 17-year-old boys who have just passed their driving test and think they know it all. (It could also be that older people with more experience commit just as many crimes but being more experienced are less likely to be caught and so 'labelled' as criminals, but this seems inadequate in accounting for the massive differences in crime levels.)

School is not merely one of society's control mechanisms countering delinquency, it may also actually be a cause of it. It is significant that as the school-leaving age has been raised, so has the age of peak delinquency. David Hargreaves (1967) noted the effect of 'streaming' in a secondary school on the emergence of sub-cultures. Pupils who did well developed a conformist sub-culture; those who did not developed an anti-academic sub-culture and became, in his word, 'delinquescent'. Writers like Stuart Hall and Phil Cohen at the Centre for Contemporary Cultural Studies at Birmingham have argued for a Marxist interpretation of this phenomenon. Schools, they argue, attempt to impose alien middle-class values on working-class children. The result is resentment against the authority of the school initially, leading later to resentment against authority in general.

## Area

Crime is a predominantly *urban* phenomenon. It therefore seems plausible to seek at least some of its causes in the social effects of urbanization. And, following Robert Park, it was in Chicago and among the Chicago School that a group of sociologists laid the foundation for an *ecological model* of crime. In their *Juvenile Delinquency and Urban Areas* (1942) Clifford Shaw and Henry McKay noted that male rates of delinquency were at the highest in the area surrounding the inner business centre. This zone, originally occupied by the well-to-do, had by the 1920s begun to fall into decay and to be occupied by immigrant workers, characterised by poverty, poor housing, unstable family conditions and social disorganisation. It was social disorganisation, they argued, that was conducive to crime.

Critics argued that since crime was part of the evidence for social disorganisation the argument ran the risk of becoming circular. Besides, not everyone who lived in a 'zone of transition' turned to crime. This, another Chicago sociologist, Edwin Sutherland (Sutherland and Cressy 1966), suggested was because crime only emerged where there were criminal associations, or gangs, which nurtured deviance. The question of why certain groups became deviant and others did not however was still not satisfactorily explained. This focused attention on what Albert K. Cohen (1955) called the 'sub-culture' within which deviance was 'learned'.

Sub-cultures emerge within society when, Cohen argued, the general culture sets goals but fails to provide adequate means for them to be fulfilled. Male working-class youths are most likely to find themselves in this position when they fail to achieve at school and find themselves at the bottom of the stratification system. Among those groups who are unable to achieve success there can be several responses, as Cloward and Ohlin argue. However some adopt a strategy of *adaptation*, rejecting the goals of society in favour of an alternative set of goals which they can achieve and which are accorded high status by their peers. The rejection of the norms of society leads them into behaviour society will regard as criminal. W. B. Miller (1958) emphasises the independent origin of such sub-cultures in a concern with 'toughness' and masculinity. Obviously such sub-cultures will more readily develop where there are many youths in similar circumstances, that is, in urban areas. Moreover, as Matza (1969) points out, one should expect delinquent subcultures to be located within what he terms 'the subculture of delinquency'. Boys whose brothers are in jail, and who grow up to find this a natural state of affairs, are more likely to drift into delinquency themselves. *At the same time*, however, they accept the 'conventional view' of society that what they are doing is 'wrong'. On that basis the majority of them exempt drunkards, the old or the infirm from their attentions.

We would therefore expect the number of youngsters convicted (or cautioned) for indictable offences to be relatively high in deprived working-class areas and low in well-to-do middle-class areas. Statistics for England and Wales show that Cleveland is, in fact, the county in which both boys and girls are most likely to be convicted or cautioned; Surrey, in the Home Counties' 'stockbroker belt', has the best record. But as usual we have to be careful in assessing the reasons for this. Crime is higher in urban areas for several reasons: there are more residents so there is more to steal, they are more anonymous, so mechanisms of informal social control are less effective; conversely formal control is more likely to be called into play if an incident occurs.

## Youth Culture in the United Kingdom

Culture has two aspects for the group of people who share it. Social relations are structured by it; they are also interpreted in the light of it. However some cultures in society are stronger than others, and all others have to struggle against the dominant culture in order to survive. Youth cultures (or sub-cultures) have a double problem; they have to struggle both against the dominant culture and against the culture of their area, class or group. Strictly speaking, the media use of the term 'youth culture' is inaccurate; even in a small country like Britain there are various youth sub-cultures.

The idea of a stage between childhood and adulthood is very recent. The period of 'youth' broadly corresponds to the 'teenage' years; when it begins is not clear and its end, the age of maturity, was brought down from 21 to 18 in the 1960s. During this time the young person is not expected to behave like a child but is not allowed to be an adult, either. In simple societies, *rites of passage* — such as a boy's first successful hunt — mark the end of childhood and the beginning of adulthood. In modern industrial society such as Britain, things are more complex. At 16, a person may leave school, get a job, marry and have children, but may not drive a car, take out a mortgage or buy an alcoholic drink. Therefore, beginning work or getting married does not in itself mark the entry to adulthood. There is no clear role for youth and therefore teenagers suffer from what Durkheim and Merton called *anomie*.

Even before the Second World War there were signs of the possible future emergence of youth as a distinct sub-culture in Britain. The rapid spread of the motor car, the motor cycle, the cinema and the dance-hall, gave 'teenagers' (originally an American term) both the ability to get away from their parents and somewhere to gather when they did. Advertisers exploited the new spending potential of youth while the mass media reinforced their sense of separateness by criticising their dress, habits and behaviour as if they were a collective group, giving rise to periodic 'moral panics'.

This development may have been accelerated by the disruption of the war, but the main influences leading to its emergence as a distinct sub-culture seem to have been:

1. *Rapid social change*, which left parents unable to provide a full and satisfactory role-model for their children, who therefore needed a period to work it out for themselves.
2. The *extension of mass secondary education* (Coleman 1961). Raising the school-leaving age meant that teenagers were isolated from the discipline of work for a longer period during which they were concentrated together and could develop distinctive values and lifestyles.
3. The *returning affluence* of the early 1950s which enabled youth to emerge as a major consumer group (Abrams 1963) for the 'hi-fi' revolution. The arrival from the United States of 'rock and roll' offered youth an alternative set of role models and a new uniform — long hair, tight blue jeans, etc. — which had a satisfyingly shocking effect upon staid English society.
4. In turn this was immediately labelled as deviant and a potential threat to society by the *mass media*. Newspapers and television, in their struggle to compete with one another, found youth a source of stories and so encouraged both new fashions and alarm at their rapid spread. As Howard Becker was to point out later, deviance was 'not a quality that lies in the behaviour itself, but in the interaction between those who commit acts and those who respond to them' (Becker 1966: 14).

A classic instance of the way in which society created its own 'folk devils' can be found in the publicity given by the media to 'mods' and 'rockers' in the 1960s. 'Mods' and 'rockers' were mainly working-class, though unlike their predecessors, the 'teddy boys' or 'teds', they did not dress in the style of the well-to-do (the 'Edwardian' look) but adapted basic articles already available: in the case of the 'rockers' black leather jackets and motor cycles, and in the case of the 'mods' short hair, mohair suits and Lambrettas. Nor when they were not at the seaside were they particularly noticeable. But after scattered incidents of violence between smallish groups in Clacton, Southend and Brighton on which they had descended in search of entertainment on wet Bank Holidays, the press turned them into two great rival movements, obligingly predicted their descent on other places (a self-fulfilling prophecy) and so sold millions of newspapers to the alarmed and outraged inhabitants of South Coast seaside resorts (Cohen, S. 1980).

In fact, most working-class youths do not spend a significant period of their lives in coherent subcultures, and even persistent offenders in delinquent sub-cultures do not spend much of their time involved in delinquent or criminal behaviour (Parker, H. 1974). Graham Murdock (Murdock and McCron 1974) argues that working-class youth is much more concerned with school and work. Paul Corrigan (1979) suggests that their main preoccupation is how to pass the time. But where they differ from earlier generations is in their ability to get away from home and school influences and youth sub-cultures therefore can be seen as attempts to distance themselves from these influences. 'Subculture is a compromise solution between two contradictory needs,' writes Phil Cohen: 'the need to create and express autonomy and difference from parents and the need to maintain the parental identifications which support them' (Cohen, P. 1972). And sub-cultures are above all defined in terms of 'style' (Hebdige 1979).

As Hall and Jefferson (1975) point out, working-class youth is brought up within working-class culture, but comes into contact with the dominant culture of society through the institutions which mediate the dominant culture to the subordinate culture, e.g. schools, work, leisure, the police, social workers, etc. The subordinate culture negotiates and resists the effect of the dominant culture. These defensive measures are adapted by youth and then become youth sub-cultures. Thus youth sub-cultures emerge where working-class youth is in contact with agencies of the dominant culture. But they remain clearly located in the parent culture. Common elements in working-class sub-cultures are an emphasis on collectivity, a stress on territoriality and an assertion of male dominance. These features of the parent culture reappear in more pronounced forms in youth sub-cultures. The skinheads of the early 1970s with their cropped heads, braces and Doc Marten boots, were merely collecting together the most exaggerated features of working-class dress of the period, while the punk rock movement of the later 1970s, rejecting work and career, reflected the working-class experience of the dole queues.

The dominant style of youth sub-cultures, then, is male. Male youth sub-culture, with its aggressive *machismo*, can hardly be shared by female youth, and in fact it is not. Women feature in the lyrics and imagery of much pop music as passive recipients of male aggression. However their own conception of themselves is an active one, and McRobbie (1991) argues that their main task, to 'escape' from the family and to assert themselves, is in direct contradiction to all that present-day youth subculture stands for and a necessary step in feminist self-realisation.

Middle-class youth has also been involved in subcultural movements which reflect cultural disaffiliation from the dominant culture. These are generally radical and politicised and thus have been called 'counter-cultures' rather than sub-cultures (after Roszak 1970). Examples are the 'beatniks' of the 1950s (associated with the ban the bomb movement), the 'hippie' movement of the late 1960s (associated with the anti-Vietnam protests and the outbreak of student unrest across the world in 1968), Gay Liberation, drug cultures, etc. Their expansive nature reflects the greater opportunities open to members of the middle class. 'Middle-class culture affords the space and opportunity for sections of it to 'drop out' of circulation. Working-class youth is persistently and consistently structured by the dominating alternative rhythm of Saturday Night and Monday Morning' (Hall and Jefferson 1975: 60−1).

# Drink and Drugs

In a democratic society, the general assumption must be that people have the right to do what they want to do, provided they do not harm anyone else. An important test case for this is the handling of addiction. Should the state be the guardian of individual liberty in this area, or should it act to ensure protection for innocent victims?

In England and Wales two important addictive substances, alcohol and tobacco, are freely sold to adults. Limited safeguards restrict their sale but these are designed only to withhold them from children and to ensure that the government enjoys a very substantial revenue from their sale. Against this tobacco-related illnesses account for over 100,000 premature deaths a year, many of them after a very high cost to the NHS. It causes more damage to public health than all other drugs put together. The consumption of alcohol almost doubled between 1950 and 1979, while at the same time a number of alcohol-related problems increased also, including accidents, drownings, addiction, medical conditions and crimes. Although alcohol is 'legal', it is an offence to drive a car (or ride a bicycle) while under the influence of drink, or to be drunk and disorderly in a public place. Some 70,000 people a year are convicted of drunken driving. In 1989 a total of 92,820 people were found guilty of or cautioned for drunkenness offences, a slight reduction on the previous year. The peak age for drunkenness offences was 20 years; the average fine £45. Areas in which one was most likely to be convicted were London, Merseyside, Northumbria and Gwent; but in the Home Counties, Norfolk, Gloucestershire, Warwickshire and Leicestershire the risk of being caught and convicted was minimal.

Attitudes towards alcohol vary according to the viewpoint of the social group concerned. Thus doctors regard alcoholism as a disease that requires treatment. The police regard it as a threat to public order, and keep addicts on the move or put them under arrest. Given the amount that is consumed annually in the United Kingdom, it appears that most people are generally tolerant towards its use, and are concerned only about its *misuse.*

Other addictive substances are regarded by the law as narcotic drugs and their manufacture and sale (except for medical purposes and then only under prescription) is strictly prohibited. In fact, possession of such substances is an absolute offence, i.e. one against which no defence is possible. Those that are banned include not only the so-called 'hard' drugs such as heroin and cocaine but also so-called 'soft' drugs like cannabis. Each of these is quite legally and freely available in other parts of the world, and in those places the manufacture and consumption of alcohol, for example, may be banned.

As with Prohibition in the United States (1920−33), this attempt to solve a social problem leads to other social problems. Making narcotic drugs illegal does not stop them from being available but it does make them very expensive. Their high 'street price' makes it worth while for giant crime syndicates to cater for the demand, while at the same time those who want to buy drugs often turn to other forms of crime to pay for their addiction. A possible remedy, it has been suggested, would be the legalisation (or, more precisely, *decriminalisation*) of some or all of the substances concerned. However, this suggestion has met with fierce resistance from the police. On the other hand, unlike some other countries, Britain allows for the legal registration of addicts so that they can be weaned off drugs under medical supervision. In 1983 5,079 people were officially notified to the Home Office to be 'narcotics addicts', and some 23,000 people were cautioned by the police or convicted for drugs offences.

Not surprisingly, it is very difficult indeed to assess the actual level of illegal drug use in Britain. In 1981 the British Crime Survey suggested that some 5 per cent of all persons aged 16 or over had at some time used cannabis. There is no evidence that the majority of people who do so go on to use other drugs, though this is widely believed to be the case by both press and police. Nor is it true that what the United States does today, Britain will do tomorrow. The explosion of 'crack' in the United States has not, despite dire warnings from across the Atlantic, been copied here (*The Sunday Times*, 1 April 1990).

From the social point of view, the most interesting thing about the misuse of narcotic drugs in Britain is that it is not evenly distributed across the country, or even concentrated in urban areas, but shows a very irregular pattern of distribution:

> Our ignorance about the *epidemiology* (that is, the characteristics of the nature and spread of heroin use) is considerable. We do not have adequate explanations as to why a quiet Lancashire town should be the site of a couple of hundred opioid users, why users inject heroin in Edinburgh or smoke it in Chester, or why women are more heavily involved in some areas than others (Parker, H. 1986).

## Suicide

Suicide is defined as the intentional killing of oneself. Official statistics suggest that it is a very rare form of deviant behaviour. However, there is probably no other form of social behaviour which is more controversial, or on which the official figures are more unreliable.

The decision as to whether a death is by suicide or not is a matter of *interpretation*. In the case of a suspicious death, and in the absence of a suicide note, it is in England and Wales for the coroner (in Scotland the Procurator-Fiscal) to interpret from the available facts (such as they are) whether the death is suicide. Even when what purports to be a suicide note is found, its authenticity has first to be determined (a murderer could have forged it).

Second, the question of *intention* has to be established from the place, timing and circumstances of the death. Atkinson, in his *Discovering Suicide* (1978), found that coroners interpret similar signs in a wide range of ways, according to their own rules-of-thumb. Thus one coroner, knowing that ten barbiturate tablets was a fatal dose, interpreted all cases in which the dead person had taken that number or more as suicide, although they might not have known what constituted a fatal dose and might indeed for a variety of reasons simply have been too confused to count properly. On the other hand, few coroners treat single vehicle motor accidents as successful attempts at suicide, though investigators believe that they form quite a high proportion of the whole — perhaps as much as one-third.

Generally speaking, the deaths of people who are unmarried, isolated or solitary are more likely to be treated as suicide than those of married people or people who lead gregarious and therefore presumably happy lives. Though this may appear to be common sense, there is no way of knowing whether or not it is in fact true. Hence statistics of suicide reflect what coroners and others *believe* to be the case rather than the actual intentions of the dead person.

Comparison of international trends in official statistics between 1964 and 1986, however, have shown up a disquieting trend. During the economic recession of the early 1980s in Britain the rate of suicide in England and Wales, which had been falling among both men and women, continued to fall among women, from 62 per million in 1973 to 49 in 1986 and 45 in 1988, but began to rise again among men, from 94 in 1973 to 118 in 1986 and 125 in 1988. The discrepancy between male and female rates increased even more in Scotland. Colin Pritchard believes this discrepancy is caused by the effects of rising unemployment, with which it is statistically associated (*The Guardian*, 9 February 1990).

Contrary to a widespread belief, the country with the highest official suicide rate in the world is not Sweden, which in overall figures ranks behind Austria, France, Belgium and Japan. In 1986 the highest recorded suicide rate among men was in Finland, among women Denmark.

## Mental Illness

Some people behave persistently over time in a way that is socially inappropriate if not deviant. At one time some if not all of these people would have been regarded as 'mad' but today many such patterns of behaviour are regarded as 'illness' and various forms of 'treatment' prescribed for them, the most common of which is the use of a wide range of behaviour modifying drugs which change the patient's personality state.

However, mental illness is a social phenomenon and therefore it is at least in part a social construct. It is also seldom associated with a definable set of physical signs such as make clear to the physician that a physical illness exists, and it very seldom directly threatens life. Moreover, behaviour that would be regarded as grossly inappropriate or offensive in one context or society may be perfectly acceptable in another context or society. It is appropriate to laugh hysterically at a party, but not at a funeral. Hence the distinction between what is 'normal' and what is 'abnormal' is itself socially defined. Such differences refer, however, mainly to the way in which various mental states are expressed. The same circumstances are likely to give rise to, say, joy or sorrow in different societies. Even in cultures where people believe very strongly in an after-life, the death of a close relative is still the occasion for keen personal grief.

Human beings have a considerable capacity to adapt to 'abnormal' circumstances, if they have the time to do so and if the circumstances are not too extreme. The way in which ordinary people in Britain adapted to the stress and privation of the Second World War has become part of the popular self-image. Significantly, it was achieved by an increased sense of solidarity and community, and was accompanied by a decline in the crime rate. However, there are limits to adaptation. The Gulf War of 1991 made it cruelly clear that even trained military personnel could not adjust to the terror deliberately engendered by a continuous modern artillery bombardment. And some people find it impossible to adapt successfully to the demands of 'normal' society.

Awkwardly, once under treatment, patients adapt to the expectations that their clinicians have of them. Treatment for mental illness teaches patients the appropriate symptoms to adopt to 'please' those who are treating them. They conform to the picture of treatment that is presented to them. In fact, Rosenhan (1973) showed it was possible for some psychologists to convince staff in a US mental hospital that they themselves were insane.

Political opposition is often labelled mental illness. The classic example over recent years has, of course, been the USSR, where it is now known that many political dissidents were subjected to physical abuse, shock treatment and massive injections of mind-changing drugs because, as defined by the political authorities, their behaviour in resisting authority was 'abnormal' and they had to be 'cured'. But even in Britain the abusive term 'loony left' has similar connotations, though, happily, not similar consequences for the individuals concerned.

Instead, in the 1990s, mental illness is likely to be a social issue in Britain for quite a different reason. Major advances in pharmacology, as mentioned above, have made it possible for many people who would previously have been treated in closed hospitals to remain in the community and to lead a normal (or near-normal) life. In consequence health authorities have rushed to close down the vast majority of the old mental hospitals, many of which were antiquated, depressing and in very poor condition, and with the aid of modern psychiatric techniques and mind-altering drugs to return as many of their former inmates as possible to 'care in the community'. However, as a result of this policy, it had become clear that many of these people could not live in normal housing, and even where they had families, they were often neither able nor willing to look after them. The ideal remedy favoured by psychiatrists, namely improved follow-up services and more special small sheltered homes for the more disturbed patients, promised to be very much more expensive than the traditional 'institutional' approach. A particularly difficult problem was presented by the large number of mentally ill people living in poverty, who wandered the streets and 'lived rough'. At the beginning of the 1990s, it appeared that an uneasy alliance was forming behind the alternative option of keeping the traditional 'asylums' open. But as the next chapter shows, there are many other calls on public funds, and it is for sociologists to ensure that the information is available on which such social policy choices can best be made.

## Suggestions for Further Reading

On deviance generally, see David Downes and Paul Rock (1982), *Understanding deviance; a guide to the sociology of crime and rule-breaking*. The relationship between crime and society is analysed in Frances Heidensohn (1989), *Crime and Society*. For a functionlist view and the problem of anomie see Robert K. Merton (1957), *Social Theory and Social Structure*. The key text for the interactionist perspective is Howard Becker (1973), *Outsiders*; see also Stan Cohen (1980), *Images of deviance* and Stuart Hall and Tony Jefferson (1975), *Resistance through Rituals*. On the 'moral panic' see Stan Cohen (ed.) (1973), *Folk Devils and Moral Panics*. K. Pryce (1979), *Endless Pressure: a study of West Indian life styles in Bristol*, discusses the difficult relationship between ethnic minority groups and the police. The problem for teenage girls of 'escaping' from home is a theme of Angela McRobbie (1991), *Feminism and Youth Culture: from 'Jackie' to 'Just Seventeen'*.

# 12 Social Policy — What of the Future?

## Social Policy

Broadly three main areas are discernible: theoretical questions, demographic issues and the role of the welfare state.

- What contribution does sociology make (or should sociology make) to social policy? Sometimes the contribution of sociology to one or more specified areas relating to social policy (such as mental illness or suicide) is considered.
- Changes in *birthrate* may be related to economic activity. *Immigration* and population growth are usually considered over a specified period, e.g. since 1945. The social consequences of a *changing age structure* may alternatively be expressed as change in the dependency ratio. Social class differences can be related to a wide range of social policy issues, e.g. *mortality* or *social mobility*. Increasingly *regional* differences are of interest with regard to variations in unemployment, health care provision, etc.
- The general contribution of the welfare state to reducing inequality may be examined, but so too may the contribution of a specific aspect of welfare such as community care. The negative side of state provision is also a frequent topic: the continuing connection between economic inequalities and health, the role of voluntary organisations in dealing with social problems and the threat to welfare services inherent in economic recession.

## What is Social Policy?

*Social policy* is the name usually given to the main principles under which the government of the day directs economic resources to meet specific social needs. It is one aspect of *public policy*, which is concerned with all the responsibilities of governments, including as well as social policy, economic policy and policy on matters of commerce, trade, defence and foreign affairs.

Between 1943 and 1979 the dominant ideology which governed social policy in Britain was that of the 'welfare state'.

The 1980s on the other hand, have been dominated by 'Thatcherism', the product of the thinking often known as the 'New Right'. Thatcherism, however, was not a clear ideology. It consisted of a number of confused strands, a cluster of often contradictory attitudes. What joined these together was the reaction to ever-increasing expectations of state provision for health, education, etc. The wish to cut state responsibilities in these and other areas was made more urgent by economic difficulties. These in turn stemmed from other factors:

1. World-wide recession, resulting from the steep price increases in oil after 1973.
2. The decline of Britain's share of world manufacturing in face of competition especially from the Far East, partly resulting from:
3. The development of new technology, which (where used) made industry more 'efficient' but at the cost of employing fewer people.

In the 1990s, however, the structure of the welfare state, though modified in a number of respects, is still largely intact, and so too is the group of ideas which gave rise to it in the first place. The end of the 'Cold War' offers a new opportunity to redirect public expenditure into welfare provision and already there are arguments that this should now be done.

# The Contribution of Sociology

What can sociology contribute to this debate?

1. Through surveys and other properly based research projects it can provide the *data* on which decisions can be securely founded. In the United States, sociological research is regarded as the essential basis for serious, informed policy-making.
2. It can, with the help of its body of theoretical knowledge based on comparisons both across time and between different societies, offer an independent critique of policies proposed by government (or opposition parties) (see e.g. Brown and Sparks 1989). In the former USSR sociology, after many years of eclipse, was called upon to help when it became clear that communist society had failed to eliminate many serious social problems, such as crime and alcoholism.
3. It can draw attention to *issues* that seem not to have been noticed or to be receiving insufficient attention. Given the very short attention-span of governments, which are primarily concerned with election and re-election, there is a special role for those outside government to point to *long-term* problems which short-term solutions may not be able to tackle. An example is the social dislocation caused by rapid economic development in countries such as Brazil.

Table 12.1   *Britain's ageing population*

| | Mid-year estimate/projection, millions, United Kingdom | | | | | |
|------|----------|-------|-------|-------|---------|-------|
| **Year** | **Under 15** | **16−39** | **40−64** | **65−79** | **Over 80** | **Total** |
| 1951 | | | 15.9 | 4.8 | 0.7 | 50.3 |
| 1961 | 13.1 | 16.6 | 16.9 | 5.2 | 1.0 | 52.8 |
| 1971 | 14.3 | 17.5 | 16.7 | 6.1 | 1.3 | 55.9 |
| 1981 | 12.5 | 19.7 | 15.7 | 6.9 | 1.6 | 56.4 |
| 1991 | 11.7 | 20.2 | 16.5 | 6.9 | 2.2 | 57.5 |
| 2001 | 12.8 | 19.2 | 18.0 | 6.7 | 2.5 | 59.2 |
| 2011 | 12.1 | 18.1 | 20.2 | 7.0 | 2.7 | 60.0 |
| 2025 | 12.1 | 18.6 | 19.0 | 8.5 | 2.9 | 61.1 |

Sources: *Annual Abstract of Statistics*, No. 90, 1953; *Social Trends*, 20, Table 1.2, p. 24.

# The Demographic Background

Britain, a member of the G7, (the 'Group of Seven' most industrialised nations), enjoys a much higher *average* standard of living than most other countries in the world.

Average life expectancy is 74 years. This means that an ordinary man or woman can expect to live nearly *twice as long* as someone in Sierra Leone, where the average life expectancy is 42 years. They will be very unlikely to die of infectious diseases, and much more likely to succumb to a heart attack or to cancer.

Britain therefore has an *ageing population* — ten million, or some 18 per cent of its citizens were classified as elderly (men aged 65 or over, women aged 60 or over) in 1991. Though this number is projected to remain roughly the same until the end of the century, it will then start to climb again. Meanwhile the very old (85 plus) will continue to increase as a proportion of the whole and by 2001 there will be more than one million. Centenarians, once extremely rare, are becoming relatively frequent as every year 2,700 more people reach their hundredth birthday.

Though in the 1980s the birth rate rose slightly, the number of babies born remained well below the peak year of 1966, when 946,000 were born. The average age of mothers has risen, with a big increase in the number of children born to mothers aged 30−4. Britain's rate of *population increase* has therefore slowed, like that of other industrialised nations whose populations are static or show a slight decline. The increase was calculated at 0.8 per cent per year between 1981 and 1986. (By contrast, the population of Nicaragua in Central America increased in the same period at some 3.6 per cent a year — the highest rate in the world.) The population of the United Kingdom estimated at 57.1 million in 1988 will at this rate take until 2011 to reach 60 million.

Inconveniently, the preliminary results from the 1991 Census, which show a drop of about a million over the decade, appear to have been distorted by the fear of officialdom engendered by new government measures to track down spurious social security claimants and by the poll tax register, and it has yet to be decided how (and where) they will be adjusted to take account of this.

These demographic trends form the starting point for both the discussion of the 1980s policy impact on health, unemployment, community, poverty, education, the environment and other issues.

# Health

During the 1980s smallpox was finally eradicated worldwide. (By a sad laboratory accident the last person to die of it was British.) World Health Organisation programmes resulted in the virtual elimination of killer diseases such as diphtheria and polio. Immunisation had cut the number of notified cases of measles from 788,800 in 1961 and 155,200 in 1971 to 15,600 in 1991, making it for the first time less common than whooping cough (pertussis) (*The Guardian*, 23 January 1992). The widening gap between rich and poor nations, however, was shown most cruelly by the continued prevalence of diseases of poverty in the Third World, such as tuberculosis. In 1991 a serious outbreak of cholera in Peru proved uncontrollable and rapidly spread to five adjoining states, where for the first time in a century it is now endemic.

In Britain mass vaccination programmes under the NHS had played a key role in eliminating the threat from infectious diseases and as a result many old hospitals could be closed or their space reallocated for other purposes. However, despite a vigorous hospital building programme, NHS beds were continually full and costs continued to rise steeply. Though improved surgical procedures and aftercare saved lives and shortened hospital stays for many people, three other problems emerged.

First, an ageing population required more expensive care. It cost some seven times as much as the average for the population as a whole to provide medical care for someone who was over 75, and the number of over 75s was increasing at a rate of some 70,000 a year.

Second, the impact of health care was not evenly spread. The Black Report (1980) showed that social class differences in mortality had not declined since the 1930s but had actually slightly increased, and calculated that almost 25,000 lives a year were being lost prematurely in social classes IV and V (Waddington 1989; see also Hart 1985).

Third, it was becoming possible to do many things that had previously been unthinkable, such as heart and liver transplants. Hence while patients' expectations expanded, new dilemmas of choice were presented to those who had to carry them out. The number of heart transplants, nil in 1978, rose from 3 in 1979 to 227 in 1986, while by comparison the number of kidney transplants, a well-established procedure, rose by only half, from 941 to 1,493 (*Social Studies Review*, May 1988). Someone had to choose between, for example, one heart transplant, which would take many hours and many specialists and cost many thousands of pounds, and a number of relatively simple hernia operations, each individually quick and cheap. Not surprisingly, doctors were not willing to make such choices, and hospital administrators were not medically qualified to do so. By 1990, of over one million people on the waiting lists for routine operations, 25 per cent had had to wait over a year. The worst area for such a wait for general surgery was West Lambeth in south London, with 72 per cent of the 872 patients on the waiting list for more than a year (*The Guardian*, 8 March 1990, citing The College of Health *Guide to Hospital Waiting Lists*).

Part of the problem was that the overall level of expenditure on health care in Britain (virtually all of it publicly funded) did not keep up with that in other countries. In 1986 Britain spent only 5.8 per cent of GDP on health care. By contrast Germany spent 8.2 per cent, France 9.1 per cent, Sweden 9.4 per cent and the United States 10.7per cent.

The 1980s solution was to try to transfer some of the burden of choice to the patients themselves. Pay beds in NHS hospitals, which had been virtually eliminated in the 1970s, were brought back, and private companies built new private hospitals. There was a substantial increase in the number of people covered by health insurance schemes, membership of which was often a key part of the remuneration package offered by companies to their executives. This is, of course, similar to the pattern in the United States, where there is no national system of medical care, and medical services for most people are funded through private insurance schemes:

> The US spends $2,354 a head on health care, nearly three times the $835 spent in Britain, and almost double the average $1,200 a year spent in France, Germany and the Netherlands. The money finances an excellent system of health care for its middle and upper classes, the world's leading medical research base and its richest doctors, and a barely adequate system for the poor (Walker 1991).

In the 1990s the next move has been to encourage hospitals and medical practitioners to opt out of the old system of regional and central control, using their allocation of the available budget as they see fit. Government assurances have, however, been given that people will not be denied medical treatment simply because the money has run out. This is fortunate for the poorer members of society, who cannot afford private medicine and do not know how to make best use of the NHS. Figures released by the Government in 1986 with the publication of the 1979−80, 1982−3 Occupational Mortality decennial Supplement showed a rise in the death rate among unskilled workers. Between the early 1970s and the early 1980s the standardised mortality rate (SMR) for social class V men rose from 137 to 165 (and, within that class, for labourers and unskilled workers, not elsewhere classified, from 201 to 355). Over the same period, the SMR for social class I fell from 77 to 66 (Preston 1986).

It has been suggested in a 1991 report that no government will be able to bear the burden of long-term care for the old, who will have to take out private insurance to pay for home helps and other social services (Laing and Hall 1991). However, for a woman recently retired at 60, with the reasonable hope of living for another twenty or thirty years, it is already too late to do so.

# Industrial Infrastructure and Unemployment

In a party political broadcast in September 1991 the Conservative Party claimed that there were one million more people *in work* than ever before in Britain's history (BBC 1, 19 September 1991). The opposition parties pointed out that the number *out of work* was just under 2.5 million and rising, which (even without allowing for the changes in definitions discussed in Chapter 6, which would make the figure well over 3.5 million) would still be one of the highest levels recorded.

Both figures are of course 'correct'. Behind them lie several problems:

1. Many of those who make up the increased number of people in work, work part-time (*Social Trends, 1990*, p. 69). In 1979 there were 25,365,000 in work compared with 26,394,000 in 1991. However in 1991 only 3.87 million worked part-time, today the figure is 5.5 million, and a further 400,000 are counted as employed because they are on the government training scheme. Comparing like with like, the number in full-time employment has actually *fallen* by some 600,000 since 1979 (*The Sunday Times*, 22 September 1991).

2. In a society in which most people still regard paid employment as the norm, being out of work carries a social stigma and the unemployed continue to be both disillusioned and depressed by what they see as their own 'failure' and distrusted and feared by government. Unemployment benefits have not been raised since 1979 in line with the general increase in income. Hence, though there has been some improvement in general living standards in the 1980s it has not been evenly spread throughout society and the long-term unemployed have been among those who have come off worst.

3. Despite the government Training Scheme, youth unemployment remains a major social problem with high visibility, as, for example, when the Archbishop of Canterbury, Dr Carey, referred to it as one of the contributory causes of the riots in Newcastle upon Tyne in the summer of 1991.

4. The recession of 1990—92 has accentuated established trends in the restructuring of British industry. There has been a further sharp decline in the number of jobs available in primary and secondary manufacturing industry. But in the 1990s the recession has also hit hard the services sector and brought steep rises in unemployment in London and the South-East.

5. In these circumstances, the desire of many older people to go on working beyond the age of 65 (or 60), cannot be fulfilled. (In the United States, the senior citizens lobby has already persuaded members of Congress, many of whom are themselves senior citizens, that 'ageism' is wrong and they they should be allowed to go on working.) Nor has a decision yet been taken on how to implement the decision of the European Court that retirement ages for men and women must be equalised.

Government economic policy remains based on the assumption that combating inflation is the primary target and that rising unemployment is a necessary part of this adjustment. In addition to established training schemes, a considerable expansion of higher education is now taking place, though without additional resources. Social policy in the 1990s will have to continue to tackle the social problems resulting from structural readjustment and continuing unemployment.

# Community, Housing and Homelessness

*Housing* underwent a dramatic change in Britain during the 1980s. There was a steep increase in *owner-occupation* — by 1988 65 per cent of all households owned their own homes, compared with 47 per cent in France and 37 per cent in West Germany. Government policy was:

1. In general, to allow the market to fill the demand for housing.
2. To restrain expenditure by local authorities in the cause of controlling inflation, with the incidental result that less money was available to those authorities for slum clearance, refurbishment of old stock, and the construction of new housing.
3. To force the sale of council houses to sitting tenants at subsidised prices.

This combination of cuts in public expenditure on housing (by 1982 new starts had fallen from over 150,000 in 1976 to under 50,000 a year) and council house sales under the Housing Act 1980 brought about a sharp decline in the public housing stock. The percentage of households in publicly-owned housing fell from 31.5 per cent of all housing in 1979 to 27.9 per cent in 1984. Although the rate of sale fell off steeply in 1985 and 1986, partly because flats have not proved as easy to sell as houses, it picked up again after new legislation had reduced the minimum period of tenancy from three years to two. Meanwhile new council house starts have declined even further and the proportion of households in council housing has continued to fall. For young people the main possibility of housing now rests with the much diminished private rented sector.

Those who entered the property market during the boom years included many who would not previously have contemplated ownership. Sale of council houses was politically very popular and is widely believed to have contributed significantly to the Conservative victory in 1987, although this has been disputed (Curtice 1987). However, some of the new owners have encountered problems for which they were not adequately prepared. Many borrowed heavily in order to buy. Rapid inflation in property prices in the private sector, however, came to a abrupt end in 1988 and since that time prices have fallen. There has been a sharp increase in the number of mortgage repossessions as new owners have proved unable to meet the repayments. Others are struggling with the problems of maintenance and in trying to keep up with them are drained of their remaining financial

Table 12.2  *Public housing stock, 1981–9*

| | Dwellings (000s) | | | | | | | | |
|---|---|---|---|---|---|---|---|---|---|
| | **1981** | **1982** | **1983** | **1984** | **1985** | **1986** | **1987** | **1988** | **1989** |
| *New construction* | | | | | | | | | |
| Private | 118 | 128 | 152 | 165 | 162 | 174 | 182 | 192 | 181 |
| Housing assns. | 19 | 13 | 17 | 17 | 14 | 13 | 12 | 12 | 13 |
| Local authorities | 58 | 36 | 37 | 35 | 29 | 24 | 20 | 21 | 17 |
| New Town corpns | 10 | 4 | 2 | 2 | 1 | 1 | 1 | — | — |
| Govt depts | 1 | — | — | — | — | — | 1 | 1 | 1 |
| *Total new* | 206 | 182 | 208 | 220 | 206 | 212 | 215 | 226 | 213 |
| *Other changes* | | | | | | | | | |
| Slum clearance | − 30 | − 26 | − 18 | − 15 | − 14 | − 11 | − 10 | − 11 | − 9 |
| Other changes incl. conversion | − 9 | − 3 | − 1 | − 6 | 5 | 4 | 1 | 1 | 1 |
| *Total* | − 39 | − 23 | − 19 | − 21 | − 8 | − 7 | − 9 | − 10 | − 8 |
| Net gain | 167 | 158 | 189 | 199 | 198 | 205 | 206 | 216 | 205 |

Sources: *Social Trends*, 20, Table 8.2, p. 128; 21, Table 8.2, p. 136.

resources (Karn *et al.* 1988) and end up in a descending spiral of debt (Ford 1990).

There is general agreement that in the 1990s a substantial number of new houses — up to two million — will be required, mainly in the south-east. The policy issue is how they are to be provided, whether by reliance solely on the forces of the market, or through a new wave of public housing, or some combination of the two.

*Homelessness* has increased. The most dramatic sign was the appearance of 'Cardboard City' outside Waterloo Station, and its counterpart under Hungerford Bridge on the Embankment (both in London). By 1986 between 500 and 5,000 people were believed to be sleeping rough, but on the definition of homelessness then in use anything up to four million people could have been regarded as lacking adequate shelter, and 200,000 households actually applied for rehousing. The Housing (Homeless Persons) Act 1977 drew the definition of homelessness more tightly, requiring local authorities only to house children or those vulnerable on account of old age or mental handicap, and excluding the single homeless altogether. In 1990 a record 43,000 homeless families spent Christmas in temporary accommodation because there was no permanent home available for them (Shelter 1990).

The decision in December 1990 of the Housing Minister, Sir George Young, to appoint Nick Hardwick, director of Centrepoint, a voluntary agency providing night shelter and hostels in Soho, and to relax housing subsidy rules to end the practice of maintaining homeless families in very expensive bed-and-breakfast accommodation, however, seemed to indicate a review of policy priorities for the 1990s.

Table 12.3 *Mortgage arrears and repossessions, 1980–91*

| Year | No. mortgages at year-end | Repossessions during year | Cases in mortgage arrears 6–12 months | 12 + months |
|------|---------------------------|---------------------------|---------------------------------------|-------------|
| 1980 | 6,210,000 | 3,480 | 15,430 | — |
| 1981 | 6,336,000 | 4,870 | 21,540 | — |
| 1982 | 6,518,000 | 6,860 | 27,380 | 5,540 |
| 1983 | 6,846,000 | 8,420 | 29.440 | 7,530 |
| 1984 | 7,313,000 | 12,400 | 48,270 | 9,510 |
| 1985 | 7,717,000 | 19,300 | 57,110 | 13,120 |
| 1986 | 8,138,000 | 24,090 | 52,080 | 13,020 |
| 1987 | 8,283,000 | 26,390 | 55,490 | 14,960 |
| 1988 | 8,564,000 | 18,510 | 42,810 | 10,280 |
| 1989 | 9,125,000 | 15,810 | 66,800 | 13,840 |
| 1990 | 9,415,000 | 43,890 | 123,110 | 36,100 |
| 1991* | 9,628,000 | 36,610 | 162,210 | 59,690 |

* First half of year only.
Source: *The Guardian*, 17 December 1991.

# Poverty and the Emerging Underclass

*Poverty* remains a problem. In 1976 a survey showed that 43 per cent of respondents believed that people were poor 'because of laziness and lack of willpower'; 16 per cent thought that it was because of bad luck; and 10 per cent because of injustice. These were attitudes which contributed to the Conservative victory in 1979.

Government policy between 1979 and 1990 was to reduce inflation through the strict control of public expenditure at central and local level. Welfare benefits were seen as a key target for cuts for three reasons. The total amount of money spent by central government in transfer payments (payments from taxes to individuals or families) was very large. Many people believed (like Mrs Thatcher herself) that welfare payments removed the incentive for individuals to help themselves. And even more believed that the welfare burden was so high because many people claiming welfare benefits were 'on the fiddle'.

Four years later, after a sharp recession, the government had pegged some welfare benefits and was still hoping to cut others. They had mounted several campaigns to root out 'social security scroungers'. Meanwhile, however, social attitudes had changed markedly. Only 23 per cent of respondents now saw welfare recipients as lazy, and 13 per cent as unlucky, while 33 per cent considered that the main cause was injustice (Lansley and Weir 1983).

In 1991 one in seven people in Great Britain were dependent for all or part of their income on state benefits. The main policy debate revolved around two issues: how far the existing level of benefit could be regarded as adequate, and how far the structure of benefit could and should be revised to target those most in need — with the necessary consequence that those less in need would be deprived of support.

*Inequality* has increased sharply during the 1980s. By the end of the decade, among *those in work* the gap between the lowest paid and the highest paid was the widest that it had been at any time since figures were first collected in 1886. Between 1982 and 1990 the amount earned by the lowest paid tenth of the population fell from 68.3 per cent of the median to 63.7 per cent — a decrease of some 28 per cent on their position in 1979. Meanwhile the rich have got richer. The 200 richest people in Britain in 1990 were collectively worth 'more than £48 billion, equivalent to 9.4 per cent of the country's total gross domestic product' (*The Sunday Times*, 8 April 1990).

The main criticism of this growing inequality has come, not from politicians, but from the Church, some of whose members have become increasingly concerned at the effects of inequality on the sense of community.

By the end of the decade there was a new concern that an 'underclass' was emerging in Britain. Interestingly, the new term came from the United States and the argument came from both ends of the political spectrum. From the Right the American political scientist Charles Murray argued that in Britain as in the United States there were, as there had been in Victorian times, two sorts of poor: those who simply had low incomes, and another group which he claimed to recognise from the Iowa of his youth:

> These poor people didn't lack just money. They were defined by their behaviour. Their homes were littered and unkempt. The men in the family were unable to hold a job for more than a few weeks at a time. Drunkenness was common. The children grew up ill-schooled and ill-behaved and contributed a disproportionate share of the local juvenile delinquents. (Murray 1989).

Murray identified this group with the 'undeserving poor' of Mayhew's time, and, though not an expert on British society, had no hesitation in stating his conclusion about it:

> Britain does have an underclass, still largely out of sight and still smaller than the one in the United States. But it is growing rapidly. Within the next decade, it will probably become as large (proportionately) as the United States's underclass. It could easily become larger.

The 'early-warning signals', he claimed, were 'the increase in illegitimacy, violent crime, and drop out from the labour force'. Illegitimacy, he argued, forces long-term welfare dependence on women. Britain already has a higher rate of crimes against property than the United States, but concern about them has been muted by the relatively low level of violent crime. Though beginning from a much lower base, however, violent crime has been rising much more rapidly than in the United States since the late 1960s, and between 1980 and 1988 it rose by 60 per cent (from 196 to 314 per 100,000). Thirdly, Murray claims, 'large numbers of young, healthy, low-income males choose not to take jobs', and when large numbers of young men do not work, the communities around them break down.

Murray does not offer a solution to the problem, if it exists. Those offered by correspondents to *The Sunday Times* (3 and 10 December 1989) included:

- A change of heart.
- Rejecting 'permissiveness'.
- Spending more money with more care on finding answers.
- Putting more effort in schools into teaching basic literacy and numeracy.
- Restoring national service.
- Making husbands and fathers pay for the upbringing of their children.
- Providing cheap accommodation for rent.
- Signing the minimum wage provisions of the European Social Charter.
- Ignoring 'the mumbo-jumbo trotted out by the social engineers who infest our seats of learning'.

For the British social historian John MacNicol, the concept of an underclass is nothing more than a refuted concept periodically resurrected by conservatives 'who wish to constrain the redistributive potential of state welfare' (McNicol 1987). Others, such as Richard Berthoud, also continue to be suspicious of the notion of an underclass and are critical of Murray's approach: 'It's a ragbag of different groups ... You have to establish that they have something in common. If each group is marginalised in a separate way, they cannot form a group culture' (quoted in *The Sunday Times*, 3 December 1989).

The moderate Labour MP, Frank Field, however, has accepted that there is an emerging underclass, though he differs substantially from Murray on the reasons for it. The one thing they both agree on is that the situation is largely out of the control of government. However Field argues that this is because the Thatcher Government has rejected the 300-year-old tradition of shared citizenship. Its policies of increasing unemployment, widening class divisions, reducing in real terms the income of those on welfare and encouraging a 'drawbridge' mentality in those who have been fortunate enough to escape poverty are actually creating an underclass (Field, F. 1989). Ralf Dahrendorf, too, believes that there is an underclass, but that its members have not rejected a role in society, they have been excluded from it (Murray, 1989).

A comparative study of poverty levels and government responses in the United States and Europe shows that in the 1980s poverty levels among families with children accelerated much faster in the United Kingdom than in any other European country, and that in its overall level of poverty Britain has shifted away from the European pattern and towards that of the United States (Lawson 1991).

# Family Breakdown

In 1991 one person in three lives in something other than the traditional 'cereal packet' family (see Chapter 8). Though there is much public argument about the consequences for the children involved in family breakdown, there is still no evidence that family breakdown accounts for their problems independently of the problems of poverty and stress which often accompany it. Moreover, there is a great deal of evidence that all age groups value the family and wish to maintain its central role in social life.

Where serious social problems arise in these as in other circumstances, the primary responsibility for social workers is the welfare of the children, and they have to work in conjunction with medical services, the police and the probation service, among other agencies, each of which have their own legal framework, their own duties and their own perspective. The 1989 Children Act seeks to make the rights of the children more central, and establishes two principles: that 'the best place for children to be brought up and cared for is within their families, wherever possible' and that 'children should be removed from their families only when this is absolutely necessary' (Department of Health 1991). But the problem for the 1990s will be to continue to reconcile these competing demands for attention, particularly in a climate of reduced local government resources.

# Education

During most of the 1980s official policy emphasised the *economic* function of education, to provide trained and skilled members of the labour force. Changes in the structure of educational management increased the responsibility of governors and with it the involvement both of parents and of representatives of business. The powers and duties of head teachers were strengthened, and with the introduction of Local Management of Schools (LMS) they became effectively school managers with little or no time for teaching. Other teachers felt they were distrusted and excluded as far as possible from decision-making processes. By an order of the Secretary of State the long-established Burnham procedure was ended and they were deprived even of the right to negotiate their own pay and conditions.

Although survey evidence was that public respect for teachers held up surprisingly well in face of this concerted onslaught, not surprisingly teachers felt demoralised and many left the profession. To meet the need for more teachers, particularly in the fields of mathematics and science, a number of options were tried: offering more pay to teachers in 'shortage' subjects, allowing untrained teachers to teach under licence, even importing teachers from abroad. In 1991, however, the Secretary of State was still publicly critical of training for teachers and teachers' salaries continued to be imposed from above rather than subject to market forces.

At the same time, with unemployment again rising many pupils clearly felt that education was a poor investment of time and resources and that their best bet was to leave school as soon as possible and get a job while they still could. Though others took advantage of the increased number of places in higher and further education, the problem for policy-makers in the 1990s remained reconciling the expectations of pupils with the reality of a society in which unemployment was still a major problem. With many of the problems of reorganisation still unresolved, the 1990s would clearly see a continuing debate about the centrality of education in social life and between those who thought the state should control education but not necessarily provide it, and those who think that it should provide education but keep central government control to a minimum.

# Environment

A whole complex of questions relating to the quality of life of individuals came in the 1980s to be seen, virtually for the first time, as various aspects of the general problem of the impact of modern industrial society on the environment. The problem transcended national boundaries. Though successive British governments were able to ignore the impact of acid rain on the environment, since the prevailing winds carried it away from these islands and killed trees in Germany instead, on the day that the nuclear reactor erupted at Chernobyl in the Ukraine the wind was blowing from the east, and sheep were contaminated with radioactive fallout in the hill country of North Wales and Cumbria.

However during the 1980s policies to promote energy saving through better insulation, to control the exhaust emissions from motor cars, to end sewage discharges direct into the sea, to regulate light industrial development on agricultural land and to maintain a national register of dogs were all rejected or abandoned. Effectively all such questions were left to the market to decide.

In 1991 the government claimed: 'Today the air we breathe is purer than at any time since the industrial revolution. The water that flows in our rivers is the cleanest in Europe' (BBC 1, 19 September 1991). In fact, this claim was at best only partly true. Though visible dirt has been largely eliminated from the British atmosphere, the 1980s saw a continuing increase in pollution from exhaust fumes, and the variation in monitoring systems in Europe made direct comparisons between water in different countries impossible (*The Sunday Times*, 22 September 1991).

The 1990s will see a renewed debate about the role of the state in caring for the environment, which will in turn require rethinking of the degree of social responsibility to be required from all citizens.

# Centralisation vs. Decentralisation of Power

The long-term trend for more and more power to be exercised by central government was not checked in the 1980s. In those areas in which government gave up *direct* control, as in the case of privatisation of the public utilities, it was forced by public opinion and the demands of a modern economy to retain an alternative system of *regulation*.

The central irony of the 1980s was that a government professing its belief in market forces and the freedom of the individual also felt the need to adopt extensive additional powers to regulate the economy and to counteract what it saw as undesirable social trends. In consequence local government lost much of its limited independence and Whitehall came to intervene more than ever before in the everyday lives of citizens. In pursuit of its economic strategy, central government decided what money could be raised from local taxes. It even forbade local authorities to spend money that they had raised from the sale of assets such as schools and playing fields unless they had permission to do so. At the same time, privatisation of bus transport, for example, resulted in a further loss of local power to private enterprise.

By taking the management of schools out of the hands of local authorities, and by imposing a national curriculum, the powers of local government were cut back, but those of central government over education were greatly increased.

In some areas, however, central influence declined markedly, and nowhere more than in the field of labour relations. The attack on trade unions since 1979, following the 'winter of discontent' which marked the end of the Labour Government, has been accompanied by attempts to delegitimise their role. The Thatcher Government legislated to try to reduce the freedom of trade unions to organise, and by its chosen measure it was successful. In 1990 1.9 million working days were lost through strikes in Britain — the lowest level since 1963. Unlike all other post-1945 governments the Thatcher Government took pride in not using its mediating position to call the two sides together when there was an industrial dispute to try to arrive at a common position. This could be seen as inconsistent with its encouragement of Japanese working practices at the new Nissan factory at Washington, Co. Durham, where workers were given an active role in the self-management of the enterprise. It remains to be seen whether with the waning of the recession and the beginnings of industrial recovery, workers will continue to be content to accept a subordinate position or would seek to renegotiate their terms and conditions of employment as soon as the economic situation allows.

# Role of the State vs. the Individual

In theory the reduction of income tax after 1979 was to give more freedom to the individual to spend money as he or she pleased. However, though top rates of tax were reduced, lower rates were not, since national insurance contributions were raised. In addition, VAT and other taxes went up to compensate the Government for the loss of revenue, and over the 1980s the overall burden of taxation on the average individual actually increased. Nevertheless, psychologically many seem to have believed that they were better off.

In other areas the reduction in state requirements was (not surprisingly) accompanied by a reduction in its responsibilities. People were given the right to buy the council houses they rented. However, if they then fell into arrears on their mortgages and their homes were repossessed, they found that a much reduced public housing stock was available to care for them and their families.

Those who control the destiny of the state, no matter what their party preference, will always have a strong interest in maintaining its powers, and extending them where convenient to them. The individual, on the other hand, has more chance than ever before to make his or her views felt, normally in conjunction with other individuals or groups. The role of sociology in the 1990s will continue to be to provide the information that the individual needs to understand the modern, complex society in which we all live.

## Suggestions for Further Reading

Much of the subject matter of this chapter is still to be written. In the meanwhile careful reading of the daily press is essential. A good starting point is Phillip Brown and Richard Sparks (eds) (1989), *Beyond Thatcherism: social policy, politics and society*. Norman Johnson (1990) in *Reconstructing the Welfare State*, looks at changes in social policy during the decade 1980−90. On the wider signifance of Thatcherism and its differences from related trends in the United States, see Kenneth Hoover and Raymond Plant (1989), *Conservative Capitalism in Britain and the United States*. Nicky Hart (1985), *The Sociology of Health and Medicine*, focuses on one of the key issues of the 1990s. Another, the mixed blessing of home ownership, is considered by Karn *et al.* (1988), *Home Ownership in the Inner City: Salvation or Despair?* On the emerging underclass, see Frank Field (1989), *Losing Out: the emergence of Britain's underclass*.

# Glossary

*absolute poverty*, insufficient means for the maintenance of physical health.

*achieved status*, position in society determined by one's own efforts.

*adolescence*, period between childhood and maturity.

*age cohort*, people in same broad age-band, usually in context of group of voters who become politically conscious at the same time.

*age sets*, division of society into groups of approximately the same age.

*alienation*, in Marxist thought the removal of the worker from her or his product by the factory process; more generally, sense of being isolated from others, or *anomie*.

*anomic*, lacking guiding *norms* or principles (see *anomie*).

*anomie*, concept introduced by Durkheim, disorientation as a consequence of the breakdown of traditional *norms* which have not yet been replaced by new guidelines for behaviour.

*anthropology*, the study of the human species.

*ascribed status*, position in society determined by some given characteristic, usually one's family's position.

*association*, a group within society organised to pursue a specific aim or aims.

*authority*, the perceived right to get someone else to do something.

*bourgeoisie*, from French '*bourgeois*' — a town-dweller; in Marxist thought the class that owns the means of production in modern capitalist society.

*bureaucracy*, from French '*bureau*' — a desk; and Greek '*kratein*' — to rule, government by officials, a form of systematic administration through rules applied by an orderly hierarchy of paid officials appointed for their qualifications.

*capitalism*, the developing industrial society of Western Europe in the nineteenth century; by extension, the system of economic organisation of society characterised by the private ownership of the means of production.

*caste*, stratification of society, originally by racial groups, subsequently by descent from groups once perceived as racially distinct.

*'cereal packet' family*, breadwinner husband, housewife and two children.

*charismatic*, from Greek '*charisma*' — gift or grace, in Weberian sociology, *authority* or the ability to lead stemming from the outstanding personal qualities of an individual leader.

*Church*, broad inclusive grouping accepting common religious doctrines.

*class*, a major group within society; in Marxist sociology united by their common relationship to the factors of production (see also *social class*).

*closed-shop*, agreement by employer to require membership of one *trade union* as a condition of employment.

*communism*, ideal end-state of society as envisaged by Marx, a classless society without internal conflict; with capital 'C', Marxism—Leninism, the belief that this condition could be attained in the former Soviet Union.

*community*, a group of people who live together and share a set of values and interests.

*compensatory education*, in the United States, programmes designed to counteract the tendency to underachievement among working-class and ethnic minority children.

*comprehensive redevelopment*, total demolition of an urban zone and its rebuilding according to a predetermined plan.

*comprehensive schools*, secondary schools in which children of different abilities are educated together.

*consensus*, from Latin '*con-*' — 'together' and '*sensus*' — 'sense', the extent to which all the members of the society share a common set of ideas about the purposes and goals of society; agreement on what is to be done.

*contest mobility*, situation in which children are educated together and self-selection takes place over time.

*conurbation*, large area over which urban areas have grown into one another.

*convergence theory*, the belief that all societies are *en route* to industrialisation and subsequently to post-industrial society.

*co-operative*, voluntary association owned by those who use it, in which the profits are redistributed to members in proportion to their use.

*crime*, breach of the formal rules (laws) of society.

*cultural capital*, in Bourdieu, information, skills and techniques which enable the invididual to make use of the institutions of society.

*culture*, in sociology, the entire pattern of behaviour of a society; also used more widely to designate the evidences of specialised forms of self-expression such as art, music, literature, etc.

*data*, raw information requiring interpretation.

*deference*, undue respect for social superiors.

*dependency theory*, explanation of the cause of the poverty of poorer countries as being caused by the existence of the developed world.

*deskilling*, replacing complex jobs by simpler ones.

*deviance*, infringing the rules or norms of society.

*deviancy amplification*, process by which the mass media create alarm at a specific pattern of social behaviour; see *moral panic*.

*discrimination*, generally, choosing; in a social context, treating one person less favourably than another on the grounds of their colour, race or ethnic or national origins.

*division of labour*, the way in which different tasks are assigned to individuals within society.

*divorce*, the legal termination of a marriage contract.

*dysfunctional*, from the Greek '*dys-*' 'away from', harmful to the proper working of society.

*elite*, a minority of people occupying the most influential and prestigious positions in a society or organisation.

*entry*, gaining access to a group for *participant observation*.

*equilibrium*, tendency of an organism (or society) to return to normal after disturbance.

*estates*, legally defined groups with specific obligations and rights formerly the basis of stratification of European societies.

*ethnic group*, from the Greek '*ethne*' 'a tribe', a social group which is held together not only by common kinship, but also by culture and/or religion.

*ethnomethodology*, the study of the methods people employ to make sense of their everyday world.

*exit poll*, public opinion poll of voters conducted as they leave a polling station after voting.

*extended family*, larger household containing in addition to the *nuclear family* one or more grandparents and/or unmarried siblings.

*family*, primary unit of society created either by contract between two adult individuals or by their reproduction or both.

*field study*, study of sociological phenomena by direct observation.

*folk devils*, groups which suddenly become the target of media attention and alarm.

*function*, a task required to ensure the satisfaction of a basic need of an organism (or organisation) and hence its survival.

*functional prerequisite*, a fundamental social need, essential for the survival of a society.

*functionalism*, the view that all social phenomena can be explained in terms of their contribution to the survival of the social system.

*fundamentalism*, insistence that a specific religious doctrine should be taken literally and applied universally.

*gatekeepers*, people who control access to an organisation; by extension, those who control the inflow of information.

*Gemeinschaft*, for Toennies, community.

*gender*, psychological, cultural or social differences between men and women in society.

*Gesellschaft*, for Toennies, association.

*government*, the central authority in society, with the power to enforce its decisions on the rest of society through means of coercion.

*grammar school*, secondary school, entry to which is by examination or test, with emphasis on academic achievement.

*homeworking*, industrial production in the home under contract; not to be confused with *housework*.

*hypothesis*, an untested expression of a causal relationship.

*ideal-type*, in Weberian sociology, the theoretical essence of a phenomenon, which does not exist in real form.

*illegitimate*, pre-1990 term for child born to unmarried couple who could not or did not subsequently marry.

*indicator*, quantity used as an indirect measure of a sociological *variable* where a direct measure is not available.

*inner city*, central zone of a city, as distinct from the *suburbs*.

*instinct*, automatic response of an organism to an external stimulus.

*intelligentsia*, term applied in the former Soviet Union to the stratum of educated people, neither workers nor peasants.

*interest group*, people who have a common political interest, see also *pressure group*.

*labelling*, the process by which society attaches a specific interpretation of their actions to an individual; this label being retained in other social contexts.

*legitimation*, the process of conferring *authority* on individuals or structures in society.

*less-developed countries (LDCs)*, those countries in Africa, Asia and Latin America, which contain 70 per cent of the world's population, but share only 17 per cent of its income.

*limited liability*, system by which each investor in an enterprise is responsible for debts only up to the amount s/he has invested.

*managerial revolution*, transfer of control of industry to paid managers arising from the transfer of ownership from individuals to shareholders of large corporations.

*Marxism*, views of the world based on the writings of Karl Marx; divisible into *Marxian* views (attributable to Marx himself) and *Marxist* views (where a substantial component is attributable to later writers),

*mass media*, agencies by which the same message can be transmitted simultaneously to a large number of people.

*materialism*, the belief that everything can be explained in terms of visible and/or measurable phenomena.

*means of production*, in Marxist thought, land, labour and capital (including tools, machinery, etc.).

*means test*, assessing the income and wealth of an individual as a condition of granting them welfare benefits.

*mechanical society*, society bound together by common tasks.

*meritocracy*, rule by the most meritorious.

*moral panic*, widespread alarm at a specific aspect or aspects of social behaviour.

*multi-national corporations (MNCs)*, large corporations that operate in many different countries.

*New Towns*, complete communities planned for people to live in and work and enjoy themselves.

*non-decision-making*, the ability to keep issues out of the public arena.

*norms*, certain organising principles by which *values* are to be realised.

*nuclear family*, parent(s) and child(ren).

*oligarchy*, rule by the few.

*operationalising*, making explicit what a *hypothesis* is and finding a suitable method to test it.

*opinion leaders*, people to whom other members of society are accustomed to look for guidance.

*organic society*, society characterised by differentiated tasks.

*organisation*, a social unit predominantly orientated to the attainment of specific goals.

*paradigm*, a major organising theory, which dominates the choice of all lesser theories until sufficient evidence accumulates to force its rejection.

*participant observation*, social research by someone who becomes a member of a group or organisation to study it from within.

*partisan dealignment*, the tendency of voters to abandon the political parties they traditionally supported.

*party*, in Weberian thought, group working together to further common interests through political action; today more specifically *political party*, organisation which seeks to further common interests through contesting for or retaining political *power*.

*patriarchy*, a system in which men have more power and influence than women; this being inbuilt in class and work roles.

*perspective*, a view of the nature of society which gives a specific interpretation to social actions.

*phenomenology*, the view that individuals create the social world around them and that it is how people see the world that is important in studying their actions and reactions.

*pluralism*, a political system in which power is widely distributed.

*politics*, contest for the ultimate power to make decisions in society.

*population*, the entire set of people who are to be subject of a survey.

*positivism*, the view that the social sciences must use the methods of the natural sciences.

*post-industrial society*, society based on the production and exchange of information rather than of material goods.

*poverty trap*, point at which, because of defects in the tax system, an increase in wages results in a net loss of income; also used to refer to the transmission of poverty from one generation to the next.

*power*, the ability to get others to do what they would not otherwise do.

*power elite*, term coined by C. Wright Mills to describe the most powerful people in politics, business and the armed forces in the United States, whom he believed acted as if they formed a single elite, even though they did not.

*pressure group*, or *interest group*, group of people actively seeking to influence the political process, but unlike a political *party* do not contest for political power on their own account.

*privatisation*, (1) in sociology, tendency for what was previously done in public, especially leisure activities, to be done within the family or home; (2) sale of state enterprises or property to private individuals.

*profession*, occupational group recognised as having skills of special social value, entry to which is by training and examination, and who are subject to the regulation of a governing body of practitioners.

*proletariat*, from the Latin '*proletarii*' — those who have no economic resources except their children (*proles*); in Marxist thought the class which is forced by economic necessity to sell its labour power to modern capitalist society.

*psephology*, from the Greek words *psephos*, — 'a pebble' or a 'vote', and *logos* — 'word' or 'field of study', the study of voting behaviour.

*public policy*, all the responsibilities of governments, including *social policy*.

*public schools*, in the United Kingdom, privately funded schools whose head teachers are members of the Headmaster's Conference (or equivalent); in the United States, state-funded schools open to all children.

*quango* (Quasi-Autonomous Non-Governmental Organisation), body of people who discharge specific functions on behalf of government.

*questionnaire*, prepared list of questions to be asked of all respondents to a survey.

*race*, in common usage, any group of human beings who are perceived as sharing a common physiognomy; see also *ethnic group*.

*racialism*, the belief that there are significant differences between 'races', with the implication that some are superior and some inferior.

*racism*, discrimination against members of specific 'races'.

*recorded crime*, breaches of the law that have been reported to the police and have been recorded as such.

*regulation*, in politics, control by *quangos* of industries or utilities which are not owned by government or have been *privatised*.

*relative poverty*, standard of living below that generally enjoyed in a specific society.

*reliable*, in statistics, statistics guaranteed to contain a record of all incidents they are defined to contain.

*religion*, any unified system of belief concerning itself with those aspects of life which are beyond proof; more specifically, belief in certain specific things, usually the existence of a supernatural being.

*restricted code*, for Bernstein, the specific vocabulary and pattern of speech of the working class.

*role*, part played by individual in society; different roles being played in different social contexts.

*salariat*, professional, administrative and managerial workers who have little capital but whose skills earn them a high income; sometimes called the 'service class'.

*satisficing*, taking the first reasonably satisfactory course of action that presents itself rather than searching all available alternatives.

*sect*, any small religious grouping defined in opposition to established larger groups; see *Church*.

*secularisation*, the process of religious thinking, practice and institutions losing social significance.

*sex*, biological or anatomical differences between men and women; see also *gender*.

*sexism*, discrimination against individuals on grounds of sex.

*social class*, major social groupings within society arising from economic inequalities, whether of wealth or income.

*social closure*, process by which people affirm their own *status* by excluding other members of society.

*social control*, process by which the values and norms of society are maintained.

*social mobility*, movement either up or down the social *class* hierarchy to a different class (*vertical mobility*) or from one occupation to another within the same social class (*horizontal mobility*).

*social policy*, the main principles under which the government of the day directs economic resources to meet specific social needs; see also *public policy*.

*socialisation*, the learning of the basic way in which society works; the process by which children learn the values and norms of society.

*socialism*, political doctrine with social equality as its central value.

*society*, the whole web of social relationships between people who live in a particular area under a single *government*.

*sociobiology*, a perspective which seeks to explain human society by reference to biological imperatives.

*source*, generally, person or thing from which information is derived; specifically, written document which forms the subject of historical inquiry.

*sponsored mobility*, condition in which education separates out at an early age candidate members of the *elite*.

*standard error*, how far a sample is likely to differ from the population from which it is taken.

*standard operating procedures*, routine and habitual tasks within an organisation.

*state*, society as an organised political entity.

*status*, social honour or esteem accorded to individual or group.

*stigma*, social disapproval attached to an individual by other members of society.

*stratification*, structured division of society horizontally into different levels which can be ranked from top to bottom.

*stratified diffusion*, process by which new ideas spread down the social class hierarchy.

*structuralism*, explanation of human behaviour in terms of social structure.

*sub-culture*, the common body of knowledge of a restricted group within society defined by its own members.

*suburbs*, built-up area on the edge of towns, from Latin 'sub-', — 'under'; and 'urbs' — 'a town', hence its singular form.

*supersession theory*, the belief that industrial capitalism has been superseded by post-capitalist society.

*symbolic interactionism*, the belief that group action is the sum of individual actions, that these actions rest on meanings held by the actors and that these meanings develop out of social interaction or subconscious negotiation with other people.

*Taylorism*, the application of time and motion study to industrial production to increase overall productivity by *deskilling* individual workers.

*theory*, general interpretation of relationships of cause and effect.

*total institution*, term applied by Goffman to closed organisations such as military units, mental hospitals, orphanages and prisons where the individual's self is rebuilt in isolation from the outside world.

*trade unions*, voluntary organisations of workers for the purpose of negotiating wages and conditions of employment with their employers.

*triangulation*, using two or more measures as a check on the reliability of each.

*underclass*, the poorest and most socially deprived members of society.

*unobtrusive measures*, methods of measuring which are not known to and therefore do not influence the activities of the people being studied.

*urbanisation*, the process by which people have moved from the country (*rural* areas) and become *concentrated* in towns or cities (*urban* areas).

*valid*, in statistics, statistics which actually measure what they purport to measure.

*values*, those things held to be usual, right or proper.

*variable*, pattern of behaviour that changes in the social environment (*independent variable*) bringing about changes in behaviour in a specific group or individual (*dependent variable*).

*Verstehen*, in Weberian thought, understanding of the actor's intentions; placing action in its social context (from German word for understanding).

*welfare state*, state which provides adequate social services to ensure a minimum standard of welfare for all citizens.

*workforce*, in the United Kingdom, all those over the age of 15 who are employed or registered as being available for employment, including persons serving in the armed forces.

# Bibliography

Abel-Smith, Brian and Townsend, Peter (1965), *The Poor and the Poorest: a new analysis of the Ministry of Labour's Family Expenditure Surveys of 1953—54 and 1960*, London: Bell.

Abercrombie, Nicholas and Urry, John (1983), *Capital, Labour and the Middle Classes*, London: Allen & Unwin.

Abercrombie, Nicholas, Warde, Alan, Soothill, Keith, Urry, John and Walby, Sylvia (1988), *Contemporary British Society; a new introduction to sociology*, Cambridge: Polity Press in association with Basil Blackwell.

Abraham, J. H. (1973), *Origins and Growth of Sociology*, Harmondsworth: Penguin Books.

Abrams, Mark, Rose, Richard and Harden, R. (1960), *Must Labour Lose?* Harmondsworth: Penguin Books.

Acker, Susan (1981), 'No woman's land: British sociology of education, 1960—70', *The Sociological Review*, 29, No. 1, pp. 77—104.

Albrow, Martin (1970), *Bureaucracy*, London: Pall Mall Press.

Allan, Graham (1985), *Family Life: domestic roles and social organisation*, Oxford: Basil Blackwell.

Allan, Graham (1989a), *A Sociology of Friendship and Kinship*, London: George Allen & Unwin.

Allan, Graham (1989b), *Friendship — developing a sociological perspective*, Hemel Hempstead: Harvester Wheatsheaf.

Allan, Graham and Crow, Graham (eds) (1989), *Home and Family: creating the domestic sphere*, Basingstoke: Macmillan.

Allan, Graham and Skinner, Chris (eds) (1991), *Handbook for Research Students in the Social Sciences*, London: The Falmer Press.

Allen, Sheila and Wolkowitz, Carol (1987), *Homeworking — myths and realities*, Basingstoke: Macmillan Education.

Althusser, Louis (1972), 'Ideology and ideological state apparatuses', in Cosin, B. R. (ed.), *Education: structure and society*, Harmondsworth: Penguin Books.

Anderson, F. S. (1977), 'TV violence and viewer aggression: accumulation of study results, 1956—1976', *Public Opinion Quarterly*, 41.

Annan Report (1977), *Report of the Committee on the Future of Broadcasting*, London: HMSO.

Appleton, Ian (1975), *Leisure Research and Policy*, London: Academic Press.

Arensberg, C. M., and Kimball, S. T. (1968), *Family and Community in Ireland*, Cambridge, MA:. Harvard University Press, 2nd edn.

Aron, Raymond (1967), *Eighteen Lectures on Industrial Society*, trans. M.K. Bottomore, London: Weidenfeld & Nicolson.

Aron, Raymond (1972), *Main Currents in Sociological Thought*, 2 vols, Harmondsworth: Penguin Books.

Atkinson, A. B. and Harrison, A. J. (1980) 'Trends in the distribution of wealth in Britain', in A.B. Atkinson (ed.), *Wealth, Income and Inequality*, Oxford: Oxford University Press.

Atkinson, J. M. (1978), *Discovering Suicide*, London: Macmillan.

Bachrach, Peter and Baratz, Morton S. (1970), *Power and Poverty: theory and practice*, New York: Oxford University Press.

Bagehot, Walter (1872), *The English Constitution*, new edn with an additional chapter, London: H.S. King (first publ. 1867).

Bakke, E. Wright (1950), *Bonds of Organization*, New York: Harper & Brothers.

Ball, Stephen J. (1981), *Beachside Comprehensive*, Cambridge: Cambridge University Press.

Banton, Michael (1987), 'The Davis–Moore theory of inequality', *Social Studies Review*, 3, No. 2.

Barker, Diana Leonard and Allen, Sheila (1976), *Dependence and Exploitation in Work and Marriage*, London: Longman.

Barnard, Chester I. (1938), *The Functions of the Executive*, Cambridge, MA: Harvard University Press.

Bauman, Zygmunt (1982), *Memories of Class*, London: Routledge.

Becker, Howard S. (1950), *Through Values to Social Interpretation: essays on social contexts, action types and prospects*, Durham, NC: Duke University Press.

Becker, Howard S. (1966), *Outsiders: studies in the sociology of deviance*, New York: The Free Press.

Becker, Howard S. (1973), 'Labelling theory reconsidered', in *Outsiders: studies in the sociology of deviance*, New York: The Free Press, pp. 177–212.

Becker, Howard S. *et al.* (1961), *Boys in White: student culture in medical school*, Dubuque, Ia., Brown Reprints, n.d., of 1st publ. Chicago, University of Chicago Press.

Bell, Colin R. (1968), *Middle Class Families: social and geographical mobility*, London: Routledge & Kegan Paul.

Bell, Daniel (1973), *The Coming of Post-industrial Society*, London: Heinemann.

Belson, William (1978), *Television Violence and the Adolescent Boy*, London: Saxon House.

Berger, Peter C. and Luckmann, Thomas (1971), *The Social Construction of Reality: a treatise in the sociology of knowledge*, Harmondsworth: Penguin Books.

Bernstein, Basil (1961), 'Social class and linguistic development: a theory of social learning', in Halsey, A.H., Floud, J. and Anderson, C.A. (eds), *Education, Economy and Society*, New York: The Free Press.

Bernstein, Basil (1973), *Classes, Codes and Control*, London: Paladin.

Berry, Brian (ed.) (1976), *Urbanization and Counter-urbanization*, Beverly Hills, CA: Sage.

Beynon, Huw (1973), *Working for Ford*, Harmondsworth: Penguin Books.

Black Report (1980), Peter Townsend and Nick Davidson (eds) (1982), *Inequalities in Health: the Black report*, Chairman Sir Douglas Black, Harmondsworth: Penguin Books.

Blau, P. M. (1963), *The Dynamics of Bureaucracy*, Chicago: University of Chicago Press, 2nd edn.

Blau, P. M. (1974), *On the Nature of Organisations*, New York: John Wiley.

Blauner, R. (1964), *Alienation and Freedom: the manual worker in industry*, Chicago: University of Chicago Press.

Blondel, Jean (1975), *Voters, Parties and Leaders*, Harmondsworth: Penguin Books.

Bottomore, T. B. (1965), *Classes in Modern Society*, London: Allen & Unwin.

Bottomore, Tom (1991), *Classes in Modern Society*, London: Unwin Hyman, 2nd edn.

Boulding, Kenneth Ewart (1970), *A Primer on Social Dynamics: essays on dialectics and development*, New York: Free Press.

Boulton, M. G. (1983), *On Being a Mother*, London: Tavistock.

Bourdieu, Pierre and Passeron, J. (1974), *Reproduction in Education, Society and Culture*, London: Sage.

Bowles, S. and Gintis, H. (1975), *Schooling in Capitalist America*, London: Routledge & Kegan Paul.

Bradley, H. (1989), *Men's Work, Women's Work*, Cambridge: Polity Press.

Bradley, Ian (1982), *The English Middle Classes are Alive and Kicking*, London: Collins.

Braverman, Harry (1975), *Labor and Monopoly Capital*, New York: Monthly Review Press.

Brittan, E. (1976), 'Multiracial Education 2 — Teacher Opinion on Aspects of School Life: Teachers and Pupils', *Educational Research*, 18, No. 3.

Britten, N. and Heath, A. (1983), 'Women, men and social class', in E. Garmarnikow, D. Morgan, J. Purvis and D. Taylorson, *Gender, Class and Work*, London: Heinemann.

Bulmer, Martin (ed.) (1984), *Sociological Research Methods*, Basingstoke: Macmillan, 2nd edn.

Brown, Colin (1984), *Black and White Britain*, London: Heinemann for Policy Studies Institute.

Brown, Phillip and Sparks, Richard (eds) (1989), *Beyond Thatcherism: social policy, politics and society*, Milton Keynes: Open University Press.

Brown, Wilfred (1960), *Exploration in Management*, London: Heinemann.

Broadbent, Lucinda (1985), *War and Peace News*, Milton Keynes: Open University Press.

Burgess, R. G. (1984), *In the Field: an introduction to field research*, London: Allen & Unwin.

Burnham, James (1945), *The Managerial Revolution*, London: Penguin.

Burns, T. and Stalker, G. M. (1966), *The Management of Innovation*, London: Tavistock, 2nd edn.

Butler, David and Stokes, D. (1974), *Political Change in Britain*, London: Macmillan, 2nd edn.

Calvert, Peter (1982), *The Concept of Class*, London: Hutchinson.

Carchedi, Guglielmo (1983), *Problems in Class Analysis*, London: Routledge & Kegan Paul.

Castells, Manuel (1977), *The Urban Question*, London: Edward Arnold.

Castells, Manuel (1983), *The City and the Grassroots*, London: Edward Arnold.

Castles, S. and Kosack, G. (1973), 'The function of labour immigration in Western European capitalism', *New Left Review*, 73, pp. 3−21.

Chapman, Leslie (1978), *Your Disobedient Servant*, London: Chatto & Windus.

Chapman, Myra with Mahon, B. (1986), *Plain Figures*, London: HMSO.

Charles, Prince of Wales (1989), *A Vision of Britain: a personal view of architecture*, London: Doubleday.

Cicourel, Aaron V. (1968), *The Social Organization of Juvenile Justice*, New York: Wiley.

Clark, David (1987), 'Wedlocked Britain', *New Society*, 13 March 1987, pp. 12−15.

Clarricoates, K. (1980), 'The importance of being Ernest . . . Emma . . . Tom . . . Jane . . . The perception and categorization of gender conformity and gender deviation in primary schools', in Rosemary Deem (ed.), *Schooling for Women's Work*, London: Routledge & Kegan Paul.

Cloward, Richard A. and Ohlin, Lloyd E. (1961), *Delinquency and Opportunity: a theory of delinquent gangs*, London: Routledge & Kegan Paul.

Club of Rome (Donella H. Meadows, Dennis L. Meadows, Jorgen Rangers and William W. Behrens III) (1974, first published 1972), *The Limits to Growth: a report for the Club of Rome's project on the predicament of mankind*, London: Pan Books.

Coard, Bernard (1971), *How the West Indian Child is Made Educationally Subnormal in the British School System*, London: New Beacon.

Coates, Ken and Silburn, Richard (1970), *Poverty; the forgotten Englishmen*, Harmondsworth: Penguin Books, new edn with intro. 1975.

Cohen, Albert K. (1955), *Delinquent Boys: the culture of the gang*, New York: The Free Press.

Cohen, Phil (1972), 'Sub-cultural conflict and working-class community', *Working Papers in Cultural Studies*, No. 2, University of Birmingham, Centre for Contemporary Cultural Studies.

Cohen, Stanley (ed.) (1973), *Images of Deviance*, Harmondsworth: Penguin Books.

Cohen, Stanley (1980), *Folk Devils and Moral Panics: the invention of the mods and rockers*, Oxford: Martin Robertson.

Coleman, A. (1961), *The Adolescent Society*, New York: The Free Press.

Coleman, A. and Gorman, P. (1982), 'Conservatism, dogmatism and authoritarianism in British police officers', *Sociology*, 16, No. 1, pp. 1–28.

Cooper, Cary L. and Lewis, Suzan (1990), *Career Couples*, London: Unwin Hyman.

Corrigan, Paul (1979), *Schooling the Smash Street Kids*, London: Macmillan.

Cotgrove, Stephen (1975), *The Science of Society*, London: Allen & Unwin.

Coyle, A. (1984), *Redundant Women*, London: The Women's Press.

Crewe, Ivor (1984), 'How to win a landslide without really trying: Why the Conservatives won in 1983', in Howard Penniman and Austin Ranney, *Britain at the Polls, 1983*, Washington, DC: American Enterprise Institute.

Crompton, R. and Jones, G. (1984), *White Collar Proletariat*, London: Macmillan.

Crosland, C. A. R. (1956), *The Future of Socialism*, London: Jonathan Cape.

Cunnison, S. (1983), 'Participation in local union organisation. School meals staff: a case study', in E. Gamarnikow *et al.* (eds), *Gender, Class and Work*, London: Heinemann.

Curtice, John (1986), 'Political partisanship', in R. Jowell, S. Witherspoon and L. Brook (eds), *British Social Attitudes; the 1986 report*, Aldershot: Gower.

Curtice, John (1987), 'Must Labour lose?', *New Society*, 19 June 1987.

Curtice, John and Steed, Michael (1986), 'Proportionality and exaggeration in the British electoral system', *Electoral Studies*, 5, No. 3, December 1986.

Dahl, Robert A. (1961), *Who Governs?* New Haven, CT: Yale University Press.

Dahrendorf, Ralf (1959), *Class and Class Conflict in Industrial Society*, London: Routledge & Kegan Paul.

Daniel, W. (1968), *Racial Discrimination in England*, Harmondsworth: Penguin Books.

Davidoff, Leonore (1976), 'The rationalization of housework', in Diana Leonard Barker and Sheila Allen (eds), *Dependence and Exploitation in Work and Marriage*, London: Longman, pp. 121–151.

Davis, H. and Scase, R. (1985), *Western Capitalism and State Socialism: An Introduction*, Oxford: Basil Blackwell.

Davis, Kingsley and Moore, Wilbert E. (1945), 'Some principles of stratification', *American Sociological Review*, 10, in Bendix, Reinhard and Lipset, Seymour Martin, *Class, Status and Power*, London: Routledge & Kegan Paul, 1967.

Deem, Rosemary (ed.) (1980), *Schooling for Women's Work*, London: Routledge & Kegan Paul.

Deem, Rosemary (1986), *All Work and No Play: the sociology of women and leisure*, Milton Keynes: Open University Press.

Deem, Rosemary (1990), 'Women and leisure — all work and no play?', *Social Studies Review*, March, pp. 139–143.

Delphy, C. (1984), *Close to Home*, London: Hutchinson.

Denver, David (1989), *Elections and Voting Behaviour in Britain*, Hemel Hempstead: Philip Allan.

Department of Health (1991), *The Children Act and Local Authorities: a guide for parents*, London: Department of Health.

Dex, Shirley (1985), *The Sexual Division of Work: conceptual revolutions in the social sciences*, Brighton: Wheatsheaf Books.

Dex, Shirley (1987), *Women's Occupational Mobility*, London: Macmillan.

Djilas, Milovan (1957), *The New Class: an Analysis of the Communist System*, London: Thames & Hudson.

Douglas, J. W. B. (1964), *The Home and the School*, London: McGibbon & Kee.

Downes, David and Rock, Paul (1982), *Understanding Deviance; a guide to the sociology of crime and rule-breaking*, Oxford: Clarendon Press.

Dunleavy, Patrick and Husbands, Christopher T. (1985), *British Democracy at the Crossroads: voting and party competition in the 1980s*, London: Allen & Unwin.

Durkheim, Emile (1893), *The Division of Labor in Society*, New York: The Free Press 1964.

Durkheim, Emile (1915), *The Elementary Forms of the Religious Life: a study in religious sociology*, London: Allen & Unwin.

Durkheim, Emile (1938), *The Rules of Sociological Method*, New York: The Free Press.

Durkheim, Emile (1966), *Suicide: A study in sociology*, trans. John A. Spaulding and George Simpson, London: Routledge & Kegan Paul.

Edgell, S. (1980), *Middle-Class Couples*, London: Allen & Unwin.

Elliott, P. (1972), *The Sociology of the Professions*, London: Macmillan.

Engels, Frederick (1972), *The Origin of the Family, Private Property and the State in the Light of the Researches of Lewis H. Morgan*, London: Lawrence and Wishart, new edn., ed. and intro. Eleanor Burke Leacock, first publ. 1884.

Erikson, Robert, Goldthorpe, John H. and Portocarero, Lucienne (1979), 'Intergenerational Mobility in Three Western Societies', *British Journal of Sociology*, 30, pp. 415−39.

Erikson, Robert, Goldthorpe, John H. and Portocarero, Lucienne (1982), 'Social Fluidity in Industrial Nations', *British Journal of Sociology*, 33, pp. 1−34.

Erikson, R. *et al.* (1983), 'Intergenerational mobility and the convergence thesis', *British Journal of Sociology*, 34, pp. 303−40.

Eron, Leonard D. (1963), 'Relationship of TV viewing habits and aggressive behaviour in children', *Journal of Abnormal and Social Psychology*, 67, pp. 193−6.

Eron, Leonard D., Huesmann, L. Rowell, Lefkowitz, Monroe, M. and Walder, Leopold O. (1972), 'Does TV violence cause aggression?', *American Psychologist*, 27, April 1972, pp. 253−63.

Eron, Leonard D., Walder, Leopold O. and Lefkowitz, Monroe M. (1972), *Learning of Aggression in Children*, Boston, Mass: Little Brown.

Esland, G., Salaman, G. and Speakman, M. (eds) (1975), *People and Work*, Milton Keynes: Open University Press.

Etzioni, Amitai (1964), *Modern Organizations*, Englewood Cliffs, NJ: Prentice Hall.

Eysenck, H. J. (1971), *Race, Intelligence and Education*, London: Temple Smith for New Society.

Farmer, M. and Barrell, R. (1981), 'Entrepreneurship and government policy: the case of the housing market', *Journal of Public Policy*, 2, pp. 307−32.

Faulkner, Wendy and Arnold, Erik (eds) (1985), *Smothered by Invention: technology in womens' lives*, London: Pluto.

Fayol, Henri (1930), *Industrial and General Administration*, London: Pitman.

Field, Frank (1989), *Losing Out: the emergence of Britain's underclass*, Oxford: Basil Blackwell.

Field, Simon (1986), 'Trends in racial inequality', *Social Studies Review*, March 1986.

Finch, J. and Groves, D. (eds) (1983), A Labour of Love, London: Routledge & Kegan Paul.

Finer Report (1974), *Report of the Committee on One-Parent Families*, Chairman Sir Morris Finer, Cmnd. 5629, London: HMSO.

Firestone, Shulamith (1972), *The Dialectic of Sex*, London: Paladin.

Florence, P. S. (1959), *Ownership, Control and Success of Large Companies*, London: Sweet & Maxwell, 1961.

Ford, Janet (1990), 'Households, housing and debt', *Social Studies Review*, May 1990.

Ford, Julienne (1960), *Social Class and the Comprehensive School*, London: Routledge & Kegan Paul.

Fox, A. (1966), *Industrial Society and Industrial Relations*, London: HMSO.

Frank, André Gunder (1978), *Dependent Accumulation and Underdevelopment*, London: Macmillan.

Frankenberg, Ronald (1957), *Village on the Border*, London: Cohen & West.

Frankenberg, Ronald (1969), *Communities in Britain*, Harmondsworth: Penguin.

Freeman, Derek (1984), *Margaret Mead and Samoa: the making and unmaking of an anthropological myth*, Harmondsworth: Penguin.

Freire, Paulo (1974), *Education, the Practice of Freedom*, London: Writers & Readers Publishing Co-operative.

French, Jane (1986), 'Gender and the classroom', *New Society*, 7 March 1986.

Fryer, David and McKenna, Stephen (1987), 'The laying off of hands; unemployment and the experience of time', in Stephen Fineman (ed.), *Unemployment: personal and social consequences*, London: Tavistock.

Fuller, Margaret (1971), *Women in the Nineteenth Century*, New York: W.W. Norton.

Galbraith, John Kenneth (1952), *American Capitalism: the concept of countervailing power*, London: Hamish Hamilton.

Galbraith, John Kenneth (1958), *The Affluent Society*, London: André Deutsch, 4th edn 1985.

Galbraith, John Kenneth (1967), *The New Industrial State*, Harmondsworth: Penguin Books.

Galbraith, John Kenneth (1974), *Economics and the Public Purpose*, London: André Deutsch.

Gallie, Duncan (1978), *In Search of the New Working Class*, Cambridge: Cambridge University Press.

Gallie, Duncan (ed.) (1989), *Employment in Britain*, Oxford: Basil Blackwell.

Gardiner, Jean (1976), 'Political economy of domestic labour in capitalist society', in Diana Leonard Barker and Sheila Allen (eds), *Dependence and Exploitation in Work and Marriage*, London: Longman, pp. 109–20.

Garfinkel, Harold (1967), *Studies in Ethnomethodology*, Englewood Cliffs, NJ: Prentice Hall.

George, Vic and Lawson, Roger (eds) (1980), *Poverty and Inequality in Common Market Countries*, London: Routledge & Kegan Paul.

Gershuny, Jonathan (1978), *After Industrial Society? The emerging self-service economy*, London: Macmillan.

Gershuny, Jonathan and Miles, Ian (1983), *The New Service Economy; The Transformation of Employment in Industrial Societies*, London: Frances Pinter.

Gershuny, Jonathan and Pahl, R. E. (1979–80), 'Work outside employment: some preliminary speculations', *New Universities Quarterly*, 34, No. 1, Winter.

Gerth, H. H. and Mills, C. Wright (1957), *From Max Weber: Essays in Sociology*, London: Routledge and Kegan Paul.

Giddens, Anthony (1982), 'Class structuration and class consciousness', in A. Giddens and D. Held, *Classes, Power and Conflict*, London: Macmillan.

Glasgow University Media Group (1976), *Bad News*, London: Routledge & Kegan Paul.

Glasgow University Media Group (1980), *More Bad News*, London: Routledge & Kegan Paul.

Glasgow University Media Group (1982), *Really Bad News*, London: Routledge & Kegan Paul.

Glass, David (ed.) (1954), *Social Mobility in Britain*, London: Routledge & Kegan Paul, 1971.

Glass, Ruth, assisted by Harold Pollins (1960), *Newcomers: the West Indians in London*, London: Centre for Urban Studies.

Glueck, Sheldon and Glueck, Eleanor (1964), *Ventures in Criminology*, London: Tavistock.

Goffman, Erving (1961), *Asylums: Essays on the Social Situation of Mental Patients and Other Inmates*, Harmondsworth: Penguin Books.

Goffman, Erving (1966), *Encounters: two studies in the sociology of interaction*, Indianapolis, Bobbs-Merril.

Goffman, Erving (1969), *The Presentation of Self in Everyday Life*, Harmondsworth: Penguin Books.

Goffman, Erving (1986), *Stigma: notes on the management of spoiled identity*, Harmondsworth: Penguin Books, first publ. 1963.

Golding, Peter and Middleton, Sue (1976), 'Why is the press so obsessed with welfare scroungers?', *New Society*, 26 October, pp. 195−7.

Goldthorpe, J. H. (1980), *Social Mobility and Class in Modern Britain*, Oxford: Clarendon.

Goldthorpe, J. H. (1983), 'Women and class analysis; in defence of the conventional view', *Sociology*, 17, pp. 456−88.

Goldthorpe, J. H., Lockwood, D., Bechhofer, F. and Platt, J. (1968a), *The Affluent Worker: industrial attitudes and behaviour*, Cambridge: Cambridge University Press.

Goldthorpe, J. H., Lockwood, D., Bechhofer, F. and Platt, J. (1968b), *The Affluent Worker: political attitudes and behaviour*, Cambridge: Cambridge University Press.

Goldthorpe, J. H., Lockwood, D., Bechhofer, F. and Platt, J. (1969), *The Affluent Worker in the Class Structure*, Cambridge: Cambridge University Press.

Gorz, A. (1982), *Farewell to the Working Class*, London: Pluto.

Gouldner, Alvin W. (1954), *Wildcat Strike: a study in worker-management relationships*, London: Routledge & Kegan Paul.

Grant, Wyn and Marsh, David (1977), *The Confederation of British Industry*, London: Hodder & Stoughton.

Griffin, Christine (1985), *Typical Girls? Young Women from School to the Job Market*, London: Routledge & Kegan Paul.

Griffith, J. A. G. (1977), *The Politics of the Judiciary*, London: Fontana, 4th edn.

Grint, K. (1991), *The Sociology of Work*, Cambridge: Polity Press.

Habermas, Jürgen (1972), *Knowledge and Human Interests*, London: Heinemann.

Habermas, Jürgen (1976), *Legitimation Crisis*, London: Heinemann.

Hakim, C. (1987), *Research Design: strategies and choices in the design of social research*, London: Allen & Unwin.

Haines, Valerie A. (1987), 'Biology and social theory: Parsons's evolutionary theme', *Sociology*, 21, No. 1, pp. 19−39.

Hall, Stuart (1980), *Culture, Media, Language: working papers in cultural studies, 1972−79*, London, Hutchinson in association with Centre for Contemporary Cultural Studies.

Hall, Stuart and Jefferson, Tony (eds) (1976), *Resistance through Rituals: youth subcultures in post-war Britain*, London: Hutchinson.

Hall, Stuart *et al.* (1978) *Policing the Crisis: mugging, the state, law and order*, London: Macmillan.

Halloran, J. D., Brown, R. L. and Chaney, D. (1970), *Television and Delinquency*, Leicester: Leicester University Press.

Halsey, A. H. (1989), 'A turning of the tide? The prospects for sociology in Britain', *British Journal of Sociology*, 40, No. 2, pp. 353−73.

Halsey, A. H., Floud, J. and Anderson, C. A. (eds) (1961), *Education, Economy and Society*, New York: The Free Press.

Halsey, A. H., Heath, A. F. and Ridge, J. M. (1980), *Origins and Destinations: Family Class and Education in Modern Britain*, Oxford: Clarendon Press.

Hamilton, M. and Hirszowicz, M. (1987), *Class and Inequality in pre-Industrial, Capitalist and Communist Societies*, Brighton: Wheatsheaf.

Hardey, Michael and Crow, Graham (eds) (1991), *Lone Parenthood: coping with constraints and making opportunities in single-parent families*, Toronto: University of Toronto Press.

Hardyment, Christina (1990), 'Squaring the family circle', *Weekend Guardian*, 16−17 June.

Hargreaves, Andy (1980), 'Review symposium', *British Journal of Sociology of Education*, 1, No. 2, pp. 211−16.

Hargreaves, D. H. (1967), *Social Relations in the Secondary School*, London: Routledge and Kegan Paul.

Harris, C. C. (1983), *The Family and Industrial Society*, London: Allen & Unwin.

Hart, Nicky (1985), *The Sociology of Health and Medicine*, Ormskirk: Causeway.

Healey, Denis (1989), *The Time of my Life*, Harmondsworth: Penguin Books.

Heath, A. (1981), *Social Mobility*, London: Fontana.

Heath, Anthony, Jowell, Roger and Curtice, John (1985), *How Britain Votes*, Oxford: Pergamon.

Heath, Anthony, Jowell, Roger and Curtice, John (1991), *Understanding Political Change*, Oxford: Pergamon.

Hebdige, Dick (1979), *Subculture: the meaning of style*, London: Methuen.

Heidensohn, Frances (1989), *Crime and Society*, Basingstoke: Macmillan.

Higgins, Joan (1978), *The Poverty Business*, Oxford: Blackwell.

Higgins, Joan *et al.* (1983), *Government and Urban Poverty: inside the policy-making process*, Oxford: Basil Blackwell.

Himmelweit, Hilde *et al.* (1958), *TV and the Child*, London: Oxford University Press.

Hindess, Barry (1971), *The Decline of Working Class Politics*, London: Paladin.

Hindess, Barry (1987), *Politics and Class Analysis*, Oxford: Basil Blackwell.

Hoogvelt, Ankie M. M. (1976), *The Sociology of Developing Societies*, London: Macmillan.

Hoover, Kenneth and Plant, Raymond (1989), *Conservative Capitalism in Britain and the United States*, London: Routledge.

Hulme, David and Turner, Mark (1990), *Sociology and Development*, Hemel Hempstead: Harvester Wheatsheaf.

Hunt, A. (1980), *A Survey of Women's Employment*, London: HMSO.

Hunter, Floyd (1953), *Community Power Structure: a study of decision-makers*, Chapel Hill, NC: University of North Carolina Press.

Hutber, Patrick (1980), *The Decline and Fall of the Middle Class and How it can Fight Back*, Harmondsworth: Penguin Books.

Hyman, Richard (1972), *Strikes*, London: Fontana.

Hyman, Richard (1975), *Industrial Relations: a Marxist Introduction*, London: Macmillan.

Illich, Ivan (1973), 'The professions as a form of imperialism', *New Society*, 13 September 1973, pp. 633−5.

Illich, Ivan (1973), *Deschooling Society*, Harmondsworth: Penguin Books.

Illich, Ivan (1977), *Medical Nemesis: the Expropriation of Health*, London: Marion Boyars.

Irwin, J. (1970), *The Felon*, Englewood Cliffs, NJ: Prentice Hall.

Jack, Ian (1988), *Before the Oil Ran Out: Britain 1977−1986*, London: Fontana.

Jackson, Brian (1982), 'Single parent families' in N. Rapoport, M.P. Fogarty and R. Rapoport, *Families in Britain*, London: Routledge & Kegan Paul.

Jackson, Brian and Marsden, David (1972), *Education and the Working Class: some general themes raised by a study of 88 working-class children in a northern industrial city*, London: Routledge & Kegan Paul.

Jacobs, Eric and Worcester, Robert (1990), *We British: Britain under the MORIscope*, London: Weidenfeld & Nicolson.

Jacques, Elliott (1978), *Health Services: their nature and organisation, and the role of patients, doctors, nurses, and the complementary professions*, London: Heinemann.

Jahoda, Marie (1982), *Employment and unemployment: a social-psychological analysis*, Cambridge: Cambridge University Press.

Jahoda, Marie, Deutsch, Morton and Cook, Stuart W. (1951), *Research Methods in Social Relations*, New York: Dryden, for the Society for the Psychological Study of Social Issues, 2 vols.

Jenkins, Clive and Sherman, Barrie (1979), *Computers and the Unions*, London: Eyre Methuen.

Jensen, A. (1969), 'How much can we boost IQ and scholastic achievement?' *Harvard Educational Review*, 39, No. 1.

Johnson, Malcolm (1983) in Robert Dingwall and Philip Lewis (eds), *The Sociology of the Professions: lawyers, doctors and others*, London: Macmillan.

Johnson, Norman (1990), Reconstructing the Welfare State: a decade of change 1980–90, Hemel Hempstead: Harvester Wheatsheaf.

Johnson, Terence (1972), *Professions and Power*, London: Macmillan.

Johnson, Terry, Dandeker, Christopher and Ashworth, Clive (1984), *The Structure of Social Theory*, London: Macmillan.

Jones, Trevor and Young, Jock (1986), 'Crime, police and people', *New Society*, 24 January.

Jowell, Roger, Witherspoon, Sharon and Brook, Lindsay (eds) (1989), *British Social Attitudes; special international report*, Aldershot: Gower, for Social and Community Planning Research.

Karn, V. *et al.* (1988), *Home Ownership in the Inner City: Salvation or despair?*, Aldershot: Gower.

Keddie, Nell (1973), *Tinker, Tailor . . . The Myth of Cultural Deprivation*, Harmondsworth: Penguin Books.

Keller, Suzanne (1963), *Beyond the Ruling Class: strategic elites in modern society*, New York: Random House.

Kennedy, Ian (1981), *The Unmasking of Medicine*, London: Allen & Unwin.

Kerr, Clark *et al.* (1962), *Industrialism and Industrial Man: the problems of labor and management in economic growth*, London: Heinemann.

Kettle, Martin and Hodges, Lucy (1982), *Uprising: the police, the people and the riots in Britain's cities*, London: Pan Books.

King, Roger and Raynor, John, with Dallas Cliff and Geoffrey Sparks (1981), *The Middle Class*, London: Longman, 2nd edn.

Knowles, K. G. J. C. (1952), *Strikes: a study of industrial conflict*, Oxford: Oxford University Press.

Konig, René (1968), *The Community*, London: Routledge & Kegan Paul.

Kuhn, Thomas S. (1970), *The Structure of Scientific Revolutions*, Chicago: Chicago University Press, 2nd edn, first published 1952.

Labov, William, (1973), 'The logic of non-standard English', in Nell Keddie, *Tinker, Tailor . . . The Myth of Cultural Deprivation*, Harmondsworth: Penguin Books.

Laing, William and Hall, Mike (1991), *The Challenges of Ageing*, London: Association of the British Pharmaceutical Industry, cited in *The Guardian*, 19 September 1991.

Lane, T. and Roberts, K. (1971), *Strike at Pilkingtons*, London: Fontana.

Lansley, Stewart, and Weir, Stuart (1983), 'Towards a popular view of poverty', *New Society*, 25 August, pp. 283–4.

Lapper, Richard (1985), *Honduras: state for sale*, London: Latin American Bureau.

Laslett, Peter (1979), *The World We Have Lost*, 2nd edn, corr., London: Methuen.

Lazarsfeld, Paul F., Berelson, Bernard and Gaudet, Hazel (1948), *The People's Choice; how the voter makes up his mind in a Presidential campaign*, New York: Columbia University Press, 2nd edn, 1960.

Leach, Edmund R. (1957), *A Runaway World?* London: BBC Publications.

Leonard, D. and Lipsey, D. (1981), *The Socialist Agenda: Crosland's legacy*, London: Jonathan Cape.

Lipset, Seymour Martin (1950), *Agrarian Socialism*, Berkeley: University of California Press.

Lipset, S. M. and Zetterburg, H. L. (1956), 'Social mobility in industrial societies', in S.M. Lipset and R. Bendix (eds), *Social Mobility in Industrial Society*, Berkeley: University of California Press, 1959.

Lipset, Seymour Martin, Trow, Martin and Coleman, James S. (1956), *Union Democracy*, Glencoe, Ill.: The Free Press.

Little, A. (1978), *Educational Policies for Multiracial Areas*, Goldsmiths' College: University of London.

Littler, C. (1982), *The Development of the Labour Process in Capitalist Societies*, London: Heinemann.

Litwak, E. (1960a), 'Occupational mobility and extended family cohesion', *American Sociological Review*, February, pp. 9–21.

Litwak, E. (1960b), 'Geographic mobility and extended family cohesion', *American Sociological Review*, June, pp. 385–94.

Livingstone, E. (1987), *Making Sense of Ethnomethodology*, London: Routledge & Kegan Paul.

Lockwood, David (1958), *The Blackcoated Worker*, London: Allen & Unwin.

Lockwood, David (1966), 'Sources of variation in working class images of society', *Sociological Review*, 14.

Lodge, P. and Blackstone, T. (1982), *Educational Policy and Educational Inequality*, London: Martin Robertson.

Lukes, Steven (1974) *Power — a Radical View*, London: Macmillan.

MacBeth, A. (1983), *The Child Between. A report on school–family relations in the schools of the European Community*, Glasgow: Department of Education, University of Glasgow.

McFate, Katherine, Lawson, Roger and Wilson, William Julius (1991), *Poverty, Inequality and the Crisis of Social Policy: summary of findings*, Washington, DC: Joint Center for Political and Economic Studies.

MacGregor, Susanne (1981), *The Politics of Poverty*, London: Longman.

MacIver, R. M. and Page, C. H. (1931), *Society*, London: Macmillan, 1950.

Mack, J. and Lansley, S. (1985), *Poor Britain*, London: Allen & Unwin.

McKenzie, Robert and Silver, Allan (1968), *Angels in Marble: working class conservatives in urban England*, London: Heinemann.

McQuail, Denis and Siune, Karen (1986), *New Media Politics*, London: Sage Publications.

McRobbie, Angela (1991), *Feminism and Youth Culture: from 'Jackie' to 'Just Seventeen'*, Basingstoke: Macmillan.

Mannheim, Karl (1948), *Ideology and Utopia*, London: Routledge & Kegan Paul (first published 1931).

Marsh, Peter (1978), *Aggro*, London: Dent.

Marsh, Peter, Rosser, Elisabeth and Harré, Rom (1978), *The Rules of Disorder*, London: Routledge & Kegan Paul.

Marshall, G. (1982), *In Search of the Spirit of Capitalism*, London: Hutchinson.

Martin, David (1967), *A Sociology of English Religion*, London: Heinemann.

Martin, David (1978), *The Dilemmas of Contemporary Religion*, Oxford: Blackwell.

Martin, F. M. (1954), 'Some subjective aspects of social stratification', in Glass, David (ed.), *Social Mobility in Britain*, London: Routledge & Kegan Paul, 1971.

Martin, J. and Roberts, C. (1984), *Women and Employment: A Lifetime Perspective*, London: HMSO.

Marx, Karl and Engels, Frederick (1955), *On Religion*, Moscow: Foreign Languages Publishing House.

Matza, David (1969), *Delinquency and Drift*, Englewood Cliffs, NJ: Prentice Hall.

Mayhew, Henry (1851), *London Labour and the London Poor*, London: n.p., 4 vols.

Mayhew, Pat, Elliot, David and Dowds, Lizanne (1989), *The 1988 British Crime Survey*, London: HMSO.

Maynard, Mary (1990), 'The re-shaping of sociology? Trends in the Study of gender', *Sociology*, 24, No. 2, May, pp. 269–90.

Mayo, Elton (1933), *The Human Problems of an Industrial Civilization*, New York: Macmillan.

Mead, George Herbert (1934), *Mind, Self and Society*, Chicago: University of Chicago Press.

Meadows, Donella H., Meadows, Dennis L., Randers, Jorgen and Behrens, William W. III (1972), *The Limits to Growth: a report for the Club of Rome's Project on the Predicament of Mankind*, London: Pan Books.

Meighan, R. (1981), *A sociology of educating*, London: Cassell, 2nd edn 1986.

Merton, Robert K. (1952), 'Bureaucratic structure and personality', in Robert K. Merton *et al.* (eds), *Reader in Bureaucracy*, Glencoe, Ill.: The Free Press.

Merton, Robert K. (1957), *Social Theory and Social Structure*, New York: The Free Press.

Michels, Robert (1962), *Political Parties: a sociological study of the oligarchical tendencies of modern democracy*, New York: The Free Press (first published 1911).

Miles, Robert (1982), *Racism and Immigrant Labour*, London: Routledge & Kegan Paul.

Miliband, Ralph (1973), *The State in Capitalist Society*, London: Quartet.

Mill, John Stuart (1879), *A System of Logic, Ratiocinative and Inductive, being a connected view of the principles of evidence and the methods of scientific investigation*, 10th edn, first published 1843.

Miller, S. M. (1960), 'Comparative social mobility', *Current Sociology*, 9, No. 1, pp. 1–89.

Miller, W. B. (1958), 'Lower class culture as a generating milieu of gang delinquency', *Journal of Social Issues*, 14.

Millerson, G. (1964), *The Qualifying Associations: A study of professionalisation*, London: Routledge & Kegan Paul.

Mills, C. Wright (1953), *White Collar*, Oxford: Oxford University Press.

Mills, C. Wright (1956), *The Power Elite*, New York: Oxford University Press.

Milner, D. (1975), *Children and Race*, Harmondsworth: Penguin Books.

Morris, Desmond (1967), *The Naked Ape*, London: Jonathan Cape.

Morris, Terence (1976), *Deviance and Control*, London: Hutchinson.

Moser, C. A. and Hall, J. R. (1954), 'The social grading of occupations', in D.V. Glass (ed.), *Social Mobility in Britain*, London: Routledge & Kegan Paul, 1971.

Mouzelis, Nicos P. (1967), *Organisations and Bureaucracy*, London: Routledge & Kegan Paul.

Murdock, Graham and Golding, Peter (1973), 'Beyond monopoly: mass communications in an age of conglomerates', in Beharrel, P. and Philo, G., *Trade Unions and the Media*, London: Macmillan.

Murdock, Graham and McCron, R. (1976), 'Youth and class: the career of a confusion', in Maugham, G. and Pearson, G. (eds), *Working Class Youth Cultures*, London.

Murdock, Graham and McCron, Robin (1978), 'Television and teenage violence', *New Society*, 14 December.

Murray, Charles (1989), 'Underclass', *Sunday Times Magazine*, 26 November.

National Association of Citizens' Advice Bureaux (1989), *One Parent Families: Benefits and Work*, London: National Association of Citizens' Advice Bureaux.

*New Society* (1977), 'Society Today', 14 January.

Newby, Howard (1977), *The Deferential Worker*, London: Allen Lane.

Newby, Howard (1980), *Green and Pleasant Land*, Harmondsworth: Pelican.

Nichols, Theo and Beynon, Huw (1977), *Living with Capitalism: Class Relations and the Modern Factory*, London: Routledge & Kegan Paul.

Nobbs, Jack (1983), *Sociology in Context*, London: Macmillan.

Nordlinger, E. A. (1967), *Working-Class Tories*, London: McGibbon & Kee.

Oakley, Ann (1972), *Sex, Gender and Society*, London: Temple Smith.

Oakley, Ann (1974, 1976), *Housewife*, London: Allen Lane; Harmondsworth: Penguin Books.

Oakley, Ann (1979), *Becoming a Mother*, Oxford: Martin Robertson.

Oakley, Ann (1982), *Subject Women*, London: Fontana.

Offe, Claus (1984), *Contradictions of the Welfare State*, London: Heinemann.

Office of Population, Censuses and Surveys (1990), *Social Trends 20*, London: HMSO.

Ollman, Bertell (1971), *Alienation: Marx's conception of man in capitalist society*, Cambridge: Cambridge University Press.

Organization for Economic Cooperation and Development (1987), *Financing and Delivering Health Care*.

Packard, Vance (1981), *The Hidden Persuaders*, Harmondsworth: Penguin Books, reprint.

Pahl, R. E. (1965), *Urbs in Rure*, London: Weidenfeld & Nicolson.

Pahl, R. E. (1970), *Patterns of Urban Life*, London: Longman.

Pahl, R. E. (1975), *Whose City?*, Harmondsworth: Penguin Books.

Pahl, R. E. (1984), *Divisions of Labour*, Oxford: Basil Blackwell.

Park, Robert E. (1915), 'The city: suggestions for the investigation of human behavior in the urban environment', *American Journal of Sociology*, 20, reprinted in Park and Burgess, (1925).

Park, Robert E., Burgess, Ernest W. and McKenzie, Roderick D., (1967), *The City*, Chicago: University of Chicago Press (first publ. 1925).

Parker, Howard (1974), *View from the Boys*, Newton Abbot: David and Charles.

Parker, Howard (1986), 'Heroin: A solution with a problem', *Social Studies Review*, November, pp. 2−6.

Parker, Mary Follett (1941), *Dynamic Administration*, New York: Harper & Brothers.

Parker, S. (1976), *The Sociology of Leisure*, London: Allen & Unwin.

Parker, S. R. *et al.* (1983), *The Sociology of Industry*, London: Allen & Unwin.

Parkin, Frank (1972), *Class Inequality and Political Order*, St Albans: Paladin.

Parkin, Frank (1979), *The Marxist Theory of Class: A Bourgeois Critique*, London: Tavistock.

Parry, Noel and Parry, José (1976), *The Rise of the Medical Profession*, London: Croom Helm.

Parsons, Talcott (1964), *Essays in Sociological Theory*, New York: The Free Press.

Pateman, Carole (1988), *The Sexual Contract*, Cambridge: Polity Press.

Patmore, J. A. (1973), *Land and Leisure*, Harmondsworth: Penguin Books.

Patterson, S. (1965), *Dark Strangers*, Harmondsworth: Penguin Books.

Pawson, Ray (1982), 'Desperate measures', *British Journal of Sociology*, 33, No. 1, March, 35−63.

Peters, Guy (1978), *The Politics of Bureaucracy*, London: Longman.

Pennington, Shelley and Westover, Belinda (1989), *A Hidden Workforce: women homworkers in Britain today*, Basingstoke: Macmillan Education.

Pheonix, A. (1988), 'The Afro-Caribbean myth', *New Society*, 4 March.

Phizacklea, A. and Miles, Robert (eds) (1980), *Racism and Political Action in Britain*, London: Routledge & Kegan Paul.

Piachaud, David (1982), *Family Incomes since the War*, London: Study Commission on the Family.

Pilkington, Andrew (1984), *Race Relations in Britain*, London: University Tutorial Press.

Plant, Raymond (1981), 'Democratic socialism and equality', in D. Leonard and D. Lipsey (1981), *The Socialist Agenda: Crosland's legacy*, London: Jonathan Cape.

Plowden Report (1967), Central Advisory Council for Education (England), *Children and their Primary Schools: a report of the Central Advisory Council for Education*, London: HMSO, 2 vols.

Policy Studies Institute (1983), *Police and People in London*, London: Policy Studies Institute, 4 vols.

Political and Economic Planning (1956), *Graduate Employment: a sample survey*, London: P.E.P.

Poulantzas, Nicos (1974) *Classes in Contemporary Capitalism*, London: New Left Books.

Prandy, K. *et al.* (1982), *White Collar Work*, London: Macmillan.

Presthus, Robert (1962), *The Organizational Society: an analysis and a theory*, New York: Alfred A. Knopf.

Preston, Barbara (1986), 'Death and the unskilled', *New Scientist*, 6 November.

Pryce, K. (1979), *Endless Pressure: a study of West Indian life styles in Bristol*, Harmondsworth: Penguin Books.

Pyle, David J. (1987), *The Political Economy of Tax Evasion*, London: Hume Institute.

Rampton Report (1981), *West Indian Children in Our Schools, Interim Report of Inquiry into the Education of Children from Ethnic Minority Groups*, London: HMSO.

Rapoport, Rhona and Rapoport, Robert (1971), *Dual-career Families*, Harmondsworth: Penguin.

Rees, Gareth and Lambert, John (1985), *Cities in Crisis: the political economy of urban development in post-war Britain*, London: Edward Arnold.

Reid, I. (1977), *Social Class Differences in Britain*, London: Open Books.

Rex, John (1970a), *Race Relations in Sociological Theory*, London: Weidenfeld & Nicolson.

Rex, John (1970b), 'The concept of race in sociological theory', in Sami Zubaida (ed.), *Race and Racialism*, London: Tavistock.

Rex, John (1982), 'The 1981 urban riots in Britain', *International Journal of Urban and Regional Research*, 6, No. 1, pp. 99–114.

Rex, John and Moore, Robert (1967), *Race, Community and Conflict; a study of Sparkbrook*, Oxford: Oxford University Press for Institute of Race Relations, London, corrected edn 1979.

Rex, John and Tomlinson, S. (1979), *Colonial Immigrants in a British City*, London: Routledge & Kegan Paul.

Richards, Martin, Burgoyne, Jacqueline and Ormrod, Roger (1987), *Divorce Matters*, Harmondsworth: Penguin Books.

Robbins Report (1963), *Committee on Higher Education*, London: HMSO.

Roberts, Ken (1979), *Contemporary Society and the Growth of Leisure*, London: Longman.

Roberts, Ken *et al.* (1977), *The Fragmentary Class Structure*, London: Heinemann.

Robertson, Elliot F. (1986), *The Family: change or continuity*, London: Macmillan.

Roethlisberger, F. J. and Dickson, W. J. (1939), *Management and the Worker*, Cambridge MA: Harvard University Press.

Rose, E. J. B. and Deakin, Nicholas (1969), *Colour and Citizenship: a report on British race relations*, London: Oxford University Press for Institute of Race Relations.

Rose, Richard (1969), *Studies in British Politics: a reader in political sociology*, London: Macmillan, 2nd edn (first publ. 1966).

Rosenfeld, E. (1974), 'Social stratification in a "classless" society', in J. Lopreato and L.S. Lewis, *Social Stratification: a reader*, New York: Harper & Row.

Rosenhan, D. (1973), 'On being sane in insane places', *Science*, 179.

Rosser, C. and Harris, C. (1965), *The Family and Social Change*, London: Routledge & Kegan Paul.

Rossi, A. S. (ed.) (1970), *J.S. Mill and Harriet Taylor; Essays on Sex Equality*, Chicago: University of Chicago Press.

Rostow, Walt Whitman (1960), *The Stages of Economic Growth: a non-Communist manifesto*, Cambridge: Cambridge University Press.

Rostow, Walt Whitman (1971), *Politics and the Stages of Growth: a non-Communist manifesto*, Cambridge: Cambridge University Press.

Roszak, Theodore (1970), *The Making of a Counter-culture: reflections on the technocratic society and its youthful opposition*, London: Faber & Faber.

Routh, G. (1980), *Occupation and Pay in Great Britain*, London: Macmillan.

Runciman, Walter G. (1966), *Relative Deprivation and Social Justice*, London: Routledge & Kegan Paul.

Rushdie, Salman (1982), 'The new empire within Britain', *New Society*, 9 December.

Rutter, Michael (1979), *Fifteen Thousand Hours*, Harmondsworth: Penguin Books.

Salaman, Graeme (1981), *Class and the Corporation*, London: Fontana.

Sampson, Anthony (1982), *The Changing Anatomy of Britain*, London: Hodder & Stoughton.

Sarlvik, Bo and Crewe, Ivor (1983), *Decade of Dealignment*, Cambridge: Cambridge University Press.

Scarman, Lord (1982), *The Scarman Report: The Brixton Disorders 10–12 April 1981*, Harmondsworth: Penguin Books.

Schattschneider, Elmer Eric (1961), *The Semisovereign People: a realist's view of democracy in America*, New York: Holt, Rinehart & Winston.

Scott, J. (1982), *The Upper Classes*, London: Macmillan.

Scott, John (1977), *Corporations, Classes and Capitalism*, London: Hutchinson (2nd edn 1981).

Scott, John (1990), *A Matter of Record: documentary sources in social research*, Oxford: Polity Press.

Scott, W. Richard (1981), *Organisations: rational, natural and open systems*, Englewood Cliffs, NJ: Prentice Hall.

Sharpe, Sue (1978), *'Just Like a Girl': how girls learn to become women*, Harmondsworth: Penguin Books.

Shaw, Clifford, R. and McKay, Henry D. (1942), *Juvenile Delinquency and Urban Areas: a study of rates of delinquents in relation to differential changes of local conditions in American cities*, Chicago: University of Chicago Press.

Shelter (1990), *Wasting Money, Wasting Lives*, London: Shelter Publications.

Silverman, David (1970), *The Theory of Organizations: a sociological framework*, London: Heinemann.

Simon, Herbert (1976), *Administrative Behavior: a study of decision-making processes in administrative organization*, New York: The Free Press, 3rd edn, new intro.

Sinclair, Peter (1987), *Unemployment: economic theory and evidence*, Oxford: Basil Blackwell.

Sivanandan, A. (1982), *A Different Hunger: Writings on black resistance*, London: Pluto Press.

Smith, Adam (1976), *An Inquiry into the Nature and Causes of the Wealth of Nations*, Oxford: Clarendon Press (first publ. 1776).

Smith, D. J. (1976), *The Facts of Racial Disadvantage*, London: Political and Economic Planning.

Smith, David (1988), 'Crime prevention and the causes of crime', *Social Studies Review*, May, pp. 196–9.

Smith, J. (1987), 'Men and women at play: gender, life-cycle and leisure', in D. Jary, J. Horne and A. Tomlinson (eds), *Sociological Review Monograph 33*, London: Routledge.

Smith, S. (1982), *Race and Crime Statistics*, Race Relations Fieldwork Background Paper No. 4, August.

Solomos, John (1989), *Race and Racism in Contemporary Britain*, Basingstoke: Macmillan.

Spender, Dale and Sarah Elizabeth (eds) (1980), *Learning to Lose: sexism and education*, London: The Women's Press.

Spiro, M. E. (1968), 'Is the family universal? the Israeli case', in Bell, N. W and Vogel, E. F. (eds), *A Modern Introduction to the Family*, New York: The Free Press.

Stacey, Margaret (1960), *Tradition and Change: A Study of Banbury*, Oxford: Oxford University Press.

Stacey, Margaret *et al.* (1975), *Power, Persistence and Change: a second study of Banbury*, London: Routledge & Kegan Paul.

Stanworth, Michelle (1981), *Gender and Schooling: a study of sexual divisions in the classroom*, London: WRRC.

Stanworth, Michelle (1984), 'Women and class analysis: a reply to Goldthorpe', *Sociology*, 18, pp. 159–170.

Stanworth, Philip and Giddens, Anthony (eds) (1974), *Elites and Power in British Society*, Cambridge: Cambridge University Press.

Stewart, A., Prandy, K. and Blackburn, R. M. (1980), *Social Stratification and Occupations*, London: Macmillan.

Stokman, Frans N., Ziegler, Rolf, and Scott, John (eds) (1985), *Networks of Corporate Power: a comparative analysis of ten countries*, Oxford: Polity Press.

Sussman, M. B. and Burchinal, L. G. (1971), 'The kin family network in urban-industrial America', in Michael Anderson (ed.), *Sociology of the Family*, Harmondsworth: Penguin Books.

Sutcliffe, D. (1982), *British Black English*, Oxford: Basil Blackwell.

Sutherland, Edwin and Cressy, Donald R. (1966), *Principles of Criminology*, Philadelphia: J. B. Lippincott.

Swann Report (1985), Committee of Inquiry into the Education of Children from the Ethnic Minority Groups, *Education for All*, Cmnd 9543, London: HMSO.

Taylor, Frederick W. (1911), *Principles of Scientific Management*, New York: Harper & Row.

Taylor, M. (1981), *Caught Between*, London: Nelson.

Therborn, Göran (1978), *What Does the Ruling Class do when it Rules? State apparatuses and state power under feudalisn, capitalism and socialism*, London: New Left Books.

Thomas, Caroline (1987), *In Search of Security: the Third World in international relations*, Brighton: Harvester Press.

Thompson, Ian (1986), *Religion*, London: Longman.

Thompson, P. (1989), *The Nature of Work: an introduction to debates on the labour process*, London: Macmillan, 2nd edn.

Thompson, P. and McHugh, D. (1990), *Work Organisations*, London: Macmillan.

Thrasher, F. (1927), *The Gang: a study of 1,313 gangs in Chicago*, Chicago: Chicago University Press.

Tiger, Lionel (1969), *Men in Groups*, London: Nelson.

Times Newspapers (1985), *The Times: Past, Present, Future*, London.

Titmuss, Richard (1962), *Income Distribution and Social Change: a study in criticism*, London: Allen & Unwin.

Toennies, Ferdinand (1955), *Community and Association*, London: Routledge & Kegan Paul.

Toffler, Alvin (1980), *The Third Wave*, London: Pan Books, 1981.

Tomlinson, Sally (1984), *Home and School in Multicultural Britain*, London: Batsford.

Touraine, Alain (1981), *The Voice and the Eye: an analysis of social movements*, Cambridge: Cambridge University Press with Fondation de la Maison des Sciences de l'Homme.

Townsend, H. E. R. and Brittan, E. M. (1972), *Organization in Multiracial Schools*, Windsor: National Foundation for Educational Research.

Townsend, Peter (1971), *Immigrant Pupils in England: the LEA Response*, London: National Foundation for Educational Research.

Townsend, Peter (1979), 'Inequality at the workplace: how white-collar always wins', *New Society*, 18 October.

Townsend, Peter (1979), *Poverty in the United Kingdom: a survey of household resources and standards of living*, London: Allen Lane.

Trenaman, J. and McQuail, D. (1961), *Television and the Political Image*, London: Methuen.

Troeltsch, Ernst (1931), *The Social Teaching of the Christian Churches*, London: 2 vols (first publ. in German, 1912).

Trowler, Paul and Riley, Mike (1984), *Topics in Sociology*, London: University Tutorial Press.

Tumin, Melvin (1967), *Social Stratification: the forms and functions of inequality*, Englewood Cliffs, NJ: Prentice Hall.

Turner, Bryan S. (1988), *Status*, Milton Keynes: Open University Press.

Turner, Ralph H. (1958), 'Life situation and subculture: a comparison of merited prestige judgments by the occupational classes in Britain', *British Journal of Sociology*, 9, December, 299–320.

Turner, Ralph H. (1960), 'Modes of social ascent through education', *American Sociological Review*.

Urry, J. and Wakeford, J. (1973), *Power in Britain*, London: Heinemann.

Urwick, Lyndall F. and Brech, E. J. L. (1948–9), *The Making of Scientific Management*, London: Management Publications Trust, 3 vols.

Veblen, Thorstein (1912), *The Theory of the Leisure Classes: an economic history of institutions*, New York: Macmillan, 1st pub. 1899.

Waddington, David (1989), 'Inequalities in health', *Social Studies Review*, January, 116–20.

Walker, Martin (1991), 'Rising health bill in US inspires calls for fairer system', *The Guardian*, 14 August.

Wallis, Roy (1985), 'The sociology of the new religions', *Social Studies Review*, September, pp. 3–7.

Walker, Robert, Lawson, Roger and Townsend, Peter (eds), (1984), *Responses to Poverty: lessons from Europe*, London: Heinemann Educational.

Wallis, Roy (1984), *The Elementary Forms of the New Religious Life*, London: Routledge & Kegan Paul.

Webb, Eugene J., Campbell, Donald T., Schwartz, Richard D. and Sechrest, Lee (1966), *Unobtrusive Measures: nonreactive research in the social sciences*, Chicago: Rand McNally.

Weber, Max (1965), *The Theory of Social and Economic Organization*, ed. and intro. Talcott Parsons, New York. The Free Press.

Weber, Max (1974), *The Protestant Ethic and the Spirit of Capitalism*, London: Allen & Unwin.

Webster, Andrew (1990), *Introduction to the Sociology of Development*, Basingstoke: Macmillan, 2nd edn.

Wedderburn, Dorothy (1970), 'Workplace inequality', *New Society*, 9 April.

Wedderburn, D. and Craig, C. (1969), 'Relative deprivation in work' in Wedderburn, D. (ed.) (1974), *Poverty, Inequality and Class Structure*, Cambridge: Cambridge University Press.

Wiener, Martin J. (1981), *English Culture and the Decline of the Industrial Spirit: 1850–1980*, Cambridge: Cambridge University Press.

Westergaard, John (1984), 'Class of '84', *New Socialist*, 15.

Westergaard, J. and Resler, Henrietta (1975), *Class in a Capitalist Society*, Harmondsworth: Penguin Books.

Westwood, Sallie (1984), *All Day Every Day*, London: Pluto Press.

Westwood, Sallie and Bhachu, Parminder (1988), *Enterprising Women: ethnicity, economy and gender relations*, London: Routledge.

Whitehead, M. (1987), *The Health Divide: Inequalities in health in the 1980s*, The Health Education Council.

Whitely, Paul (1983), *The Labour Party in Crisis*, London: Methuen.

Whyte, William Foote (1956), *Street Corner Society: the social structure of an Italian slum*, Chicago: Chicago University Press, enlarged edn.

Whyte, William H. (1956), *The Organization Man*, New York: Doubleday Anchor.

Wilensky, H. (1964), 'The professionalisation of everyone', *American Journal of Sociology*, 69.

Wilkins, Leslie T. (1964), 'The deviance-amplifying system', *Social Deviance*, London: Tavistock, pp. 87–94.

Will, J., Self, P. and Datan, N. (1976), 'Maternal behaviour and perceived sex of infant', *American Journal of Orthopsychiatry*, 46.

Williams, Nigel (1991), 'Skin deep', *The Guardian*, 13 December.

Williams, William Morgan (1963), *A West Country Village, Ashworthy: family, kinship and land*, London: Routledge & Kegan Paul.

Willis, P. (1977), *Learning to Labour: how working class kids get working class jobs*, Farnborough: Saxon House.

Willis, P. (1978), *Profane Culture*, London: Routledge & Kegan Paul.

Willmott, Peter (1966), *Adolescent Boys of East London*, London: Routledge & Kegan Paul.

Willmott, Peter (1988), 'Urban kinship past and present', *Social Studies Review*, November, pp. 44–46.

Wilson, Bryan (1966), *Religion in a Secular Society*, London: C.A. Watts.

Wilson, Bryan (1970), *Religious Sects*, London: Weidenfeld & Nicolson.

Wilson, Bryan (1982), *Religion in Sociological Perspective*, Oxford: Oxford University Press.

Wirth, Louis (1938), 'Urbanism as a way of life', in P. Hatt and A. Reiss (eds), *Cities and Society*, New York: The Free Press, 1957.

Wollstonecraft, Mary (1792), *A Vindication of the Rights of Woman*, Harmondsworth: Penguin Books, 1985.

Wood, S. (1982), *The Degradation of Work*, London: Hutchinson.

Woodward, Joan (1980), *Industrial Organisation*, Oxford: Oxford University Press, 2nd edn.

Worsley, Peter (ed.) (1971), *Introducing Sociology*, Harmondsworth: Penguin Books.

Wright, Erik Olin (1978), *Class, Crisis and the State*, London: New Left Books.

Wright, Erik Olin (1979), *Class Structure and Income Determination*, New York: Academic Press.

Wright, Erik Olin (1985), *Classes*, London: Verso.

Yeandle, S. (1984), *Women's Working Lives*, London: Tavistock.

Young, Jock (1971), 'The role of the police as amplifiers of deviancy', in Cohen, Stan, *Images of Deviance*, Harmondsworth: Penguin Books.

Young, Michael (1961), *The Rise of the Meritocracy, 1970–2033: an essay on education and equality*, Harmondsworth: Penguin Books.

Young, Michael (1971), *Knowledge and Control: new directions for the sociology of education*, London: Collier-Macmillan.

Young, Michael and Willmott, Peter (1956), 'Social grading by manual workers', *British Journal of Sociology* 7, 337–45.

Young, Michael and Willmott, Peter (1957), *Family and Kinship in East London*, London: Routledge & Kegan Paul.

Young, Michael and Willmott, Peter (1975), *The Symmetrical Family*, Harmondsworth: Penguin Books.

Zaehner, R. C. (1971), *Concise Encyclopedia of Living Faiths*, London: Hutchinson, 2nd edn.

Zubaida, Sami (ed.) (1970), *Race and Racialism*, London: Tavistock.

Zweig, Ferdynand (1961), *The Worker in an Affluent Society*, London: Heinemann.

# Index